Cases on the Resurgence of Emerging Businesses

Shefali Saluja
Chitkara Business School, Chitkara University, India

Dhiresh Kulshrestha
Chitkara Business School, Chitkara University, India

Sandhir Sharma
Chitkara Business School, Chitkara University, India

A volume in the Advances in Business Strategy and Competitive Advantage (ABSCA) Book Series

IGI Global
PUBLISHER of TIMELY KNOWLEDGE

Published in the United States of America by
IGI Global
Business Science Reference (an imprint of IGI Global)
701 E. Chocolate Avenue
Hershey PA, USA 17033
Tel: 717-533-8845
Fax: 717-533-8661
E-mail: cust@igi-global.com
Web site: http://www.igi-global.com

Library of Congress Cataloging-in-Publication Data

Names: Saluja, Shefali, 1991- editor. | Kulshrestha, Dhiresh, 1975- editor. | Sharma, Sandhir, 1974- editor.
Title: Cases on the resurgence of emerging businesses / edited by Shefali Saluja, Dhiresh Kulshrestha, Sandhir Sharma.
Description: Hershey, PA : Business Science Reference, [2023] | Includes bibliographical references and index. | Summary: "This book will strengthen the research in the following fields: 1. Understanding the culture, expectations, and priorities of customers within a country when taking the business into emerging markets. 2. Establishing strategies for the business managers in guiding a business to success. 3. Boosting the creator's economy keeping a special focus on the recent trends in the businesses"-- Provided by publisher.
Identifiers: LCCN 2023003372 (print) | LCCN 2023003373 (ebook) | ISBN 9781668484883 (hardcover) | ISBN 9781668484890 (paperback) | ISBN 9781668484906 (ebook)
Subjects: LCSH: Entrepreneurship--Developing countries. | Economic development--Developing countries.
Classification: LCC HB615 .C35 2023 (print) | LCC HB615 (ebook) | DDC 338/.04091724--dc23/eng/20220318
LC record available at https://lccn.loc.gov/2023003372
LC ebook record available at https://lccn.loc.gov/2023003373

This book is published in the IGI Global book series Advances in Business Strategy and Competitive Advantage (ABSCA) (ISSN: 2327-3429; eISSN: 2327-3437)

British Cataloguing in Publication Data
A Cataloguing in Publication record for this book is available from the British Library.

Advances in Business Strategy and Competitive Advantage (ABSCA) Book Series

Patricia Ordóñez de Pablos
Universidad de Oviedo, Spain

ISSN:2327-3429
EISSN:2327-3437

Mission

Business entities are constantly seeking new ways through which to gain advantage over their competitors and strengthen their position within the business environment. With competition at an all-time high due to technological advancements allowing for competition on a global scale, firms continue to seek new ways through which to improve and strengthen their business processes, procedures, and profitability.

The **Advances in Business Strategy and Competitive Advantage (ABSCA) Book Series** is a timely series responding to the high demand for state-of-the-art research on how business strategies are created, implemented and re-designed to meet the demands of globalized competitive markets. With a focus on local and global challenges, business opportunities and the needs of society, the **ABSCA** encourages scientific discourse on doing business and managing information technologies for the creation of sustainable competitive advantage.

Coverage

- Foreign Investment Decision Process
- Business Models
- Core Competencies
- Innovation Strategy
- Resource-Based Competition
- Economies of Scale
- Tacit Knowledge
- Ethics and Business Strategy
- Customer-Orientation Strategy
- Cost Leadership Strategy

IGI Global is currently accepting manuscripts for publication within this series. To submit a proposal for a volume in this series, please contact our Acquisition Editors at Acquisitions@igi-global.com or visit: http://www.igi-global.com/publish/.

The Advances in Business Strategy and Competitive Advantage (ABSCA) Book Series (ISSN 2327-3429) is published by IGI Global, 701 E. Chocolate Avenue, Hershey, PA 17033-1240, USA, www.igi-global.com. This series is composed of titles available for purchase individually; each title is edited to be contextually exclusive from any other title within the series. For pricing and ordering information please visit http://www.igi-global.com/book-series/advances-business-strategy-competitive-advantage/73672. Postmaster: Send all address changes to above address.

Titles in this Series

For a list of additional titles in this series, please visit: www.igi-global.com/book-series

Strategic Management and International Business Policies for Maintaining Competitive Advantage
Ailson J. De Moraes (Royal Holloway University of Londo, UK)
Business Science Reference • © 2023 • 340pp • H/C (ISBN: 9781668468456) • US $250.00

Handbook of Research on Digital Natives as a Disruptive Force in Asian Businesses and Societies
Omkar Dastane (UCSI Graduate Business School, UCSI University, Malaysia) Aini Aman (Universiti Kebangsaan Malaysia, Malaysia) and Nurhizam Safie Bin Mohd Satar (Universiti Kebangsaan Malaysia, Malysia)
Business Science Reference • © 2023 • 400pp • H/C (ISBN: 9781668467824) • US $295.00

Handbook of Research on Sustainability Challenges in the Wine Industry
Bartolomé Marco-Lajara (University of Alicante, Spain) Armand Gilinsky (Sonoma State University, USA) Javier Martínez-Falcó (University of Alicante, Spain & Stellenbosch University, South Africa) and Eduardo Sánchez-García (University of Alicante, Spain)
Business Science Reference • © 2023 • 435pp • H/C (ISBN: 9781668469422) • US $295.00

Opportunities and Challenges of Business 5.0 in Emerging Markets
Sumesh Dadwal (Northumbria University, UK) Pawan Kumar (Lovely Professional University, India) Rajesh Verma (Lovely Professional University, India) and Gursimranjit Singh (Lovely Professional University, India)
Business Science Reference • © 2023 • 357pp • H/C (ISBN: 9781668464038) • US $250.00

Embracing Business Sustainability Through Innovation and Creativity in the Service Sector
Pankaj Kumar Tyagi (Chandigarh University, India) Vipin Nadda (University of Sunderland, UK) Vishal Bharti (Chandigarh University, India) and Ebru Kemer (Niğde Ömer Halisdemir University, Turkey)
Business Science Reference • © 2023 • 329pp • H/C (ISBN: 9781668467329) • US $250.00

Strengthening SME Performance Through Social Media Adoption and Usage
Sikandar Ali Qalati (School of Business, Liaocheng University, Shandong, China) Dragana Ostic (School of Finance and Economics, Jiangsu University, China) and Rohit Bansal (Vaish College of Engineering, Rohtak, India)
Business Science Reference • © 2023 • 291pp • H/C (ISBN: 9781668457702) • US $250.00

Bankruptcy and Reorganization in the Digital Business Era
Fahri Özsungur (Mersin University, Turkey) Nevzat Tetik (Inonu University, Turkey) and Ersin Kanat (Zonguldak Bulent Ecevit University, Turkey)
Business Science Reference • © 2023 • 300pp • H/C (ISBN: 9781668451816) • US $250.00

IGI Global
PUBLISHER of TIMELY KNOWLEDGE

701 East Chocolate Avenue, Hershey, PA 17033, USA
Tel: 717-533-8845 x100 • Fax: 717-533-8661
E-Mail: cust@igi-global.com • www.igi-global.com

Table of Contents

Detailed Table of Contents

NLP for talent management and leadership development in an IT organization. In this case, learners will identify the tools of NLP and understand their integration into leadership development programs for the HiPO employees.

This case study focuses on Mr. Sharma, a retail investor who has been investing in the Indian stock market for the past 10 years. Recently, Mr. Sharma has been making emotional investment decisions and has fallen victim to a stock market scam. The case explores the factors that may have contributed to Mr. Sharma's emotional decision-making, such as a lack of confidence in his investment choices and external influences from media and social pressure. The case also highlights the importance of conducting proper research and analysis before making investment decisions, and the risks associated with falling victim to common types of stock market scams in India. Through this case, students can develop strategies for avoiding falling victim to stock market scams and understand the importance of building investor confidence and trust in the stock market.

The case narrates a comparative study of Battle Royale: Harley-Davidson v/s Triumph. It is of their product launch and marketing strategies used by Harley-Davidson and Triumph, two leading brands in the Indian premium motorcycle segment. For the purpose of this study, data were gathered from both primary and secondary sources. This study used secondary sources dominantly for extracting related information of Harley-Davidson and Triumph brands. Secondary sources include company reports, their promotional events, social media, news reports, etc. The author of the case also interacted with users of these two brands. Feedback from these brand users was discussed in the case explicitly. This case was discussed with UG and PG students in a classroom. It helped them to understand branding strategies of these two brands specifically.

Content marketing is an eye opener to various customers and prospecting consumers to give them the viewpoint of understanding and knowledge. Consumers are educated due to the awareness of digital media and easy access to it. In today's era, this digital platform is also taking advantage of camouflaging the content as per their viewpoint, which needs to be put at the forefront. Today shoppers' various reports show that these associations are vulnerable to acts of neglect and may take on substitute freak procedures like a disguise. This case study makes salient contributions by integrating various portals of digital marketing with the concept of camouflaging and through which channel consumers' interest gets hampered. Every organization should use digital platforms with their uniqueness intact so that it should not be driven to another meaning of a message. Digital marketing is a spokesperson which is one way so it should be guided and directed with objectivity.

This case study highlights a few prominent cognitive biases influencing investor behavior in India during the COVID-19 pandemic. Financial decisions of an investor are affected by cognitive factors and not just knowledge. Decision-making is not always necessarily rational by nature. Investors are inclined towards irrational decision making quite frequently due to the impact of various cognitive factors. Moreover, the ongoing COVID-19 pandemic has made situations around us extremely precarious. Every business segment has been affected by it, including financial markets. This case study emphasizes significant cognitive biases faced by Stella while investing her and her clients' hard-earned money in the Indian capital markets and expanding her business during COVID-19. She had numerous thoughts and questions in her mind while going through the investment and expansion process ranging from investment amount and options available at her disposal to the level of risk and return involved in each of them. Such apprehensions are also faced by several other investors in India and the world.

Bipin Preet Singh and Upasana Taku, the power couple of the FinTech world, had sought to differentiate their wallet company by turning it into a microloan disbursement platform. Simultaneously, they had been extending the number of physical stores that accept MobiKwik payments. Mobikwik's image suffered a big blow in February 2021 when it was reported to have compromised the KYC details of over 3.5 million users, in addition to making personal details of 100 million phone users public, which landed the startup on the radar of the regulator Reserve Bank of India following an RTI (Right to Information Act 2005) petition. This also had an impact on its future IPO. The markets had not been receptive to FinTechs accessing capital markets, and its competitor company Paytm's IPO was a disaster. Crises planning and associated risk management was vital for MobiKwik. Was the response to the crises appropriate and effective? Bipin and Upasana were dealing with issues impacting their brand reputation and a possible fallout and impact on their upcoming IPO.

Chapter 11

Motivational leaders who consider not only company development but also societal and national development as a whole are needed in the current tumultuous climate. Motivational leaders see the best in their employees and also facilitate society's efforts to breed compassionate and transformational leaders for inclusive growth. This case study highlights the major motivational leadership style adopted by Reliance Industries Limited (RIL) chairman Mukesh Ambani at different stages of his business deployment. Through his tactics and wisdom, he has not only changed the complete face of Indian industries but also helped society stand up during the pandemic. This case discusses four motivational leadership approaches, i.e., compassionate leadership, inclusive leadership, transformational leadership, and value-based leadership. A motivational leader understands that people and society are the sources of all progress and innovation and thus the key to success in the future. This case study may be used in MDPs, FDPs, and academic programmes to highlight the value of motivational leadership.

Chapter 12

The case revolves around the reactionary measures taken by an Indian IT services company based in Pune in an attempt to stay afloat during the COVID-19 pandemic. The case, in particular, brings to light the effect of the employee-related managerial decisions on their well-being and work involvement amidst the unprecedented health crisis. The pronounced role of leadership, decision making, communication, conflict management, employee perceptions, and HR policies is well brought out in the narrative. Apart from the key takeaways, the readers are provoked to analyze the case and deliberate on novel ways to manage a business within India's unique socio-economic scenario. The in-depth account acquires significance in the light of rapid digital transformation due to the pandemic and its impact on business and management. It paves the way for empirical research on the newer constructs in the areas of organizational behavior and has implications for human resource policies in the VUCA environment.

Chapter 13

Every organisation has leadership succession issues. This is more challenging in social entrepreneurship. This case addresses leadership succession issues in social enterprise. Social entrepreneur Padmshree Phoolbasan Bai Yadav fought poverty and empowered rural women. Her 2 million rurally disadvantaged and uneducated women's network earned 40 crore rupees through social business until 2018. She concentrated on education, health, hygiene, fighting addiction, and independent jobs. She designed a four-layer framework to fulfil these societal tasks. She worried about replacing leaders at each level. As she sought leadership succession, she stressed that a leader should shun politics, work from the heart, not be arrogant or self-driven, and be willing to give her life to society. Her successor and leadership transitions scared her.

It was in the year 1977 in October that the Toyota Motor Corporation entered India. Toyota entered into a joint venture with the Kirloskar Group, therein establishing Toyota Kirloskar Motor Private Limited. Carving their place in the Indian automobile sector, Toyota has successfully carved its place known for their dependability and durability likewise as it was globally. In India, the cars like Corolla Altis sedan, Innova Crysta premium MPV, and the Fortuner premium SUV are one of the most popular models that run successfully. In addition to being the largest automobile manufacturer in the world, the Toyota camp has always been renowned for the cutting-edge technology and brilliant production practices it employs in its manufacturing operations. Toyota has always been a path finder propagating and manufacturing eco-friendly automobiles. Over the years Toyota has developed and mastered developing incredible and refined power plants, which empowers it to deliver tremendous power while minimising fuel consumption.

This case study focuses on a major challenge faced by Yes Bank as a result of increasing NPAs, a 30-day moratorium imposed by the RBI on its operations, and withdrawal limits of Rs. 50,000 from their accounts. This situation downgraded the value of the bank and built a bad image among its customers. Yes Bank was the UPI companion for almost 20 apps, according to the National Payments Corporation of India (NPCI). However, as a result of its failure, Yes Bank has suspended most of its UPI accounts. Now the government is trying to fix the problem and looking into what went wrong at Yes Bank. Altman's Z-Score, developed by American professor Edward Altman in 1968, is a numerical measurement that can be used to predict the chances of bankruptcy, and after calculating the z-score, it is possible to conclude that Yes Bank is still safe from going bankrupt.

This is a case study on the relevance of the culture and heritage of a city to overall happiness and comfort of the citizens. India ranks at 136 in the World Happiness Ranking as per 10th World Happiness Report 2022. A happy city is a city that focuses on building infrastructure for get-togethers, interactions, parties, and socializing of the residents. This case study takes a look at the evolution of culture of Bikaner city and identifies key elements of this culture. It is located in Thar Desert and has extreme climatic conditions. It has geographical disadvantage but has many distinct advantages also. The city has been able to maintain its unique identity and culture despite the changes and pandemic the world has undergone over the decades. This city has been able to preserve its heritage and its deeply rooted traditional values. The authors have highlighted unique cultural characteristics of the city and also raised some concerns to be addressed to develop it as a preferred destination while developing it as modern city of happiness. The case study leaves many questions to ponder.

The case study focusses upon the control of inflation in India during the time of higher inflation rates globally. Post pandemic and Russia-Ukraine war have had a great negative impact on ongoing slow growth of the economies globally. All the economies all over the world are facing economic instability, having higher inflation and increasing unemployment in the economy. The study discusses the policy regarding crude oil, which is a major contributor in Consumer Price Index for inflation, increase in exports of agricultural products, and gains in trade from the trade of fertilizers. The case will try to study the impact of Russia-Ukraine war on the economy in context of India, draw attention towards the situation faced by the countries after the sanctions on Russia implemented by them. How the countries globally are facing energy security and India through its policy is importing many of the commodities at discounted prices compared to prices in the international market.

Cacao has been cultivated in Malaysia for almost two centuries, with the first pods being discovered in a garden in Malacca in 1778. The arrival of the fruit on these beaches is generally dated to 1770, when it was introduced by sailors from Sri Lanka, then known as Ceylon. In 2021, the worldwide cocoa and chocolate industry was estimated to be worth 46.91 billion USD. The market is expected to increase at a compound annual growth rate (CAGR) of 4.98% between 2022 and 2029, from USD 48.29 billion to USD 67.88 billion. This chapter will be comprehensive about the cocoa industry. It will widely cover the history of cocoa, the types of cocoa, and an understanding of cocoa throughout the overview of the cocoa industry in the world. This case study concludes by discussing the issues and threat of the cocoa industry in Malaysia from the economic perspectives.

The case provides an opportunity to evaluate the accuracy of business performance and financial position of Yes Bank, the situation of window dressing in financial statement, and the regulatory role to ensure the investors' protection of Yes Bank, as well as analyzes the role of promoters and different regulators

Foreword

It is my honor to foreword the upcoming book *Cases on the Resurgence of Emerging Businesses*, an up-to-date compilation of 20 unique case studies that apply various multidisciplinary ways to conduct business from various sectors, covering the most current trends in emerging markets.

I had the chance to meet one of the editors, Dr. Shefali Saluja, following her reference to my highly cited research paper "Advancing theory of fraud: the SCORE model". As a well-known fraud expert, I was invited to collaborate with her in various research projects, having the ability to share ideas and spread my expertise. Through this process I was able to understand the deep knowledge of Dr Dhiresh and Dr Sandhir on the subject matter stemming from their long academic experience and involvement in several related projects. So, from the very first moment I heard about this book I was looking forward to reading it. Focusing on emerging firms, this book covers a wide range of case studies, from startups and entrepreneurs to successful measures tackling the Covid-19 pandemic and the ongoing Russia-Ukraine war. As a result, it offers the readers a unique opportunity to explore one of the hot topics nowadays concerning the business world, shedding light to contemporary business models and assisting every stakeholder in converting the thoroughly analyzed case studies into win-win situations.

To conclude, I totally suggest reading this book to anyone interested in getting a holistic view of emerging businesses by real-life case studies, turning theory into practice.

Georgios L. Vousinas
National and Kapodistrian University of Athens, Greece

***Georgios L. Vousinas** is fraud leading expert and author of the world's latest fraud theory, the S(C)CORE Model or Fraud Hexagon Theory, whose papers include "Advancing theory of fraud: the SCORE model", "Shadow economy and tax evasion. The Achilles heel of Greek economy. Determinants, effects and policy proposals" and "Supervision of financial institutions: The transition from Basel I to Basel III. A critical appraisal of the newly established regulatory framework".*

Preface

Nearly 40% of the global GDP, measured in terms of purchasing power, comes from emerging businesses, whose markets are seeing rapid growth. Even the COVID-19 pandemic and the economic unrest caused by Russia and Ukraine have not had a significant influence on the expansion of emerging businesses. As a result, they have continued to develop rapidly for the previous six years on average at a rate of over 7% per year. Continuous economic and infrastructure progress in these countries has been fueled by rising foreign direct investment as well as the local social demographic dividend. The region has abundant natural and human resources, which draws the interest of international business and management stakeholders. To protect the planet from climate change, the corporate organisations in these nations are under pressure to match their predictions and service operations with the sustainable development goals (SDGs). Various measures have been taken by management practitioners in this area to comply with the SDGs, however they have both positive and bad effects on staff management and the performance of firms. Additionally, the performance of organisations as a whole as well as the operations of individual employees have been significantly impacted by changing technologies, the rise of industry 4.0, and cyber-physical production and operational systems. As a result, governments and organisations are taking a variety of steps to harmonise all the concerns for the growing countries' economies to flourish more smoothly. However, both governmental and commercial organisations can continue to be successful if they focus on specific issues related to business and management in this area. We are therefore narrating the various chapter contributions in emerging businesses in order to give the most recent research, theories, and case studies on business and management challenges in rising countries in one case handbook. This case book offers chances for scholars, academicians, and practitioners to widen their knowledge and foresee the various dimensions of the businesses, especially those that concern rising nations.

Relevance of the Case Book on Emerging Businesses

It's fascinating to see how the corporate world is developing at a rapid rate as we set off in 2023. Some businesses are thriving as a result of technological improvements and shifting consumer preferences, while others are battling to stay afloat. Since the epidemic, e-commerce has grown to be an essential part of our life. The e-commerce sector has seen extraordinary growth as consumers increasingly choose to shop online rather than go to physical locations. The rapidly changing financial industry is being driven by fintech. The way we manage our accounts is being revolutionized by fintech startups, who are making it easier and more accessible for everyone. Fintech is growing in importance as a result of the rise of digital banking, mobile payments, and blockchain technology in our daily lives. In addition, the firms have benefitted from social enterprises and many others. The focus of corporations looking for development possibilities has turned to emerging markets because the majority of developed global economies will only grow slowly in the following ten years under the weight of public and private debt. Financial indications already indicate that emerging markets will contribute significantly to increases in sales and profits. The case book examines the megatrends followed in the emerging economy and includes 20 unique case studies from various industries. It demonstrates the most effective ways for businesses to seize the growth opportunities in developing nations and how to allocate resources according to geography to maximize short-, medium-, and long-term profits. To know about the most recent case studies of developing enterprises, academics, practitioners, researchers, and students must read this book. Moreover, in academics and particularly in the case based teaching the students are also involved in the discussion of certain scenarios that resemble or are often examples from the actual world. This approach is learner-centered and features strong interaction between participants as they increase their knowledge and analyse the case as a group.

Target Audience

The book is anticipated to be helpful to a wide range of industries, including academia, business, policymakers, and society at large. This will be especially helpful for the subject matter specialists who may use this book as a foundation to progress these disciplines to a high level of awareness and comprehension. The focus of corporations looking for development possibilities has turned to emerging markets because the majority of developed global economies will only grow slowly in the following ten years under the weight of public and private debt. This case book investigates "what will change economically" and "what are the overarching business megatrends that will impact organisations and their strategies in global marketplaces" with the case studies of different enterprises. Financial indications currently predict that a major portion of sales and profit growth will come from emerging markets. In order to help readers build a critical awareness of the growth economies featured in the book, as well as their common traits, development, and importance in the global economy, the authors give analytical frameworks, tools, and best practice insights. The authors examine the distinct difficulties and opportunities for emerging markets throughout the world today, including the growing middle class, partnership, and negotiation strategies, using original instances embracing various situations and scenarios. For students, scholars, and practitioners of international business who are interested in doing business in emerging markets, this case book is required reading.

Chapter Contribution

The case book has received 20 case studies on the emerging businesses and the challenges faced by these businesses to grow their worth in the economy. The first case study narrates the journey of a woman academician turned into Edupreneur in the field of higher education in the developing economy. The case also discusses the challenges faced by the woman Edupreneur to successfully build her business empire. The second case study examines the competitive strategies to protect themselves from incidents related to collapse of FTX and other financial institution because they explored the structural weaknesses existing in the system. The third case study highlights the journey of an organization and how its founders have created a whole new set-up for BPO organizations that is changing the rules of the game. The fourth case study highlights the major challenges faced by the start-up for funding, expansion and adoption of green technology while promoting social media marketing post Covid19 revival in the fashion industry. The fifth case study examines the neuro linguistic programming (NLP) tools and techniques used by the IT Organization. It also explores the behavioral challenges and outcomes in leadership development for the HiPo employees. The sixth case study focuses on an entrepreneur's emotional decision making which became a lack of confidence in him for his investment choices and external influences from media and social pressure. It talks about the challenges he faced to regain his business in the economy. The seventh case study narrates a comparative study of Battle Royale "Harley Davidson" vs "Triumph" branding strategies while playing in the competitive market. The eighth case study makes salient contributions by integrating various portals of digital marketing with the concept of Camouflaging and through which channel the customers interests gets hampered. The ninth case study highlights few prominent cognitive biases influencing investor behavior during Covid 19 in India. The tenth case study shows the story of power couple of FinTech world who had sought to differentiate their wallet company by turning into a microloan disbursement platform. The case also shows the fallout and impact of their IPO fall. The eleventh case study highlights the major motivational leadership style adopted by Reliance industries Chairman at different stages of his business development. The twelfth case study revolves around the reactionary measures taken by an Indian IT services company based in Pune, in an attempt to stay afloat during Covid19 pandemic. The case reflects the efforts of employee and related managerial decisions on their well being and work involvement amidst the health crisis. The thirteenth case study addresses the leadership succession issues in social enterprise. The story of a woman entrepreneur who fought poverty and empowered the rural woman in the area. The fourteenth case study discusses the challenges of product cannibalization for Suzuki as the launch of Hybrid "Glanza" that leads to decrease in sales of original model of "Baleno" which is Suzuki's best-selling car in the hatchback segment. The fifteenth case study focuses on the major challenge faced by the Yes Bank as a result of increasing NPAs. The situation downgraded the value of Yes Bank and build a bad image among its customers. The sixteenth case study highlights the relevance of culture and heritage of a city to overall happiness and comfort of citizens. The case study takes a look at the evolution of culture of Bikaner city in India and identifies key elements to their culture. The eighteenth case study shows the history of Cocoa, types of cocoa and an understanding of cocoa throughout the world. The nineteenth case study provides an opportunity to evaluate accuracy of business performance and financial position of Yes Bank, the situation of window dressing in financial statements and the regulatory role to ensure investors protection of Yes Bank as well as analyses the role of promoters of different regulators. The twentieth case study using the real-world cases, this research emphasis the importance of disciplined innovation land proposes a framework to integrate the characteristics into the function al procedures and operational mechanisms of the organization.

Conclusion

The case book *Cases on the Resurgence of Emerging Businesses* is expected to be extremely useful for all participants in the education and business ecosystem across all product categories and service areas. It will have far-reaching consequences in business and academia, and its theoretical and practical framework contributions suggest it will be welcomed by a diverse spectrum of readers around the globe. The breadth of topics covered is another strength of the study, and its all-encompassing approach means it will provide fresh avenues for progress for a wide variety of interested parties. By guiding administrators and regulators towards the best framework for fostering growth, our book will significantly advance the policymaking process. This method can be applied to the development of novel business models that provide benefits to all stakeholders (customers, partners, and society at large). In sum, the case book is the best place to look if you're interested in learning about a wide range of case studies and getting unique insights on how to turn them into a win-win for everyone involved in the relevant fields of study, practice, and policymaking.

Shefali Saluja
Chitkara Business School, Chitkara University, India

Dhiresh Kulshrestha
Chitkara Business School, Chitkara University, India

Sandhir Sharma
Chitkara Business School, Chitkara University, India

Chapter 1
Marking a Legacy as an Edupreneur: Dr. Madhu Chitkara

Shivani Inder
https://orcid.org/0000-0002-4805-4118
Chitkara Business School, Chitkara University, India

Shefali Saluja
https://orcid.org/0000-0002-8560-5150
Chitkara Business School, Chitkara University, India

Sandhir Sharma
https://orcid.org/0000-0002-3940-8236
Chitkara Business School, Chitkara University, India

Harkiran Kaur
Office of Alumni Affairs, Chitkara University, India

EXECUTIVE SUMMARY

This case study reflects the journey of a woman academician turned into edupreneur in the field of higher education in a developing economy. Dr. Madhu Chitkara has developed a high-quality educational ecosystem for nurturing talent by co-establishing and leading the development of higher education institutions in India. At the time of the case, she has achieved a number of milestones and is trying to chalk out the future steps so as to pass on the legacy to next generation leaders. The case is written to illustrate an example of a woman entrepreneur in the field of education and provide insights on her philosophy, leadership style, and strategy.

INTRODUCTION

As 2023 marks a New Year, Dr. Madhu Chitkara dives into deep thoughts of how her small steps towards being an academician has led to a NAAC A+ Accredited University which has several 'Centers of Excellence', achieved strong stand on several rankings like QS Asia University Rankings, Times Higher

DOI: 10.4018/978-1-6684-8488-3.ch001

Education Impact Rankings, WURI, Green Metric, NIRF (National Institutional Ranking Framework), The Business India, Outlook-ICARE India, Dataquest, Business World, India Today, and other national rankings, bagged 'The Confederation of Indian Industry National Award for Excellence in Water Management', and many such prestigious recognitions.

On the journey, she has led several international collaborations, held Global Week for students for bringing internationalization at home, facilitated faculty interactions, and has also adopted five villages to work on sustainability issues, taken care of emotional health of students with 'Centre of Happiness'. With clear focus on research & innovation, she has been emphasizing on the areas such as farming, lifestyle, health, assistive technology by filing more patents, paper publications, copyrights, start ups at university level. Her passion is into making the world better for living.

While She is happy to acknowledge that many action points of NEP 2020 are already in place at Chitkara University yet she is pondering over opportunities of enhancing and implementing NEP 2020 with more rigor to increase academic outcome. She acknowledged the contribution of around 500 academicians at the 'Excellence Awards' February 2023 for their contribution to the world of academia.

At the same time, the words of her life partner, co-founder, the renowned academician and entrepreneur Dr. Ashok K Chitkara were ringing in her ears that "Life is a journey. So, it was their belief in education, knowledge and abilities that has given them enough wisdom to make generations of their students settle well in corporate world because of their education and knowledge."

The actual founding of the Chitkara University, Punjab (See Exhibit 1) is on 2002, with establishment of Chitkara Institute of Engineering and Technology, Punjab. In just 20 years, shared vision of Dr. Madhu Chitkara and Dr. Ashok K Chitkara has manifested itself into two universities, two international schools in three states and one UT with 25,000 students, 1,500 faculty members and more than 1200 support staff. In year 2013, based on having a flair of highly exceptional acumen of being an entrepreneur, Dr. Madhu Chitkara was honored with South East Asia Award by Washington School of Business. She has also been recognized as a visionary edu-leader of India by former Lt. President, Sri Pranab Mukherjee during Rethink INDIA Fifth Estate Summit 2017.

Twenty years earlier, standing on milestone of setting up Chitkara University, Punjab in 2002, Dr. Madhu Chitkara and Dr. Ashok K Chitkara announced that their goal for Chitkara University is "To be a globally recognized organization promoting academic excellence through interdisciplinary applied research and to expand realms of knowledge through innovation."

The Formative Years

Dr. Madhu Chitkara vividly remembered her first day on the job as the newly appointed teacher of a government school. Her sharp focus on creating academic excellence pushed her to take turns in life and place herself on the journey of entrepreneurship. Dr. Madhu Chitkara expresses herself:

I would like to define myself as an accidental entrepreneur. I am the first in my family and that too a woman, to take up education as a profession, initially as an employee, and later as an entrepreneur. I call myself an 'accidental entrepreneur' because so much was not planned. I have been instrumental in creating more than 68 relevant industry-linked programs in the fields of Engineering, Management, Architecture, Art & Design, Nursing, Healthcare, Education, Mass Communication, Hospitality, Law, Psychology, Liberal Arts, and Pharmacy & Marine Engineering at Graduate, Postgraduate and Doctorate Level.

Recalling her journey, she mentions that they started Chitkara Institute of Engineering and Technology (CIET) affiliated to Punjab Technical University in 2002. Quantity, quality and discipline were every important watchwords, Dr. Madhu Chitkara took up the challenging job of setting up an exemplary example in the field of education by surrendering 'Management Quota' seats[1]. She mentions that "I did it to ensure equity and meritocracy." In 2003, she began her journey with Chitkara College of Education for Women which became immensely popular and her success emboldened her to launch 'Chitkara School of Planning and Architecture' in 2004. During the same year, Dr. Madhu Chitkara felt resonance of her vision with global standards when she visited Cambridge University and Oxford University, London. She returned with much stronger conviction and mindset of making Chitkara and India shine globally. She rolled the carpet for 'Chitkara International School'.

One more such episode fueled the growth of Chitkara University. Dr. Madhu Chitkara recalls:

How does one begin to conceive a new university! The nagging thought was giving me insomnia. In 2008, I and my team of educators travelled to the United States of America and visited many best universities to see what best practices they follow. It was then that I understood and prioritized building an institutions with a collaborative global model. I came back and in the same year, established Chitkara University in Himachal Pradesh. With the University, I got the autonomy to adopt means to provide quality education. In 2010, I was able to set up Chitkara University, Punjab. It was no mean achievement to rise from a school teacher to create two Universities.

Dr. Madhu Chitkara restated its mission in 2008 to give a larger emphasis to leadership development alongside more traditional education, and to widen its geographic reach. This mission drafted the path for further development of institutions (See Exhibit 4). Accolades for both the universities and international schools offer a plentiful evidence of Dr. Madhu's dedication and devotion to education.

Tough Challenges

Quick to embark on the entrepreneurial journey of being an edupreneur, Dr. Madhu Chitkara was not having only teething issues for Chitkara University but confronting the new economic realities and changes, and had to face complex mesh of rules, laws and regulations constructed by education regulatory agencies, both at state and central governmental level. She was dealing with officials from different governmental departments like land and revenue department, real estate laws, population, and environmental regulations, etc., which was a very daunting and uphill task. Over and above, being a female, it was more difficult and resistance was huge. She elaborates further:

It was very hard time for me and there were times when I felt that I was losing it. But it was my commitment towards the higher purpose and support of my family that kept me going. Thankfully I never learnt to put my weapons down. I wanted that my educational institutions should be known for quality education. Thus, hiring of good faculty, drawing up the curricula for different courses and equipping the laboratories were major challenges. Being a mathematician, I was not familiar with the nuances of other disciplines and it was a herculean task to get that done.

As she talked about the challenges and hurdles, Dr. Madhu Chitkara pointed proudly also to her support system. She refers her family as her strongest critics and support system in her journey of becoming an entrepreneur. She recalls:

When I look back, I remember that though my brother was younger to me, abiding by the Indian Patriarchal society, he was considered superior and the preferred one. My father never differentiated between us, but mother was a little biased. Not that she did not love me or care for me, but he was given more preference. While I was studying, my parents were least interested in whatever I was doing. In my world, education wasn't important for a girl child. But I wanted to become a doctor. Unfortunately, due to the then prevailing environment of limited accessibility and financial constraints of the family, I could not realize my dream. But that didn't stop me.

Indeed, Dr. Madhu Chitkara was self-committed in and around academics, not only in pursuing her own studies, but also opening doors of good quality education for generations to come. "I was always very good in Maths", she said, "and took up undergraduate programme with mathematics as majors in Maitreyi College New Delhi. I got my bachelor's degree in 1975 and then Bachelor of Educaton (B.Ed.) soon after. For my exceptional contribution as a teacher, I was honored with State Award for Teachers as a "Teacher of Outstanding Merit" in 1987". Indeed Dr Madhu herself was ever-present in and around classrooms and students, not only opening and closing programs, but greeting guests from academics and industry, talking with stakeholders, checking and rechecking the smallest details, and overseeing staff and faculty. Dr. Madhu Chitkara believes in prompt feedback. So those who fail to meet up to her high standards receive prompt feedback in clear manner so as to channelize their efforts. This brings in clarity on how to do things differently. Further, through timely and appropriately feedback interests of all can be aligned.

Around the same time, Dr. Madhu Chitkara got married to Dr. Ashok K Chitkara. Dr. Ashok K Chitkara was her classmate in B.Ed. She smiled and said, "He had been and still is my biggest supporter. I completed M.Sc. (Mathematics), M.Ed. and later Ph.D. by working on a topic related to Education. Having armed myself with these degrees, I was soon employed by a college as a lecturer. But, the entrepreneur inside me was imploring to take on bigger challenges in life. Now my son, daughter in law, son-in-law, and grand-children are my biggest cheerleaders." Further, she elaborates, "I believe behind every man's success, there is a woman. Similarly, on the other hand, behind every woman's success, there is a man. I believe it's Dr. Ashok's faith and belief in me that has consistently fueled me to pursue my dreams."

Dr. Madhu and Her Philosophy

On a fire-side chat, the interviewer asked Dr. Madhu what connect does she find in professional and personal life. She recounted:

Both roles that is of an entrepreneur and home-maker call for passion, personal touch and progressive approach. I am yet to come across anyone who doesn't possess these attributes and is successful. An entrepreneur nurtures the ideas as a mother nurtures a child. It's all about values. What values are the most important to you? What are you willing to do, to sacrifice, to dare? And who are you willing to be? It's a roller coaster of emotions, experiences, mistakes and successes. All we have to do is just take the chance. Go with our instincts, guts or hearts, whatever we like to call it, and simply dare. Knowing we will never know how it actually turns out, when being on the outside, but ensuring and trusting it will work out as soon as we gain some first hand experience.

Establishing work life balance has been at core of Dr. Madhu Chitkara's philosophy. As she juggles different roles, i.e., entrepreneur, mother, wife, administrator, academician, at the same time. During 2002, Dr. Madhu Chitkara and Dr. Ashok K. Chitkara took a big leap of entrepreneurship. They resigned from their respective jobs so as to establish Chitkara Institute of Engineering and Technology (CIET) affiliated to Punjab Technical University. At that time, their children had not completed their education. They took calculated risk. She underlines:

It was as full time job and without any extended family support, I had to muster all my skills to arrive at a work life balance. I realized that it was not easy, and for a woman, it was probably twice as hard. But it was my love for teaching that kept me going. The dimensions of being an entrepreneur and mother are strikingly similar- long days, endless nights and the continual blurring of it all. Strike that, may be there aren't so many differences and maybe they are quite compatible. Your kids grow up. Actually, if you manage it well, your venture grows up too by leaps and bounds.

She is deeply attached to her roots. She ensures that Chitkara University engages and contributes in the development of nearby villages Jhansla, Thuha, Ramnagar, Kalo Majra and Fatehpur Garhi.

The Way Ahead

Even if the Chitkara's guiding principles (e.g., vision, mission, values, etc.) were to remain relatively intact, many important issues still had to be resolved if these were to be included in coming years, along-with nurturing the next generation of leaders in university to continue the journey.

Exhibit 1(a): About Chitkara University, Punjab

Figure 1. About Chitkara University, Punjab

Exhibit 1(b): About Chitkara University, Punjab

Figure 2. About Chitkara University, Punjab

VISION

To be a globally recognized organization promoting academic excellence through interdisciplinary applied research and to expand realms of knowledge through innovation

MISSION

- To carry out the academic processes in accordance with global standards through active teacher-student-industry participation
- To promote research, innovation and entrepreneurship in collaboration with industry, research laboratories and academic institutions of global repute.
- To be a globally recognized organization promoting academic excellence through interdisciplinary applied research and to expand realms of knowledge through innovation.

MISSION

- To carry out the academic processes in accordance with global standards through active teacher-student-industry participation.
- To promote research, innovation and entrepreneurship in collaboration with industry, research laboratories and academic institutions of global repute.
- To inculcate high moral, ethical and professional values amongst our students, faculty & staff.
- To contribute in building skillful society

LOGO

CHITKARA UNIVERSITY

EXPLORE YOUR POTENTIAL

Our logo depicts the arrows in soaring heights, promising everlasting progress. It also illustrates the interlinking of our key stakeholders namely Students, Parents, Faculty, Alumni, Industry and Society as a whole, working in synergy towards a common goal which is the "Everlasting Success of Each Chitkara Student and creating them as responsible citizens". The colour Red denotes Energy & Passion to "Explore Our Potential"

UNIVERSITY'S CHARTER

The learning environment at Chitkara University represents unique blend of distinguished faculty, brilliant and intellectual students with a proactive collaboration with industry. All stakeholders at Chitkara University abide by our charter.

CHITKARA UNIVERSITY

OUR CHARTER

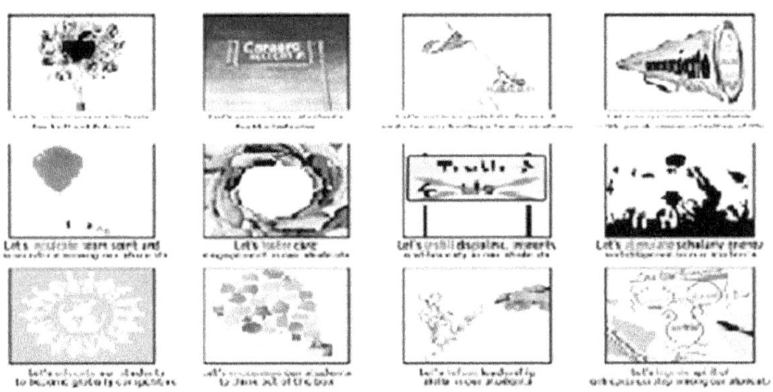

Exhibit 2: Milestones in Entrepreneurial Journey of Dr. Madhu Chitkara

Figure 3. Milestones in entrepreneurial journey of Dr. Madhu Chitkara

Exhibit 3: Key Accolades Achieved by Institution (Latest Achievements)

Figure 4. Key Accolades achieved by institution (latest achievements)

Key Rankings of Chitkara University
International Rankings **QS Asia University Rankings 2023: Southern Asia:** Chitkara University has been ranked 145th in the QS Asia University Rankings 2023: Southern Asia, announced by QS in QS Higher Education Summit- APAC 2022 in Jakarta, Indonesia.
World's Universities with Real Impact (WURI) ranking Chitkara University has been ranked in the 101-200 bank in the list of "Top Innovative Universities" and 2nd in India by the coveted World's Universities with Real Impact (WURI), and ranked 51-100 band in the 'Student Mobility and Openness' category in the WURI Ranking 2022.
UI GreenMetric World Universities Rankings Chitkara University has been ranked 12th in India and 337th in the world in the "UI GreenMetric World Universities Rankings". The university has been ranked 97th rank in the world for "Water Conservation" and "Recycling Processes & Policies".
Time Higher Education World University Rankings Chitkara University has been ranked 4th in India in the Times Higher Education World University Rankings 2022 and is among the top 5 in almost every individual SDG.
Key National Rankings
NAAC A+ Ranking Chitkara University has been ranked NAAC A+

Exhibit 4: Journey of Being a Woman Edupreneur

Figure 5. Journey of being a woman edupreneur

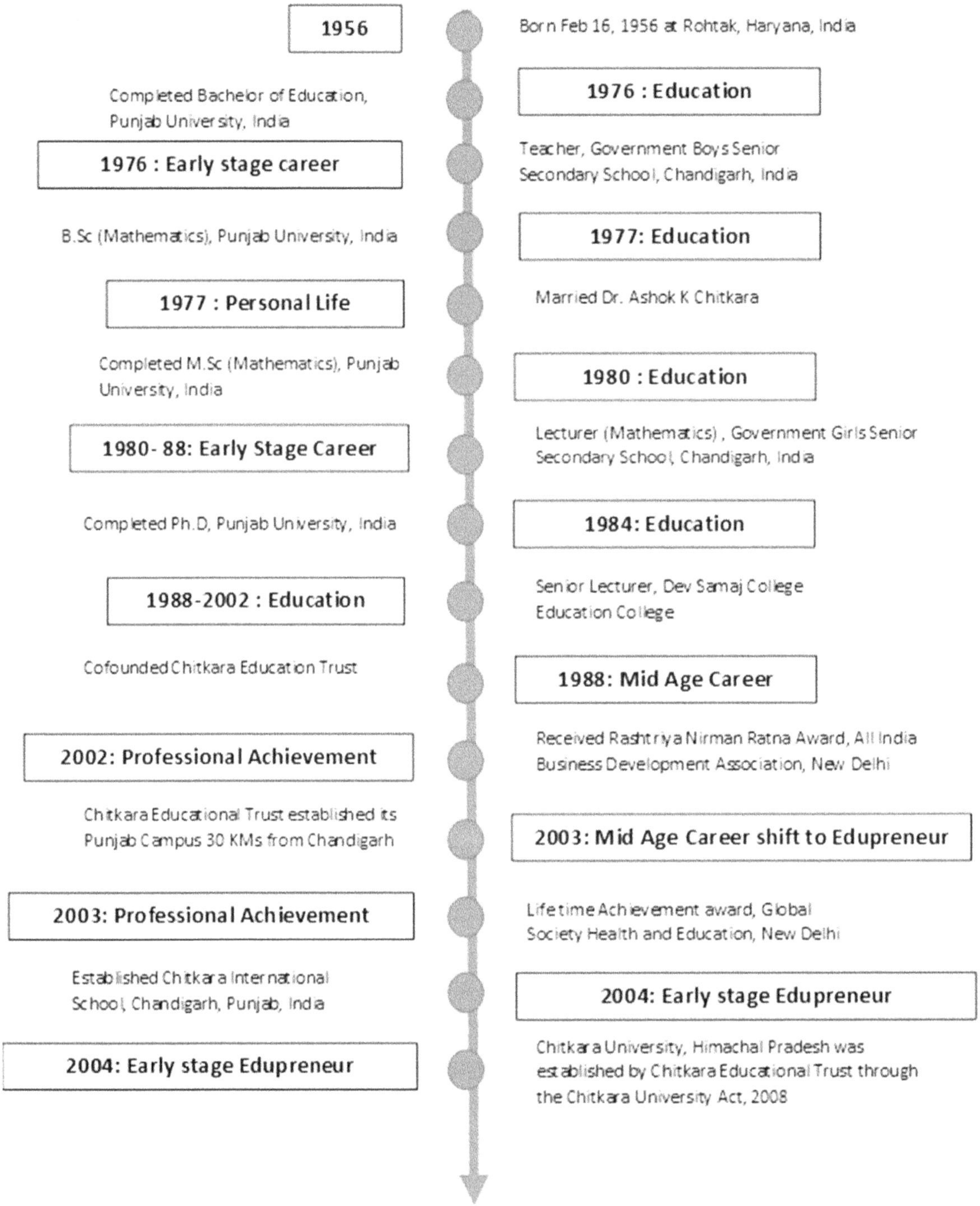

Figure 6. Journey of being a woman edupreneur

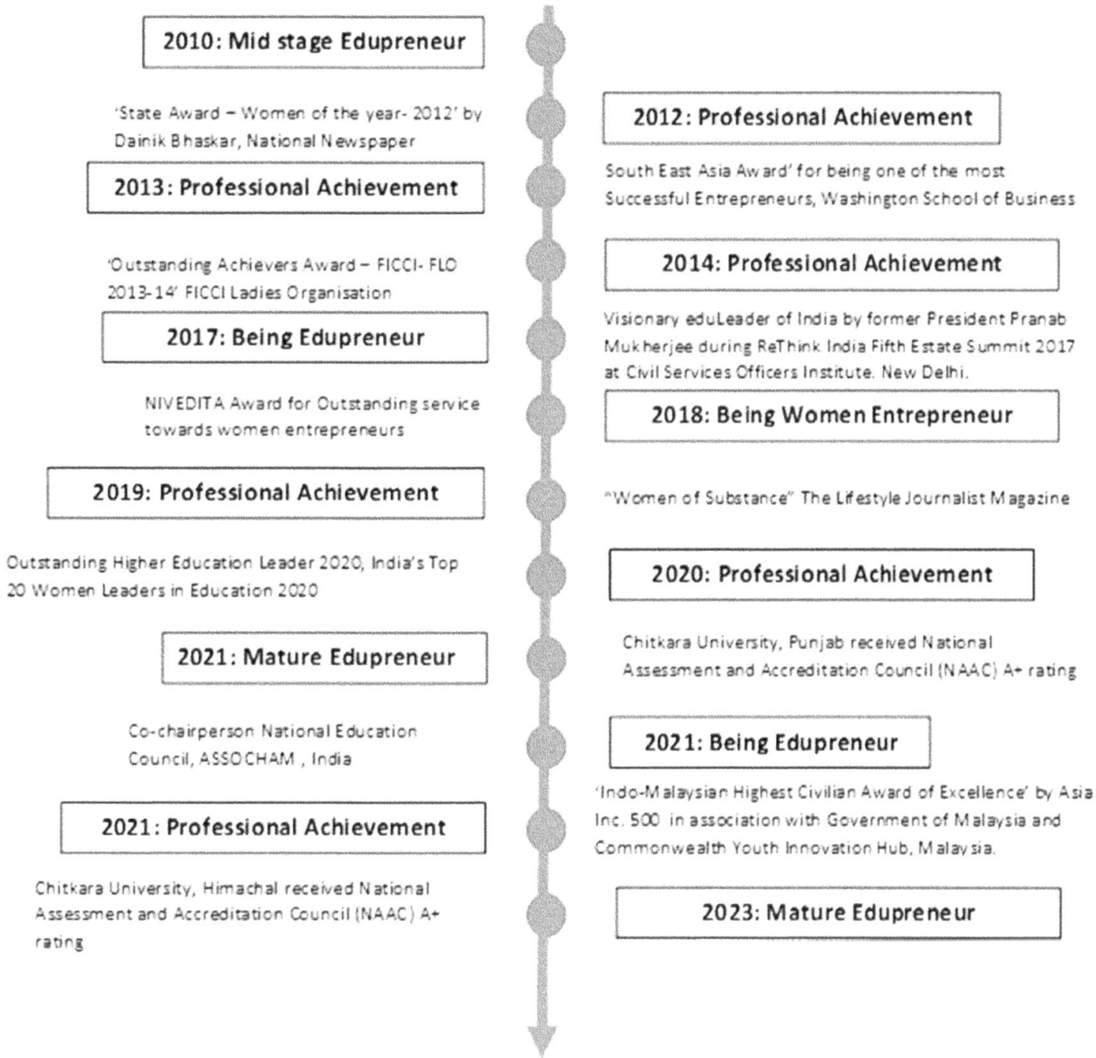

Exhibit 5: Important statistics

Figure 7. Important statistics
(Approximate values as on March 2023)*

Important Statistics for Intellectual Property for Chitkara University, Punjab*	
Patents	2111 patents filed 521 patents granted
Research Papers	1682 Conference papers 2687 papers in journals 244 book chapters 26 books
International collaborations	198
Industry Partners Number of courses - UG - PG Regulator's Affiliations	200 58 32 • UNIVERSITY GRANTS COMMISSION (UGC) • NATIONAL ASSESSMENT AND ACCREDITATION COUNCIL (NAAC) – GRADE A+ • COUNCIL OF ARCHITECTURE (COA) • PHARMACY COUNCIL OF INDIA (PCI) • NATIONAL COUNCIL FOR TEACHER EDUCATION (NCTE) • INDIAN NURSING COUNCIL (INC) • NATIONAL COUNCIL FOR HOTEL MANAGEMENT & CATERING TECHNOLOGY (NCHMCT) • ASSOCIATION OF UNIVERSITIES OF ASIA AND THE PACIFIC (AUAP) • RECOGNITION OF "INSTITUTIONAL ANIMAL ETHICS COMMITTEE (IAEC)" BY CPCSEA, MOFAHD • RECOGNITION OF "INSTITUTION'S INNOVATION COUNCIL (IIC)", MINISTRY OF EDUCATION, GOVT. OF INDIA • RECOGNITION OF THE INSTITUTE AS BUSINESS INCUBATOR (BI)/ HOST INSTITUTE (HI) FOR IMPLEMENTATION OF THE SCHEME "SUPPORT FOR

TEACHING NOTE

Marking a Legacy as an Edupreneur: Dr. Madhu Chitkara

Synopsis

The case describes an exceptional women edupreneur Dr. Madhu Chitkara. Dr. Madhu Chitkara and Dr. Ashok K Chitkara are an exceptional duo who are standing on the point of training upcoming leaders and academicians in the education sector while keeping their feet firm on grounds of quality of education. As they look ahead to the celebration of Excellence Awards in Feb 2023, Dr. Madhu Chitkara revisit her journey of being an edupreneur.

Case Objectives

The main objective of the case is to instill the zeal of entrepreneurship and leadership in the students.

Table 1. Teaching objectives

Major Teaching Objectives	
Entrepreneurship	To discuss entrepreneurial journey, style of a women edupreneur in a not-for-profit sector in a developing economy.
Leadership futures, leadership development and university strategy	To bring challenges and management requirements in leadership positions while developing strategy for university.
Strategic management, Inspiration	To specifically discuss strategic management decisions, inspiration and leadership development.

Position in the Course

This case can be referred for both undergraduate (during final year) and postgraduate (during first year) courses in management, leadership, entrepreneurship and strategic management. This can be part of 'Strategic Management' or 'Entrepreneurship' or 'Leadership' courses and can be used for a 90- minute session.

The case may be used in business schools, schools of education, public policy. Further, it can be referred by HR executives holding key responsibilities for leadership, entrepreneurial development, and a key reading for deans, directors etc. preparing for key responsibility position in an educational institution.

Suggested Readings

Students can be assigned the following pre-reading to get a basic understanding on entrepreneurship:

Gutterman, A.S. (2018). *Founder's Preformation Duties and Liabilities.* Business Expert Press, Harvard Business Publishing.

Stevenson, H.H., & Gumpert, D.E. (1985). The Heart of Entrepreneurship. *Harvard Business Review,* 1-11.

Hamori, M., Bonet, R., Cappelli, P., & Sambare, S. (2022). Women are Scaling out on the way to the Top. *MIT Sloan Management Review,* 1-12.

Inder, S., Singh, A., & Sharma, S. (2022). *Institutions, Resilience, and Dynamic Capabilities of Entrepreneurial Ecosystems in Emerging Economies.* IGI Global Publishers

Mittal, A., Mantri, A., Tandon, U., & Dwivedi, Y. K. (2022). A unified perspective on the adoption of online teaching in higher education during the COVID-19 pandemic. *Information Discovery and Delivery*, *50*(2), 117-132.

Kumar, P., Tandon, U., & Taneja, A. (2022). Underpinning the relevancy of the NIRF rankings in higher education management institutions in India. *Journal of Public Affairs*, *22*(3), e2579.

Teaching Plan

The case can be first introduced as pre-read along with other relevant material suited to subject. The best plan to initiate discussion is to trigger participants with thoughts on being a women entrepreneur, leader and the style, beliefs, strengths, weaknesses.

Bringing this analysis on table, participants can be called to have broad and diverse class discussion on leadership style and capacities that would be most effective. Participants will soon sense that Chitkara University is a personification of its leader and that its' strategic intent mirrors closely her own predispositions. They should understand that strategy making for an entrepreneur results not only from the analytical aspects of what can be done (resources/competencies) and what could be done (segments of opportunity) but also from large doses of want (passion for) and should (a sense of broader responsibility).

Wherever appropriate and possible, the instructor should call for alternative assumptions and future leadership challenges, on what leaders need, how their capacities develop. The instructor can also have a quick survey of class by asking following questions and gauging the responses by show of hands from class participants.

- Is Dr. Madhu Chitkara viewed as social entrepreneur, women entrepreneur, or an academician turned entrepreneur?
- Does she hold a centralized or decentralized leadership style?
- Do you find gender equality in her leadership style? If yes, then why? If no, then why?

Suggested Time Plan

Following time plan is suggested for 90 minutes discussion session.

Table 2. Suggested time plan

Exhibit TA1: Suggested Time Plan	
Initial Discussion	10 minutes
Study groups discussion on entrepreneurial aspect of Dr. Madhu Chitkara	20 minutes
Discussion on 'University' as personification of Dr. Madhu Chitkara journey.	25 minutes
Discussion on challenges faced by women leaders	20 minutes
Discussion on future challenges and possibilities	15 minutes

Pre-class assignment questions:

1. Describe and evaluate Madhu Chitkara as an entrepreneur. Analyse her style, beliefs, strengths and weaknesses.
2. Where do you feel she has succeeded and what might she had faced as difficulties?
3. Describe and evaluate the key steps taken by Dr. Madhu Chitkara in shaping Chitkara University strategy- what makes Chitkara different?
4. What assumptions does this strategy make about the future challenges that leaders will face the type of leadership needed, and how these abilities can be developed.

Case Analysis

There are five parts suggested for analysis of case:

1. Dr. Madhu Chitkara as an edupreneur. Her story, style and current profile.
2. Discussion over the assumptions on being a women edupreneur and challenges that women leaders face.
3. An analysis of Dr. Madhu Chitkara's journey and her responsibilities
4. Discussion on key assumptions, steps in philosophy of Dr. Madhu Chitkara.
5. Choices among the future which Dr. Madhu Chitkara is considering at the close of the case

Landscape: Dream for Quality Education

It would be great to start by setting up the context for the case. Instructor can introduce the students with a brief history on the foundation and growth of Chitkara University. For building up the discussion on this, students can capture many instances on the milestones for Chitkara University. For instance, laying the foundation of Chitkara Institute of Engineering and Technology, with affiliation from Punjab Technical University in 2002. This was followed by Chitkara College of Education for women and Chitkara School of Planning and Architecture and ultimately Chitkara University in 2003, 2004 and 2010 respectively (Refer to Appendix ##2). One point to be brought to attention here is each milestone achieved by Chitkara University, Chitkara International School is linked with an experience, episode or emotion of Dr. Madhu Chitkara. Hence, the growth of Chitkara University is fueled by vision of Dr. Madhu Chitkara.

From this, discussion can be extended with students on the personality, style and profile of Dr. Madhu. A brief outline for discussion is provided below:

Madhu Chitkara: Her Style and Fit Into Current Profile

This case presents plentiful information on background, style, personality and journey of Dr. Madhu Chitkara. Dr. Madhu Chitkara has a lot to handle on her plate, she is juggling a number of roles and yet maintain firm footing on each role. This brings our focus on understanding her persona as a whole and thus, discussion on strengths and weakness must come as a whole, and students must understand that an entrepreneur's personality cannot be observed in piecemeal. Considering the context and term of fit, the following points are important to note:

1. Madhu founded Chitkara University, and has been the entrepreneurial spirit the fueled the growth and journey over a time span of approximately 20 years from its foundation. We notice here that entrepreneurship revolves around taking responsibility and initiatives to bring dreams into reality with decisions that call for a lot on stake. Entrepreneurial decisions are risky decisions and an entrepreneur is called to take responsibility of consequences before the results of decisions are reaped. For instance, in order to manifest the dream of building up an educational institution, both Dr. Madhu Chitkara and Dr. Ashok K Chitkara gave up their hard earned and well paying jobs. This decision was not an easy decision as this decision held the capacity to change the course of their further lives. But with her determination and conviction, Dr. Madhu Chitkara worked hard to turn the sequence of events and manifested her dream into reality. Students must note that stakes pinned onto this decision were emotional as well as financial.
2. Dr. Madhu Chitkara calls herself as accidental entrepreneur, but she is also a change agent who held an uncanny ability to achieve her goals and make out follow and work. She is also a women edupreneur with a humble background. Dr. Madhu Chitkara and Dr. Ashok K Chitkara are first generation entrepreneurs who had to struggle to arrange for resources. Dr. Madhu fits into the definition of entrepreneur as someone "who pursues opportunity beyond the resources currently available" by Harvard Business School professor 'Howard Stevenson'.
3. Dr. Madhu's dedication to quality makes her a tough boss who values quality to a greater extent. For instance, it's her dedication to quality of education that made Chitkara university gave away management quota seats. Students may further be made to recall the events which led to establishment of Chitkara International School as a consequence of Dr. Madhu's love for quality education.
4. Dr. Madhu Chitkara holds administrative skills and had dealt with tough challenges of dealing with the governmental processes and other allied processes in establishing institutions. Students must understand that establishing an organization is not all about placing feet into the shoes of CEO, but one has work on each dimension of building up an organization. For example, Dr. Madhu had to deal with complex web of rules and regulations, deal with different government bodies, understand laws, affiliations, setting up administrative processes for the departments, course structures etc.
5. Dr. Madhu does not work for monetary rewards. She has always placed her stakeholders over and above the monetary aims. Her devotion to society and education also inclines her to be a women social entrepreneur.
6. Though she is woman, yet she is gender neutral entrepreneur who believes in equality. This can be indicated by her statement indicating 'a man behind success of a woman and vice versa'.
7. The case suggests that Madhu has acquired little of her unique leadership competences via a number of channels. First, formal education held a very important part of her journey. She pursued her PhD at time when women were not into on forefront in pursuing higher education. This gave her an edge in understanding the leverage education can place in an individual's life. Second, the value system from her family is still embedded in vision of Chitkara University. Third, social capital cultivated by her in the university. She has nurtured social networks in institutions along with formal systems so as to establish harmony and an ecosystem to enable a sustainable survival of organization.

Additional points suggested by students can be jotted down on blackboard plan to draw a comprehensive picture of the case. Additionally, at this point instructor can bring thoughts on the point that it's personality of entrepreneur, leader that gets personified into operations of an enterprise.

The Journey of an Entrepreneur

There will be many diverse comments about the journey, decisions taken, responsibilities handled and leadership styles followed. In this discussion, the instructor should encourage participants to think up across different perspectives and differently about the needs for managers, entrepreneurs and leaders who aim to complete their journey of establishing a legacy. The following question and points can be employed to guide the discussion:

"Where do you feel she has succeeded and what might she had faced as difficulties?"

She calls herself as accidental entrepreneur. This indicates her style of making most of every situation, taking advantage of:

- **Preference to Merit:** She stick to her gut in establishing quality of education. One remarkable example of this is her giving up management quota seats and preferring to merit.
- **Giving Back to Society:** Chitkara University fulfills its social responsibility. It has adopted five villages surrounding Chitkara university and carry out many social service events.
- **On Personal Front:** She risked her job in order to pursue her dream of being an entrepreneur.
- **Dedication to Quality and Meritocracy:** Her dedication for meritocracy can be reflected in strong and bold choices she made during her leadership.
- Juggling between different roles as entrepreneur, academician, administrator, mother and wife, while keeping the spirit of being teacher running deep down as foundation stone.
- **Holding Multiple Skills Simultaneously:** Facing challenges of different regulatory authorities like red tapism, societal stereotypes, dealing with officials etc. call for altogether different set of skills.
- Challenged the societal norms, expectations during 1980s and 1990s in India. Dr. Madhu's responsibilities are strectched in two ways: horizontally by broad responsibilities at Chitkara University and Chitkara International School and Home as well, and vertically, because she looks after many details as an mother, wife, academician, administrator and entrepreneur. She is continuously juggling these roles.
- Family as support system is a big aspect of Dr. Madhu's personality, which is reflected in the strength and conviction exhibited by her during entrepreneurial journey.

Key Steps in Philosophy of Dr. Madhu Chitkara

It is therefore recommended that for a typical executive session the instructor attempts to organize the discussion along the following analytical lines:

1. How would Chitkara University's focus on quality education was developed?

Students should be asked to consider the context while responding to this question. Other competing institutions and a general discussion on understanding the student profile in a developing economy must be considered for discussion. Additionally, considerations of Chitkara University in past and the accolades achieved by Chitkara University in establishing itself as an institutions providing quality education must be considered.

2. How do you think the focus of entrepreneurs remains over a period of time?

In all likelihood, students would recognize the multiplicity of roles handled by Dr Madhu Chitkara, her achievements, and the progression of institution.

3. How Dr. Madhu Chitkara handled the context of social responsibility?

This will be heightened when students would focus on 'inclusiveness' on growth of an institution. In all likelihood, the current focus on corporate social responsibility can be brought to understand that Chitkara University has adopted villages surrounding it and has been contributing its bit in creation of a better world.

4. How will the role on personal front and professional front be balanced?

Answer: It was a tough call. But participants should be encouraged to think "and" instead of "or"- with respect to management versus leadership and entrepreneurship; with respect to balancing roles of being women entrepreneur, leader, mother, wife,....

5. What balance will be needed between managers, leaders, and entrepreneurs, and will we really be looking for those who can combine all three?

Answer: The need for decentralized entrepreneurial leadership is likely to grow as the world and business become more segmented, and impossible to manage from the top down alone. As more initiative taking is required from the bottom up, top management roles and responsibilities will also be redefined.

An overall conclusion is that leadership is not going to become any easier, and that the faint of heart need not apply! The world will require legions of outstanding individual entrepreneurial leaders lower down in organizations, as well as entrepreneurs who start and build their own enterprises.

Instructor can, at this stage, encourage a discussion on leadership development and succession planning. In all likelihood, students should be guided to combine (not to be selective or choose between):

1. The traditional view of universities
2. Shifts and change management structures
3. New and innovative focus on dilemmas faced by leaders.
4. Enhancing understanding in change patterns, creativity, unconventional thinking, vision.

An overall conclusion here is that students should be made to think on terms of inclusivity i.e. "and" and not "or" while taking various decisions on way forward in entrepreneurial activity.

With at least some of these issues on the table, participants will be in a stronger position to evaluate Dr. Madhu's current and future strategy and plans for university. We could certainly say that she is on the right general track, particularly with the current configuration of an exceptionally experienced visiting faculty teaching the more traditional school management and entrepreneuship programs, and plans for an expanded permanent faculty to research and teach her broader agendas.

Blackboard Plan

Figure 8.

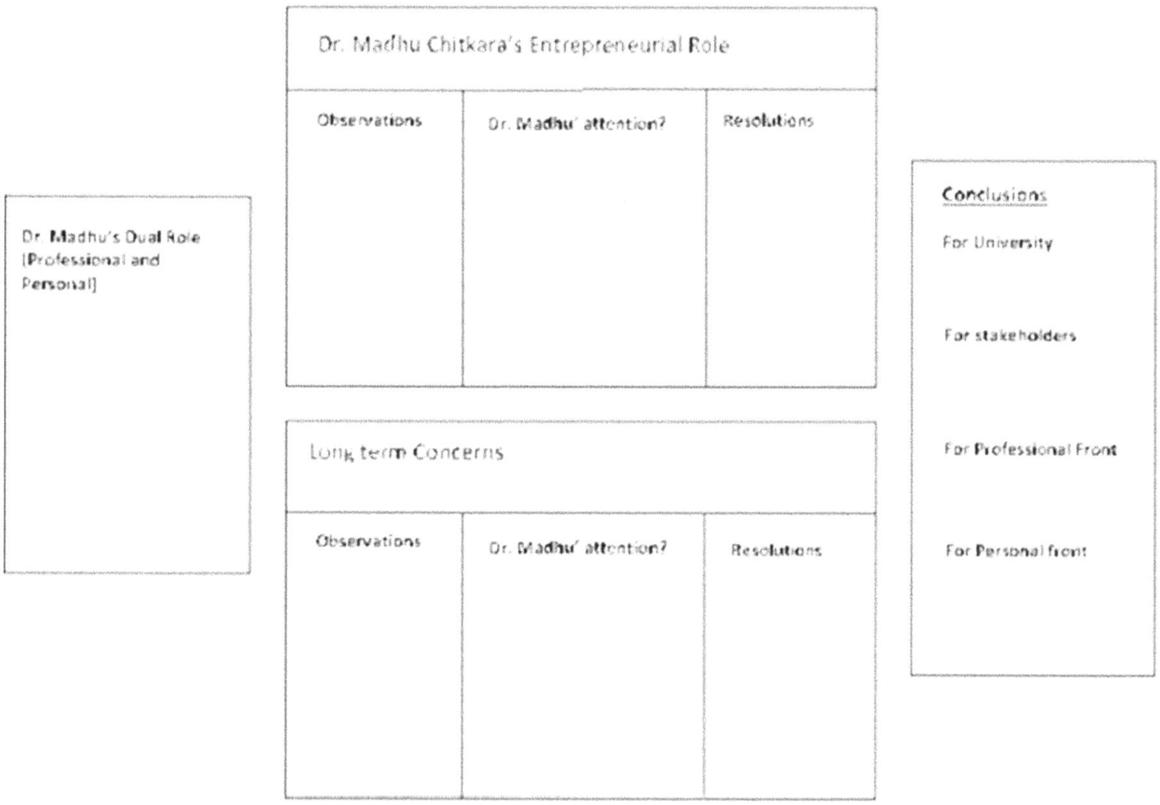

Take home/final wrap up/lesson learnt

1. The kind of entrepreneurial style that Dr. Madhu exhibits is not universally applicable in all managerial and leadership situations. It has fitted and worked with great success at Chitkara University during past 20 years. As the educational institution scales up and expands its horizons across new fields and extend its network with more industry partners, the entrepreneurial capacities and leadership is going to take a wide shift. Dr. Madhu's style seem appropriate particularly in growing field of social entrepreneur and edupreneur. The ties with corporate sector or industry, which is profit driven, must be strengthened to balance the primary stakeholders i.e. students and society, which are non-profit driven.
2. The choices, decisions, actions, strategies and perspectives are developed in the case on the assumptions about the education ecosystem of a developing nation. The success of an edupreneur depends on the evolving shape of the world, business created and deepening roots of technology

in education. Industry and educational institutions should follow the ‘hand in glove’ approach to guide the fate of students. Thus, edupreneurs would not have extend their understanding on these fronts as well.

3. Entrepreneurship and strategic choices are greater than matching competencies, arranging resources and opportunities. Edupreneurs like Dr. Madhu teach us that we also need to include substantial doses of passion and social responsibility. The same is applicable in the profit driven corporate world, if the bigger global problems are to be offered with appropriate and adequate solutions in time.

Word Map for the Case

Figure 9. Word map

ENDNOTE

[1] Management quota refers to mechanism that has been authorized by government through which student can secure direct admission in an institute. This was made available to educational institutions as such institutions did not receive any governmental grants. These seats allow institutes to charge excess fees despite comparatively lower marks obtained by students.

Chapter 2
Lessons From the FTX Cryptocurrency Exchange Collapse

Vijaya Kittu Manda
https://orcid.org/0000-0002-1680-8210
GITAM School of Business, GITAM University (Deemed), India

Lubza K. Nihar
GITAM School of Business, GITAM University (Deemed), India

EXECUTIVE SUMMARY

Governments and market regulators are debating and deliberating on matters of concern and benefits of treating cryptocurrencies as an asset or a currency so that they can tax them accordingly. 2022 has shaken the financial markets with the onset of the worst crypto winters in cryptocurrency history on one hand and the collapse of a few cryptocurrencies and the exchanges that facilitate investing and trading in them. These events brought chills to the stakeholders, who began questioning the stability of the cryptocurrency and the functioning of various exchanges. Cryptocurrencies promise to be the future of currency, and hence, there is an immediate need to protect investors by regulating them – especially those cryptocurrency exchanges running in a centralized form. The case examines the collapse of FTX and other financial institutions because they exposed the structural weaknesses existing in the system. The case also examines competitor business strategies to protect themselves from such incidents and stresses the need for governmental and regulatory interventions.

INTRODUCTION

"A year ago, Sam Bankman-Fried ditched his trademark shorts and T-shirt for a suit and sat before the U.S. House of Representatives as the acceptable face of crypto. Lawmakers could not see that, under the table, his shoelaces were untied." – Joshua Oliver & Stefania Palma, Financial Express Weekend, U.K., December 17, 2022

DOI: 10.4018/978-1-6684-8488-3.ch002

The financial services industry has transformed due to innovative and disruptive financial engineered products that use emerging technologies of Web 3.0 and the Metaverse era. These have given rise to new-generation financial instruments such as cryptocurrencies and Non-Fungible Tokens (NFTs) that are backed by the fundamental concepts of blockchain and Distributed Ledger Technology (DLT). These digital currencies and assets have led to the emergence of newer forms of businesses, such as cryptocurrency exchanges and Distributed Autonomous Organizations (DAO). Cryptocurrency exchanges, also known as Digital Currency Exchanges (DCE), are online marketplaces that let investors purchase and sell cryptocurrencies in return for fiat money or other cryptocurrencies.

THE DILEMMA

FTX is the world's second-largest cryptocurrency exchange. Its sudden and surprising collapse before the end of 2022 affected millions of its investors globally and has put billions of dollars invested by them into limbo. The unprecedented situation pushed the cryptocurrency community to review the concept of cryptocurrencies, the industry, and the dangers of centralized exchanges. Their faith and confidence levels were already put to the test as cryptocurrencies were experiencing the most prolonged crypto winter period. The previous crypto winter was in 2017 and lasted several months, and the present ongoing one started at the end of 2021. Extreme turbulence in the cryptocurrency markets was observed in 2021 and 2022 - particularly between May to June 2022. The bearish trend was ongoing till November 2022. Some leading digital asset market players, including Vauld, Three Arrow Capital, Terra-Luna, Celsius Network LLC, BlockFi Inc, Voyager Digital Ltd, Genesis Global Holding LLC, and Gemini Trust, have collapsed due to the crypto meltdown. Experts believe that another year of crypto winter is likely before a turnaround can be seen (Cornelius, 2022). This means crypto asset traders and investors face a wall of worries until the digital asset market revives. The investigations into the activities of FTX were univocally pointing toward the biggest fraud in American history! Parallels were drawn to the Ponzi scheme architect Madoff and the bankruptcy of Enron. The poster boy who sat before the U.S. House of Representatives giving visionary speeches is now testifying about what exactly led to the collapse of his own FTX.

INDUSTRY DYNAMICS

"The great crypto crisis is upon us." — Hyun Song Shin, Financial Express Weekend, U.K., December 17, 2022

Cryptocurrency origins can be traced to 1998. However, they emerged as an instrument for alternative investment after the post-Financial Crisis of 2008. While Cryptocurrencies have had a tumultuous journey so far, they are undoubtedly considered marvelous creations of technology. However, their global acceptance is still debatable because of the lack of proper acceptance or support, particularly by Governments and regulators of various countries. Due to the complexity of the instrument, only some countries could take a clear stand. Some have officially accepted them (such as El Salvador), and few ban them (such as in China and Turkey, amongst others) or make moves towards regulating them (U.S., U.K., South Africa, South Korea, India, amongst others). Despite the mixed reactions and actions by governments and regulators, the meteoric rise in the prices of Bitcoin and other cryptocurrencies has led investors worldwide to invest heavily in cryptocurrencies due to the fear of missing out (FOMO) effect.

The uncertainty of the Governments in taking a firm decision on cryptocurrency and the wait-and-watch mode of financial regulators led startups, small companies, and corporations to begin offering platforms in the name of cryptocurrency exchanges that allowed customers to trade and invest in cryptocurrencies. In most countries, these young cryptocurrency exchanges were registered as legal entities at places outside the original jurisdiction of their target market. As a result, the business ownership, financial data, and location are often masked and cannot be tracked. Nevertheless, the success of these businesses allowed the unchecked and free flow of value across borders, resulting in government and regulators taking a keen interest in this digital asset. Table 2 shows the list of the top 10 cryptocurrencies being traded globally. Table 3 shows the list of the top 10 cryptocurrency exchanges.

LEGISLATION AND REGULATIONS

The cryptocurrency that started as a technological experiment started gaining momentum in terms of volumes and amount invested. Before the growth, cryptocurrency regulators were strictly against exchanges dealing with uncommon financial instruments. In 2004, three exchanges - Stevens I.T. Pty Ltd, Sydney Gold Sales Pty Ltd, and Fountainhead Management Pty Ltd – voluntarily closed their business. Australian Securities and Investments Commission (ASIC) investigated the *modus operandi* and found that these exchanges did not hold the appropriate license to allow digital currency transactions. Gold Age (2006), E-Gold (2007), and WebMoney (2008) were chased, investigated, and made to close their business in the U.S. for not adhering to due regulations. This global phenomenon of a crackdown on uncommon financial instruments was common because financial regulators have a clear mandate to tackle such products under legislation that permit them to take measures to regulate.

However, the complexities involved in cryptocurrencies in regulatory recognition, digital market infrastructure, money laundering issues, security and investor protection concerns, and the use of emerging technologies have created divided views among governments and financial regulators.

The first cryptocurrency was Bitcoin, created in 2009 by a person or group using the pseudonym Satoshi Nakamoto. A white paper on Bitcoin (BTC) claimed that the blockchain system would be behind the operationalization of the entire cryptocurrency market. The first reported real-world financial transaction involving Bitcoin occurred on May 22, 2010, when a Florida man negotiated to pay 10,000 BTC for two pizzas priced at about $25. This was when cryptocurrency enthusiasts understood the financial value of digital assets and their financial engineering and technology value. The online exchanges started trading in Bitcoin in the year 2011. The growth of Bitcoin led to the introduction of other cryptocurrencies in the market.

CME Group Inc. announced that it would launch Bitcoin Futures contracts in 2017, a first-of-a-kind financial product offered by a United States-regulated financial institution. Binance is one of the first established exchanges for cryptocurrencies.

THE COLLAPSE OF FTX

"At first, most people ignore it, and then suddenly everyone gets more excited until it becomes obvious that promises cannot keep up with reality." — Jarek Hirniak, founder and CEO of Generation Lambda, The U.S. News, August 31, 2022

According to Jarek Hirniak, the crypto bubble was inevitable as Bitcoin followed a common innovation trajectory known as the Gartner Hype Cycle. Whenever there is an innovation with new technology, there is an increase in the visibility of a product or service. It is followed by very high expectations that are way beyond reality, creating a mismatch of expectations and actuals. This happened with Bitcoin and other cryptos. As the gap widened, investors realized they would face liquidity issues with their cryptocurrency investments. The possibilities of market manipulation in the crypto market increased as the investors did not get their expected returns combined with a low level of regulation.

Mt. Gox (2014), MyCryptoWallet (2021), and FTX (2022) are some modern cryptocurrency exchanges that stopped their operations and, in some cases, were liquidated for scandal or other reasons.

The collapse of FTX is believed to be caused by its former CEO, "crypto king" Sam Bankman-Friedand (SBF), who was also named as the "next Warren Buffet" and the hedge fund he co-founded - Alameda Research – that was intentionally deceiving/cheating their customers and investors. The linkage between the exchange and hedgefund became a dangerous business model for investors. The FTX makes money from transaction fees on users' assets, and Alameda seeks to profit from actively trading or investing funds it controls. As per the Chapter 11 bankruptcy filing, as many as one million investors are believed to have lost their investments held in FTX.

The exchange was founded in 2019 by Sam Bankman-Fried (SBF) high-profile figure in the cryptocurrency industry known for his political ties, celebrity endorsements, and bailouts of other struggling firms and Zixiao "Gary" Wang. The Bahamas-based cryptocurrency exchange was run from a luxury penthouse with about nine housemates, including the Director of Engineering, Nishad Singh (F.P. Explainers, 2022), Caroline Ellison, the CEO of Alameda Research, and Gary Wang, the Chief Technical Officer and Co-founder of FTX, amongst others. A gang of kids ran the exchange, but it was able to attract funds from several marquee venture capitalists who invested in the company (Crunchbase, 2022). The 30-year-old SBF had a net worth of US$ 10.5 billion in October 2022, but the collapse of his empire eroded 94% of his net worth in a single day. Bloomberg Billionaires Index reported the collapse as the most significant one-day drop in its history.

Cracks began to surface when in September 2022, Coindesk, a crypto news desk, reported there were irregularities with FTX. Customers were seen rushing to cash in their investments though the number and volume were low then. On November 2, 2022: Alameda Research finance data was leaked, exposing its relationship with FTX. Many of the assets of Alameda Research, a trading firm, were held in FTT - the native token of FTX. Only a tiny portion of FTT was traded, and as much as 40 percent of Alameda Research's assets are in FTTs, which made the media suspect since this is an unusual quantity of its holding. This implied that these assets were impossible to sell in the open market, but the Balance Sheets presented by SBF showed them at fictitious market prices. These FTT were also used as collaterals for loans that included loans of customer funds from FTX to Alameda. Investigations revealed that the customer funds at FTX are channeled to Alameda Research so they can trade. Alameda also enjoyed priority treatment in terms of – faster transactions, negative ledger balances, exemption from liquidity and margin requirements, exemption from paying interest to FTX, allowed to overextend trade, and an unlimited supply of loans (Joshua & Stefania, 2022).

Bank Run Situation and Solvency Crisis

FTX followed the business model of depending too much on fresh/new investor money pouring into the company to run its operations. Such business models ought to fail sooner or later because of liquidity reasons. This way of running a business is not a sustainable one. What is believed to be the real trigger for the FTX collapse is the "bank run" or "run for deposits" situation. Binance, the world's leading cryptocurrency exchange and the immediate competitor of FTX, announced that it would be dissolving its holdings in FTX Token (FTT) following speculation of the liquidity of FTT in early November 2022. At that time, Binance held 23 million FTX tokens worth about $529 million. FTT is the native currency of FTX. SBF countered with a tweet saying, "FTX is fine. Assets are fine. A competitor is trying to go after us with false rumors." However, the announcement made by Binance was seriously considered by the market. The result is the collapse of FTX as the investors, in a panic reaction to the news, withdrew 90% of all FTTs. The market crashed as the price fell from $22 on November 7, 2022, to $5 on November 8, 2022 –a whopping 80% erosion in value.

FTX had $900 million in sellable assets against liabilities of $9 billion. It came under immense pressure because panic withdrawals amounting to US$ 6 billion in a 72-hour window led to a sudden cash-strapped situation. Cryptocurrency exchanges are not banks. Unlike banks, the exchanges do not lend securities that the investors own. So, ideally, the case of a "run for deposits" should not happen. On November 8, FTX stopped allowing customers to take money out of the platform.

Additionally, FTX has promised its investors that their securities will never be lent out or used by the crypto entrusted to the exchange. However, the turn of events and its evidence tell a different storyline than the promise made by the FTX. The investor-owned cryptos are lent to Alameda Research, which "gambled away" the cryptos. SBF said he stepped down as CEO of Alameda in 2019 and nominated Ms.Ellison as its CEO. He, however, maintained discretionary decision-making authority but, after the collapse, could not explain what went wrong there or how customer funds ended up in Alameda. Commodity Futures Trading Commission (CFTC) asserts that SBF had regular (often daily) participation in various in-person and mobile chat communication with senior personnel at Alameda and thereby remained the ultimate decision maker at Alameda.

On November 8, he announced that Binance would purchase FTX for an undisclosed amount in what would essentially constitute a bailout for the beleaguered firm. However, Binance quickly backed out, with Zhao citing reports that FTX had mismanaged user funds and information gleaned during the standard due diligence process that accompanies such deals. The sudden collapse tempted Binance to announce that it would be interested in buying FTX, a bailout for the troubled firm. However, Binance did not proceed with the deal citing reports of mismanagement of user funds by FTX. A series of group chats that were disclosed to the media showed some alleged conversations between Changpeng Zhao ("C.Z."), the CEO of Binance, and SBF. C.Z. and SBF often publicly spar and taunt each over Twitter. However, considering the gravity of the situation, SBF reached out to C.Z. for help "for the sake of the industry and users" (New York Times, 2022). While C.Z. initially agreed to give a loan and even buy FTX, there was a change of mind apparently after examining the books. The alarming text revealed that C.Z. warned SBF, "Stop now, don't cause more damage…The more damage you do now, the more jail time."

Bankruptcy Announcement and Implications

A series of announcements were out that the U.S. Securities and Exchange Commission (US SEC), Commodity Futures Trading Commission, and Department of Justice (DoJ) have launched an investigation into the company. On November 11, 2022, FTX and about 100 related entities filed for bankruptcy protection under Chapter 11 in the Delaware bankruptcy court. In January 2022, the company published its valuation at $32 billion. Institutional investors who lost money due to their stakes in FTX include Tiger Global Management, the Ontario Teachers' Pension Plan, SoftBank Group, BlackRock, Lightspeed Venture Partners, Temasek, and Sequoia Capital. The effect was felt on Cryptocurrencies too. Tether dropped below its peg price of $1.00 to $0.97, and Bitcoin sank to its lowest price in two years.

Royal Bahamas Police Force started an investigation into the operations of a subsidiary - FTX Digital Markets Ltd - after its Chairman, Ryan Salame warned the authorities. The authorities felt that Mr. Salame had advised that transferring funds from FTX Digital to Alameda was contrary to corporate governance and operations at FTX Digital. The SEC released the letter before the U.S. Bankruptcy Court later. FTX Digital is not one of the 100-odd companies of FTX that filed for bankruptcy, though (Jonathan, 2022).

In September 2022, FTX announced it had received approval from the Cypriot regulator to operate as a Cyprus Investment Firm, allowing the company to own a local investment firm it had previously acquired fully. This allowed FTX EU to serve the European Economic Area. Cyprus's Securities and Exchange Commission asked FTX EU to suspend its operations on November 9, 2022.

Amongst the list of investors who fell prey to FTX included the Belfer family, famous for their legendary oil dynasty. The Belfer family lost $2 billion in the Enron episode, and two decades later, they (Belfer Investment Partners) lost because of their exposure to FTX through equity shares. Documents showed that the family business invested in the 2021 and 2022 fundraising rounds of FTX and later in the U.S. business of the crypto exchange. What is worrisome is the ability of FTX to woo families showing signs of the far reach of SBF. Of course, some are lucky. Founders Fund, a venture capital firm founded by billionaire Peter Thiel, exited almost all its cryptocurrency investments in March 2022, bringing in $1.8 billion in returns.

Lavish Spending Chasing Ambitious Dreams

On November 20, 2022, Zhao tweeted, "#bitcoin is not dead. We are still here". He said one need not be a genius to understand that things at FTX are wrong. He pointed at spending practices at FTX, especially marketing & 'partnerships,' luxurious offices in Chicago, exclusive residences in the Bahamas, fancy parties at the Bahamas resorts, trips across the globe, and mansions for all of their senior staff (and his parents)." FTX even purchased a five-acre plot to construct housing (which could not happen) for its staff.

SBF had global expansion plans and was willing to spend money on sports sponsorship. Media reported SBF negotiations with English Premium League to sponsor the Manchester United and Liverpool football teams in early 2022. Of course, the sponsorship deal did not happen, but $100 million was earmarked for the engagement. FTX worked numbers to consider being the leading partner for Liverpool FC for the 2023 season and beyond. Liverpool managers were happy to go with the deal and even flew to the Bahamas to give a corporate presentation and expressed favoritism for the FTX deal.

SBF appeared confused about the success rate of such sponsorships when he referred to NBA Miami Heat sponsorship in an internal email. He asked for a customer survey to measure the conversion rates of the deal. FTX has spent millions of dollars for a football stadium at the University of California Berkeley and got its logo on Formula 1 racing team Mercedes-AMG Petronas to patches worn by Umpires at Major League Baseball teams. They are a title sponsor for an esports team called TSM. A $135 million 19-year deal was signed in 2022, and the Miami Heat basketball team was renamed FTX arena. NFL quarterback Tom Brady became an ambassador of the crypto brand. Ratings and Data agency Nielsen in February 2022 said sports sponsorship deals with crypto, blockchain, and digital asset companies would turn 9x of the 2021 levels – to $5 billion by 2026. The disgrace of SBF and the collapse of FTX has made sports teams think twice before taking digital asset companies as sponsors (Samuel, 2023). The situation surely warranted the need for careful vetting of sponsorships before sports teams ink the deal. Seven Leagues says the crypto winter has reduced the appetite for sports collectibles and that the conversion of sports fans to NFT enthusiasts is expected to be slower. In a December 2022 survey by European Sponsorship Association, reflections of a bleak picture of the industry were surfacing, with many feelings that alliance with digital asset companies is negatively affecting.

The Confession

In early December 2022, SBF said that he finished reviewing the collapse and was ready to testify before the U.S. Congress (Aljazeera, 2022). In his first appearance (live interview with *The New York Times*) after filing for bankruptcy, he said that he was unaware of the extent of transactions going on in his business. He blamed management failure and sloppy accounting for the collapse. He said he "did not ever want to do a crime" and that he "did not knowingly commingle funds." Speaking to the BBC in his so-called media apology tour, SBF said he is ready to start a new business/venture to repay the customers he owes.

The Contagion Effect

The collapse of FTX has started a domino effect in the crypto industry. Days after the collapse of FTX, another leader – BlockFi – filed for bankruptcy because of significant exposure to FTX (Natalie, 2022). At the same time, Maple Finance was reported to have ties with crypto firm Orthogonal Trading and is alleged to have "misrepresented its financial position." Since the collapse of FTX, corporations in the crypto space are keeping watch on one another as to who will be the next collateral victim. The cryptocurrency empire of Barry Silbert, led by Digital Currency Group, is reported to be under the radar by DoJ and SEC. Lender Genesis stopped allowing customers to withdraw money and issue new loans in November 2022.

The collapse of FTX only extended the crypto winter, and industry elephants are shivering. November 2022 saw the highest amount of withdrawals in Bitcoin, with 91,363 tokens worth nearly $1.5 billion pulled off exchanges. On the day the shocking FTX announcement was made, Bitcoin fell by 14%, while its immediate competitor, Ether, fell by 16%. Bitcoin lost 25% of its value in those two days, extending its bearish trend to the sub-$15,000 territory. Post the week of collapse, cryptocurrencies such as Solana, Bitcoin, and Polygon have seen increased inflows, while Ethereum-based products recorded outflows. Hedge fund Galois Capital said that nearly half of its assets (about US$ 100 million) were trapped in FTX.

Post-Collapse Revival of FTX

John J. Ray III took up the onerous task of cleaning up the mess at FTX after assuming the charge of CEO. He had earlier seen Enron Corporation in the early 2000s through the bankruptcy process after its collapse. Asked why he took up the job that no one would want to, he said he is "drawn to crisis" and that "there is something about the sheer chaos and human panic that creates an unbridled energy" (Ben, 2022). While Enron and FTX have bankruptcy filing as common, FTX is a modern new generation mess. However, Mr. Ray says that FTX issue is an "old-fashioned embezzlement" and just taking customer money and using it for their own purposes. Ms. Ellision was fired from Alameda. Ray says that FTX lacked cash management controls, poor tracking of disbursements and records, lack of employee records, and high-level auditing failures.

By mid-January 2023, the new management of FTX was in a position to have hold of $5 billion in liquid assets and $4.6 billion in investor funds. Mr. Ray engaged investment banks to try to liquidate as much of the $5 billion investments that FTX has made in about 150 startups. Another $250 million is believed to be in LederX, a U.S.-regulated crypto derivatives company. Clearly, the identification and valuing assets of FTX appeared as a pandora box for the lawyers (Goldstein & Yaffe-Ballany, 2023).

Corporate Governance Issues

Corporate governance is the structure of rules, practices, and processes used to direct and manage a company. Businesses are expected to follow the rules of fair practices in the delivery of goods and services. However, FTX was found to have flouted various corporate governance norms. The biggest allegation against FTX is the diversification and use of customer funds for investment in hedge fund Alameda Research, which SBF used "as his personal piggy bank to buy luxury condominiums, support political campaigns, and make private investments, among other uses."

The lack of records of employees, disbursements, and low cash management controls showed the failure on the part of the leadership to put systems and processes in place for transparency and disclosure requirements. In addition, the new CEO Mr. Ray pointed out the lack of any purchase agreements or agreements signed when the old management made about $5 billion in investment in about 150 startups. In some cases, there was no proof of transactions or proper record of why funds were transferred to specific firms.

Treasury Secretary Janet Yellen called FTX's collapse a "Lehman moment" for the cryptocurrency industry. Experts believe the mistake made is a "diabolical" mixture of securities and banking fraud. SBF said that lawyers at Sullivan and Cromwell had pressured him to nominate John Ray III as the Chief Executive Officer of the crypto exchange. Shortly after the announcement, he got a "potential funding offer for billions of dollars to help make customers whole." However, the firefighting offer appeared late to rescind the move (Reuters, 2022c).

Prosecutors in the middle of December 2022 were investigating if any violations, such as improper transfer of funds, happened because hundreds of millions of dollars were moved from the U.S. to the Bahamas at the FTX collapse.

Arrest and Prosecution

On December 12, 2022, the SEC authorized charges against SBF. He was arrested the same day at Nassau, Bahamas, by the Bahamian authorities on a wide range of criminal charges upon a formal request from the U.S. Government based on a sealed indictment filed by the southern district of New York. The arrest came on the eve of his scheduled appearance at the House Financial Services Committee and Senate Banking Committee. At the hearing, he is to testify under oath about the crypto exchange's overnight demise. The Securities Commission of the Bahamas froze the assets of FTX Digital Markets, the group's local unit, and appointed a provisional liquidator.

U.S. prosecutors, who usually take months before indicating criminal charges, are super-fast in this case, highlighting the importance of one of the biggest financial frauds in American history. The Department of Justice charged SBF with eight counts, including conspiracy to commit wire fraud, money laundering, and violations of campaign finance rules by making illegal political contributions. Bahamanian and U.S. regulators argued in court filings about who should lead the hunt for FTX assets. Bahamanian liquidators said they need access to FTX data controlled by their American counterparts to clean up FTX Digital, a locally-based subsidiary (Bloomberg, 2022). They asserted they had jurisdiction over the millions of dollars of company real estate and wanted the oversight by the U.S. judge to be removed from it. The scuffle is because whichever liquidator wins will get access to controlling millions of dollars of assets of FTX.

The judge in the Bahamas denied him bail since he posed a flight risk. Fleeing in another jurisdiction will make it difficult for the U.S. to extradite him. However, reports that emerged after a week of his arrest suggested that SBF is dropping his fight against U.S. extradition and facing the charges. Apart from the FTX collapse investigation, Prosecutors in Manhattan are looking into his links with the collapse of Luna stablecoin and the Terra blockchain (Meghmala, 2022).

FTX is reportedly paying the law firm partners and special counsel from $1,575 to $2,165 per hour, an unusually high rate for a company that cannot afford to repay its debts. These rates are far higher than the $1,300 per hour new CEO John Ray is billed. The total legal fees in the FTX case likely exceed $100 million.

In the last week of December 2022, SBF entered into FBI custody and flew from the Bahamas to the U.S. to face charges. Two of his associates, Caroline Ellison (CEO of Alameda Research) and Gary Wang (co-founder of FTX), pleaded guilty (Reuters, 2022d). SBF pleaded not guilty (Reuters, 2023a) in the case, while his lawyers claimed that money leaked into Alameda by mistake and that SBF is largely unaware of how the trades happened at Alameda. However, some internal documents show SBF saying that bad trades at Alameda Research cost the firm more than the money it made or will ever make! SBF was in a catch-22 situation, and "given the amount that Alameda is doing, we can't really shut it down." The U.S. alleges that the separation between FTX and Alameda Research is "cosmetic."

A mini-legal battle cropped up regarding 56 million shares of FTX that the federal government has seized (or is in the process of seizing). However, it was disputed that they are not part of the bankruptcy estate by the new FTX management and BlockFi. Another court hearing looked into $93 million of an FTX unit that was keeping an account with Silvergate Capital Corp (Alexander et al., 2023).

Opportunity for Competitors

Traditional financial companies see the collapse of FTX as an opportunity for themselves. Investment bank Goldman Sachs said it felt an increasing need for trustworthy and established players to be in the crypto market. The company began considering investing tens of millions of dollars in discounted crypto investments (Gkritsi, 2022). It believes in blockchain technology and is doing due diligence on some small players.

Laser Digital, the crypto unit of Nomura Holdings that began operations in September 2022, says its crypto unit will break even in two years because it is now easier to hire talent and acquire assets at a lower valuation. However, the interconnectedness and over-leveraging between cryptocurrencies require much untangling.

To take advantage of the situation, C.Z. acquired a Japanese cryptocurrency exchange, allowing Binance to enter the Japanese market "as a regulated entity." In addition, Binance increased its advertising and good public relations helping it to establish credibility at the expense of FTX's collapse.

While it is opportunities galore for some, few other businesses are turning increasingly risk averse. Insurance companies have tightened their wording leaving digital currency traders and exchanges uninsured or turned reluctant to underwrite protection policies to key personnel of digital asset companies having crypto exposure. Some insurance companies were asking for additional disclosures and information for transparency (Reuters, 2022a).

WHY ARE THE EXCHANGES FALLING?

Skepticism by the Renowned

"Follow them, the shining ones, the wise, the awakened, the loving, For they know how to work and forbear." — Gautama Buddha

Some renowned and notable personalities expressed skepticism about bitcoin and cryptocurrencies, calling them a speculative bubble, mirage, or fraud. The list included investors like Warren Buffett, George Soros, Jack Ma, Bill Gates, and others and eight Noble laureates. Factors leading to skepticism include volatility in prices, trustworthiness, and security. But, of course, some people support it strongly too. Investment billionaire Peter Theil lashed out at Warren Buffett, Jamie Dimon, and Larry Fink at the Bitcoin 2022, saying the trio forms a "financial gerontocracy" and have conspired to intentionally hold down cryptocurrency prices.

Pump and Dump Activities

Over social media, many groups target specific crypto, do a staggering accumulation, and then start to dump the accumulation. Because cryptocurrencies are not regulated, there is no stopping them from doing this artificial rigging of prices.

Crypto Exchanges Are Not Like Stock Exchanges

Unlike stock exchanges, where securities are held with custodians and securities are transferred from one investor to another through a stock market purchase/sale transaction, cryptocurrencies are to be transferred to the exchange for the trade to happen. This means that the investor will no longer be holding the cryptocurrency in the wallet but will give it to the exchange to facilitate the exchange (with another cryptocurrency or fiat currency). Hence, the investors will not be like a depositor but a creditor.

WAY FORWARD FOR STAKEHOLDERS

When the industry is heading toward a collapse, all stakeholders have built trust among themselves and work together to ensure stability, thereby preventing future collapse. Experts suggest all stakeholders take up some changes for this.

1. Check if the cryptocurrency exchanges are truly decentralized exchanges or not.
2. Check Government policies and regulations concerning investor protection
3. Cryptocurrency exchanges should over-collateralize their holdings to ensure minimum levels of asset values are maintained in case of a sudden collapse
4. Cryptocurrency exchanges should increase their disclosures and transparency levels to win the faith of their investors

The FTX episode, will create an environment where the regulators will be monitoring every crypto company. The SEC reminded publicly listed companies of their disclosure obligations and told its investors about their direct or indirect involvement with cryptocurrency firms (IANS, 2022).

KEY LEARNINGS

1. Cryptocurrencies and their exchanges are not regulated (or poorly regulated), posing risks to investors. The collapse of cryptocurrencies and their exchanges is a wake-up call for regulators and policymakers to come forward and show a direction to investors.
2. Cryptocurrencies still are far from real-life adoption and use. Unless they become a public token of exchange, they will only be like play coins, and their prices depend on the willingness of those who trade with them (eye of the beholder).
3. Investors who do not have private keys with them do not have control over their assets.
4. Mere venture capital funds investing in the company do not qualify that the company has robust corporate governance.
5. The bubbles are popping off at places with centralization (such as with the exchanges). However, blockchain technology remains to get the trust as a futuristic technology that promises decentralized finance, allows the running of decentralized organizations, and brings solutions far beyond cryptocurrencies.

TEACHING NOTE

Synopsis

World's second-largest cryptocurrency exchange FTX announced bankruptcy for multiple reasons - misuse of investor funds, not adhering to blockchain-based decentralization systems, no proper corporate governance practices, lavish spending and expensive sports sponsorships, and a bank run situation. In addition, the founders and key personnel were arrested after differences as to who owns jurisdiction – the Bahamas or the U.S. The FTX story once again has brought to the fore the risks involved in investing in cryptocurrencies and the need for coordination between Governments and financial regulators worldwide.

CASE OBJECTIVES

1. To make students understand the higher level of risks involved in cryptocurrencies.
2. To explain the risks involved in dealing with unregulated products and how the unfavorable market environment (crypto winter) makes the market players (exchanges) sink.
3. To help students understand jurisdiction and other legal dimensions involved in global businesses that span multiple geographies.

POSITION IN THE COURSE

This case is suitable for students of postgraduate business management courses who take up functional areas in finance, fintech, international business, and strategy. In addition, it fits well with multiple elective courses such as financial markets and services or financial engineering (for those opting finance), international trade laws (international business), competing in global markets (strategy), and for courses related to cyber laws, and blockchain (fintech).

SUGGESTED PRE-READINGS

Students can be encouraged to have some basic understanding of various concepts discussed in the case so that they can understand it better when it is being discussed in the classroom. Considering the case to be a diversified one, the selection of chapters from various books that can be suggested as pre-reading and can span from various disciplines:

1. Lowe, C. (July 1, 2021). *Bitcoin and Cryptocurrency Trading for Beginners: How to Make Money Investing in Crypto Exchanges, Using Technical Analysis, and Reading Trends & Indicators.* Independently Published.
2. Ottina, M., Peter, J.S., & Jesper, K. (2023). *Automated Market Makers: A Practical Guide to Decentralized Exchanges and Cryptocurrency Trading*. APress Media LLC
3. Markham, J.W. (2006). *A Financial History of Modern U.S. Corporate Scandals: From Enrol to Reform.* M.E. Sharpe, Inc.

TEACHING PLAN

Students are asked to go through the information on the internet about cryptocurrencies and how they work. They are encouraged to read as much as possible from the suggested pre-reading. They are then taken through the class in the form of a case presentation by the trainer, followed by a classroom discussion by posing questions.

SUGGESTED TIME PLAN

The case fits for a 90-minute session during which the instruction can follow the below suggested time plan to present the case study.

Table 1. Suggested teaching plan

Topic	Duration
Introduction to Financial Engineering, Cryptocurrencies & Crypto Exchanges	10 minutes
How did the trouble start at FTX?	15 minutes
The issues and fraud element in FTX operations. How does bankruptcy work?	15 minutes
Competitors and what they did during the FTX crisis	15 minutes
Why are cryptocurrencies seen in a bad light, in general?	15 minutes
What is the way forward for various stakeholders?	10 minutes
Conclusions	10 minutes
TOTAL	**90 minutes**

Source: Authors proposed teaching plan

SUGGESTED QUESTIONS FOR DISCUSSION

Q1) Are Cryptocurrency Exchanges Decentralized Exchanges?

Expected Answer

The collapse of cryptocurrency exchanges was because the assets which ought to be stored or managed in a decentralized environment are actually managed in a centralized atmosphere – usually in the hands of its founder or a small number of venture funds that back them. The collapse of Terra and FTX are examples to show that decentralization is only on paper but not in practice. Investors need to crosscheck with the crypto exchanges in regard to the storage practices of the exchanges. Similarly, exchanges have to clearly disclose if their cryptocurrency storage network is centralized or decentralized.

Q2) What is Governmental Policies and Regulations's Role in Cryptocurrencies and Cryptocurrency Exchanges?

Expected Answer

Despite being highly liquid and boasting of being "the most regulated exchange on the planet," FTX experienced a quick collapse. Learning from the episode is essential for stakeholders because it exposes the structural weaknesses that exist in the system. Fixing these weaknesses through policy and regulations is the job of the Governments and Regulators. Stakeholders' interests are to be protected in any business, and investor expectations, in this case, are transparency and protection.

Goldman Sachs (G.S.) believes that regulation is "needed at the point of trust." Expressing satisfaction with the blockchain industry and its developments, they said the centralized elements of the blockchain are to be regulated instead of the technology itself. Exchanges act as gatekeepers of the crypto world and need to be regulated. A lack of regulations can give scope for fraud to take place. This is an inevitable requirement for regulation when public money is involved. It is agreed that in a decentralized system, the decision-making authority is not concentrated in one or a few persons, but that should not come at the cost of investors losing their money. The U.S., U.K, and the E.U. are already started to regulate cryptocurrency activities actively. India is asking for a global coordinated effort towards regulations, while Japan is asking global regulators to regulate crypto institutions on the same serious lines as that of banking (Reuters, 2023b).

Unlike the dot-com bubble that took place within the ambit of the well-regulated equity markets, cryptocurrency bubbles could cause widespread global panic as the exact amount invested and the number of investors is still a matter of concern. Regulators need to decide which aspect of cryptocurrency should be regulated and which should not. G.S. says that financial instruments promising yields should be regulated, just like any other security. In contrast, Decentralized Finance (Defi) need not be regulated because smart contracts usually do not result in counterparty risk.

Once basic regulations are in place, slow tightening and softening of regulations will be required amidst changing market situations. Regulations should be coupled with investor education so that awareness is brought into place.

In some cases, even when some regulations exist, the action by the regulators was considered slow and inadequate. The collapse of FTX, Genesis Global and Gemini Trust is seen as a case of failure on the part of the SEC to act quickly. Sometimes, the regulators had to face the blame that they were working to protect their turf than to protect investors (Scott & Gulliver, 2023).

Even when the regulators find violations, companies can quickly settle with the regulator and escape blame by paying the penalty and getting a clean chit without admitting or denying any charges – a common practice in the capital market industry. In mid-January 2023, Crypto lender Nexo Capital, for example, agreed to pay $45 million to settle charges with SEC (Michaels, 2023).

Q3) How Can Exchanges Over-Collateralize Their Assets?

Expected Answer

In finance, collateral is something pledged as security for repayment of a loan, to be forfeited in the event of a default. Cryptocurrencies are very volatile products whose prices could go up or down drastically. So, it is common for exchanges to collateralize the cryptocurrency with that of another asset (such as fiat currency or gold) so that the pledged security protects in the case of a sudden shortfall in the margin funding of a crypto trade. The collapse of FTX has forced crypto exchanges to prove how stable and collateralized they are. In addition, other cryptocurrency exchanges began increasing collaterals to avoid a potential collapse. Stronger risk management practices are the need of the hour.

Q4) How Can Exchanges Increase Their Transparency Levels?

Expected Answer

Any business that has to show that they are clean will require to reveal or share more information than what is required for statutory reasons. Being transparent by making frequent disclosures can go a long way in establishing trust. Investors are worried about the safety of their cryptocurrencies. Binance made some moves towards this by publicizing details about its crypto-wallet address in November 2022. In addition, it hired an accounting firm to prepare a "proof of reserve report" that shows the customer if their assets with the exchange are not loaned out. However, experts believe that these reports are just a snapshot and cannot be a statement of lack of risk and oftentimes can be misleading too. Such reports will not reveal in-and-out asset movements, nor does it list liabilities against assets. Other steps include covering a portion of its assets and liabilities, including a small financial data set.

Q5) What Should a Bankrupt Company Do? Can a Company That Filed for Bankruptcy Revive?

Expected Answer

One usual task for a company that has filed for Chapter 11 filing is to wind up all the operations and return as much money as possible back to customers and investors. Liquidation appears to be a simple possibility, but in most cases, the funds would not be sufficient to return to all stakeholders to which the company is due to the fullest extent.

It is indeed possible for companies that have filed for bankruptcy to revive and restart their business. There are several instances where debt-stressed companies have filed for bankruptcy and made a good comeback. Some famous examples include Hostess, Marvel, Converse, and G.M., who have declared bankruptcy and bounced back stronger than ever. The new CEO of FTX, John J. Ray III, said he is seriously considering the possibility of restarting the operations of FTX. As a first step towards this, a task force is a setup to check into the possibilities of FTX.com international operations, to begin with. He said customers see "value in rebooting the platform" (Saeedy & Osipovich, 2023).

A large part of either returning funds to stakeholders or to revive operations depends mainly on the successful recovery of cash and assets. Mr. Ray says he has received support from Gary Wang and Caroline Ellison to track company funds.

Q6) Is Binance a Safer Cryptocurrency Exchange?

Expected Answer

Most exchanges, including Binance, do not disclose the location where they are located.

Binance was in the middle of an investigation regarding anti-money laundering and sanctions against it since 2018. A series of cases said that criminals used Binance to transfer illicit funds. However, a split between U.S. Department of Justice prosecutors is delaying the conclusion. This is because a segment of prosecutors wishes to wait to collect more evidence. Binance refuted the charges that aired in the media about this. However, it hired former employees of IRS Criminal Investigation's Cyber Crime Unit who help the platform fight crimes and work closely with law enforcement (Reuters, 2022b).

Additionally, Binance hired former officials with the FBI and the Treasury; two former officials from the Financial Conduct Authority, a United Kingdom regulator; and a former CEO of the financial regulator for the United Arab Emirates.

It raised the compliance headcount by 500% and boasted of its team as "possibly even the strongest in the entire financial sector." (Parikshit & Oliver, 2022)

Cryptocurrency exchanges often have strict secrecy rules on employees, telling them to use email as little as possible and to communicate using encrypted messaging services.

EXHIBITS

Table 2. Top 10 cryptocurrencies by market capitalization

Rank	Cryptocurrency	Market Capitalization
1	Bitcoin (BTC)	$435,685,478,667
2	Ethereum (ETH)	$202,680,590,599
3	Tether (USDT)	$66,497,548,683
4	BNB (BNB)	$48,136,605,019
5	USD Coin (USDC)	$43,182,060,255
6	XRP (XRP)	$20,872,892,214
7	Binance USD (BUSD)	$16,336,738,741
8	Cardano (ADA)	$12,574,833,856
9	Dogecoin (DOGE)	$11,446,276,486
10	Solana (SOL)	$9,330,693,379

Data Source: CoinMarketCap; Market Capitalization data is as of January 21, 2023

Table 3. Top 10 cryptocurrency spot exchanges

Rank	Name	Volume(24h)	Number of Coins (Cryptocurrencies) Supported	Fiat Currencies Supported
1	Binance	$20,376,067,803	384	11
2	Coinbase Exchange	$2,375,029,142	239	3
3	Kraken	$704,836,520	220	7
4	KuCoin	$935,551,169	787	48
5	Bitstamp	$221,569,047	73	3
6	Bitfinex	$209,243,633	187	4
7	OKX	$1,496,055,373	357	46
8	Gate.io	$746,531,450	1582	2
9	Bybit	$489,685,398	344	6
10	Binance.US	$434,877,449	153	1

Data Source: CoinMarketCap; 24-hour traded volume is as of January 21, 2023 at 08:01 hrs IST

REFERENCES

Alexander, S., Becky, Y., & Peter, R. (2023, January 5). Authorities move to seize funds tied to FTX. *WSJ*.

Aljazeera. (2022, December 5). FTX's Bankman-Fried says he will testify before U.S. Congress. *Aljazeera*. https://www.aljazeera.com/economy/2022/12/5/ftxs-bankman-fried-says-he-will-testify-before-us-congress

Ben, C. (2022, December 17). The New CEO of FTX on How to Clean Up a Mess. *WSJ*.

Bloomberg. (2022, December 15). FTX downfall: Bahamas challenges the U.S. Case. *Mint*.

Cornelius, C. (2022, December 6). Another year of Crypto Winter likely before turnaround—Anastasios Papakonstantinou. *Kitco*. https://www.kitco.com/news/2022-12-06/Another-year-of-Crypto-Winter-likely-before-turnaround-Anastasios-Papakonstantinou.html?sitetype=fullsite

Crunchbase. (2022, December 14). FTX Ventures. *Crunchbase*. https://www.crunchbase.com/organization/ftx-ventures

Explainers, F. P. (2022, November 14). Who is Nishad Singh, the Indian-origin techie under scrutiny for crypto exchange FTX's collapse? *First Post*. https://www.firstpost.com/explainers/nishad-singh-indian-origin-engineer-crypto-exchange-ftx-collapse-sam-bankman-fried-11622961.html

Gkritsi, E. (2022, December 6). Goldman Sachs to Spend "Tens of Millions" on Discounted Crypto Investments After FTX Implosion: Report. *Coindesk*. https://www.coindesk.com/business/2022/12/06/goldman-sachs-to-spend-tens-of-millions-on-discounted-crypto-investments-after-ftx-implosion-report/

Goldstein, M., & Yaffe-Ballany, D. (2023, January 19). FTX assets: Billions in cash and crypto located. *Business Standard*.

IANS. (2022, December 12). FTX collapse: U.S. asks listed companies to disclose exposure to beleaguered crypto firms. *Money Life*. https://www.moneylife.in/article/ftx-collapse-us-asks-listed-companies-to-disclose-exposure-to-beleaguered-crypto-firms/69152.html

Jonathan, R. (2022, December 15). FTX Executive Warned Funds were Mixed with Alameda's. *Wall Street Journal*.

Joshua, O., & Stefania, P. (2022, December 17). U.S. watchdogs outline sprawling case against Bankman-Fried. *Financial Times Weekend*.

Meghmala. (2022, December 12). FTX's Sam Bankman-Fried under Criminal Probe for Market Rig. *Analytics Insight*. https://www.analyticsinsight.net/ftxs-sam-bankman-fried-under-criminal-probe-for-market-rig/

Michaels, D. (2023, January 20). Crypto lender Nexo settles with SEC. *Wall Street Journal*.

Natalie, S. (2022, November 28). Crypto firm BlockFi files for bankruptcy after FTX collapse. *BBC*. https://www.bbc.com/news/business-63786201

New York Times. (2022, December 13). Explained: How the collapse of FTX is giving Binance a chance to become the new face of crypto. *First Post*. https://www.firstpost.com/world/explained-how-the-collapse-of-ftx-is-giving-binance-a-chance-to-become-the-new-face-of-crypto-11800601.html

Parikshit, M., & Oliver, K. (2022, December 12). *U.S. Prosecutors Look to Charge Binance, Executives on Possible Money Laundering Violations: Reuters*. https://www.coindesk.com/business/2022/12/12/us-prosecutors-look-to-charge-binance-and-cz-for-possible-money-laundering-violations-reuters/

Reuters. (2022a, December 9). Insurers shun FTX-linked crypto firms as risk mounts. *Business Line*.

Reuters. (2022b, December 13). Binance under scrutiny by US Justice department, prosecutors split. *Business Today*. https://www.businesstoday.in/crypto/token/story/binance-under-scrutiny-by-us-justice-department-prosecutors-split-356124-2022-12-13

Reuters. (2022c, December 13). Sam Bankman-Fried says lawyers pressured him to name new CEO. *Money Control*. https://www.moneycontrol.com/news/world/sam-bankman-fried-says-lawyers-pressured-him-to-name-new-ceo-9694951.html

Reuters. (2022d, December 22). *Two Bankman-Fried associates plead guilty to fraud*.

Reuters. (2023a, January 5). Bankman-Fried pleads not guilty in FTX fraud case. *Financial Express*.

Reuters. (2023b, January 17). Regulate crypto, Japan tells U.S., E.U. *Business Standard*.

Saeedy, A., & Osipovich, A. (2023, January 20). New FTX chief calls reboot of exchange a possibility. *Wall Street Journal*.

Samuel, A. (2023, January 4). FTX failure forces rethink on global sports sponsorship by digital asset groups. *Financial Express*.

Scott, H., & Gulliver, J. (2023, January 19). A Question for Congress: Why Didn't the SEC stop FTX? *Wall Street Journal*.

Chapter 3
People Side-Up:
A Case Study on TaskUs

Divya Juneja
Chandigarh University, India

Sukhjeet Kaur Matharu
Prestige Institute of Management and Research, Indore, India

EXECUTIVE SUMMARY

The case is all about a company called TaskUs and how its founders have created a whole new setup for BPO organizations that is changing the rules of the game. With their innovative approaches, the founders Bryce Maddock and Jaspar Weir created a value centric work culture that includes striving for excellence, believing that teamwork makes dreams work, inspiring others by believing in yourself, working hard, and being ridiculous. With its beautiful, culture-driven ambience and amazing office aesthetics, the founders have redefined the BPO for the needs of 21st-century youth. The case highlights the journey of Bryce and Jaspar, elaborating on how these high school pals built an award-winning global organization with more than 20,000 employees across the world. It also underlines the role of work culture and people's focus in organization's success. The case can be used with undergraduate, graduate, and startup founders and HR managers to make them understand the concept of organizational culture, and how innovative thinking can change the entire phenomenon of outsourcing work.

INTRODUCTION

"Being a great place to work is the difference between being a good company and a great company." – Brian Kristofek, President and CEO, Upshot

"Be Ridiculous" and "Sexiest outsourcing", what could be the fanciest word that can define the most happening and employee centric culture of any company that is breaking all the traditional rules and redefining the work life of the youths of 21st Century. "Welcome to TaskUs, Together. You and Us, Delivering Ridiculously Good next-generation digital outsourcing to the most innovative brands in the

DOI: 10.4018/978-1-6684-8488-3.ch003

world", with this tag line, started in 2008 by 2 high school pals, from Santa Monica, CA, TaskUs is now running its successful outsourcing business in six countries namely United States, Philippines, Taiwan, Europe, Mexico and India. With more than 24 offices and 20,000+ employees across the globe, it is not failing to show its ridiculously high spirit at any corner of the world. TaskUs is supporting world's most disrupting companies like Uber, Tinder and Whisper and serving lots of industries that include Media & Entertainment, Gaming, HiTech, FinTech, Insurance, HealthTech, Retail, Consumer Products, E-Commerce, Social Media, On-Demand Travel & Transportation, Professional Services Industry and Edtech.

Figure 1. TaskUs office
Source: TaskUs.com

TaskUs has partnered with world's most innovative brands and with the support of its highly qualified human capitals, solving their business problems through deploying technology and data. The company provides support in the domain of Digital CX, Data operations, AI Operations, Content Security and Consulting and thriving continuously in an ever changing world.

TaskUs is not like an old traditional kind of BPO, it is a new breed of outsourcing that is changing the complete customer and employees' experience. The most prominent and thrilling characteristic of the company is its 'People first" policy, which is changing the definitions of office working culture and resulted into 4.7 Glassdoor rating and 75 eNPS score. From the most vibrating premises to most happening work culture, the success of TaskUs is hidden in keeping its People Side Up and that's ridiculous.

Bryce Maddock and Jaspar Weir started their business journey when they were 17. From selling designer belts in school yards to setting up real Night Club experience for high school students, their entrepreneurial spirit never let them look down. Later they moved around the Europe, dropped their high-class jobs and started their startup "TaskUs".

The journey was not a cake walk for them. After leaving the jobs, they were in shear confusion and thought that they might have to live to their parent's house for long time but universe moved them in different direction.

TaskUs is not like traditional outsourcing and virtual assistant firm, it has broken all the traditional prototypes and came up with a novel kind of customer and employees' experience to provide the back-end support to the most unruly startups. The idea itself is very new and unique. When Bryce and Jaspar were 22, they wanted to start business about virtual assistance and have their own VAs but due to lack of money, they couldn't hire VAs for themselves. The business model is designed in such a way that clients can feed the task into the TaskUs and that task would be assigned to the most skilled person. The clients will not be dependent on one person's skills but task can be performed by anyone who is an expert.

Initially they were not sure about the idea, in first year they could make only $100,000 and after paying to the freelancers, they left with $1000 only. Even after 3 years, they were living with their parents and were thinking about giving up (Atson, (Date:NA)). Bryce asked the Jasper to give it another thought but Jasper was determined and did not want to go alone. He assured Bryce that they will make it a success.

They went for trial and error of outsourcing in 16 different countries in initial two years; ultimately they realized that understanding clients' expectation is at most important to deliver high class services. Later they expanded their scope of delivery and started offering complete solution that includes customer service, content moderation and photo editing, and hired new teams to provide full functional supports to their clients. Their other bigger clients are Oscar Health, MailChimp, Hotel Tonight, Eventbrite and Turo. Half of the TaskUs employees handle customer service through phone, emails and live chat, rest half work as back office support.

Okay to Be Ridiculous

"We knew nothing about anything, so we voraciously read everything and were obsessed with building this cool place to work." Jasper said.

Call centers are considered to be a boring place to work. The entire industry itself was known for ugly offices and high turnover of employees. Bryce and Jasper created a value driven culture. Those values are different from any other outsourcing firms. The values talk about striving for excellence, teamwork makes dream work, inspire others by believing in yourself, work hard and be ridiculous.

"Everything we do now is centered around our employees and we think that allows us to be better than our competitors," Jasper said.

When they had their first office at Santa Monica, they wanted to put a lot of energy in it. Later they started their working in Philippines. To track their culture they measured their Net Promoter Score (NPS) They conducted an employee survey to measure their happiness. The NPS score scale ranges from -100 to +100. They thought that they are doing really good but their first score survey was 4. Realization of reality made them work more dedicatedly on the culture.

TaskUs came up with most happening offices in the world, for example the office in Anonas, Philippines is named as "Chateau Ridiculous" which looks like a café and office in Indore, India is named as "Rangreza", which defines the culture of color and happiness. They worked on building the culture from very basics.

Apart from ambiance, they have also introduced employee referral policies. They believe that happy employees attract good employees. The employee referral rate of TaskUs is 71 percent against the average industry rate which is just 30 percent. They constantly battle to hire the best talent by taking thousands of interviews to hire hundreds. Hiring executives is even more difficult. They always make sure that the new employee should fit into the system well. They believe that the practice, process and structure do not build the culture but it's the people.

"I would love to see us become not only a great company but globally recognized as one of the best cultures in the world." Jasper said.

Ridiculous Culture

"One of our core values is 'Be Ridiculous' which is actually a callout to all our employees to think different and challenge the status quo." ~– TaskUs

At TaskUs, inspiration, openness and fun are the core values on which the management styles are based. There is not red tape or office politics and self improvement is the key for perfections. The leaders always lead by examples and employees learn from the leaders by seeing them performing their daily tasks and professionalism.

The offices are equipped with game rooms, lounges and cafeterias. Everyone feels that the culture has a family vibe and a proper balance between work and recreation. A blend of empowerment, recognition and consideration for employees along with Cowboy Breakfast, Golf with CEO and Taco Tuesday there is a lot to look at for employees.

From Management styles to the company's layouts, everything is transparent. Two way communication, health improvement and global parties are cherry on the top. The core essence of TaskUs policies is simple, "Work hard and have fun".

It's not only happening culture or friendly department that TaskUs has provided to the employees, it continuously works for development of employees, works on reduction of absenteeism and make them tech geeks so that they can deliver the best customer experience.

According to ICMI (International Customer Management Institute), more than 60% of the customers do not like to wait for longer period of time. To deliver the best Average Handle Time (AHT) performance, TaskUs provides continuous Innovation delivery training to the employees. As the long AHT might result into losing the customers, training engagement technologies paired with continuous evolution and refinement of training experience for the teammates, result into skill building, better resolving of the client issues and retention check exercises. This kind of creative effective learning experience is one of the biggest competitive advantages with the company.

To avoid burnouts, absenteeism and poor customer support, TaskUs ensures People-First Culture. Taking care of employees wellbeing, increasing quality of output, motivating employees by encouraging them continuously and celebrating their contributions resulted into saving of costs upto $2,660 each year and reduces the client attrition upto 31%.

Awards

This is not first time TaskUs has received these awards, TaskUs won 6 awards in 2020, 12 awards in 2019, 3 awards in 2018, one award in each 2017 and 2016. All these awards are for best culture, diversity, empowering the women and best leaderships. Not only this, it has won 2020 Stevie® Awards for Great Employers and LA's 100 Fastest-Growing Private Companies. In 2021, TaskUs Won Two Gold Stevie® Awards, "People-Focused CEO of the Year" by his founder Brayce and "Achievement in Workplace Health & Wellbeing" along with that it has also won the Bronze for the "Chief Happiness Officer of the Year." According to Entrepreneur 360, it ranks #3 worldwide in 2017.

Figure 2. Awards from 2016-2021
Source: https://www.comparably.com/companies/taskus/awards

Ridiculous Competitors

24-7 Intouch, Concentrix, Transcom, Sutherland Global Services and Teleperformance are the biggest competitors of the TaskUs. When it comes to Culture, TaskUs is on the first position but other companies have their own advantages, like market size and revenue. Teleperformance is one such competitor that is a 42 year old company with more than 33K employees and annual revenue is 6.05 billion, which is far ahead in existence and market share as compare to TaskUs. If they improve their employee culture, who knows how future might turn-up for TaskUs.

Though TaskUs is breaking all the records when it comes to managing people, but satisfying human is never an easy task (Bhambani, 2020). Still we can find a lot of negative comments on Glassdoor, indeed and other site against the company. A company which is driven by people and lead by thousands of leaders worldwide, how can be so assure about their leaders that they would be committed to keep up the same culture everyday everywhere.

Synopsis

The case study is on organizational culture of TaskUs. It is a story of a firm that provides outsourcing and virtual assistance to the world's most innovative startups to provide back office support to them. TaskUs has changed all the traditional norms of call center and outsourcing and has created world's most happening offices and people oriented firm. It's continuous support from development of employees to offer them transparent culture, it is winning all the games by following a philosophy of "work hard and have fun".

Case Objectives

- To make students understand the challenges faced by BPO companies related to organisational culture and employee retention.
- To explain how start-ups are solving the major employment issues with innovative solutions.
- To help students understand the need of healthy organisational culture.
- To give them an insight about the evolution of new type of office spaces.
- To help students gain knowledge of the strategic actions required by companies to hire and retain employees.

Position in the Course

This case can be used for both undergraduate and postgraduate management programs and also for any sessions to be conducted to start-up entrepreneurs, HR professional and managers. For undergraduate students, this case can be used for the second and final year as by then they would have gained a broad knowledge this subject. For post graduate students this case can be used towards the end of the first year.

The case can be used in classroom for demonstrating the importance of organizational culture, transparent HR policies and how traditional organizations are turning themselves into most happening places to work. Startups are not only coming up with innovative products but their ideas regarding work life is also very innovative. The case serves in the area of HRM, Organizational Behavior and Entrepreneurship.

Suggested Pre-Readings

Students can be assigned the following pre-readings to get a basic understanding on BPO Industry, Organisational Culture and Startup Culture.

Pre-Reading Material

1. Leaders, Stop Rewarding Toxic Rock Stars, Harvard Business Review. https://hbr.org/2022/04/leaders-stop-rewarding-toxic-rock-stars.

2. Culture Is A Company's Single Most Powerful Advantage. Here's Why, Forbes. https://www.forbes.com/sites/benjaminlaker/2021/04/23/culture-is-a-companys-single-most-powerful-advantage-heres-why/?sh=50216937679e.
3. The BPO Industry in India. Outsource to India. https://www.outsource2india.com/india/bpo-industry-india.asp.
4. Seven Ways To Create A Startup Culture Of Innovation, Forbes. https://www.forbes.com/sites/alisoncoleman/2021/07/20/seven-ways-to-create-a-startup-culture-of-innovation/?sh=131566034042.
5. The Negative Impacts of A Non-Productive Culture in the Outsourcing Industry. Time Doctor. https://www.timedoctor.com/blog/lack-of-a-productive-culture/.

Teaching Plan

The instructor can ask the students if they have seen how call centers work and they know about their working style, culture or ambience. After discussion, instructor can provide the case to the students to read along with other relevant course reading materials.

Suggested Time Plan

The time plan includes 120 minutes for reading, analysis and discussion. The below Table 1 exhibits the time division for the case study:

Table 1. Time plan

Exhibit 1: Time Plan	
Initial discussion of BPO culture and working	10 mins
Reading of case	45 mins
Split class into 5 groups – allocate one question to each group to brainstorm	5 Mins
Group analysis	15 mins
Discussion on question 1_Value driven employee centric culture	10 mins
Discussion on question 2_ Strategies for hiring and retaining of the employees	10 mins
Discussion on question 3_ Possible threats	10 mins
Wrap Up	15 mins

Organisational Culture of BPO Companies

The traditional work culture of any BPO organisations consists of repetitive tasks, strict following of SOPs, Target based work, Alternative shifts, low opportunities of learning and growth, health issues and fewer increments. Many of the employees feel that they hardly get time for their well being, which results into stress and depression. The organisations generally focus on deadlines and targets.

The companies also suffer from high employee turnover. Researches shows that in country like India, many well educated people are performing low skill and low cost jobs. Employees do not consider BPO jobs as a long term career option for themselves.

The office setup mostly remains traditional, congested and boring. According to study conducted by Rahayu (2018) on 100 BPO frontline staff, it was found that 52% of the employees display low performance and performance improvement is required at immediate level. Apart from that more that 70% of the employees couldn't complete their sales target in terms are money whereas 68% couldn't achieve in terms of accounts and customers. Lack of productive culture signals serious problems especially when competition is very high. Report published by HBR highlighted that American businesses bear more that $50 billion losses annually due to toxic corporate culture. It also decreases the employee productivity by 38% (hbr.org, 2020). Not only this, 25% of employees reported that they took out their frustration on clients that caused huge negative impact on company's good will and bottom line of the business due to bad customer experience.

SUGGESTED QUESTIONS FOR DISCUSSION

To discuss the questions, instructor can divide the class into group of 5s. Class should be given time as mentioned in the proposed timelines to discuss and write their answers. Then instructor can facilitate the discussion, where each group can present their views and counterviews. The instructor can refer the solution given below to discuss the missed out points.

Question 1. How did TaskUs create a value driven employee centric culture?

Expected Answer

TaskUs works on 'People First' policy. The most prominent characteristic of the company is to have a most vibrant and happening work culture. Where call centers are considered to be the boring place to work, ugly offices and high employee turnover, the founders of the company Bryce and Jasper created a value driven culture which are different from all other outsourcing firms.

They created the value driven culture by focusing on defining their own unique values which includes striving for excellence, teamwork makes dream work, inspire others by believing in yourself, work hard and be ridiculous etc. For this they provide continuous training and mentoring to their new and existing employees. The leaders always lead by examples and employees learn from the leaders by seeing them performing their daily tasks and professionalism.

The entire organisation centered on employees. They want their organisation to be recognized as world's best culture organisation. Most happening office spaces equipped with game room, cafeteria and cultural vibes such as Rangreza reflects the core values like inspiration, openness and fun clearly.

Question 2. What strategies has TaskUs used to hire and retain best fit employees?

Expected Answer

It is clear that BPO industries suffer from serious attrition issues; to deal with this TaskUs has come up with some innovative strategies.

To hire right fit for the company, task us implements employee referral policies, with a faith that happy employees attract good employees. Their employee referral rate is 71% against the market benchmark at 30%. They do not afraid to take thousands of interviews to hire the right fit. Their belief about creating the right culture revolves around people more than practice process and structure. Higher eNPS and Glassdoor rating also helps them to attract best talent.

Apart from hiring the right fit that can stay with the organisation for longer period of time, happening organisations culture, exquisite ambience, continuous learning and growth opportunities and remarkable employer branding help TaskUs to retain their employees.

Question 3. What could be the possible threats for TaskUs?

Expected Answer

The possible threats of the TaskUs are:

- Competition from existing larger and older companies like Teleperformance
- Threats of new entrance
- Its challenging to please people and get the high performance from them
- Negative comments on social media can impact the employer brand
- Very difficult to maintain the same culture everywhere when leaders have their own styles

Wrapping Up

The case can be concluded by recapping the key concepts discussed in case about organisation culture, BPO working in India, innovative work environment and value driven employee centric culture. Instructor can ask each group to revise one concept. At the end, key learning can be discussed.

REFERENCES

Aston, D. (n.d.). *How The Founder of TaskUs Went From Zero to 1500 Employees in 5 Years*. https://www.incomediary.com/bryce-maddock-interview/

Bhambani, S. (2020). *Challenging corporate policies with people-first practices with Us in India*. TaskUs. https://www.taskus.com/blog/challenging-corporate-policies-with-people-first-practices-with-us-in-india/

Businesswire. (2019). *TaskUs Wins 2019 Best Places to Work For Second Year in a Row*. https://www.businesswire.com/news/home/20191213005067/en/TaskUs-Wins-2019-Best-Places-to-Work-For-Second-Year-in-a-Row

Comparably. (n.d.). *TaskUs Competitors*. https://www.comparably.com/companies/taskus/competitors

Entrepreneur 360™. (2017). *Entrepreneur India*. https://www.entrepreneur.com/360/2017

Forbes. (2021). https://www.forbes.com/sites/billconerly/2021/11/13/oil-forecast-2022-and-beyond/?sh=4bc9bf616a67

IndiaE. https://www.entrepreneur.com/company/taskus

Kelly, L. (2022). *Overcome Outsourcing Cost Limitations: The Competitive Advantage of Quality Over Price.* https://www.taskus.com/insights/overcome-outsourcing-cost-limitations-the-competitive-advantage-of-quality-over-price/

Overcome, O. C. L. (2017). *The Competitive Advantage of Quality Over Price.* TaskUS. https://www.taskus.com/insights/overcome-outsourcing-cost-limitations-the-competitive-advantage-of-quality-over-price/

Rahayu, M., Rasid, F., & Tannady, H. (2018). Effects of self efficacy, job satisfaction, and work culture toward performance of telemarketing staff in banking sector. *South East Asia J. Contemp. Business. Econ. Law*, *16*(5), 47–52.

Ranganathan, A., & Kuruvilla, S. (2008). *Employee Turnover in the Business Process Outsourcing Industry in India.* https://www.igi-global.com/chapter/management-practices-high-tech-environments/25651

Reviews. (n.d.). https://in.worldorgs.com/catalog/indore/park/taskus-india

Sie, E. (n.d.). *GE Ep 71: How TaskUs CEO Bryce Maddock Went from Living With His Parents to $15M in Revenue.* https://www.levelingup.com/growth-everywhere-interview/bryce-maddock-taskus/

Simplr. (n.d.). *TaskUs vs Teleperformance? Which is the Better Enterprise Call Center?* https://www.simplr.ai/learn/taskus-vs-teleperformance-which-is-the-better-enterprise-call-center

TaskUs. (n.d.a). https://www.taskus.com/

TaskUs. (n.d.b). https://www.taskus.com/locations/india/

TaskUs. (2016). *Facebook official page.* https://m.facebook.com/TaskUsPH/posts/one-of-our-core-values-is-be-ridiculous-which-is-actually-a-callout-to-all-our-e/1165676483502070/

TaskUs. (n.d.c). *Entrepreneur India.* https://www.entrepreneur.com/company/taskus

TaskUs boosts employee Perks & Benefits amid COVID-19 pandemic. (2020). TaskUs. https://ir.taskus.com/news-releases/news-release-details/taskus-boosts-employee-perks-benefits-amid-covid-19-pandemic

TaskUs Competitors. (n.d.). *Comparably.* https://www.comparably.com/-companies/taskus/competitors

TaskUs Facebook. (n.d.). https://m.facebook.com/TaskUsPH/posts/one-of-our-core-values-is-be-ridiculous-which-is-actually-a-callout-to-all-our-e/1165676483502070/

TaskUs India. (n.d.).. https://in.worldorgs.com/catalog/indore/park/taskus-india

TaskUs vs Teleperformance? Which is the Better Enterprise Call Center? (n.d.). Simplr. https://www.simplr.ai/learn/taskus-vs-teleperformance-which-is-the-better-enterprise-call-center

TaskUs Wins. (2019). Best Places to Work For Second Year in a Row. *Business Wire.* https://www.businesswire.com/news/home/20191213005067/en/TaskUs-Wins-2019-Best-Places-to-Work-For-Second-Year-in-a-Row

Chapter 4
Simple Kaur:
The Growth of Start-Ups Through the Adoption of Sustainable Fashion, Technological Innovation, and Social Media Marketing

Navpreet Kaur Sidhu
Chitkara Business School, Chitkara University, India

Devesh Bathla
https://orcid.org/0000-0003-3990-5934
Chitkara Business School, Chitkara University, India

Sandhir Sharma
Chitkara Business School, Chitkara University, India

Harpreet Singh Bhatia
Human Resources, Chitkara University, India

EXECUTIVE SUMMARY

In India, technology developments and resource sustainability are the most crucial factors for any startup or emerging organization for decent work and economic growth. To survive in a competitive market, it is essential to exploit the resources effectively. Even though a start-up is a complex organism with many heterogeneous forces acting in concert to progress it, the likelihood of failure rarely outweighs the likelihood of success. International trade benefits greatly from the usage of technology. Sustainable technology benefits an international company. This case study highlights the major challenges faced by the start-up, for funding, expansion, and adoption of green technology while promoting social media marketing (SMM) strategy post-COVID-19 revival in the fashion industry. It discusses how the start-up got additional funding for the expansion of its successful growth internationally. It concludes by discussing strategic actions required to ensure Simple Kaur's entrepreneurial uninterrupted growth.

DOI: 10.4018/978-1-6684-8488-3.ch004

INTRODUCTION

When Simple Kaur heard in the News on television that the country (India) had been placed under lockdown due to COVID in March 2020, she suffered a significant setback. She had a profitable start-up that expanded to Canada and India. She needed to pay her bank loan, staff salaries, utility bills, and huge client orders that needed to be processed right away. When the lockdown was imposed, the business was shut down, which made her realize how important sustainability is by implementing green technology, which lowers the cost and friction. Eliminating waste and creating clothing from repurposed materials.

In recent years, academia and practice have given much attention to the consumption of unsustainable fashion and wasteful activities. The global fashion market is predicted to increase from $1.5 trillion in 2020 to over $2.25 trillion in 2025, demonstrating a persistent increase in demand (Ikram, M. 2022). The transition to a green economy and the advancement of a movement for ecologically friendly fashion are both aided by new technology breakthroughs. Technology may seem counterintuitive, but becoming more sustainable is crucial for fashion, which is often an accelerant of waste. Sustainable fashion technologies significantly impact waste reduction through materials, products, and consumer experiences. Material changes made by environmentally conscious businesses improve longevity and reduce resource consumption. Fashion start-up managers can use the proposed model to gain a deeper understanding of how technological innovations help achieve a successfully sustainable fashion, while simultaneously improving sustainability practices. Recent years have been difficult for many traditional stores due to unprecedented competition and emerging technologies. Managing demand uncertainty, inventory management, and rapid market responses are all problems that existing push supply chains and forecast-based, inventory-driven systems are unable to solve on their own.

Green technology utilization has been crucial to the growth and operation of start-ups. An information culture that is supported by technical breakthroughs and is swiftly spreading is now exemplified by industrialized nations. In India nowadays, technology developments and resource sustainability are the most crucial factors for any start-up or emerging organization. To survive in a competitive market, it is essential to exploit the resource effectively. Even though a start-up is a complex organism with many heterogeneous forces acting in concert to progress it, the likelihood of failure rarely outweighs the likelihood of success. International trade benefits greatly from the usage of technology.

FASHION TRENDS IN INDIA

Despite having a young fashion industry, India has a long history of creating apparel. Although there were a few designers before the 1980s, there was a growing boom in the latter half of the 1980s and early 1990s. This resulted from more exposure to international design as well as the economic boom that followed the economic liberalization of the Indian economy in 1990. Sequins and gold thread are frequently used in fashion to draw clients and make a statement about the Indian fashion scene. The practice of stitching distinctive thread designs is known as embroidery and is a hallmark of Indian fashion. Applying embroidery to various dresses, skirts, blouses, and pants is one method to incorporate the traditional style and make a fresh fashion statement that reflects both western and Indian cultural influences.

- Ritu Kumar, a designer and textile print specialist based in Kolkata started working on resurrecting the old hand block printing techniques of Bengal and establishing "ethnic chic" as a part of the wider restoration movement in the Indian textile sector. In Delhi, she started her first store in 1966.
- The first wave of Indian fashion designers, notably Satya Paul, began to emerge towards the beginning of the 1980s. But Rohit Khosla (1958-1994), together with Tarun Tahiliani, Abu Jani-Sandeep Khosla, and others, co-founded Ensemble in 1987, becoming a pioneer in the fashion business.
- With assistance from the Fashion Institute of Technology in New York, the Ministry of Textiles of the Government of India established the National Institute of Fashion Technology (NIFT) in Delhi in 1986. It was crucial in attracting fashion designers with local training. By 2010, it had established 15 branches around India, and there were also smaller private fashion institutes.
- The Indian economy underwent economic liberalization in 1990, which fuelled the growth of the fashion sector. The next decade saw a boom in the fashion business in terms of both volume and styles.

THE GENESIS OF SIMPLE KAUR

Simple Kaur started her brand in 2003. For her, it was a brand-new beginning in terms of style. She has always been a really creative person. She grew up seeing her uneducated grandmother sew clothing for the entire household. Additionally, she did not know the expensive and glamorous world of the fashion industry, including facts and numbers. When she was a young girl and used to attend school, her grandmother made her school scarves with lovely motifs, about which all the nuns at her school inquired and took to be copied. She noticed how her grandmother's crotia and knitted outfits gained popularity among the Nuns and teachers at her school. Her grandmother sewed clothes using the Usha sewing machine, which she to date has kept with her as an inspiration and motivation at her studio. She then made up her mind to pursue her studies in the fashion industry to become a leading designer one day. For her to become a business entrepreneur was not difficult as she hailed from a business family, but the challenge was to start her start-up in the field of fast fashion as a woman entrepreneur with limited funds and high-grade competition. She started with a market survey before launching her brand, to understand the local market and trends, and to study the demography, income expenditure, lifestyle, and pattern of the customers around. She met local artisans, textile suppliers, and various fabric distributors to understand the financial requirement needed for her start-up.

SIMPLE KAUR FOUNDATION

In 2003, simple kaur launched her brand under her name, opening her first showroom in Chandigarh's sector 35, a popular destination for shoppers thanks to its proximity to the ICICI Bank, Dollar Store, and the Memorable Moments restaurant, a gathering place for women who enjoyed attending kitty parties and wearing designer clothing. People that frequented the marketplace paid her name a lot of attention and made sure to check out her business to learn more about what it is all about. It was one of the first stores in the city center to provide custom apparel built to customers' preferences and tastes rather than standard-issue clothing. Chandigarh never catered to the needs of customers when it came to designing exclusivity in apparel. She created her website, had her logo produced, and acquired the trademark and patent rights for it thanks to her technology-oriented attitude. For city dwellers, receiving all the exclusivity, quality, and custom clothing design was brand-new. She was able to carve out a place for herself because of the quality, location, timeliness, and technology-driven approach. She introduced a line with Kashmiri embroidery that drew many NRI customers, including some members of the high-end upper class who had expensive tastes and were aware of clothing's formality. That's when she began to receive a large number of clients from outside of India, who eventually assisted her in growing her business from local catering to a worldwide market.

INDIAN FASHION INDUSTRY COMPETITION

Due to the high danger of substitutes, increased consumer bargaining power, high level of competitive rivalry, and high threat of new entrants, the Indian fashion business has very high levels of industry competitiveness. These various circumstances are all having a bad effect on the fashion business. The market's low level of negotiating power among textile and fabric vendors is the only thing to be pleased about. A sizeable portion of the market, Simple Kaur viewed this as a danger and realize she must take an action by improving her products to fit modern consumers' wants while preserving the competitive edge that led to her early success, she can plow into the general market.

Businesses carried out demand forecasting closer to the time of sale when customer demand fluctuates continually, as it happens in the fashion business, to effectively predict requests. Simple Kaur has been seeking ways to reduce lead times to reduce excess inventory or missing sales that arise from poor forecasts. Utilizing artificial intelligence (AI) in demand forecasting and product creation is one emerging remedy that worked for her. The focus from standardization to customization using "Vocal for Local" was the key niche that helped her start-up to flourish and expand locally to globally. The main thing that set her apart from the rest of the competition was her network of fabric sellers, the workshop of craftsmen working for her, and her emphasis on using locally made excellent quality fabrics and original bespoke designs.

EXPANDING SIMPLE KAUR

The size of the worldwide clothing market is anticipated to increase by 4%, or $2.6 trillion, by 2025. India will be the second-most appealing clothing market in the world by 2025, generating almost $121 billion.

Regular NRI clients who also provided her with many other clients sought a joint venture and the expansion of her franchise to the international market. She launched her first international store in Calgary, Canada, in 2011. By charging a franchise owner a fee for utilizing her brand name and providing the infrastructure required for branding and shop setup, franchising assisted her in growing both in India and beyond. Simple Kaur focused on growing her brand internationally by offering the fabric, designing online, and assisting with marketing. Customization was her key differentiator. Additionally, she sent a lot of inquiries from clients throughout the world to her businesses wherever they were. She customized it once consumers gave their choices for size, design, and pricing; that served as her USP (unique selling proposition) for growing her start-up. She examined visual and textual information in addition to the preference profiles, including Pinterest boards connected to customers' profiles, written feedback, and request notes. Purchase histories and fit input from repeat consumers are further factors that influence the curating process. Data analytics powers various commercial aspects, including demand forecasting, inventory management, and product design. Forecasting demand and product development with AI. Before being packed and sent to clients, the finished goods were then checked for quality control by her staff at the store.

Simple Kaur's operational approach eliminated the need to create a new collection for unidentified customers each season or to get rid of unsold inventory at the end of each season, which automatically alleviated the main difficulties with inventory management in the conventional clothes company model. Simple Kaur was also able to minimize returns, obtain more sell-through, and further eliminated inaccuracies in demand forecasting, all of which contributed to profitability, by developing designs in-house that best reflect the most recent Innovations in the fashion retail business.

By repurposing the scraps of fabric that are left behind and creating a new costume out of them, she is sustainably growing her start-up. By adopting the John Elkington triple bottom line theory—people, planet, and profit—and using environmentally friendly color dyes for printing, she has carved out a niche for herself in the boutique industry of customized apparel designing worldwide. She has also adopted technology that enables sustainable production and expansion while maintaining corporate social responsibility towards society with utilitarian values.

OPPORTUNITIES FOR FUNDING THE EXPANSION OF SIMPLE KAUR

Using the money needed for her start-up, simple Kaur attempted to put her idea into action. Before pitching the business idea for expansion and obtaining funding from other sources, there were few, largely unofficial techniques for generating money during the early phases of starting up her business.

- Bootstrapping a start-up is the process of growing a business with little or no outside capital. It involves depending on one's income and savings to survive and develop.
- **Family and Friends:** A popular source of funding for entrepreneurs. The inherent level of trust that exists between investors and business owners is this investment source's key benefit.
- **Crowdfunding:** It was the process of getting money from a lot of individuals (NRI and high-end clients) whom each gave a modest amount. Usually, internet crowdsourcing sites are used for this sought financial funding for any start-up.

She received financial support from the government loan funding program that supported her startup under the start-up India Seed Fund Scheme and SIDBI Fund of Funds, which was a government-sponsored program for ambitious entrepreneurs to access low-cost financing, during the gestation period of her business as it was starting, evolving, and expanding from the period from 2014 onwards.

In the meantime, she had already expanded into the global market. As a part of her investment in low-cost manufacturing for the personalized operation of her designing garments, she also worked on credit purchases from different fabric vendors and employed pre-paid advances from her client base located all over the world. As a starting business, she used the pre-paid advances as a liquid buffer to access other NBFC and Bank funding alternatives.

MARKETING PLAN FOR SIMPLE KAUR

Simple Kaur started and grew her firm using the marketing mix method. She had the popular face of the Indian fashion business at the time, Top Model Mehr Bhasin, open her store, which helped her earn a lot of credibility in the market and popularity with the residents of the city because the entire event was covered by the print media and journals.

She examined visual and textual information in addition to the preference profiles, including Pinterest boards connected to customers' profiles, written feedback, and request notes

She established herself as a frequent contributor to print publications in India, such as Hindustan Times and Economic Times, which included her articles on page 3 throughout every blossoming season on the newest and emerging trends in Indian fashion. Her plot was covered by magazines like Glimpse, which also assisted in drawing in and keeping clients.

From her logo to personalized bags with her name on them, she has provided value through a customer-focused approach.

Using the Blue Ocean strategy, she concentrated only on her business and the customization of her products more sustainably, not paying attention to or seeing the threats from her regional competitors. Instead, she worked on improving her business and services to adopt a green technology-driven approach, by expanding internationally using social media, creating pages on Facebook, and Instagram, using chatbots on her website, and providing answers to customers' questions there. Just in time improved the business bottom line by getting rid of dead stock and cutting the price of making tailored clothing.

She held a workshop in advance of festival season to introduce her new clothing line, and many students worked under her. Models also wore her creations on the catwalk. The citizens of the city and the nation heard a lot about this.

CHALLENGES FACED BY SIMPLE KAUR

The whole world's businesses, commerce, and markets were shut down owing to the imposition of lockdown in 2020 after covid had emerged internationally. The closing of borders prevented trade from flowing across them, which affected how the economy operated. The craftsmen and migrant workers were ordered back to their home villages, and the fashion sector, like other industries, had a huge stop in operations, resulting in significant losses in both people and money. It affected both trade and manufacturing activities. The country's distribution and logistics activities were suspended, and significant supplies were reduced as a result, forcing the operations to cease. There were no operations, which caused a significant loss of customers. Due to a lack of revenue creation on a worldwide scale, consumers cut back on their spending and switched from buying expensive goods to buying cheaper alternatives offered by online retailers.

Simple Kaur was forced to close her business since it became too difficult to pay her rent, other monthly bills, and bills to banks and other NBFCs. As there were few significant customer orders, she partnered with Amazon, who also provided free photoshoots of her designed clothes to sell on their platform. However, this may not have worked out well for her as customers' spending patterns had changed as a result of the lockdown and psychological behavioral changes brought about by Covid. Due to reduced significant supplies of fabrics and textiles, which made it impossible to execute orders on time, there were fewer online orders, which led to a loss of consumers.

REVIVAL OF SIMPLE KAUR POST COVID-19

Rising industrial activity and changes in lifestyle that have resulted in environmental harm are directly linked to rising carbon footprints (Vyas et al., 2023). During the lockdown in the year 2020, Simple Kaur researched and used sustainable technological practices to reduce the cost of creating clothing and boost business margins while enhancing the quality and customer service, by keeping an environment-friendly clothing line. Eco-friendly materials and a reasonable price range helped it regain its pre-covid status. Her leadership style was based on a comparison of consumer sentiments toward organic goods, which were further divided into likes and dislikes and positive or negative viewpoints on organic vs. conventional products. Consumers view organic products favorably because of the negative effects of conventional goods. Due to the harm that conventional products cause to people's health and the environment, some consumers opt to buy organic products instead of conventional ones (Nedra et al., 2015). This stated that people purchase organic goods because they believe they are unquestionably healthier and more environmentally friendly than conventional goods. She was able to reclaim her place in the business with the aid of worldwide webinars, online courses, and seminars. She partnered with Tantra, a company that provided unisex personalized t-shirts that drew customers of all ages, to rebuild the client base that was lost during the lockdown By providing free tips on how to take care of their wardrobes and pricey outfits by producing and re-using them in different ways, she engaged with clients by sharing DIY (do it yourself) hacks on social media platforms including Instagram reels, Facebook page, and video logs. She participated in the resurgence of ancient Indian weaving, printing, dyeing, and embroidery methods such ikat, patola (double-ikat), bandhani (tie-and-dye), and shisha (mirror embroidery).

For her adoption of technology that met the demands of the customers while helping to promote sustainable fashion. She established herself as a successful female entrepreneur who started a business, took it global, and received a major award from the Punjab government. This honor helped her acquire more exposure and strengthened her brand more than before.

TEACHING NOTE

Outline

An Indian start-up named Simple Kaur was founded in Chandigarh in 2003. Fashion enthusiast Simple Kaur desired to launch her brand to serve the Indian market and expanded globally. She opened her first store in a prime location for shoppers that had proximity to the ICICI Bank, Dollar Store, and the Memorable Moments restaurant, a gathering place for women who enjoyed attending kitty parties and wearing designer clothing. She opened her business with the assistance of top fashion model Mehr Bhasin, who received extensive media attention and gave her venture a successful start. She started with local customers, then extended to all of India before launching her first business outside of India in Canada. She employed a variety of funding sources for her start-up and growth. Her Vocal for Local strategy was used to attract customers. She experienced setbacks throughout the covid and was forced to close her business; she worked with Tantra and Amazon but failed. How she embraced using eco-friendly technologies and pursuing sustainable fashion enabled her to get back into the business after covid.

CASE OBJECTIVES

- To educate students about the obstacles to growth faced by start-ups in India
- To teach students the strategic steps founders must take to establish and expand start-up businesses.
- To aid students in comprehending the possibilities available to finance a start-up expansion and the benefits and drawbacks of the same
- To educate students, on how to implement the blue ocean strategy
- Start-ups must continue growing their businesses to gain or maintain market share.

PLACE OF THE COURSE

This can be utilized for undergraduate and graduate management programs as well as for any workshops that will be held for new business owners. This can be used by undergraduate students in their last semester since they will thoroughly understand all courses by that point. This instance can be applied to graduate students near the conclusion of the first year. This might be a 90-minute lesson that is included in a course on entrepreneurship or start-up funding.

Suggested Pre-Readings

The following pre-readings can be given to students to help them grasp the basics of start-up expansion finance and the possibilities available for it.

PRE-READING MATERIAL

1. Kaur, S. (2023). *Simple Kaur.* Chandigarh: Simple Kaur. Retrieved from https://simplekaur.com/Kaur
2. Cassar, G. (2014). Industry and startup experience on entrepreneur forecast performance in new firms. *Journal of Business Venturing*, *29*(1), 137-151.
3. Hottenrott, H., Rexhäuser, S., & Veugelers, R. (2016). Organizational change and the productivity effects of green technology adoption. *Resource and Energy Economics*, *43*, 172-194.
4. Henninger, C. E., Alevizou, P. J., & Oates, C. J. (2016). What is sustainable fashion? *Journal of Fashion Marketing and Management: An International Journal*, *20*(4), 400-416.
5. Ikram, M. (2022). The transition toward green economy: Technological Innovation's role in the fashion industry. *Current Opinion in Green and Sustainable Chemistry*, 100657.
6. Jin, B. E., & Shin, D. C. (2020). Changing the game to compete: Innovations in the fashion retail industry from the disruptive business model. *Business Horizons*, *63*(3), 301-311.
7. Le Xuan, T. (2019). *Digital marketing strategies of luxury fashion brands in China: The Gucci brand.* Academic Press.
8. India, S. (2016). *Ministry of Commerce and Industry.* Government of India, Delhi, India https://www. startup India. gov. in/content/sih/en/about_us/about-us. html
9. Chantia, S. (n.d.). *Fashion in India: From tradition to sustainable contemporisation: An appraisal.* Academic Press.

10. Billatos, S. (1997). *Green technology and design for the environment.* CRC Press.

TEACHING PLAN

The case may be given to the class as pre-reading together with other resources pertinent to the course's theme. The instructor can begin the class by conducting a quick poll of the students by posting the following question on the board and asking them to raise their hands if they have any responses.

RECOMMENDED TEACHING PLAN

To conduct the class for 90 minutes utilizing this case study, instructors may adopt the proposed plan shown in Table 1.

Table 1. Recommended time plan

Preliminary survey: Should the business grow?	10 Minutes
Divide the students into five groups and give each group a question to think about	5 Minutes
Group Discussion	15 Minutes
Discussion on SWOT Analysis	10 Minutes
Benefits and Drawbacks of the available funding alternatives	10 Minutes
Alternative sources of support	10 Minutes
Required funding and equity dilution	10 Minutes
Foreseeable difficulties	10 Minutes
Wrap-up	10 Minutes

Sources – Authors Analysis

SUGGESTED QUESTIONS

The following series of questions can then be used by the instructor to facilitate class discussion on the case. If necessary, the teacher can also provide one question to each of the five groups in the class and ask them to work together to determine the answer. The remaining students can then hear each group's analysis. Based on the answers provided below, the instructor can then conclude the lesson and recap any points that were missed. If the instructor chooses to adopt this method, a sample lesson plan with suggested timelines is also included toward the end of this teaching note.

Q1) What Motivated Simple Kaur to Grow Her Business? Did She Adequately Expand Her Start-Up?

Expected Answer

Simple Kaur founded her start-up in 2003, but her early memories of watching her grandmother create garments for the entire family served as motivation for the venture. She was inspired to pursue this career by the attention she received from instructors and nuns at her school while wearing knitted scarves. As a result, she enrolled at the National Institute of Fashion Designing where she studied fashion and eventually became a fashion designer.

She established her business in her name and obtained a trademark for it. Her business was founded on the slogan "Vocal for Local," which promoted handicrafts, textiles, and art made locally. She traveled around India, researched market needs, and made connections with fabric vendors.

Yes, she successfully expanded her start-up by channeling her resources and making the most use of them, by deciding on a suitable site for her new business and attending to the demands of the clients.

Q2. How Did Simple Kaur Implement the Blue Ocean Strategy to Resurrect the Business?

Expected Answer

Simple Kaur implemented the Blue Ocean Strategy to resurrect the business by the following:

- Create a market with no competition: Simple Kaur utilized her fashion degree to its fullest potential by comprehending the demands, likes, and preferences of the clientele. She used a customized approach to her company strategy while all of the linked business entrepreneurs continued to use standardization and sold their goods, such as garments, based on production principles. As a result, she customized her specialty, picked a prime location for her business venture, and focused on her target market.
- Make the opposition unimportant: Instead of concentrating on what rivals were doing, Simple Kaur concentrated on adopting the technology that encouraged the usage of scrap fabrics
- (leftover) and the creation of clothing out of it. She concentrated on improvising and improving her business to provide higher-quality goods and prospering it by gaining market share using her voice for local strategy.
- Elicit and seize fresh demand: By wearing her designed clothing line made from locally sourced sustainable fabrics on models, Simple Kaur increased demand for it among locals and across India. She also led a workshop for students at the Indian Institute of Fashion Design to highlight the rich heritage of the Indian fashion industry, which was covered by the media.
- Achieve value-cost parity: Simple Kaur strikes a balance between cost- and utility-conscious design or service innovation and delivering new value for the consumer. Word-of-mouth marketing can raise demand as more people buy what you're selling. the price of making clothing and selling it to consumers while obtaining economies of scale.

- Align the whole system of business operations to achieve distinctiveness and cheap cost: In addition to the preference profiles, Simple Kaur incorporated textual and visual data, such as Pinterest boards linked to customer profiles, written comments, and request notes. Additional elements that affect the curating process include purchase histories and fit feedback from returning customers. Demand forecasting, inventory control, and product creation were just a few of the commercial activities that were powered by data analytics. Using AI to predict demand and product creation. The final items were then examined by her personnel at the store for quality control before being packaged and sent to customers. Developing and promoting the reuse and sustainable fashion, which lowers total cost, helped her use her resources as efficiently as possible and eliminate the need for inventory build-up.

Q3) What Are the Benefits and Drawbacks of The Financing Choices Selected by Simple Kaur?

Expected Answer

The benefits of the financing choices selected by Simple Kaur are as follows:

1. **Book Strapping:** It is a great funding strategy since it keeps ownership domestic and reduces debt. One obtains 100% of the earnings and it is one of several excellent funding solutions that don't dilute ownership. Improved management of business direction. One won't have to worry about receiving approval from others if they want to attempt a different product design, modify their company strategy, or altogether change where their business is going. To establish business credit or for one-time transactions, it could open a credit card. However, they never rely on outside finance to advance their business. One won't have to worry about owing on a sizable loan if things don't go as planned because the majority of the debt they accumulate (if any) will be rapidly paid off.
2. **Funds From Family and Friends:** There may be no interest to repay. Paying back a high-interest loan or credit card with relatives and friends is significantly less expensive.
3. **Crowdfunding:** One of the main benefits of holding a start-up fundraising event is that you can consolidate all of your investor discussions in one location for the welfare cause and for venturing out the business. One will be aiming their crowdfunding endeavor at a group of people who are already interested in becoming early adopters.
4. **Bank Loan:** The funds borrowed from the bank for business help to maintain complete control and be free from outside meddling. When a borrower pays off a loan, there is no further obligation or engagement with the bank lender, unless the borrower wants to take out another loan, which is determined by the worth of the firm and its perceived capacity to service the debt by making payments on schedule and in full. Tax deductions are available for business bank loans' interest. In addition, loan servicing payments stay the same for the duration of the loan, particularly with fixed-rate loans where the interest rate is constant for the period of the loan. Because of this, it is simple for firms to plan their budgets and make monthly loan payments. Even if the loan has an adjustable rate, business owners may still calculate future payments in the case of a rate change using a straightforward spreadsheet.

The drawbacks of the financing choices selected by Simple Kaur are as follows:

1. Bootstrapping involves investing your own money in the company directly, which carries the greatest visible risk. When one's business suffers, whether, from a drop in sales or an unforeseen expenditure, it will have an immediate impact. Self-funded enterprises are more likely to have sluggish cash flow and even run out of money despite having less debt to worry about. Finding the contacts, you need to develop your business may be more difficult without the support of seasoned investors. One might not be able to meet the high demand if one's budget is very little.
2. If money is borrowed from family or friends and is not returned, it could damage such relationships. Sometimes, things might elude our control if we cannot repay a friend's debt.
3. Failed initiatives run the danger of harming the reputation of the company and the investors. Someone could notice one's company idea on a crowdfunding website and steal it if one hasn't registered a patent or copyright for it.
4. Business Banks Loans are a tedious process and not many businesses and start-ups qualify for obtaining it. There is a high rate of interest and loans are obtained using collateral as security, with high processing charges and strict repayment plans

Q4) How Did Simple Kaur Revive Her Start-Up Post-Pandemic?

Expected Answer

Simple Kaur conducted research and employed sustainable technology techniques to lower the cost of producing the garments and increase company margins while boosting the quality and customer service during the lockdown in the year 2020. To replace the clientele that was lost during the lockdown, she teamed up with Tantra, a business that offered unisex customized t-shirts that attracted clients of all ages. It was able to reclaim its pre-covid status because of eco-friendly building materials and an affordable price range. With the help of international webinars, online courses, and seminars, she was able to restore her position in the industry. She interacted with clients by posting DIY (do it yourself) hacks on social media platforms including Instagram reels, Facebook page, and video logs. She gave free advice on how to take care of their wardrobes and expensive clothing by making and reusing them in various ways. She adopted green technologies that satiated client needs while advancing sustainable fashion. Sustainable manufacturing is described as the production of manufactured goods using procedures that minimize adverse environmental effects, preserve energy and natural resources, are secure for workers, communities, and customers, and are financially viable. She made a name for herself as a successful female businesswoman who launched a company, expanded it internationally, and won a significant honor from the Punjabi government. She received additional visibility as a result of this distinction, which also improved the power of her brand.

Q5) What Tactics Simple Kaur Used to Make Sure the Simple Kaur Brand Name Endures Forever During Her Launch? How Did Social Media Marketing Assist Simple Kaur in Growing Her Start-Up?

Expected Answer

Simple Kaur launched her business under the signature "Simple Kaur," which garnered a lot of interest. She had her logo created and registered the trademark for it. Because the entire event was covered by the print media and journals, she was able to gain a lot of credibility in the market and popularity among city residents when she opened her store of designer clothing in a prominent Chandigarh location with a well-known face of the Indian fashion industry, Top Model Mehr Bhasin. The focus from standardization to customization using "Vocal for Local" was the key niche that helped her start-up to flourish and expand locally to globally. The main thing that set her apart from the rest of the competition was her network of fabric sellers, the workshop of craftsmen working for her, and her emphasis on using locally made excellent quality fabrics and original bespoke designs.

She improved her business and services to embrace a green technology-driven strategy by leveraging social media to develop globally, building pages on Facebook and Instagram, employing chatbots on her website, and responding to inquiries from clients there. By getting rid of dead stock and lowering the cost of creating fitted apparel, Just in Time enhanced the company's bottom line.

REFERENCES

Gansky, L. (2010). *The mesh: Why the future of business is sharing*. Penguin.

Gleasure, R. (2015). Resistance to crowdfunding among entrepreneurs: An impression management perspective. *The Journal of Strategic Information Systems*, *24*(4), 219–233.

Henninger, C. E., Alevizou, P. J., & Oates, C. J. (2016). What is sustainable fashion? *Journal of Fashion Marketing and Management*, *20*(4), 400–416.

Hottenrott, H., Rexhäuser, S., & Veugelers, R. (2016). Organizational change and the productivity effects of green technology adoption. *Resource and Energy Economics*, *43*, 172–194.

Ikram, M. (2022). The transition toward green economy: Technological Innovation's role in the fashion industry. *Current Opinion in Green and Sustainable Chemistry*, 100657.

India, S. (2016). *Ministry of Commerce and Industry*. Government of India, Delhi, India https://www. startup India. gov. in/content/sih/en/about_us/about-us. html

Jin, B. E., & Shin, D. C. (2020). Changing the game to compete: Innovations in the fashion retail industry from the disruptive business model. *Business Horizons*, *63*(3), 301–311.

Kalkreuter, B. (2020). Anyone's Heritage? Indian Fashion Design's Relationships with Craft between Local Guardianship and Valorization of Global Fashion. *Fashion Practice*, *12*(2), 264–287.

Kaur, S. (2023). *Simple Kaur.* Chandigarh: Simple Kaur. Retrieved from https://simplekaur.com/Kaur

Le Xuan, T. (2019). *Digital marketing strategies of luxury fashion brands in China: The Gucci brand.* Academic Press.

Nedra, B. A., Sharma, S., & Dakhli, A. (2015). Perception and motivation to purchase organic products in Mediterranean countries: An empirical study in Tunisian context. *Journal of Research in Marketing and Entrepreneurship.*

Pozzo, B. (2020). Fashion between inspiration and appropriation. *Laws*, *9*(1), 5.

Vyas, V., Mehta, K., & Sharma, R. (2023). The nexus between toxic-air pollution, health expenditure, and economic growth: An empirical study using ARDL. *International Review of Economics & Finance*, *84*, 154–166.

Chapter 5
Cohort-Based Leadership Development for High Potential (HiPO) Employees Through Neurolinguistic Programming (NLP)

Shuchi Dawra
https://orcid.org/0000-0001-9296-6838
Chitkara Business School, Chitkara University, India

Sandhir Sharma
https://orcid.org/0000-0002-3940-8236
Chitkara Business School, Chitkara University, India

EXECUTIVE SUMMARY

In organizations, leadership development is considered one of the critical success measures for the growth of high potential employees. This case study examines the neuro linguistic programming (NLP) tools and techniques used by IT organization, behavioural challenges, and outcome in leadership development for the high potential (HiPO) employees. The aim of this study is to illustrate characteristics of HiPO employees, importance of neuro linguistic programming for the leadership roles, and integration of NLP for talent management and leadership development in an IT organization. In this case, learners will identify the tools of NLP and understand their integration into leadership development programs for the HiPO employees.

DOI: 10.4018/978-1-6684-8488-3.ch005

INTRODUCTION

The Global Information Technology Market is growing in double digits, especially in emerging technologies. Growth in the software, hardware, and services market is driven by the growth in mobile and cloud markets. These cloud and mobile technologies have given impetus to the software development market. Software continues to hold the highest percentage in IT spending along with digital transformation technologies. Over the next few years, the surge in IT products and services will be there due to expanded innovations in Augmented Reality, Virtual Reality, and Artificial Intelligence (AI) enabled products. These technologies will not only lead to cost savings for organizations but also to gain competitive benefits.

As per the IBEF report (2022) on IT and BPM, in India the Information Technology industry contributed for 7.4% of India's GDP', as of Financial Year 2022 and it is expected to account 10% to India's Gross Domestic Product by 2025. The IT industry employs 5 million people. As per the estimates of National Association of Software and Service Companies (NASSCOM), the Indian IT industry's revenue touched US$ 227 billion in FY22, a 15.5%YoY growth. The Indian IT Exports stood at US$254.4 billion in FY22.The Business Process Management(BPM) sector currently employs more than 1.4 million people, while IT and BPM together have more than 4.5 million workforce as of FY21.The software and hardware sector in India has attracted cumulative foreign direct investment(FDI) inflows worth US$85.51 billion from April 2000 till March 2022.Also the sector ranked 2nd in Foreign Direct Investment inflows as per the data released by Department for the Promotion of Industry and Internal Trade (DPIIT).

Complex Environment

The disruptive technologies and subsequent adoption of new transformational strategies, processes and value chain has reshaped the nature of work around the globe. These have also brought in the new challenges for the leaders as well as employees. Thus, increasing concern for organizational and employee wellbeing. The torpedoing of the jobs, and disruption creating business models are the dynamic phenomena (Bruckner et al., 2017). Some of the challenges of this sector include- traditional approach to work design and digital transformation work in the services firms; cutting edge competition from the bigger fishes in the market; New-age IT firms who adopt work based on latest technologies; changing concept of workspaces towards remote locations (Sull et al., 2020) and work from home(WFH); the independent work mindset (Aggarwal et al., 2020), and outsourced HR function; Talent acquisition, management and engagement (Pillai & Paul, 2023).

Organizational Challenge

Peter Anderson as a CEO is running a well-established IT firm Ambit Technologies, with operations in India and serving for the development of software applications and services across the globe. He has a flamboyant team in leadership looking after business clients, and a Team of Product Managers and Software Engineers building the organization at different locations including US, Canada and UK. Team includes 5 leaders looking after sales, 10 Product Managers and 30 Software Engineers with varied experience. Recently, Peter had a discussion with the Leaders and Product Managers face to face in which he has identified the following challenges:

- Though profitability increased, leaders have lost the zeal to innovate and play their best in the field as an organizational team due to the dynamic and complex environment.
- There are a lot of conflicts due to gaps in the communication amongst the Leaders and the Product Managers. Some team members shared a great bond whereas others were aloof.
- Though Product Managers were well acquainted with the technical skills, there was an urgent need to train them in soft skills.

Being concerned, Peter consulted one of his industry colleagues Joseph N, who is a Certified Global Organization Change Consultant with an experience of over 15 years in the Leadership Development and Team Management. His area of expertise included behavioural modification amongst Business Leaders in the organizations through Neuro Linguistic Programming (NLP). He has conducted 28 Leadership Development Programs with the corporate leaders in various FMCGs and global IT firms ranging from one week to two months. Looking at the growth prospects and opportunities in the sector, Peter deployed Joseph N as a consultant to conduct a leadership program for the candidates for leadership profiles -10 Product Managers and 5 existing business leaders.

Identifying the Gap

Joseph initiated the open discussions with Peter to understand his requirements to conduct the leadership program. He created dummy profiles of 5 leaders and 10 Product Managers through their performance records, achievements and observation method. After the preliminary investigation and discussions with Peter, Joseph decided to conduct the leadership development program for these High Potential(HiPO) employees by using the tools of neurolinguistic programming (NLP) (Malik et al., 2017).The objective of this program would be to help these future leaders to understand the concept and relevance of situational leadership to be more effective.

Characteristics of HiPO Employees

High Potential (HiPO) employees are the employees in an organization which are driven to outperform their previous targets (Silzer & Church, 2010). They have dominant characteristics of maturation, motivation, mandates and moxie. Maturation refers to growth of an individual through his/her are of expertise and experiences over time. They are self-starters who have an inherent drive to perform par excellence. HiPOs have a better understanding of the organization's vision and policies (Cummings & Oldham, 1997). Also, they have the characteristics of 'moxie'-better conceptual skills to understand and observe complex patterns. Looking into the personalities of 10 Product Managers and 5 Leaders combined with a preliminary research, Joseph observed the presence of 4 Ms-characteristics of HiPOs in them.

Adopting Neuro Linguistic Programming (NLP)

During the Leadership Program especially designed with an objective of further developing the HiPO employees through neuro-linguistic programming (NLP), he kept the challenges faced by an organization in the platter amongst the 15 participants he had interacted with before. The idea was to address these issues from the forefront to put an organization in the growth path (Kaur et al., 2021). NLP refers to three words- Neuro-Linguistic Programming. The term 'neuro' refers to the neurological system, i.e., how you experience five senses. The neuro system of an individual gets affected by both conscious and unconscious thought process which has an influence on how an individual feels, what they say and do (Kang et al., 2020; Linder-Pelz, 2010). Linguistics refers to verbal and non-verbal cues through which we communicate our experiences. An individual's thinking pattern and how an employee codes, evaluates, learns and communicates his experience is known as the programming process. There are five stages through which NLP practitioners work on behaviour modification which are given in Figure 1.

Figure 1. Stages of changing through NLP
Source: Elfaki (2008, pp. 35-40)

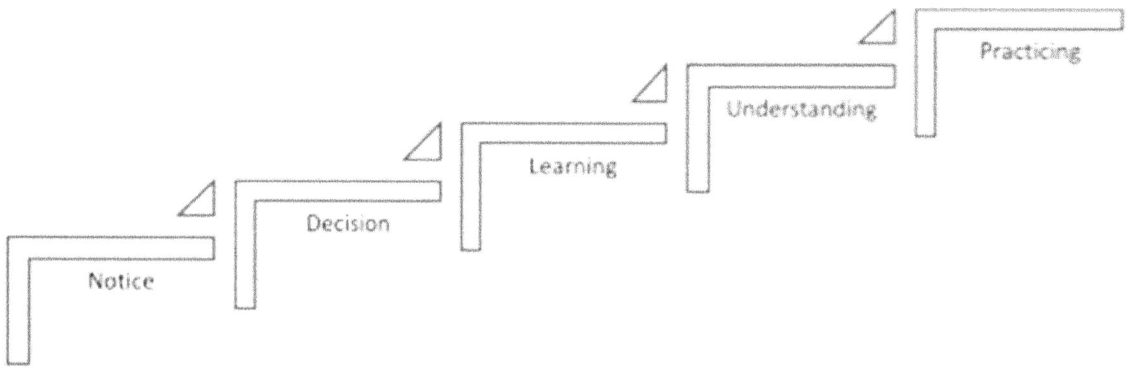

To begin with, participants were told to notice their workplace conversations and start keeping a journal of their observations. Once they have got into the habit of maintaining a journal, they are being guided to make decisions related to counter work behaviours and conversations with colleagues that they want to modify. After that they were asked about the willingness and ways to adopt new behaviours in the same situations and pace up their learnings. Next step adopted by Joseph was to help participants understand the situation and how it affects the communication and response of the participant. Participants at this stage must understand the behaviour change will not come at once, rather it includes understanding of previous stages. In the final stage participants were made to understand the power of practicing the desired behaviours. For four weekends, Joseph worked tirelessly with 15 participants for 10 hours to guide and monitor their behavioural challenges and changes.

Tools and Techniques for Neuro Linguistic Programming (NLP)

Joseph planned to implement various tools of NLP like-Mirroring/Modelling, Confidence building, anchoring, loop breaking. Neuro-linguistic programming (NLP) is a communication model which can be used to work on an employee's thinking pattern, language, and behaviour (Murray, 2013; Mahony, 2007). The techniques of NLP are highly recommended for developing leaders across the globe. Joseph started using these techniques of NLP in his two months weekend leadership development program with Representational system of NLP (five senses-hearing, taste, sight, smell and feeling)-Visual constructed, visual remembered, Auditory Constructed, Auditory remembered, Kinesthetic (feelings), Auditory Digital (self-talk).

Mirroring

Mirroring is a technique in which one person copies the style of words, speed patterns, volume, body language, face expressions and gestures of the other person. It is also a positive reinforcement technique. Participants were trained to observe the behaviours and decide what they will copy from others following the representation system of audio, visual or kinesthetics. This helped participants in understanding the cues to build better rapport and communication with the other person.

Confidence

Building confidence amongst the participants is the core of any leadership development program. This part included situations inherent to organizational challenges. Participants understood the various aspects of overconfidence and undermining the self (Saluja et al., 2022). They have been introduced to the interrelationship of confidence and fear while making business decisions, and how to act rationally in challenging situations (Robbie, 2017).

Anchoring

In anchoring technique, participants were asked to recall the situations in their life that exuded happiness-any successful project, accomplished tasks etc. Anchoring is used to bring one situation from the previous experiences and make it a current situation to generate similar feelings. This technique is essentially useful for leaders managing the crisis situation, to relax and think deeply to solve the present problems.

Loop Break

Participants were also introduced to the concept of 'loop break' as a technique for the neuro-linguistic programming. Loop break helps the participants to break the pattern consciously. For example, if an employee is angry because of work pressure he can break the pattern consciously by starting counting. This may lead to his diverted attention towards some funny situation in the past that has happened with him. Thus, reactivating his energy to return to his work as a normal routine.

The representational system of NLP as shown in Figure 2 is based on the five senses, that include hearing, taste, sight, smell and feelings. These representational systems are used by people to process the information all the time. But they do not use all the senses together, either two or three. Due to this, they do not process all the information together. This also leads to ignoring certain aspects of information, thus storing incomplete information in the conscious mind (Tosey et al., 2009). The lack of information thus leads to biases and conflicts at the workplace, especially in the interrelationships and communication amongst the team.

Joseph, attuned the participants with the effect of how an individual visually constructs, visually remembers, auditory constructs, auditory remembers, kinesthetics (feelings), auditory digitalise (self-talk) on his decisions through various activities during the 5 hrs session every weekend for consecutive four weeks. Joseph very specifically used various business challenges and observations to improvise the communication amongst self and teams, to build their leadership skills especially focused towards developing situational leadership skills (Middleton, 2011). In situational leadership, there is no best

Figure 2. Representational system of NLP
Source: Jun et al. (2010)

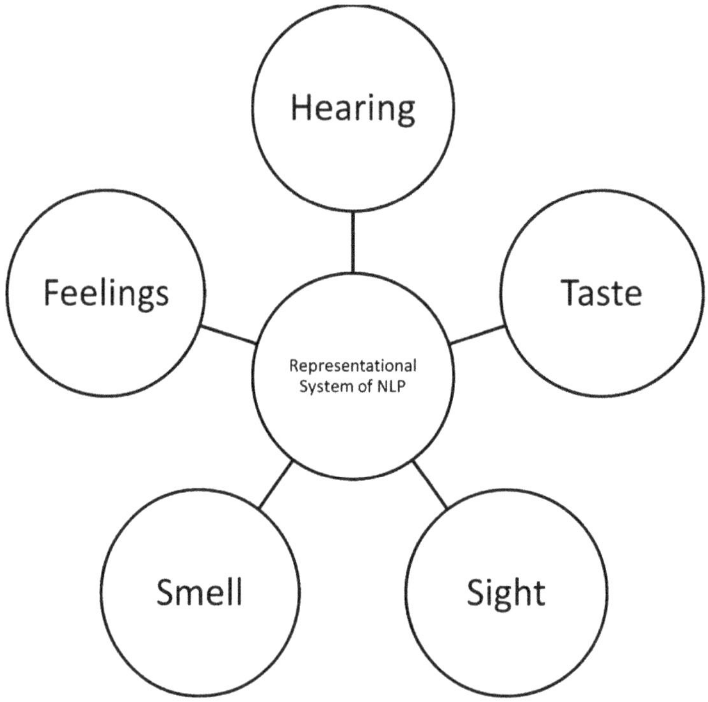

style for command, but leaders can use different forms depending on different situations; the style of leadership can vary from one case to another. Leaders must process the information and act accordingly.

After continuous eight weeks' weekend leadership development program, Joseph was asked to observe and monitor the participants. The following benefits were observed amongst the participants-increased self-awareness and understanding of individual wellbeing, improved communication amongst the team members, better rapport with business leaders, enthusiastic approach towards leading the teams and build better professional networks (Kotera & Van Gordon, 2019; Oberholzer, 2014). Also, after undergoing these sessions participants were more in sync with the organizational requirements, especially there was change in their attitude while handling the workspace communication and business clients. Peter was happy with the outcomes and investment he has made in the program. In one to one discussion with Joseph, both discussed the concerns and challenges underlying the change in the behaviour of the participants. If not practiced well, the behaviour might revert to the past behaviours. The core of using NLP techniques is to teach future leaders to build rapport with others and manage their responses to the dynamic environment in the positive state which requires understanding and regular practice (Hall & Rowland, 2016; Grant, 2019). Thus, using neuro linguistic programming (NLP) facilitates communication, brings in more commitment and cooperation from all spheres for an organization to become more sustainable.

TEACHING NOTE

Synopsis

Mr. Peter Anderson is a CEO of an IT firm Ambit Technologies; he has a team of 5 Business Leaders looking after business clients across the globe and 10 Product Managers for product development with a team of 30 software engineers. He faced a lot of conflicts and lapse in the work communication. Due to which he has realised the need for team building and rapport building in his Organization amongst the HiPO employees-5 Business Leaders and 10 Product Managers to prepare them for the dynamic and complex environment in the IT industry to sustain the organization. This is a case study about the challenges in leadership in an organization. Furthermore, this case discusses the use of Neuro Linguistic Programming (NLP) as behavior modification strategy amongst the employees.

CASE OBJECTIVES

- To make learners understand the behavioral challenges faced by the Leadership and High Potential (HiPO) employees,
- To help learners understand the concept of Neuro-linguistic Programming (NLP) and various tools for behavior modification,
- To help learners gain insights into the use of Neuro-linguistic Programming (NLP) for building Situational leadership skills amongst the High Potential (HiPO) employees.

POSITION IN THE COURSE

This case can be used for undergraduate and postgraduate management and psychology programs. Also, this case is useful for any sessions to be conducted for leadership development and training. For undergraduate learners, this can be used towards the final semester as by then they must have been through the basic concepts of human behaviour and organizational behavior. For post graduate learners, this case can be used towards the end of the first year. This case can also be used in the corporate leadership development programs at large.

SUGGESTED PRE-READINGS

Learners can be assigned the following pre-readings to get a basic understanding on behaviour modification strategies, neuro-linguistic programming (NLP) and high potential (HIPO) employees.

1. Abraham, J., Renaud, S., & Saulquin, J. Y. (2016). Relationships between organizational support, organizational commitment and retention: Evidence from high-potential employees. *Global Journal of Business Research*, *10*(1), 11-26.
2. Ahmed, H. (2017). *Improving leadership skills by using neuro linguistic programming (NLP).* Academic Press.

3. de Andreis, F., & Leopardi, F. (2020). Situational leadership and organizational behavior. *Limen 2020*, 223.
4. Dries, N., Vantilborgh, T., & Pepermans, R. (2012). The role of learning agility and career variety in the identification and development of high potential employees. *Personnel Review*.
5. Downs, L. (2015). Star talent: Investing in high-potential employees for organizational success. *Industrial and Commercial Training*.
6. Potter, D. (2018). *Neuro-linguistic programming for change leaders: The butterfly effect*. Routledge.

TEACHING PLAN

The case can be assigned to the class as a pre-reading material along with other relevant materials suitable to the subject being taught. The instructor can initiate the conversation with the discussion, and writing down the following questions on the board and gauge into the responses through the participation of learners. Table 1 shows the Suggested Time Plan.

Table 1. Suggested time plan

Initial Discussion and survey of learners' understanding	5 minutes
Split class into the group of 5-and randomly allocate one question to each group	5 minutes
Group analysis	20 minutes
Discussion on the SWOT of IT industry and it's challenges in context to human resources	10 minutes
Discussion on the characteristics of HIPO employees	10 minutes
Discussion on the various behaviour modification strategies and use of Neurolinguistic programming(NLP)	15 minutes
Discussion on the Situational Leadership and Neuro-linguistic Programming	10 minutes
Challenges in using NLP	10 minutes
Wrap-up-Summarizing the learnings	5 minutes
Source: Author's Analysis	

Source: Author's Analysis

SUGGESTED QUESTIONS FOR DISCUSSION

1. What are the behavioural challenges IT industry leaders face while managing human resources?
2. What are the characteristics of High Potential Employees in an organization?
3. Discuss the concept of Neuro-linguistic Programming (NLP) as behavioural modification strategy?
4. Discuss how situational leadership development programs are useful for the high potential employees in an organization.
5. What are the advantages and disadvantages of using neuro-linguistic programming as a behavioural modification strategy?

EXPECTED POINTS OF DISCUSSION FOR THE QUESTIONS AND THEIR ANSWERS

Both the teacher and learner can discuss the following points to further understand and introspect into the case study

1. **Behavioural challenges in IT Industry in managing human resources:**
   – High stress work environment
   – Communication Challenges
   – Conflicts in the teams
   – People Management
   – Employee retention
   – Mental wellness
2. **Characteristics of high potential employees:**
   – Maturation
   – Motivation
   – Mandates
   – Moxie
3. **Use of neuro-linguistic programming (NLP) as behavioural modification strategy:**
   – Relates to thoughts, language and patterns of behaviour
   – Psychological approach
   – Positive reinforcement
   – Focused towards specific outcomes
4. **Leadership development program-Building situational leadership skills:**
   – Continuous observation
   – Self-Awareness tools
   – Emotional Intelligence
   – Team Activities
   – Business Games
5. **Advantages and disadvantages of using neuro-linguistic programming (NLP) as behaviour modification strategy:**
   Advantages:
      – Helps in identifying and overcoming the limitations quickly
      – Increased Self-awareness
      – Mastering subliminal mind
      – Effective communication
      – Enhances confidence
      – Improves workplace and personal relationships
   Disadvantages
      – Requires a belief change
      – Complex behavioural transition
      – Requires intention as well as practice

REFERENCES

Aggarwal, A., Chand, P. K., Jhamb, D., & Mittal, A. (2020). Leader–member exchange, work engagement, and psychological withdrawal behavior: The mediating role of psychological empowerment. *Frontiers in Psychology*, *11*, 423. doi:10.3389/fpsyg.2020.00423 PMID:32296361

Bruckner, M., LaFleur, M., & Pitterle, I. (2017). Frontier issues: The impact of the technological revolution on labour markets and income distribution. Department of Economic & Social Affairs, UN.

Cummings, A., & Oldham, G. R. (1997). Enhancing creativity: Managing work contexts for the high potential employee. *California Management Review*, *40*(1), 22–38. doi:10.2307/41165920

Elfaki, I. (2008). *Magic of leadership: How to become effective leader*. Certainty House for Publishing and Distribution.

Grant, A. (2019). A personal perspective on neuro-linguistic programming: Reflecting on the tension between personal experience and evidence-based practice. *International Coaching Psychology Review*, *14*(1), 45–56. doi:10.53841/bpsicpr.2019.14.1.45

Hall, R. D., & Rowland, C. A. (2016). Leadership development for managers in turbulent times. *Journal of Management Development*, *35*(8), 942–955. doi:10.1108/JMD-09-2015-0121

IBEF. (2022). *Report on IT and BPM*. Retrieved from https://www.ibef.org/industry/indian-it-and-ites-industry-analysis-presentation

Jun, F., Chunmei, G., & Jun, Z. (2010). *A Study of Oral Communication Re- search Based on Representational Systems.* IEEE. https://ieeexplore.ieee.org/abstract/document/5660840/

Kang, Y., Cai, Z., Tan, C. W., Huang, Q., & Liu, H. (2020). Natural language processing (NLP) in management research: A literature review. *Journal of Management Analytics*, *7*(2), 139–172. doi:10.1080/23270012.2020.1756939

Kaur, M., Verma, R., & Otoo, F. N. K. (2021). Emotions in leader's crisis communication: Twitter sentiment analysis during COVID-19 outbreak. *Journal of Human Behavior in the Social Environment*, *31*(1-4), 362–372. doi:10.1080/10911359.2020.1829239

Kotera, Y., & Van Gordon, W. (2019). Japanese managers' experiences of neuro-linguistic programming: A qualitative investigation. *The Journal of Mental Health Training, Education and Practice*, *14*(3), 174–185. doi:10.1108/JMHTEP-06-2018-0033

Linder-Pelz, S. (2010). *NLP coaching: An evidence-based approach for coaches, leaders and individuals*. Kogan Page Publishers.

Mahony, T. (2007). *Making your words work: Using NLP to improve communication, learning and behaviour*. Crown House Publishing.

Malik, A. R., Singh, P., & Chan, C. (2017). High potential programs and employee outcomes: The roles of organizational trust and employee attributions. *Career Development International*, *22*(7), 772–796. doi:10.1108/CDI-06-2017-0095

Middleton, C. (2011). *Analysis of the Identification and development of High Potential Employees* [Doctoral dissertation]. University of Wisconsin-Stout.

Murray, P. (2013). Leading by design: Cultivating self-leadership for sustainability. In Motivating Change: Sustainable Design and Behaviour in the Built Environment (pp. 159-184). Routledge.

Oberholzer, C. (2014). *The role of Neuro Linguistic Programming in improving organisational leadership through intrapersonal communication development* [Doctoral dissertation]. University of Pretoria.

Pillai, R., & Paul, B. (2023). Industry 4.0 and the Changing Employment Relations: A Case of the Indian Information Technology Industry. *NHRD Network Journal*, *16*(1), 92–110. doi:10.1177/26314541221134849

Robbie, S. (2017). *Mindful business leadership*. Routledge.

Saluja, S., Aggarwal, A., & Mittal, A. (2022). Understanding the fraud theories and advancing with integrity model. *Journal of Financial Crime*, *29*(4), 1318–1328. doi:10.1108/JFC-07-2021-0163

Silzer, R., & Church, A. H. (2010). Identifying and assessing high-potential talent. *Strategy-driven talent management: A leadership imperative, 28*, 213-280.

Sull, D., Sull, C., & Bersin, J. (2020). Five ways leaders can support remote work. *MIT Sloan Management Review*, *61*(4), 1–10.

Tosey, P., Mathison, J., Tosey, P., & Mathison, J. (2009). Organisational Applications of NLP. *Neuro-Linguistic Programming: A Critical Appreciation for Managers and Developers*, 25-34.

Chapter 6
Falling Prey to Scams:
The Perils of Emotional Decision-Making in the Indian Stock Market - Retail Investor Perspective

S. Baranidharan
Presidency Business School, India

EXECUTIVE SUMMARY

This case study focuses on Mr. Sharma, a retail investor who has been investing in the Indian stock market for the past 10 years. Recently, Mr. Sharma has been making emotional investment decisions and has fallen victim to a stock market scam. The case explores the factors that may have contributed to Mr. Sharma's emotional decision-making, such as a lack of confidence in his investment choices and external influences from media and social pressure. The case also highlights the importance of conducting proper research and analysis before making investment decisions, and the risks associated with falling victim to common types of stock market scams in India. Through this case, students can develop strategies for avoiding falling victim to stock market scams and understand the importance of building investor confidence and trust in the stock market.

BACKGROUND

Certainly, the case study can be a valuable tool for introductory lectures on behavioral finance. It can be used to illustrate the impact of emotional biases on investment decision-making, and to highlight the importance of understanding and mitigating these biases.

The target audience for this case study could be students of a behavioral finance course, as they will be learning about the ways in which human behavior can affect financial decision-making. The case study can help to bring these concepts to life and make them more concrete and relatable.

DOI: 10.4018/978-1-6684-8488-3.ch006

By analyzing the case study, students can gain a deeper understanding of the various emotional biases that can impact investment decision-making, as well as the consequences of falling victim to stock market scams. They can also learn about strategies and techniques for mitigating these biases, such as developing a long-term investment plan, seeking professional advice, and diversifying their portfolio.

An emotional investor in the Indian stock market might make decisions based on their feelings rather than careful analysis of the market and individual investments. This can lead to poor investment choices and financial losses. For example, an investor might buy a stock because they feel good about the company's future prospects, without considering the potential risks or doing thorough research on the company's financial health.

Scams in the Indian stock market can also be a concern for investors. Some common types of stock market scams in India include pump and dump schemes, insider trading, and fraudulent initial public offerings (IPOs). In a pump and dump scheme, a group of individuals or entities manipulate the price of a stock by artificially inflating demand for it through deceptive marketing tactics. Insider trading occurs when an individual with inside information about a company trades the company's stock based on that information, which was not available to the general public. Fraudulent IPOs involve a company issuing false or misleading information in order to sell its stock to unsuspecting investors.

Retail Investor's in India

Investing in the stock market can be a great way to grow your wealth over time, but it can also be a complex and risky endeavor. As a retail investor in present-day India, it's important to understand the basics of investing and to develop a solid strategy to help you achieve your financial goals.

First, it's important to have a clear understanding of what the stock market is and how it works. In India, the stock market consists of two major exchanges – the Bombay Stock Exchange (BSE) and the National Stock Exchange (NSE) – where investors can buy and sell shares in publicly traded companies.

As a retail investor, it's important to conduct your due diligence before investing in any stock. This means researching the company's financial performance, management team, and industry trends to help you make an informed decision about whether to invest. It's also important to develop a long-term investment strategy that aligns with your financial goals and risk tolerance. This may involve diversifying your portfolio across different asset classes, such as stocks, bonds, and mutual funds, to help mitigate risk and maximize returns over time.

In addition to these basic principles of investing, there are also a number of legal and regulatory considerations that retail investors in India should be aware of, such as taxes on capital gains and the rules surrounding foreign investment. Overall, by taking a systematic approach to investing and developing a solid strategy that is tailored to your individual needs and goals, you can navigate the stock market with confidence and potentially achieve significant returns over time.

Evaluation of Retail Investor Behaviour in the Indian Stock Market

The behavior of retail investors in the Indian stock market has been a subject of interest and analysis for many years. There are several factors that can influence the behavior of retail investors, including market conditions, investor sentiment, and personal financial goals.

One common behavior among retail investors is a tendency to be swayed by short-term market fluctuations and news events. This can lead to impulsive buying and selling decisions, which may not align with a long-term investment strategy. Another common behavior is a lack of diversification in investment portfolios. Many retail investors in India tend to invest in a limited number of stocks or sectors, which can increase the risk of significant losses if those stocks or sectors experience a downturn. There is also evidence to suggest that retail investors in India may be more susceptible to scams and fraudulent investment schemes, particularly in the absence of adequate investor education and awareness. However, it's important to note that not all retail investors exhibit these behaviors. Many individuals have successfully navigated the Indian stock market by developing a solid investment strategy and sticking to it over the long term. Overall, while there may be some challenges and pitfalls associated with retail investor behavior in the Indian stock market, there are also opportunities for individuals to achieve significant returns and build long-term wealth with the right approach and mind-set.

According to a report by the National Stock Exchange (NSE) of India, retail investors constitute a significant portion of the Indian stock market. As of December 2020, retail investors held 47.5% of the total market capitalization of the Indian stock market. This is a significant increase from the 38.3% share held by retail investors in December 2019. Another report by the Securities and Exchange Board of India (SEBI) shows that the number of retail investors in the Indian stock market has been steadily increasing over the past few years. As of September 2021, there were over 5.5 crore (55 million) retail investor accounts in India. [1]

Indian Stock Market: Retail Investors Scams

Unfortunately, retail investors in the Indian stock market have been victims of various scams and fraudulent schemes in the past. These scams can take many forms, from Ponzi schemes to pump-and-dump schemes, and can result in significant financial losses for investors.

One common scam in the Indian stock market is the "tips and rumors" scam, in which investors are given false information or rumors about a particular stock or sector in order to manipulate the market and drive up the price. This can lead to a surge in demand for the stock, causing its price to rise, after which the scamsters sell their shares at a profit, leaving the unsuspecting investors with a significant loss.

Another common scam is the "multi-level marketing" scheme, in which investors are promised high returns on their investment in exchange for recruiting other investors to the scheme. In reality, the returns are generated through the recruitment of new investors, rather than through any legitimate investment strategy.

In recent years, there has also been an increase in the number of cryptocurrency scams targeting retail investors in India. These scams can take many forms, including fake initial coin offerings (ICOs), Ponzi schemes, and fake cryptocurrency exchanges.

To protect themselves from these scams, retail investors in the Indian stock market should always conduct thorough research before investing in any stock or scheme. This may involve reviewing the company's financial performance, management team, and regulatory compliance, as well as seeking advice from a financial advisor or reputable investment firm.

It's also important for investors to be wary of unsolicited investment offers, and to never invest money that they cannot afford to lose. By taking a cautious and informed approach to investing, retail investors in the Indian stock market can help minimize their risk of falling victim to scams and fraudulent schemes.

Traps for Retail Investors in the Indian Stock Market

There are several traps that retail investors in the Indian stock market should be aware of, in order to avoid falling victim to scams and fraudulent schemes. Some of these traps include:

1. **Tips and Rumors:** As mentioned earlier, investors may be given false information or rumors about a particular stock or sector in order to manipulate the market and drive up the price. Retail investors should always conduct thorough research before investing in any stock, and be wary of any unsolicited investment tips or advice.
2. **Multi-Level Marketing Schemes:** These schemes promise high returns on investment in exchange for recruiting other investors to the scheme. Investors should be cautious of any scheme that relies on the recruitment of new investors, rather than any legitimate investment strategy.
3. **Pump-and-Dump Schemes:** This is when a stock is artificially inflated by the scamsters, who then sell their shares at a profit, leaving unsuspecting investors with a significant loss. Retail investors should be wary of any sudden surges in demand for a particular stock, and should always research the company's financial performance and regulatory compliance.
4. **Ponzi Schemes:** These schemes promise high returns on investment, but are actually funded by the recruitment of new investors, rather than any legitimate investment strategy. Retail investors should be cautious of any scheme that promises guaranteed returns or high rates of return with little or no risk.
5. **Fake ICOs and Cryptocurrency Exchanges:** In recent years, there has been an increase in the number of cryptocurrency scams targeting retail investors in India. Investors should be wary of any ICO or cryptocurrency exchange that has not been properly regulated or vetted by reputable financial institutions.

Retail investors in the Indian stock market should always conduct thorough research and seek advice from reputable financial advisors or investment firms before investing their hard-earned money. By being aware of these traps, investors can help minimize their risk of falling victim to scams and fraudulent schemes.

Securities and Exchange Board of India (SEBI)

The Securities and Exchange Board of India (SEBI) is the regulatory body that oversees and regulates the Indian securities market, including the stock market, with the aim of protecting the interests of investors and maintaining market integrity. To control and prevent stock market scams and protect retail investors, SEBI has implemented various measures, including:

1. **Regulations and Guidelines:** SEBI has put in place various regulations and guidelines that govern the conduct of market participants, including stockbrokers, listed companies, and mutual funds. These regulations help to maintain market discipline and prevent fraudulent activities.
2. **Surveillance and Monitoring:** SEBI has set up a robust surveillance and monitoring system to track trading patterns and detect any irregularities or unusual activities in the market. SEBI also has a market surveillance department that monitors the market in real-time to detect any market abuse or manipulation.

3. **Investor Education and Awareness:** SEBI has taken various initiatives to educate and create awareness among retail investors about the risks involved in the stock market and the measures they can take to protect themselves from scams and frauds. SEBI conducts investor awareness programs and provides educational material on its website to help investors make informed decisions.
4. **Investigation and Enforcement:** SEBI has the power to investigate and take enforcement action against any violations of securities laws and regulations. This includes imposing fines, initiating legal proceedings, and even revoking the registration of market intermediaries.
5. **Prohibition of Insider Trading:** SEBI has put in place regulations that prohibit insider trading, which is the practice of buying or selling securities based on non-public information. SEBI ensures that the companies and market intermediaries comply with these regulations and takes strict action against any violation.
6. **Disclosure and Transparency:** SEBI mandates that listed companies and market intermediaries provide timely and accurate information to investors. This ensures transparency in the market and helps investors make informed decisions.
7. **Redressal Mechanism:** SEBI has established a redressal mechanism to resolve disputes between investors and market intermediaries. Investors can approach SEBI for any grievances related to investments in the stock market.

In addition to these measures, SEBI has also set up a special cell to investigate and take action against stock market scams. The SEBI Investor Protection and Education Fund (IPEF) also provides compensation to investors who have suffered losses due to fraudulent activities. SEBI's investor protection measures have helped to build investor confidence in the Indian stock market and have prevented many fraudulent activities. However, investors must also exercise caution and due diligence while making investment decisions and seek professional advice if needed. Overall, SEBI plays a crucial role in regulating and controlling the Indian stock market, and its efforts to protect the interests of retail investors have helped to prevent scams and fraudulent activities. However, it is important for investors to also exercise caution and due diligence while making investment decisions and seek professional advice if needed.

In the case study, Mr. Sharma is a retail investor who has been investing in the Indian stock market for the past 10 years. Recently, he has been making emotional investment decisions and has fallen victim to a stock market scam.

Scams in the Indian stock market can also be a concern for investors. Some common types of stock market scams in India include pump and dump schemes, price bubbling, insider trading, and fraudulent initial public offerings (IPOs). In a pump and dump scheme, a group of individuals or entities manipulate the price of a stock by artificially inflating demand for it through deceptive marketing tactics. Insider trading occurs when an individual with inside information about a company trades the company's stock based on that information, which is not available to the general public. Fraudulent IPOs involve a company issuing false or misleading information in order to sell its stock to unsuspecting investors.

Mr. Sharma's investments had become a source of emotional attachment for him, which caused him to hold on to losing stocks in the hope of a rebound. Emotional investing is a common mistake made by many retail investors who tend to become emotionally attached to their investments and fail to make rational decisions. He had made some profits in the past and had developed an overconfidence bias, which caused him to take more risks than he could handle. This is a common mistake made by many investors who become overconfident after making some successful investments.

Mr. Sharma had invested a significant portion of his savings in stocks, which lacked diversification. This means that he had not spread his investments across different asset classes or sectors, which increased his risk exposure. He had Herd Mentality and had invested in some stocks based on tips and recommendation from friends and relatives, which shows a tendency towards herd mentality. Many investors tend to follow the crowd and invest in popular stocks without conducting proper research.

The case study of Mr. Sharma's emotional decision-making and experience with a stock market scam in India would fall under the category of financial economics, as it deals with the financial decisions and risks faced by an individual investor. It would also be classified under financial institutions and services, as it relates to the stock market and investing. The case study touches on topics such as portfolio choice, asset pricing, and market efficiency, which were all relevant to the field of financial economics. It also relates to insider trading and event studies, which were relevant to the study of market efficiency.

Overall, this case study can be a valuable addition to any course on behavioral finance, providing students with practical insights into the ways in which human behavior can impact financial decision-making, and the steps that can be taken to mitigate these effects.

Challenges

- Emotional decision-making of retail investors in the Indian stock market
- Lack of understanding of fundamental analysis and valuation techniques among retail investors
- High levels of uncertainty and volatility in the Indian stock market
- Prevalence of stock market scams and fraudulent activities in India
- Insufficient regulatory oversight and enforcement in the Indian stock market

Issues

- The financial losses suffered by retail investors as a result of emotional decision-making and stock market scams
- The erosion of trust and confidence in the Indian stock market as a result of widespread scams
- The need to educate and inform retail investors about proper investment techniques and risk management strategies
- The need for more effective regulation and enforcement in the Indian stock market to prevent fraud and misconduct
- The role of media and social pressure in influencing retail investors' investment decisions and behavior.

Case Questions

1. Why might Mr. Sharma be making emotional decisions about his investments?
2. What are some common types of stock market scams in India?
3. How can Mr. Sharma protect himself from making emotional investment decisions and falling victim to stock market scams in the future?
4. What role do cultural and societal factors play in shaping an individual's investment behavior and decision-making? How might Mr. Sharma's cultural background have influenced his emotional investment decisions and vulnerability to scams in the Indian stock market?

5. What ethical considerations are at play in stock market scams, and how can investors balance their desire for high returns with their responsibility to act ethically and avoid fraudulent schemes? How might Mr. Sharma have approached his investment decisions differently if he had taken a more ethical perspective?

LEARNING OBJECTIVES

Learning Objectives of the Case Could Include:

- Understanding the risks and consequences of making emotional investment decisions in the stock market.
- Learning about common types of stock market scams in India and how to protect oneself from them.
- Developing strategies for conducting thorough research and analysis on potential investments.
- Understanding the importance of developing a long-term investment plan and sticking to it.
- Recognizing the value of seeking the advice of financial professionals when making investment decisions.
- By studying the case of Mr. Sharma, students can learn about the potential pitfalls of emotional decision-making and scams in the stock market, and how to mitigate these risks through careful planning and analysis. This can help students to become more informed and successful investors in the future.

CASE DESCRIPTION

Mr. Sharma was a retail investor who has been investing in the Indian stock market for the past 10 years. Recently, he has been feeling very emotional about his investments and has been making decisions based on his feelings rather than careful analysis. As a result, he has made some poor investment choices and has incurred financial losses. Mr. Sharma has also fallen victim to a stock market scam, in which he invested in a fraudulent initial public offering (IPO).

Mr. Sharma was now looking for ways to protect himself from making emotional investment decisions and falling victim to stock market scams in the future. He was seeking guidance on how to conduct thorough research and analysis on potential investments, how to identify common types of scams, and how to develop a long-term investment plan.

Facts

Mr. Sharma was a retail investor who has been investing in the Indian stock market for the past 10 years. Recently, he has been feeling very emotional about his investments and has been making decisions based on his feelings rather than careful analysis. As a result, he has made some poor investment choices and has incurred financial losses. Mr. Sharma has also fallen victim to a stock market scam, in which he invested in a fraudulent IPO.

Case Analysis

This case raises important questions about the factors that contribute to emotional decision-making and the role that it plays in investors falling prey to scams.

One key factor that may have contributed to Mr. Sharma's emotional decision-making was a lack of confidence in his investment choices. This was a common issue for retail investors who may not have the same level of financial knowledge or resources as professional investors. The uncertainty and risk associated with the stock market can lead to feelings of anxiety and insecurity, which in turn can lead to emotional decision-making. In Mr. Sharma's case, this emotional decision-making may have led him to make impulsive or irrational investment choices that ultimately resulted in financial losses.

Another possible factor that contributed to Mr. Sharma's emotional decision-making was external influence, such as media or social pressure. The stock market was a highly publicized and competitive arena, and investors may feel pressure to make certain investment decisions in order to keep up with the market or fit in with their peers. This pressure can lead to emotional decision-making and potentially poor investment choices. In Mr. Sharma's case, this external pressure may have contributed to him falling prey to a stock market scam.

The case of Mr. Sharma also highlights the importance of understanding and identifying stock market scams. Scams can take many forms, and it can be difficult for retail investors to detect them. In India, common types of stock market scams include pump and dump schemes, insider trading, and fraudulent IPOs. These scams can cause financial losses for investors and can erode trust in the stock market as a whole.

In case, Mr. Sharma illustrates the dangers of emotional decision-making and the importance of understanding stock market scams. It highlights the need for investors to be aware of the factors that can lead to emotional decision-making and to take steps to manage their emotions during the investment process. Additionally, it emphasizes the importance of research and due diligence in identifying and avoiding stock market scams.

Emotional Biases That Can Affect Investment Decision-Making

Here is a discussion of the different types of emotional biases that can affect investment decision-making:

- **Loss Aversion:** The tendency to strongly prefer avoiding losses over acquiring gains. This can lead to investors holding onto losing investments for too long or selling winning investments too soon.
- **Overconfidence:** The tendency to overestimate one's ability to make accurate predictions or assess risks. This can lead to investors taking on too much risk in their investments or failing to adequately diversify their portfolio.
- **Self-Control:** The difficulty in resisting the temptation to act impulsively or make emotional decisions. This can lead to investors making hasty investment decisions based on short-term market trends rather than long-term analysis.
- **Status Quo Bias:** The tendency to stick with familiar investments or strategies even when new information suggests a change is warranted. This can lead to investors missing out on opportunities for higher returns or failing to adapt to changing market conditions.

- **Endowment Bias:** The tendency to overvalue investments that one already owns, often leading to a reluctance to sell even when the investment is no longer performing well.
- **Regret Aversion:** The tendency to avoid making decisions that could result in regret, often leading to inaction or delaying decisions. This can lead to missed opportunities for higher returns or failure to cut losses when necessary.

It's important for investors to be aware of these emotional biases and to take steps to mitigate their effects on their investment decision-making. This can include developing a long-term investment strategy, diversifying their portfolio, and seeking advice from financial professionals.

Fundamental Analysis

Fundamental analysis is a critical aspect of making investment decisions, and it can have a significant impact on the success or failure of an investment.

In the case study, more emphasis can be placed on the importance of fundamental analysis, and how it can help investors to make informed decisions about which companies to invest in. The case study can discuss the various components of fundamental analysis, such as analyzing a company's financial statements, assessing its competitive position in the market, and evaluating its management team and overall strategy.

Furthermore, the case study can provide examples of how to use fundamental analysis to value a company. This can include discussing different valuation techniques, such as discounted cash flow analysis or price-to-earnings ratios, and how to apply them to real-world investment scenarios. The case study can also explore the limitations of fundamental analysis, such as the challenges of predicting future trends and the impact of unforeseen events.

Overall, by incorporating more discussion on the importance of fundamental analysis, and providing examples of how to apply it in practice, the case study can help to enhance the quality and scope of the case, and provide students with valuable insights into the role of fundamental analysis in investment decision-making.

Case Answers

1. Mr. Sharma might be making emotional decisions about his investments for a variety of reasons. He may be experiencing a lack of confidence in his investment choices, or he may be influenced by the media or social pressure to make certain investment decisions. He may also be influenced by his own biases or past successes and failures in the stock market.
2. Some common types of stock market scams in India include pump and dump schemes, insider trading, and fraudulent initial public offerings (IPOs). In a pump and dump scheme, a group of individuals or entities manipulate the price of a stock by artificially inflating demand for it through deceptive marketing tactics. Insider trading occurs when an individual with inside information about a company trades the company's stock based on that information, which was not available to the general public. Fraudulent IPOs involve a company issuing false or misleading information in order to sell its stock to unsuspecting investors.

3. To protect himself from making emotional investment decisions and falling victim to stock market scams in the future, Mr. Sharma can take several precautions. One important step was to do thorough research on any investment before making a decision. This can include reading company financial reports, consulting with financial advisors, and considering the potential risks as well as the potential rewards of the investment. Mr. Sharma should also be aware of common stock market scams and be cautious of unusual or too-good-to-be-true investment opportunities. Finally, it can be helpful for Mr. Sharma to develop a long-term investment plan and stick to it, rather than making impulsive decisions based on short-term market fluctuations or emotions.
4. Culture and societal factors can significantly influence an individual's investment behavior and decision-making. In the case of Mr. Sharma, his cultural background as an Indian might have influenced his emotional investment decisions and vulnerability to scams in the Indian stock market. Indian culture places a high emphasis on collective decision-making, which means that Mr. Sharma might have relied on advice from his peers and family members when making investment decisions. Additionally, the Indian culture also values respect for authority figures, which might have led Mr. Sharma to blindly trust his broker without conducting proper due diligence.
5. When it comes to stock market scams, ethical considerations are paramount. Investors must balance their desire for high returns with their responsibility to act ethically and avoid fraudulent schemes. In Mr. Sharma's case, he might have been more cautious if he had taken an ethical perspective. For instance, he could have conducted proper research on the company and asked his broker to provide a detailed analysis of the investment opportunity. Additionally, he could have sought the advice of a financial advisor to get an unbiased opinion on the investment opportunity. Ultimately, it is the investor's responsibility to act ethically and make informed decisions that align with their personal values and beliefs.

To protect himself from making emotional decisions and falling victim to scams in the future, Mr. Sharma can follow several precautions.

First, Mr. Sharma can do thorough research on any investment before making a decision. This can include reading company financial reports, consulting with financial advisors, and considering the potential risks as well as the potential rewards of the investment. By taking the time to carefully analyze his investments, Mr. Sharma can reduce the chances of making impulsive or irrational decisions based on his emotions.

Second, Mr. Sharma can be aware of common stock market scams and be cautious of unusual or too-good-to-be-true investment opportunities. Scams can take many forms and can be difficult to detect, but by being vigilant and doing his due diligence, Mr. Sharma can reduce the chances of falling victim to one.

Finally, Mr. Sharma can develop a long-term investment plan and stick to it. By having a clear investment strategy and goals, Mr. Sharma can avoid making impulsive decisions based on short-term market fluctuations or emotions. This can help him to make more informed, successful investment decisions over the long term.

In summary, Mr. Sharma can protect himself from making emotional investment decisions and falling victim to stock market scams by doing thorough research, being aware of common scams, and developing a long-term investment plan.

To protect himself from making emotional investment decisions and falling victim to scams in the future, Mr. Sharma can take several precautions. One important step was to do thorough research on any investment before making a decision. This can include reading company financial reports, consulting with financial advisors, and considering the potential risks as well as the potential rewards of the investment. Mr. Sharma should also be aware of common stock market scams and be cautious of unusual or too-good-to-be-true investment opportunities. Finally, it can be helpful for Mr. Sharma to develop a long-term investment plan and stick to it, rather than making impulsive decisions based on short-term market fluctuations or emotions. By following these steps, Mr. Sharma can reduce the risks of financial losses and increase the chances of making informed, successful investment decisions.

TEACHING NOTES

- Introduce the case study and present the background information on Mr. Sharma's emotional decision-making and experience with a stock market scam in India.
- Ask students to consider the following questions: Why might Mr. Sharma be making emotional decisions about his investments? What are some common types of stock market scams in India? How can Mr. Sharma protect himself from making emotional investment decisions and falling victim to stock market scams in the future?
- Lead a discussion on the various factors that can contribute to emotional decision- making, such as lack of confidence, external influence, and personal biases.
- Discuss common types of stock market scams, such as pump and dump schemes, insider trading, and fraudulent IPOs, and how investors can protect themselves from falling victim to these scams.
- Present strategies for conducting thorough research and analysis on potential investments, such as reading company financial reports, consulting with financial advisors, and considering the potential risks and rewards of the investment.
- Emphasize the importance of developing a long-term investment plan and sticking to it, rather than making impulsive decisions based on short-term market fluctuations or emotions.
- Conclude the case discussion and summarize the key takeaways for students.

Certainly, incorporating real-world examples can help to illustrate the concepts discussed in the case study and provide students with a deeper understanding of how emotional biases and fundamental analysis impact investment decision-making.

Some Real-Time Case Examples

Here are some examples from the post-2010 era that can be included in the teaching note:

GameStop Short Squeeze (2021): The GameStop short squeeze was a highly publicized event that occurred in early 2021, where a group of retail investors on Reddit coordinated to drive up the price of GameStop's stock, causing significant losses for hedge funds that had bet against the company. This event highlights the impact of social media and herd mentality on investment decision-making, as well as the risks associated with short selling.

Tesla's Rise to Dominance: Tesla's stock price has seen significant growth in recent years, driven by factors such as the company's innovative technology, strong brand, and the growing demand for electric vehicles. However, the company's valuation has been a subject of debate among investors, with some arguing that the company is overvalued due to its high price-to-earnings ratio.

COVID-19 Pandemic and Its Impact on Markets: The COVID-19 pandemic has had a significant impact on global markets, causing unprecedented volatility and uncertainty. The pandemic has highlighted the importance of assessing a company's financial stability and management team, as well as the need to diversify one's investment portfolio to manage risk.

Rise of ESG Investing: Environmental, social, and governance (ESG) investing has gained popularity in recent years, as investors increasingly focus on the long-term impact of their investments on society and the environment. This trend highlights the importance of considering non-financial factors when making investment decisions and the potential impact of ethical investing on financial returns.

Overall, these examples can be used to help students understand how emotional biases and fundamental analysis play out in real-world investment scenarios, and to explore the complexities and challenges of investment decision-making in today's dynamic markets.

The Teaching Objectives

- To understand the risks and consequences of making emotional investment decisions in the stock market.
- To learn about common types of stock market scams in India and how to protect oneself from them.
- To develop strategies for conducting thorough research and analysis on potential investments.
- To understand the importance of developing a long-term investment plan and sticking to it.
- To recognize the value of seeking the advice of financial professionals when making investment decisions.

Positions in The Course

This case study could be positioned in a course on Behavioral Finance, Investments, or Financial Markets. In a Behavioral Finance course, the case study can be used to highlight the impact of emotional biases on investment decisions and the consequences of such biases on investment outcomes. In an Investments course, the case study can be used to highlight the importance of fundamental analysis and proper research in making investment decisions. Additionally, the case study can be used in a Financial Markets course to discuss the role of scams and frauds in the market and the need for investor protection.

The case study can be used as a standalone reading or can be integrated into a larger discussion on investment decision-making, behavioral biases, and market frauds. It can also be used as a basis for a class discussion or group exercise, where students can analyze and discuss Mr. Sharma's investment decisions and the potential consequences of those decisions. Overall, the case study can be a valuable tool for teaching important concepts related to investment decision-making and market frauds.

Pre-Reading Materials

Here are some pre-reading materials that can be suggested for students before analyzing this case study:

- **Behavioral Finance:** Concepts and Theories by H. Kent Baker and John R. Nofsinger - This book covers the basics of behavioral finance and provides an understanding of how investors make decisions based on emotions, biases, and heuristics.
- **Fundamental Analysis for Investors:** How to Make Consistent, Long-term Profits in the Stock Market by Raghu Palat and Sunita Abraham - This book provides an in-depth understanding of how to evaluate a company's financial statements, industry trends, and other factors that impact the stock market.
- **Securities and Exchange Board of India (SEBI) Website:** SEBI is the regulatory body that oversees the Indian stock market. The website provides information on various regulations, investor education programs, and alerts related to scams and fraudulent activities.
- **Financial News Websites Such as Moneycontrol, Economic Times, and Bloomberg Quint:** These websites provide real-time updates on the Indian stock market, including company news, market trends, and expert opinions.
- Case studies on previous stock market scams in India - Students can analyze previous scams such as the Satyam Scandal or the Harshad Mehta Scam to gain a deeper understanding of how such scams work and their impact on investors.

TEACHING PLAN FOR DURATION 90 MINUTES

Table 1. Introduction

Introduction (10 minutes):
• Introduce the topic of emotional decision making in the Indian stock market and its potential to trap investors and lead them to scams.
• Highlight the importance of understanding the impact of emotions on investment decisions in order to make informed and rational choices.
Lesson 1: Understanding Emotions in Investment Decision Making (30 minutes):
• Define and explain the concept of emotional decision making in the context of the stock market. Discuss the most common emotions that can influence investment decisions (e.g. fear, greed, hope, regret) and how they can lead to poor investment choices.
• Provide examples of emotional decision making in the Indian stock market and its consequences.
• Provide strategies for managing emotions during the investment process to avoid making impulsive decisions.
Lesson 2: Identifying and Avoiding Scams in the Indian Stock Market (30 minutes):
• Define and explain the concept of stock market scams.
• Discuss the most common tactics used by scammers in the Indian stock market (e.g. pump- and-dump schemes, insider trading, Ponzi schemes).
• Provide examples of stock market scams in India and their consequences.
• Provide strategies for identifying and avoiding stock market scams, including researching companies and consulting with financial advisors.
Conclusion (20 minutes):
• Summarize the key points of the lesson and emphasize the importance of understanding emotional decision making and identifying and avoiding stock market scams in order to make informed and rational investment choices.
• Encourage students to ask questions and further research the topic

Assessment:

- A short quiz or exam on the topics covered in the lesson
- A group discussion or presentation on a specific scam case in Indian stock market
- An individual reflection on how one can improve emotional decision making while investing

Note: This is a general outline of a teaching plan and can be modified based on the audience's level of knowledge and understanding of the topic.

NEED OF THIS CASE

1. **Understanding Emotional Biases in Investment Decision-Making:** The case study provides insights into the emotional biases that can influence investment decisions and highlights the importance of rational decision-making in the stock market.
2. **Awareness of Stock Market Scams:** The case study sheds light on the common types of stock market scams in India and the ways in which investors can fall prey to them. This can help investors identify warning signs and take proactive measures to protect themselves.
3. **Importance of Fundamental Analysis:** The case study emphasizes the significance of fundamental analysis in making informed investment decisions. By highlighting the need for proper research and analysis, the case study underscores the importance of a thorough understanding of the company's financials, industry trends, and other relevant factors.
4. **Need for Investor Education:** The case study underscores the importance of investor education in building investor confidence and trust in the stock market. By educating investors about the potential risks and pitfalls of investing, the case study can help foster a more informed and cautious investment culture.
5. **Ethical Concerns in the Stock Market:** The case study raises ethical concerns regarding fraudulent activities in the stock market and emphasizes the need for ethical conduct among market participants. This can help promote greater transparency and accountability in the stock market and enhance investor protection.

TARGET AUDIENCE

The target audience could include students studying finance or business, particularly those interested in investing and financial decision-making. The case study could also be relevant to professional investors or financial advisors who wish to learn more about the risks of emotional decision-making and stock market scams, and how to protect themselves and their clients from these risks.

The case study may be particularly useful for students who were new to investing and were looking to learn more about the potential pitfalls of the stock market and how to make informed, successful investment decisions. It could also be beneficial for professionals who were looking to improve their investment strategies and better serve their clients.

TEACHING APPROACH AND STRATEGY

The teaching approach and strategy for the case study "Investor's emotional and scam in Indian Stock Market" could involve a combination of lecture, discussion, and case analysis.

To begin, the instructor could provide a lecture on the risks and consequences of emotional decision-making and stock market scams, using the case study of Mr. Sharma as an example. The instructor could also discuss strategies for conducting thorough research and analysis on potential investments, and the importance of developing a long-term investment plan.

Next, the instructor could lead a discussion on the case study, asking students to consider the various factors that may have contributed to Mr. Sharma's emotional decision-making and his experience with a stock market scam. The instructor could ask students to brainstorm ways in which Mr. Sharma could have protected himself from these risks, and encourage them to share their own experiences or insights on investing and financial decision-making.

Finally, the instructor could facilitate a case analysis, in which students work in small groups to analyze the case study and develop recommendations for Mr. Sharma. The groups could present their recommendations to the class, and the instructor could facilitate a discussion on the various approaches and strategies presented.

Overall, the teaching approach and strategy for the case study should be interactive and allow for the exchange of ideas and perspectives among students. By engaging in discussion and case analysis, students can better understand the risks and challenges of investing.

Financial News Articles:

- *Why Emotional Investing is a Recipe for Disaster by Greg McFarlane (Investopedia).* (2019).
- *How to Avoid Falling for a Stock Market Scam by Matt Frankel (The Motley Fool).* (2020).

Government or Industry Reports:

- *SEC Investor Alert: Social Media and Investing - Avoiding Fraud.* (2013). U.S. Securities and Exchange Commission.
- Rani, S., & Arora, R. S. (2015). Stock Market Scams in India: A Review. *Journal of Financial Crime.*

REFERENCES

Erb, K. P. (2015, August 24). *Debt, Equity and Startup money.* Retrieved 29 May 2023, from Forbes website: https://www.forbes.com/sites/kellyphillipserb/2015/08/24/debt-equity-and-startup-money/

Loewenstein, Weber, Hsee, &Welch. (2001). *The Role of Emotions in Financial Decision Making.* Academic Press.

Martins, A. T. (2018, February 8). *Advantages/disadvantages of raising fund from angel investors.* Retrieved 29 May 2023, from Profitable Venture website: https://www.profitableventure.com/advantages-raising-fund-angels/

Rangaswamy, U. S. (2021). Chai Thela: The Might "Tea" Problem of Start-up Expansion. *South Asian Journal of Management*, 1.

Ward, S. (2003, December 13). *The pros and cons of angel investors*. Retrieved 29 May 2023, from The Balance website: https://www.thebalancesmb.com/angel-investor-2947066

Xe: Currency exchange rates and international money transfer. (2019). Retrieved 29 May 2023, from https://www.xe.com/

Yadav, A. (2018, January 30). *Why every Startup should host A crowdfunding campaign*. Retrieved 29 May 2023, from Forbes website: https://www.forbes.com/sites/ajayyadav/2018/01/30/why-every-startup-should-host-a-crowdfunding-campaign/

KEY TERMS AND DEFINITIONS

Behavioral Finance: A field of finance that examines how psychological factors influence financial decisions, including biases, emotions, and cognitive errors.

Emotional Decision-Making: The process of making a decision based on personal feelings or emotions rather than rational analysis or objective facts.

Endowment Bias: The tendency to overvalue what one already possesses, such as stocks or investments, leading to holding onto them even when they may no longer be a good investment.

Fundamental Analysis: A method of evaluating the value of a company or security by examining its financial and economic factors, such as revenue, earnings, assets, and liabilities.

Investor: An individual or entity who puts money into an investment with the expectation of making a profit or gaining some other financial return.

Loss Aversion: The tendency to experience greater emotional pain from losing money than pleasure from gaining the same amount of money.

Overconfidence Bias: The tendency to overestimate one's abilities or knowledge, leading to excessive risk-taking or overtrading.

Regret Aversion: The tendency to avoid making decisions that may lead to regret or disappointment, even if it means missing out on potential gains.

Scam: A fraudulent scheme or deceptive practice intended to deceive or defraud individuals, often resulting in financial losses.

Stock Market: A marketplace where publicly traded stocks and other securities are bought and sold by investors.

ENDNOTE

1 National Stock Exchange (NSE): The NSE regularly releases reports on the Indian stock market, including data on retail investor participation. Their website is https://www.nseindia.com/. Securities and Exchange Board of India (SEBI): SEBI is the regulatory body for the Indian securities market and also provides information on retail investor participation. Their website is https://www.sebi.gov.in/.

Chapter 7
Battle Royale:
Harley vs. Triumph

Potnuru Rama Krishna Gupta
GITAM School of Business, GITAM University (Deemed), India

Sunil Kumar
https://orcid.org/0000-0002-8881-2761
GITAM School of Business, GITAM University (Deemed), India

Surendar Gade
NMIMS University, India

EXECUTIVE SUMMARY

The case narrates a comparative study of Battle Royale: Harley-Davidson v/s Triumph. It is of their product launch and marketing strategies used by Harley-Davidson and Triumph, two leading brands in the Indian premium motorcycle segment. For the purpose of this study, data were gathered from both primary and secondary sources. This study used secondary sources dominantly for extracting related information of Harley-Davidson and Triumph brands. Secondary sources include company reports, their promotional events, social media, news reports, etc. The author of the case also interacted with users of these two brands. Feedback from these brand users was discussed in the case explicitly. This case was discussed with UG and PG students in a classroom. It helped them to understand branding strategies of these two brands specifically.

INTRODUCTION

The Indian automobile industry is the largest in the world. The two wheelers segment leads the automobile market of India with an 81% market share due to increasing number of middle class and a youth population in the country. Furthermore, companies are developing interest in rural markets and exploring it to establish their brands specifically. Exports of commercial vehicles and two-wheelers increased by 18.36% in 2016 compared to 2015. Furthermore, the Government of India's initiatives paving the way

DOI: 10.4018/978-1-6684-8488-3.ch007

for major players in the automobile segment in the Indian market are expected to propel India to the global leader in the Two-Wheeler and Four-Wheeler markets by 2020. Harley-Davidson, Triumph, and Ducati are among the major players in the premium motorcycle segment.

The premium bike segment is one of the fastest growing in the Indian market, with virtually every player worth their salt seizing the prospect to use this profitable category to increase margins and have an advantage. Rising income levels, easy financing, and increased access have prompted India's large bike market to surpass 10,000 units in fiscal year 2016. At present census, the Harley-Davidson has a slender lead over its rivals with a market share of 60% and a growth rate of 15.04% whereas its rival Triumph is holding a market share of 27.5% and a growth rate of 6.89% for the fiscal year 2016-2017 in the premium motorcycle segment. These leading brands have been using unique marketing strategies for their competitive advantages in the Indian market. Though Triumph entered Indian market 5 years later, it has been making its rival Harley-Davidson run for its money. There is a competitive struggle by two leading brands to build up their brand image in the Indian market.

The Battle Royale "Harley-Davidson v/s Triumph" is a comparative study of product launch and marketing strategies used by Harley-Davidson and Triumph, two leading brands in Indian premium motorcycle segment.

Harley Davidson

Harley-Davidson considered entering the Indian market in 2007, but the Indian government objected due to high import duties levied on its motorcycles. The high import duty was viewed as a "daunting trade barrier" by the company. According to company representatives, India currently has a 60% duty on heavyweight motorcycles. Due to high import duties with additional taxes of 30 percent on registration would double the price of Harley-Davidson. The Indian government has linked permission to allow the bikes with the export of Indian mangoes, because Indian mangoes were lacked concession with U.S Food and Drug Administration requirement. Indian government even tried to link the entry of Harley-Davidson for the progress on banking licenses for some of the Indian banks, such as ICICI bank, SBI and Bank of Baroda which needed fresh branch licenses for their expansion in the United States. Though the Indian government did not agree to reduce the taxes but allowed the Harley to enter the Indian market through third party distributors. Indian Government has lifted the emission norms on bikes for more than 800cc, this move has changed the face of the heavy motorcycle segment, giving more opportunities to the new entrants with variety of products lining for the Indian market.

The first dealership store was established in Hyderabad in 2010. In the same year Harley-Davidson started its 4 more Dealership outlets across the country in Delhi, Bangalore, Chandigarh, Mumbai. The company even brought its Harley Owners Group (H.O.G) to India during the same year. For each and every store the access has been given to H.O.G along with a manager to take care of the H.O.G Group. After entering the Indian market Harley-Davidson has faced the competition from BMW, Kawasaki and KTM. In the beginning of first two years the focus of Harley-Davidson was to create brand awareness among the consumers, where the company launched its famous model "Fat boy." The company confirmed its Indian strategy in line with the global strategy of introducing new models and beginning of complete Rock-bottom operations in the country. The company formed a strategic alliance with HDFC Bank. It is one of India's leading banks for a widespread range of financial services. Which help customers to realize their dream of owning a Harley brand. The company began its completely knocked-down (CKD) assembly operations at the Indian Factory in January 2011.The Strategies of Harley Davidson that implemented globally, in regards of personal accessories, clothing and tattoos, which was delivered same from its launch in India. The desire to own a Harley is extremely high in smaller towns. Markets like Ludhiana, Lucknow and Dehradun have opened for Harley-Davidson. In general, demand is extremely high in the North and West of the country.

"The Voyage of Beast in India"

Customers can customize their Harley-Davidsons by choosing from a variety of colors, wheels, seats, racks and backrests, windshields, exhausts, and intakes. Harley-Davidson currently has 1,435 dealerships worldwide, with the company targeting on escalating its dealerships in the Indian market. Harley Davidson hosts a "Learn to Ride" event for new Harley riders. At select Harley-Davidson dealers, new riders receive professional guidance from Harley-Davidson certified coaches. Customers of Harley-Davidson are men over the age of 35, but the company is making concentrated efforts to associate with consumers of all ages, including young, adults and women. The company also sells women's gear and apparel on its website. The Harley Owners Group is an organized group for Harley motorcycle enthusiasts run by Harley-Davidson (or HOG). The company organizes a variety of events for HOG members in order to keep the spirit of Harley riders alive.

"Rebel by Choice" – Clear brand positioning by bikers, for bikers

The identity of Harley-Davidson was portrayed as the vehicular embodiment of 'freedom,' 'individualism, "rebellion,' and the 'American way.'

Because Harley-Davidson is aware of its superior image, it has pursued unconventional marketing tactics that both pasteurize and reinforce its 'outlaw' status.

Build a Loyal Following and Allow Them to Take Ownership: The Harley Owners Group

Harley-Davidson established the Harley Owners Group (H.O.G.). The Harley-Davidson club will allow to connect with its customers as well as the general public. At the time, hard-core Harley bikers chastised H.O.G for softening and stealing the company's obstinate character. Through H.O.G., Harley-Davidson have sponsored various biker rallies, organized charity drives, and have offered various special promotions to its different group of fan base. In addition, people newly becoming their members may be eligible for a free first year. H.O.G. has been a commercial smash. This company is having over million members in twenty-five countries across the world, where half of them regularly attending Harley-Davidson programs/events. Members of the Harley-Davidson Owners Group are also stimulated to offer direct information into how Harley-Davidson develops unique products and advances existing ones. Therefore, as a result of H.O.G. and its effort for better customer ownership and engagement. Advertising is highly required for such kind of customer segment. But even less than a million dollars spent by Harley-Davidson on advertising each year. The Harley Owners Group (HOG) which is around one million make it possible for this group to have adequate replacement order for their bikes. The biggest advertising happens of Harley through word of mouth. It brings brand loyalty among their customers and win over the heart of new customers and develop loyalty towards the brand.

Becoming the embodiment of an ideal: Easy Rider's "Captain America" bike features product placement.

"Easy Rider," the cult film, had a significant effect on Harley-Davidson and the global motorcycle division. It is usually found that bikers instantly started modifying their bikes to resemble the ones in Easy Rider. By introducing similar-looking motorcycles, Harley-Davidson profitably exploited the market.

Harley Davidson, A Struggling Icon

Harley-Davidson is one of the few brands that people are willing to tattoo on themselves, and it has an iconic, cult status that most other brands aspire to. Customers prefer used motorcycles or the recently relaunched Victory and Indian brands to new Harleys. As a result, overall market share and sales are down from the previous year. In 2016, the company plans to increase its product development budget by 35% (compared to 2015) and its marketing budget by 65%. Harley-Davidson has established and created a "category of one" for itself over the years. The recent revitalization and relaunch of the Victory and Indian brands, which have begun to successfully eat into Harley's market share. Harley-Davidson has excelled at brand loyalty, customer engagement, and brand community development. On a regular basis, the company sponsors and organizes community bike rallies, social events, donation drives, and other related activities to influence the interest of bikers. Harley-Davidson effectively socializes with both old and new customers and fans. Visitors to the rally can test-drive Purchase Harley-Davidson motorcycles and other Harley-Davidson merchandise. Owners of Harley-Davidson motorcycles are also proud of their machines. Harley-Davidson strengthens its loyal customer base by considering them as family members and equal contributors in the brand's promotion and production practices. The test ride campaign allows them to try out all of the company's new products. Every time the company launches a new product, we conduct a test ride campaign with our lead base because he may not be a customer today, but he will be a customer tomorrow.

Customers of Harley-Davidson in Tier II cities are between the ages of 35 and 45. It's worth noting that 98 percent of the brand's customers are men. The company is now attempting to attract more female riders as customers. To that end, Harley-Davidson recently hosted a women-only riding event in which forty women from various cities participated. Harley-Davidson has introduced a wide range of motorcycle variants on Indian roads (table-1). With a 60% market share in the 601+cc motorcycle segment, Harley-Davidson India has celebrated 12 years of success and remains the market leader in the premium two-wheeler category. According to the Society of India Automobile Manufacturers, Harley-Davidson India has a market share of 10%. (SIAM).

Triumph: For the Ride

Triumph Motorcycles is, like other premium bike makers, bullish on the Indian market. The company began commercial sales in India in April 2014. The entry of this iconic British brand in the Indian market, which was till then largely restricted to heavy cruisers and track-focused, fully faired, liter-class sports bikes as the two most popular categories, exposed professional and seasoned riders to several new genres of motorcycling. The company's philosophy is centered on a strong dedication to creating completely original motorcycles that are outstanding in terms of appearance, design, and performance. Triumph wants to build bikes that are enjoyable to ride, so they pair strong, flexible engines with well-balanced, easy-to-handle chassis. Triumph Motorcycles has established itself as one of the top three premium motorcycle brands in India. Besides offering a wide portfolio of big bikes, the company achieved this scale thanks to quick penetration through its retail network across the country. It currently has a network of sixteen dealerships, all fully equipped to provide aftersales services. Nine of these dealerships are situated across Tier 1 and 2 cities.

Changing Rules of the Game

In Triumph classic range, which was the old generation of Bonneville's, the company have now loaded modern technologies such as traction control, liquid cooling, LED lamp, immobilizer etc. It is a modern generation classic and will attract both old and young buyers. New styling and technologies improve the value proposition in our bike. Unlike rival companies in the country, Triumph sells five categories of bikes such as the Classic, which accounts for about 45 per cent of the sales, Roadster, Super Sport, Cruiser and Adventurer. "The last four categories account for about 11 per cent each of companies total sales". The selling mantra of Triumph: "one size does not fit all" philosophy. It has bikes for every rider. If you want to stand out in a parking lot, buy any superbike, but if you want to stand out on the road, get a Triumph.

Triumph was one of the first motorcycles in India to be assembled locally via the CKD route. Triumph became an official MotoGP engine supplier in 2019, and the Street Trips is built on the same platform. It is the lightest and fastest motorcycle in its class, with a number of rider-focused technologies aimed at ensuring safe riding. Ride-by-wire, traction control, ABS, riding modes, and automatic headlamp on are some of the technologies that will ensure rider safety. In India, Triumph used a three-pronged strategy. The first is in bringing products to market from all segments, such as classic, cruiser, roadster, and adventure. The second strategy is to bring more CKD models into the country for assembly. The final strategy was to combine dealerships and after-sales centers. The company has launched a wide range of brands in the Indian market (Table-2).

The company focus is to increase this premium industry by getting good products and a good network, by ensuring that we have riding schools, training sessions. The company also want to have riding groups in place and make bikes affordable. The company have tied up with HDFC bank recently for a seven-year finance scheme. The company's multi-pronged approach also includes excellent service and dealerships in all of India's major cities. Triumph Company is excited about CKDs because the impact of import duties on CBUs has been reduced from 100% to 30%–40%. (completely built Units). Customers are not inconvenienced by CKD, and more people can buy our products because they are available on the market. The company intends to open dealerships in small towns where it has noticed HNI (high net worth income) customer trends emerging. Bajaj Auto and Triumph have formed a partnership to manufacture Triumph-branded motorcycles in India for the global market. The concept of combining Triumph Global's brand image and Bajaj's expertise in low-cost manufacturing. Triumph bikes start at 675 cc globally, and this collaboration will allow them to scale down the capacity curve.

Triumph has increased its share of total marketing expenditure for digital marketing from 5% to 20% in three years. It has established its assembly units in India in order to reduce the heavy taxes and to provide the customers the bike at affordable price. The company has been conducting the training the rider in association with California superbike school these training classes has be conducted for prompting safe and responsible riding. Customers are not permitted to purchase a bike in a Triumph store if they are not prepared to wear a helmet, riding boots, or if they do not possess a valid driver's license.

Bajaj Auto and Triumph have formed a partnership to manufacture Triumph-branded motorcycles in India for the global market. When announcing their partnership with Bajaj, Triumph said, "We hope to bring to bear on global markets the individual strengths of the partners, including brand position and perception, design and development technology, quality and cost competitiveness, and global distribution." Here are some facts:

- Though few UK riders are aware of it, Bajaj is the world's fourth largest motorcycle manufacturer.
- In 2021, Triumph Motorcycles India Private Limited sold 1,112 motorcycles across the country. There was an increase in sales volume. It had a market share of 30 percent in its segment, just behind Kawasaki. The company was expected to have twenty dealerships by the end of 2022. Its Indian arm was one among its 15 subsidiaries across the world.
- With the help of its new international partnership, Triumph will be able to enter new, higher volume market segments, particularly in developing nations all over the world. In order to better serve its domestic and international markets, Bajaj will have access to the renowned Triumph brand and its excellent motorcycles.
- Triumph holding a market share of 30% called as market follower in the premium motorcycle segments.

Table 1. Products of Harley Davidson

Model Name	cc
Street	750
Street Glide	1745
Iron	883
Road King	1745
Street Rod	749
Street Bob	1585
Road Glide Special	1202
Roadster	1202
Forty-Eight	1202
Fat Bob	1585
Fat Boy	1690
Softail Classic	1690
CVO	1868
1200 Custom	1202

Source (Harley-Davidson India Official site)

Table 2. Products of Triumph

Model Name	cc
Street Twin	900
Street Scrambler	900
Street Triple	765
Bonneville	1200
Daytona	675
Street Triple RS	765
Thruxton R	1200
Speed Triple	1050
Tiger	800
Thunderbird strom	1699
Rocket III Roadster	2294

Questions

1. What are the strategies used by the Harley-Davidson and Triumph to enter the Indian market?
2. What are the unique strategies of Harley-Davidson and Triumph to Gain Cult brand position in Indian Market?
3. Why Harley Davidson Has been the leader in premium Motorcycle segment?
4. What are the Unique Strategies used Triumph to compete with its Rival brand Harley?
5. What are the major players in these premium Motorcycle segment?

Teaching Notes

All authors of this case have collaborated to produce this teaching note to aid instructors in the classroom use of the case "Battle Royale: Harley vs. Triumph."

ABSTRACT/CASE SYNOPSIS

The case narrates a comparative study of Battle Royale "Harley-Davidson v/s Triumph". It is of their product launch and marketing strategies used by Harley-Davidson and Triumph, two leading brands in Indian premium motorcycle segment.

LEARNING OBJECTIVES

To understand

1. The product launch and marketing strategies used by Harley-Davidson in Indian premium motorcycle segment.
2. The product launch and marketing strategies used by Triumph in Indian premium motorcycle segment.
3. The brand positioning by both the brands in India market to cater the aspiration of young India.
4. The marketing, partnering, technology transfer, government regulations for global brands in India.

Research Methodology

For the purpose of this study data was gathered from both primary and secondary sources. Here this study used secondary sources dominantly for extracting related information of Harley-Davidson and Triumph brands. Secondary sources include companies reports, their promotional events, social media, news reports etc. The author of the case also interacted with users of these two brands. Feedback from these brand users were discussed in the case explicitly. This case was discussed with UG and PG students in classroom which helps them to understand branding strategies of these two brands specifically.

POSITION IN COURSE

This case shall address the students at the Undergraduate and Post-Graduate level. This shall also be helpful for Industry practitioners (Marketing and Sales function) at an early stage of their career as part of training and MDP (Management Development Programs) for capability development. To be used as credits of International Marketing, Branding, Positioning, and segmentation in the area of marketing majorly. Additionally, the case offers a scope of conveying issues related to market positioning, market penetration strategies, and significance of Porter's Five Forces model for new entrant.

SUGGESTED TEACHING STRATEGY

The instructor can share the product launch and marketing strategies used by Harley-Davidson and Triumph. List out all the strategies used by both the companies for market penetration. An ideal time of 60-90 minutes with a break of 5-15 minutes can act counter-intuitive in the thinking process. What is critical is setting the ball rolling in the students' minds. An apt method would be to do a role play by different students and look from their perspective learning from this case.

RELEVANT READINGS

1. Paley, N. (2021). *The manager's guide to competitive marketing strategies*. Routledge.
2. Tiffany, J. (2021). *Marketing Strategy, Overcome Common Pitfalls and Create Effective Marketing*. Kogan Page
3. Economic times by PTI | Updated: Sep 19, 2014, 08.59 AM IST
4. ET Bureau Feb 24, 2016, 01.09 PM IST
5. Forbes India by Ashish k Mishra published: Feb 6, 2014

TEACHING PLAN

The ideal class session will be 60 minutes. A tentative teaching plan to discuss the case:

Table 3. Discussion point durations

Discussion Point	Time (Minutes)
Introduction	10
Q- 1	10
Q- 2	10
Q- 3	10
Q- 4	10
Closing	10-20

ANALYSIS

The case includes various theoretical underpinnings, which have significant implications. The case highlights a few significant issues pertinent for effective marketing strategies. Here, it reflects a specific important phenomenon of business. Practices like, product launch, marketing strategies, branding, targeting, and understanding aspirations of young Indians towards sport bikes. Harley Davidson revival and relaunch in Indian market happens successfully. The company uses a variety of strategies to draw customers to its brand, including customer engagement, brand loyalty, and community building. In the Indian market, some routine social behaviors like bike rallies, donation drives, and other social events promote customer affinity. They targeted both old and new customers in the market. Test ride campaign that is done for them to experience all of company's new products. Company's approach towards customer was very unique like today maybe they are not the customers but in future they are going to be the customer of the company. Harley-Davidson logo By treating its followers as members of the family and full partners in the creation and promotion of the brand, Davidson's actions strengthen the bonds between them and the brand.

Triumph was very bullish on the Indian market since the inception of their operations in India. The company's focus was on truly unique motorcycles that stand out in terms of appearance, design, and performance. Triumph wants to make bikes that are enjoyable to ride, so they pair strong, flexible engines with a well-balanced, easy-to-handle chassis. Because of their unique strategies, company could position in the top three in India. The company's major emphasis was on retail network to have wide reach in the country. It has very wide network of showrooms across the country. Currently 16 dealers are operating in India as of May 2022. The showrooms of it spread across 13 states and 14 cities of the country. Nine of these dealerships are situated across Tier 1 and 2 towns. The selling mantra of Triumph: "one size does not fit all" philosophy. It has bikes for every rider. The classic category account 45 percent of total sales and other account for 11 per cent each of company's total sales. It was one of the first motorbike in India assembled through Completely Knocked Down Unit (CKD). It is the lightest and fastest motorcycle in its segment and brings in several rider-focused technologies mainly aimed at safe riding. Triumph used three major strategies in India which are products in all segments to the market, such as classic, cruiser, roadster and adventure, assembly of more CKD models into the country and dealerships and after-sales centers in tandem. For financing their products company have tied up with HDFC bank. The Knocked Down Unit (CKD) has brought down import duties to 30-40 per cent. Keeping in mind the growth and emerging trends company is planning to open showrooms in small town as well. They (Triumph and Bajaj) entered in partnership for global market. The partnership was established to enhance the companies' brand recognition and perception, design and development capabilities, cost and quality competitiveness, and global product distribution. They prioritized digital marketing and increased the budget from 5% to 20%. Company develops associating with California superbike school for prompting safe and responsible riding. Triumph is very particulars about customer's outlooks.

ASSIGNMENT QUESTIONS

1. What do you think is the core issue in this case?
2. What are the strategies used by the Harley-Davidson and Triumph to enter the Indian market?
3. What are the unique strategies of Harley- Davidson and Triumph to Gain Cult brand position in Indian Market?
4. Why Harley Davidson Has been the leader in premium Motorcycle segment?
5. What are the Unique Strategies used Triumph to compete with its Rival brand Harley?
6. What are the major players in these premium Motorcycle segment?

ANSWERS TO THE QUESTIONS

1. What do you think is the core issue in this case?

As the case enumerates, the core issue has been their product launch and marketing strategy in Indian Market. Here, Harley Davidson was relaunching its product in the market where in contrary to this Triumph was new to the Indian market. What are their marketing strategies and how these brands could able to penetrates their product in Indian market was the core issues?

2. What are the strategies used by the Harley-Davidson and Triumph to enter the Indian market?

These two companies have used various marketing strategy to enter the Indian market.

Harley-Davidson Strategy

a) Harley enters the Indian market through third party distributors.
b) Dealership was established in 5 major cities of India (Hyderabad, Delhi, Bangalore, Chandigarh, Mumbai).
c) Company brought its Harley Owners Group (H.O.G) to India.
d) Focus on creating brand awareness among the consumers
e) Launching of famous model "Fat boy".
f) Rock-bottom operations in the country
g) Strategic alliance with HDFC bank for financial services
h) Knocked-down (CKD) assembly operations
i) gives customers the option to customize their vehicles by choosing from a range of colors, wheels, seats, racks, and backrests, as well as windshields, exhausts, and intakes.
j) For new Harley riders, Harley-Davidson organizes a "Learn to Ride" event.
k) The organization plans a variety of events for HOG members in an effort to preserve the spirit of Harley riders.
l) Harley-Davidson promoted its brand by portraying its products as the motorized representation of "freedom," "individualism," "rebellion," and the "American way."
m) Aware of its superior image, it pursues eccentric marketing strategies for its "outlaw" status, n) sponsoring biker rallies, running fundraising campaigns, and providing exclusive discounts to its varied fanbase.
o) Harley-Davidson and the international motorcycle scene were significantly impacted by the cult classic "Easy Rider."
p) In terms of customer engagement, brand loyalty, and community building, Harley-Davidson has excelled.

Triumph Strategy

1. A key component of the company's philosophy is its unwavering dedication to creating motorcycles that are truly exceptional in terms of their appearance, design, and performance.
2. The coupling of strong, adaptable engines with a chassis that is well-balanced and simple to control.

3. Quick penetration through its retail network across the country
4. The selling mantra of Triumph: "one size does not fit all" philosophy
5. It has bikes for every rider
6. Triumph is one of the first motorcycles to be assembled locally through the CKD route in India
7. It is the lightest and fastest motorcycle in its segment, and brings in a number of rider-focused technologies mainly aimed at safe riding
8. Products across all segments to the market, such as classic, cruiser, roadster and adventure
9. Assembly of more CKD models into the country
10. Dealerships and after-sales centers in tandem

Q.3. What are the unique strategies of Harley- Davidson and Triumph to Gain Cult brand position in Indian Market?

Harley-Davidson

1. Clear Brand Positioning
2. Building Brand Loyalty and Maintaining It
3. Organising Phenomenal Events
4. Marketing to the Military
5. Diversification of Business
6. Loyal customer base
7. HOG rallies (Harley Owners Group)
8. Uniqueness and customization
9. High customer pull
10. Increased number of young and women riders

Triumph

1. Enhanced market penetration
2. Improved brand recognition
3. Increased reliance on digital marketing
4. TRIUMPH Retail Growth Segmentation
5. Targeting and positioning by Triumph
6. Economic Effectiveness
7. Creativity
8. Consolidated market research and consumer comprehension
9. Using emotional appeals to good effect
10. Distribution Strategy of TRIUMPH
11. Competition Analysis in the marketing strategy of TRIUMPH
12. Promotional tactics
13. Monitoring and evaluation of the marketing strategy
14. Completely knocked down (CKD) products
15. Partnership between Bajaj Auto and Triumph

16. Triumph enter products at sub ₹2 lakh and a range of bikes under a new engine platform of 200cc to 750cc engines.
17. Triumph has showrooms in Chandigarh, Ahmedabad, Indore, Pune, Jaipur, Kochi, Bhubaneshwar, Hyderabad, and Jaipur, in addition to major metros Delhi, Mumbai, Bengaluru, Chennai, and Kolkata.
18. Increasing our dealer network

Q.4. Why Harley Davidson Has had been the leader in premium Motorcycle segment?

Customers who buy a Harley-Davidson motorcycle can customize it by choosing from a variety of colors, wheels, seats, racks, and backrests as well as windshields, exhausts, and intakes. Harley Davidson holds "Learn to Ride" events for novice riders. The majority of Harley-core Davidson's customers are men over the age of 35, but the company is working hard to establish relationships with people of all ages, including teenagers and women. According to Harley-Davidson, its brand represents "freedom," "individualism," "rebellion," and the "American way" in a vehicle. Harley-Davidson has pursued unconventional marketing strategies that both pasteurize and reinforce its 'outlaw' status as a result of its self-awareness of its superior image. Harley-Davidson spends less than $1 million on advertising each year. The Harley Owners Group (HOG), which has a membership of one million people, ensures that there is a healthy market for the company's motorcycles, and word-of-mouth marketing and brand loyalty help to win over new followers of the cult.

Q.5. What are the Unique Strategies used Triumph to compete with its Rival brand Harley?

In India, partnering with Bajaj Auto was a critical move to gain an advantage over Harley Davison. To put this in context, Triumph sold a record 54,432 motorcycles in 2016, with India accounting for 1300 of those sales last year across 12 models sold in 10 key Indian cities. Triumph offers adventure bikes, scramblers, café racers, and even naked streetfighters. Harley-Davidson is primarily known for its cruisers and touring motorcycles.

Q.6. What are the major players in these premium Motorcycle segment?

The majority of Harley-Davidson and Triumph competitors were based in Europe and Japan. BMW (Germany), Ducati (Italy), and KTM (Australia) focused on engineering precision and racing performance, producing both heavyweight and sport bikes. Honda, Kawasaki, Suzuki, and Yamaha were the "big four" Japanese manufacturers.

REFERENCES

Chauhan, C. P. (2016, Sep 29). Premium Motorcycles Gaining in Popularity and Sales. *Business Today*. https://www.businesstoday.in/opinion/perspective/story/premium-motorcycles-gaining-in-popularity-and-sales-144791-2016-09-29

Mishra, A. K. (2014, Feb 7). Triumph wills sells 1,000 bikes by End of 2014. *Forbes India*. https://www.forbesindia.com/article/auto-expo/triumph-will-sell-1000-bikes-by-end-of- 2014/37117/1

Philip, L. (2015, April 17). Harley Davidson Rolls out Two Years Extended Warranty. *Economic Times*. https://economictimes.indiatimes.com/harley-davidson-india-rolls-out-extended- warranty/articleshow/46837332.cms

PTI. (2013, July 24). India to be World's 3rd Largest Automotive Market by 2016. *The Economic Times*. https://economictimes.indiatimes.com/india-to-be-worlds-3rd-largest-automotive- market-by-2016-ihs/articleshow/21306611.cms

Saxena. (2016). Triumph Motorcycles India's Vimal Sumbly says the company has turned down customers wearing slippers. *Economic Times*. https://economictimes.indiatimes.com/magazines/panache/triumph-motorcycles-indias-vimal-sumbly-says-the-companyhas-turned-down-customers-wearing-slippers/articleshow/52613978.cms

Thakkur, K. (2016). Small Time Buyers Add to Sales of Super Bikes. *Economic Times*. https://economictimes.indiatimes.com/small-town-buyers-add-to-sales-of-super-bikes- like-harley-davidson-ducati-and-others/articleshow/52875844.cms

Chapter 8
Camouflaging Marketing: An Essence of Sales Issues and Perspectives

Shenki Tyagi
ITS Ghaziabad, India

Ashish Kumar
Chandigarh University, India

Shilpi Sarna
LYOD Institute, India

EXECUTIVE SUMMARY

Content marketing is an eye opener to various customers and prospecting consumers to give them the viewpoint of understanding and knowledge. Consumers are educated due to the awareness of digital media and easy access to it. In today's era, this digital platform is also taking advantage of camouflaging the content as per their viewpoint, which needs to be put at the forefront. Today shoppers' various reports show that these associations are vulnerable to acts of neglect and may take on substitute freak procedures like a disguise. This case study makes salient contributions by integrating various portals of digital marketing with the concept of camouflaging and through which channel consumers' interest gets hampered. Every organization should use digital platforms with their uniqueness intact so that it should not be driven to another meaning of a message. Digital marketing is a spokesperson which is one way so it should be guided and directed with objectivity.

INTRODUCTION

Creating and disseminating appropriate articles, accounts, electronic communications, and other media, content advertising is an elevating technique used to attract attention, interact with, and maintain the mindset of individuals. When there is a perfect opportunity to acquire what you sell, this method creates an inclination, advances brand care, and maintains your company at the forefront of customers' minds.

DOI: 10.4018/978-1-6684-8488-3.ch008

Content marketing is the development and distribution of media to online consumers. The content combines an unexpected variety of consumable media and distributing that material through advancement calls for knowledge of every top-tier showcasing channel obtainable. Every authentic piece of material that you discover online might be categorized as advanced content. There is a wide overview of media that we refer to as content, which implies that the job of a substance creator demands a remarkable breadth of abilities. Each promoter may apply their style and fitness to content distribution strategies known as content advancement. You are helping your potential prospects and customers with their problems by providing them with actually substantial and crucial substance rather than just promoting your products or organizations. The effective use of content promotion fosters and maintains relationships with your planned and current consumers. Your group will undoubtedly pick you when the moment is appropriate to buy if they view your business as a successful assistant who is a terrific source of guidance and counsel. The most well-known method of producing, disseminating, sharing, and appropriating content on web platforms is content advancement. There is a lot more to it than just the media, places, things to go, computerized accounts, things to apply for, and official justifications. The objective is to attend your invested party and enhance your brand of care, planning, responsibility, and endurance.

Definition and explanation of content marketing:

Content marketing is a marketing strategy that involves creating and sharing valuable, relevant, and consistent content to attract and retain a clearly defined audience. The aim of content marketing is to drive profitable customer action, such as purchasing a product or service or subscribing to a newsletter. Content marketing can take many forms, including blog posts, social media updates, videos, podcasts, and infographics.

Purpose and objectives of the chapter:

The purpose of this chapter is to provide an in-depth overview of content marketing and its importance in today's business landscape. The objectives of the chapter are to:

1. Define content marketing and its key components
2. Explain the benefits of content marketing for businesses
3. Provide examples of successful content marketing campaigns
4. Offer recommendation for creating and implementing a content marketing strategy

In this chapter, we will begin by defining content marketing and exploring its key components, including audience research, content creation, and content distribution. We will then discuss the benefits of content marketing for businesses, such as increased brand awareness, customer engagement, and lead generation. Next, we will examine several successful content marketing campaigns from different industries, including B2B and B2C companies.

After that, we will provide practical tips and best practices for creating and implementing a content marketing strategy, including setting goals, identifying the right channels, and measuring success. Finally, we will discuss some common challenges and pitfalls of content marketing, such as lack of strategy, poor content quality, and ineffective distribution.

Overall, this chapter will provide a comprehensive guide to content marketing, including its importance in today's business landscape and best practices for creating and implementing a successful content marketing strategy.

The Evolution of Marketing: From Traditional Marketing to Content Marketing

Marketing has come a long way since the days of traditional advertising. In the past, companies would rely on mass media outlets such as television, radio, and print to promote their products and services to a broad audience. However, with the rise of the internet, marketing has evolved to become more targeted, personalized, and interactive. Content marketing has emerged as one of the most effective ways for businesses to engage with their customers and build long-term relationships. The first edition of Benjamin Franklin's yearly Poor Richard's Almanac was simply issued in 1732. He justified his actions by stating that he wanted to promote his newly established printing company. He reasoned that printing his Almanac and potentially encouraging others to do the same was the best way to do this. This is the first instance of real substance marketing, according to the events described by the Content Marketing Institute. It occurred only around 300 years ago. For a very long time, businesses and individuals alike have made an effort to stand out by producing free or low-quality content. Franklin accomplished something quite comparable to John Deere, the manufacturer of work vehicles, in 1895 when They brought "The Furrow," a magazine on ranchers' way of life. During the past few decades, there have been numerous content promotion initiatives. It's a similar formula for encouraging people to buy your goods.

1. Apply pressure on the person's paint point.
2. Stir up that irritation.
3. Address their issue.

Significance of Content Marketing in India

Content marketing is a marketing strategy that involves creating and sharing valuable, relevant, and consistent content to attract and retain a clearly defined audience - and, ultimately, to drive profitable customer action. Unlike traditional marketing, content marketing is not focused on promoting a specific product or service. Instead, it aims to educate, inform, and entertain customers by providing them with valuable content that addresses their pain points, interests, and needs.

Some key characteristics of content marketing include:

1. **Focus on Creating Value:** The primary goal of content marketing is to provide value to the audience by creating content that addresses their needs and interests.
2. **Relationship Building:** Content marketing is focused on building long-term relationships with the audience by providing them with valuable content on an ongoing basis.
3. **Targeted Approach:** Content marketing is targeted towards a specific audience or buyer persona, allowing businesses to create content that resonates with their target market.

Benefits of Content Marketing to Businesses

Content marketing offers numerous benefits to businesses, including:

1. **Improved Brand Awareness:** By creating and sharing valuable content, businesses can increase their visibility and attract new customers.

2. **Increased Website Traffic:** Creating high-quality content can help businesses improve their search engine rankings, which can drive more traffic to their website.
3. **Lead Generation:** Content marketing can be used to generate leads by offering valuable content in exchange for contact information.
4. **Thought Leadership:** By creating valuable and informative content, businesses can establish themselves as thought leaders in their industry.

Strategies for Successful Content Marketing

To be successful with content marketing, businesses should consider the following strategies:

1. **Define Their Target Audience:** Businesses should have a clear understanding of their target audience and create content that speaks directly to them.
2. **Develop a Content Strategy:** A well-planned content strategy can help businesses create content that aligns with their business goals and resonates with their audience.
3. **Create High-Quality Content:** Businesses should focus on creating high-quality, engaging content that provides value to their audience.
4. **Promote Their Content:** Businesses should promote their content through various channels, including social media, email marketing, and paid advertising.

The Role of Storytelling in Content Marketing

Storytelling is a powerful tool in content marketing. Stories can help businesses connect with their audience on an emotional. Comprehending the explanation for why content promoting is critical to your organization is perhaps more important than understanding what content displaying is. To begin, we must comprehend the four stages of the purchasing cycle:

- **Mindfulness.** A customer may have a need prior to receiving care, but they are unaware that a response exists.
- **Research.** When a consumer receives notification that a response has been received, they will do a test to prepare themselves. A car buyer, for example, will look into what kind of vehicles are available and which ones will match their needs.
- **Thought.** Now the buyer begins to distinguish between items from various vendors in order to ensure that they are getting a high-quality item at a reasonable cost.
- **Purchase.** Finally, the customer makes a decision. Their decision is upheld, and the trade is carried out.

In terms of the two phases that follow, traditional publicising and exhibiting are outstanding. By finding issues of course of action and instructing clients about something they may have never considered, content exhibiting exploits the underlying two periods of the buying framework.

At any point when done correctly, the value of experience for content display can be amazing. We haven't spent a dollar, or even that much time, on our own content promotion. A small bundle of articles I've written, totaling approximately 20 hours of work, can account for 95 percent of the success we've had with content promotion.

Why Content Marketing Is an Essence

Maybe more crucial than knowing what content showing is, understanding the justification for why it is essential to your company. We must first understand the four phases of the buying cycle:

- **Being Present.** Before obtaining treatment, a consumer could have a need yet be ignorant that a solution is available.
- **The Study.** A customer will conduct a test to get ready for receiving news that a response has been received. For instance, a car buyer will research the types of automobiles that are offered and which ones will suit their needs.
- **I Pondered.** To ensure they are purchasing a high-quality item at a fair price; the buyer now begins to distinguish between products from various providers.
- **Buy.** Lastly, the client makes a choice. Their choice is maintained, and the transaction goes through.

Reason Why Content Marketing Is Popular in India

The traditional public relations and exhibitions are exceptional in terms of the next two phases. Content showcasing takes use of the fundamental two phases of the purchasing framework by identifying concerns of course and educating customers about something they may never have thought about.

The value of the experience for the display of content can be remarkable whenever it is done correctly. We haven't made a lot of financial or even physical efforts to promote our owner. A small bundle of articles I generated that took me about 20 hours to complete is responsible for 95% of the success we've had with content promotion.

The benefit of maintaining additional automatic progressive paths is another advantage of content displaying. It offers to tolerate consistent inbound links and develop outstanding content on your

You may provide more weight to SEO and online media promotion efforts by placing a webpage that is listed in web directories. It goes without saying that for certain associations, the success of their SEO efforts should depend on the material they are displaying. Content displaying is a tried-and-true method that has been successful. Like that, it provides a benefit. Have a look at what the data about presenting material says:

- Web diaries are 67% more likely to generate leads for organizations than other associations.

Companies that employ content showcasing have about 30% higher advancement rates than organizations utilizing it and 47% of buyers read 3 to 5 pieces of information before engaging with a salesperson.

According to 72% of B2B publicists, content advancement affects responsibilities and the volume of leads they generate.

- Content Creativity has advanced greatly during the previous few years. The cornerstone of SEO has increased in importance from being a curiosity to what 47% of buyers do today: study up to five in-depth articles before speaking with a salesperson.

Content poses a different kind of difficulty for advertisers now that it has established a presence. It has become challenging to stand out and succeed at SEO showcasing due to the massive amounts of information that are now available and the speed at which new content is produced. To ensure they begin off on the right foot, marketers need to understand how important it is to create appealing, high-quality content.

- SEO without interesting content is like a standing jug of nothing. The foundation upon which SEO methods are created and used is content. Marketers need to make sure that each word, phrase, article, and another piece of content they use for their substance campaign appeals to their target demographic in this way.
- You will initially need to understand how online search technologies operate to offer great content. Also, SEO advertisers need to be aware of the sporadic calculation adjustments that Google and other online search engines make to improve their accuracy. The next task is to incorporate the learnings into how you package and deliver content once you have finished the challenging job and understood the fundamentals. According to a Nokia study, the average person spends close to 5 hours every day using their devices.

TYPES OF CONTENT MARKETING

There are various types of content marketing that businesses can use to engage with their audience. Some common types of content marketing include:

Social Media Content Marketing

Social media platforms such as Facebook, Twitter, and Instagram are great channels for sharing content with a large audience. Businesses can use social media to share blog posts, videos, infographics, and other types of content with their followers.

It is understandable why so many businesses spend on online media marketing given that there are more than 3.6 billion users of online media worldwide. On each of the numerous platforms (including Facebook, Instagram, Pinterest, LinkedIn, and Snapchat), you can produce and post content in a variety of ways (for example photographs, live recordings, prepare-record recordings, and stories).

Infographic Content Marketing

Infographics are visual representations of data and information that are designed to be easily digestible and shareable. They can be used to present complex information in a simple and engaging way. Infographics present facts, statistics, and information in a clear, practical layout. Infographics are a fantastic way to properly communicate your content since they combine straightforward language with concise sentences and clear images. They work brilliantly when you're seeking to condense a complex or illuminating idea so that everyone in the audience can understand it.

Blog Content Marketing

Creating and publishing blog posts on a regular basis is a popular content marketing strategy. Blogs can help businesses establish thought leadership in their industry, provide valuable information to their audience, and improve their search engine rankings.

Websites are a fantastic form of inbound content that requires a lot of creativity in terms of their inspiration and purpose. With a blog, you may build more internal and external material, blog posts through partnerships, add social deal affixes, and wire item facts, among other things.

Computerized Recording Content Marketing

According to a 2020 audit, 49% of 12- to 32-year-olds in the U.S. concentrated on an online recording over the past month, spending an average of six hours per day listening. As a result, several organizations and news outlets have started creating and disseminating their digital communications. Computerized accounting takes a lot of imagination into account because it may cover any topic of the user's choice. Also, you decide on different aspects of the online recording, such as the length of scenes, the tempo of scenes, who is on the computer broadcast, where you move the webcast, and so on.

Video Content Marketing

Videos are a highly engaging and effective way to communicate with an audience. They can be used to showcase products and services, educate customers, and provide entertainment Wyzowl's research indicates that 69 percent of consumers prefer to watch videos to understand more about a brand's services or business. Also, video advertising may assist you with maintaining adjustments, boosting ROI, and fostering relationships with a huge number of people. You can choose to make public appearances, use electronic media platforms, or use a co-website to distribute your video material.

Content Marketing With Paid Ads

Paid advertisements can help you reach a large audience and position yourself where you need to stand out; they work best when combined with inbound marketing. Websites, presentation pages, banners, and support content are just a few of the places where you can share sponsored adverts.

HOW TO BEGIN USING CONTENT MARKETING

Campaigns to promote substances must follow common sense and logic. Start by taking into account these possibilities:

- **Be Aware of Your Audience.** You need to have a thorough awareness of the needs, issues, and preferences of your target audience before you can generate content for them. Choose one or two of your regions from your detailed descriptions to write for. In any case, before you begin, create profiles of the people in your crowd and their potential.

- **Decide on the Right Groups.** Depending on the sort of content you are producing and the stage of the business cycle you are in, you may choose the best organizational structure. A vital extra factor is what arrangements will assist you to display the most. Some people could find this problematic. An agenda for some; a movie for others.
- **Decide Who Will Draft, Revise, and Proofread Your Material.** The quality of your work will be evaluated by a sizable audience. Find the appropriate asset, whether it is anything from the inside or outside, to make this work. No matter who wrote it, get a pro editor to look it over before it leaves the building.
- **Choose Your Course of Action for the Circumstance.** Will the information be printed for a specific event, published on your website, or sent through email? Decide "where" your crowd will likely be first before making preparations that will be practical. For instance, posting an article through email is excellent, whereas sharing an agenda or worksheet
- **Decide on a Budget-Friendly Timetable for Pitch Development.** It is simple to develop an excessively targeted substance marketing plan. Establish a short-term (3-6 months) strategy for the number of content components you'll be able to generate based on your budget and resources once you've identified your target consumers and organizations. To include it in your plan, keep track of the time it takes you to produce each piece of content.
- **Follow Best Practices.** Clear writing in a language that only you and your friends will understand is a sign of persuasive content. A how-to section should be included. The ideal piece of information is brief, important, and remarkable.

Isn't That Just a Fancy Word for an Advertorial?

Comparable are advertorials, which are longer-form advertising written in an article format to evoke an experience similar to the distribution they are placed in. As they have been around since the 1940s, you have undoubtedly heard of them (and are antecedent to the present infomercial). The duration of advertorials is often much shorter. They regularly push for sales and, for the most part, focus on the benefits of the service or product being sold.

Local marketing, on the other hand, frequently focuses on intensely targeted material from which the pursuer might get respect. Little emphasis is placed on the object behind the piece, and there is no attempt to make a sale. Companies earn respect by establishing themselves as thought leaders in their field, creating brand loyalty.

What Are the Advantages?

- **They Are Attractive.** Customers pay greater attention to local advertising than to national campaigns.
- **They Give You Power.** When done properly, local advertisements help potential customers find solutions to their problems.
- **Excellent Leads Are Provided.** You receive more top-notch leads since the content is important and well-targeted. This is particularly obvious if you place local adverts on the recipients of payouts from specialist exchanges.

What Are the Negative Aspects?

- **Scalability.** Making local advertisements might be difficult. Every advertisement needs to blend in with the period it is playing. That indicates that if you push for a certain quantity, especially if there is a deadline, you run the danger of losing credibility or worth.
- **It May Appear Difficult.** Those people would prefer not to be misled. Your material should flow normally with the distribution at a delicate balance. Nevertheless, you also can't make your pursuer feel betrayed when they see that it's endorsed. Your content should be useful, wise, or beneficial in any other way.
- **One Corrupt Person Enriches the Group.** Several companies produce too unique local ads. Due to this, some consumers are wary of local ads in general. In any case, according to Forbes, local principles are expected to grow, making it crucial for promoters to follow rules and regulations.

What Does This All Mean for Your Brand?

Finally, if local advertising is done correctly, it might land just in the sweet spot of your prospect. Provide something from the beginning, be beneficial to your customer, and you'll gain their loyalty and name recognition. (Also, direct them to your business channel.) Local advertising, however, requires expertise, testing, and assessment to monitoring your success rates, just like any other form of marketing.

THE VALUE OF CONTENT MARKETING DATA ANALYTICS

According to a new study, content marketing has taken center stage in India's image advertising over the past year as web-based media's reputation as a showcasing strategy declines. According to the assessment conducted by Times Internet and DMA Asia, 57% of respondents said that content marketing had surpassed online media marketing as India's most popular system throughout the 2017–2018 period.

The summary included the thoughts of 150 brand advertising in India from various classes, including FMCG, medicines, land, vehicle, and retail. Combining their content marketing strategies was listed as the primary focus of over 30% of the advertisers for 2018, closely followed by evaluating ROI (27%) in both categories. Advertisers in the country acknowledge that online media is a less effective strategy than in previous years, despite the explosion in mobile phone and web infiltration, particularly in provincial India.

Just 36% of surveyed advertisers cited web-based media promotion as a method that was successfully serving their needs in 2017–18, a 30% decline from the previous year's research. Nonetheless, multi-level computerized marketing continues to be necessary for Indian firms. More than 40% of respondents said they spend more than a fourth of the average advertising budget on electronic stages and equipment

To secure or advance their computerized ad campaigns, advertisers are also giving greater thought to proving ROI in their marketing initiatives. Obtaining sufficient funding for advanced showcasing and calculating ROI rank as two of the biggest challenges (32% and 27%, respectively).

Weekly and monthly estimates of ROI for computerized marketing were the most popular options, at 38% each. In 2013, there were more than 60 advertising channels; two years later, in 2020, there will be more than 100. 78% of CMOs believe that Custom Content (individual content having a position inside the business) is the best way to reach their clients across this wide range of media. destiny of promotion.

Magazine advertising is thought to be 72% less effective than branded content. Typically, it costs $250 and $500, respectively, to reach 2,000 people via paper and magazine. 69% of advertisers believe it to be superior to even fantastic snail mail campaigns. “Unique constructed material” was cited as the primary type of content by 58% of advertisers. As new college graduates are wary of joining groups with self-serving goals, the tailored content should be presented honestly.

What Are the Content Marketing Channels?

Any path that allows the distribution of manufactured goods to a crowd is known as a channel. Plan out the outlets that will be used to spread your messages while putting together a substance marketing strategy. The top 5 channels include, regular:

- Organic Search

Without any assistance from the provider, natural traffic is built. Every material that is disseminated on your website is indexed by web crawlers, who at that point determine how relevant your company and content are for a client search.

- Pay-Per-Click

putting money behind a production to display your content upfront or to place your content in advertisement spots throughout other websites.

- Social Media Sharing Sites

Facebook, Twitter, and LinkedIn are generally welcoming platforms that almost every customer uses.

- Messages

the initial sophisticated inbound marketing campaign. Sending information via email allows you to reach a set of individuals who have successfully shown interest in your information/items by reading follow-up messages.

- Establishing external links

each time a different online component links to your content and sends visitors from that foundation to yours. When you provide valuable, useful content, other people will notice and start teaching their audiences.

Does Content Marketing Disguise Content?

- Extremely unique material

Whatever your objectives for using online media, it's crucial that you give your audience something of value. Managing the Increasing Impact of Influencer Marketing. Although social business transactions are predicted to increase by 34.8 percent this year, many store executives are unclear about how to increase their budget for their powerful marketing and monitor results. You can learn more from this review report.

Some companies make the error of believing that what is significant to them is equally significant to their audience, and as a result, they utilize social media to communicate and "sell, sell, offer" instead of considering what is significant to the target audience. Pay attention to the topics that are currently being discussed by your audience, read what the industry leaders are writing, and then pitch your content to respond.

heed these indications it's important to take into account the 5-3-2 rule, which stipulates that out of every 10 items you publish, number five should be curation—that is sharing information created by others.

- The third item should be the original work that you have produced yourself.
- The second item has to be refined, with original, engaging, and loose material that suits your brand. Every organization acting in bad faith damages trust (Higgins et al., 2020). 2020 (Kougiannou and Wallis). People's minds are torn apart when the disguise technique is revealed (in both covering and murdering). Expected and obtained outcomes This is likely to annoy present trust goals and beliefs, which will cause trust to erode (Kim et al., 2009)
- If it is a strictly political or substantive issue

Concerns about legislation and religion are two fields of knowledge that people are enthusiastic about. If you publish anything that is openly political or strict, you're unlikely to connect with the rest of your audience and you'll almost surely come out as small or hostile to people who don't share your ideas.

Avoid broadcasting anything that may be construed as troublesome unless you're a political or strict group (in which case it's unexpectedly advised to be careful); otherwise, you run the risk of upsetting and losing followers. Considering everything that might be useful, it will examine the preferences of your audience (and those of your rivals) so you can start distributing information they will like.

- Including a malicious or defamatory comment

Expressing complaints about customers or rivals has its proper place and time, which is not on social media. If When a dissatisfied consumer criticizes you on Twitter, avoid the desire to reply. You could see that you can win them back if you treat them with respect and reverence and, if it's feasible, take it away.

- Articles that include spelling or grammar mistakes

Like your website, your online media accounts act as online stores. Making a content error, whether it's a straightforward grammatical mistake or a serious mistake. Linguistic errors might create the impression that you don't care.Make careful to proofread your work after you've finished it before publishing it. Nonetheless, it is far preferable to share it with a colleague to edit before posting.

- Information that doesn't adhere to the brand

Profiles are an extension of your brand, and you do have creative control over the voice and tone of your image, even though you are constrained by the structure of the social media platform you are presenting on. Revert to your image identity whenever you publish social media content. Consider what they would say and how they would say it if they were using digital media. Make sure your material follows these trends as closely as it can. subjects, as one might anticipate.

According to Trocianko et al. (2013), a convincing disguise procedure delays or avoids the identification step until after some time has elapsed during which confidence is dynamically developed through repeated interactions. The limitation of our research was that repeated contacts had some probability of occurrence.

- Throughout interpersonal organizations, the message is consistent

No matter how important it is to have a consistent brand voice, publishing the same content across all media is a mistake. It's been said that every relationship association is unique. They each independently identify themselves to distinct substances and speak to various economics for a certain something. Instagram is more copy-heavy and professional than LinkedIn, whereas Twitter is better suited to bite-sized delights, even if Instagram is mostly visual and casual. Make sure your content is appropriate for everyone by evaluating each item of internet media you have. Make sure your message suits the tone and style of each stage, whether or not you have a set line.

- Unapproved drugs and substances

Sharing other people's content is acceptable, and, believe it or not, not, I would suggest you to. Nonetheless, such enduring brands copy material without giving a credit from several sources. The same is true for explanations; while persuasive statements have their uses, they look messy when you don't indicate where they came from.

Photos that are preserved fade over time. If you include a photo in your work that you are not allowed to use, you run the danger of receiving harsh legal consequences. In light of everything, be sure to get your photographs from open-source websites like Creative Commons and follow the credit guidelines. Take advantage of the opportunity to create an interface the next time you come across something you want to share. The source will be disclosed if you want to share this content and a link back to your article is included. Connect to the source's online media handle, of course, and include a link to the details of your profile.

- Content that is hashtag-heavy

Hashtags are crucial because they enable your work to be shared and disguised throughout online media, they let you build your community, and they may expose your content to more in-depth discussion. Considering everything, adding endless lists of pointless hashtags to your social media posts will fail. You run the danger of having a fragmented message and losing the impact of the most crucial points.

INDIAN CONTENT MARKETING COMPETITION

India is a country facing a multitude of problems, ranging from social, economic, environmental, and political issues. These problems affect various aspects of life and create challenges that impact the country's development and growth.

One example of a problem in India is the issue of air pollution. India is home to some of the world's most polluted cities, with Delhi being one of the worst affected. The air pollution in these cities has been linked to respiratory illnesses and premature deaths, which can have a significant impact on public health and the economy.

Another problem that India faces is the issue of poverty. Despite significant progress in recent years, poverty remains a significant problem in India, with millions of people living in extreme poverty. This problem affects access to basic necessities such as food, clean water, and healthcare, and also hinders the country's development and growth.

India also faces challenges in the area of gender equality. Women in India face discrimination and violence, including sexual assault, domestic violence, and forced marriages. These issues impact women's ability to access education, employment, and other opportunities and contribute to a significant gender gap in India.

In addition to these problems, India also faces challenges related to political instability, corruption, and infrastructure development. These issues can impact business operations and create challenges for companies looking to invest in the country.

Camouflaging marketing and sales strategies that ignore or downplay these issues can be problematic. Consumers are becoming increasingly aware of social and environmental issues, and they are more likely to support companies that demonstrate a commitment to addressing these issues. Ignoring or camouflaging these problems can undermine consumer trust and damage a company's reputation.

Instead, companies should take a more transparent and proactive approach to addressing these issues. This could involve implementing sustainable and socially responsible business practices, partnering with NGOs to address social and environmental challenges, and engaging in advocacy efforts to promote policy change. By demonstrating a commitment to these issues, companies can build trust with consumers and contribute to positive social and environmental outcomes in India.

Amul Dairy Cooperative Society

The recognizable cartoon girl from Amul, who commonly appears on the packaging of their dairy products, is well-known to everyone. Yet, did you know she has a significant internet presence for them? Amul regularly announces its stance on current affairs.

India Oreo

Do you remember the former Oreo television commercials that showed viewers how to properly eat an Oreo cream biscuit? This expression means to twist, lick, or dunk. In the ones that came after these, Ranbir Kapoor and other characters who were described as relishing the flavor of a brand-new Oreo cookie made an appearance.

They were able to establish a presence in the market that was previously held by Thanks to their advertisements, Parle and Britannia. This is one of the best content marketing examples in digital media marketing.

Flipkart

Flipkart is another business that dominates television advertising. Despite having well-known actors like Alia Bhatt and Ranbir Kapoor, the moments that focused on the kids and how successfully they emulated adult situations and conversations stood out.

So, the material from Flipkart may be regarded as one of the greatest illustrations of content marketing that incorporates the tastes and ideas of users. They were effective in increasing public awareness of their most recent trends and offers thanks to their most recent "India Ka Fashion Capital" motto and celebrity endorsements in their advertising. Flipkart is more than just an online marketplace for goods and services. Given that their present advertising places a strong emphasis on apparel accessories. It is a significant online retailer of homes in India. Appliances are included with food, electronics, and apparel. This might also be a great example of how content marketing influences how customers perceive a brand.

Shaadi.com

Shaadi.com's marketing believed that Women's Day would be the perfect occasion to introduce the hashtag #takethepressureoff. In their most recent campaign, a mother congratulates her daughter for turning down a marriage proposal she didn't want. The paragraph that followed this revealed the proportion of women who acknowledged feeling coerced into accepting a marriage proposal when they didn't want to.

As a result of marriage, you'll find that the majority of their commercials are directed at women. is sometimes harder for a female to decide and commit to than it is for a boy. Shaadi.com can establish a connection with its audience by understanding this basic concept. Also, they focused on showing how their characters could easily navigate through numerous profiles and traits by utilizing the application's structure in their advertising.

Why wouldn't prospective customers download their app after seeing their advertisement? Shaadi.com has also taken care to remain active on social media platforms. YouTube serves as their main content marketing tool. Without a question, this is one of the greatest examples of customer-focused content marketing.

Simplify360

Top businesses use Simplify360 to simplify communications with consumers and clients across a variety of social media channels. With this, you can also keep track of and react to customer reviews. They usually publish humorous memes with animated characters to engage their followers and connect with their audience. Amul is a fantastic illustration of content marketing that makes use of news related to each of the social media platforms, Amul has a substantial following and has promoted its content on Twitter, Instagram, and Facebook. They typically create customer-focused content to show their comprehension of and concern for the nation.

CHANCES FOR CONTENT MARKETING

Content marketers are without a doubt the driving force behind the economy. You could think that as time passes and the world becomes more digital, content marketing will become more in demand. This demonstrates unequivocally that content marketers must do the following to compete in this intensely competitive environment: possess extensive knowledge and well-honed skills. It consists of several elements, the most important of which is content marketing. These elements include the use of social media marketing, influencer marketing, SEO tactics, and content marketing. Content marketers are therefore essential to the accomplishment of digital marketing. Many content marketing strategies may be used in your strategy; the most well-liked ones are as follows:

Examples of content marketing include online content marketing, social media content marketing, infographic content marketing, blog content marketing, podcast content marketing, video content marketing, and more.

CAMOUFLAGING MONITORING

Internet media is a gift, and we should be thankful for it. There is unequivocally no question about it. But unquestionably when something bad happens.

- **Difficult Management:** Managing web-based media accounts is a complex nightmare similar to managing executives, associations, and building projects. The more internet presence you have, the more difficult it will be to keep your documents organized.
- **Profiting From Human Sorrow:** Current scientific developments are frequently a heated topic of conversation. But, there comes a time when having too many arguments might be detrimental, especially if you're attempting to capitalize on someone else's terror. "Everyone impacted by #Sandy, remain safe," tweeted Opening Inc. in response to this. We'll shop on Gap.com a lot today. You ought to do it.
- **With Sneak Attacks**

It's sensible to start searching for a sneak attack given the prevalence of internet media and the wide range of fads available. Moderate Insurance is aware of how rapidly a situation like this may develop.

- **Unfavorable Public Opinion:** People occasionally can't help but disagree with what you're doing. It's insane to think that more than a few people are aware of what you're doing. President John Pepper announced on Twitter that his chain of burrito eateries would remain open throughout Hurricane Sandy. His crowd wasn't as enthused as he had hoped, and he received a great deal of criticism for putting his delegates in danger.
- **Constructing a Wall:** CVS made an effort to choose wisely. Consumers' safety may be ensured by maintaining their social hidden media profiles.

RESULTS AND CONCLUSION

Outbound marketing strategies, or anything else that intrudes on your group of people, are no longer as effective in connecting with and influencing large groups of people. Your content must now connect with your viewers so strongly that it seems natural (a.k.a. inbound). A popular method for achieving this is to create a record for your material or to describe a tale. Acting in that position will make your content seem more obvious, charming, and uniquely crafted for your group. are less effective than they formerly were in connecting with and affecting crowds of people. Your message must now resonate with your audience so strongly that it comes off as natural (also known as "authentic" inbound). A popular method for achieving this is to create a record for your material or to describe a story. To do this, your group will see your content as being more evident and specially created. A single piece of content isn't enough to generate significant growth; nevertheless, one must make a consistent effort to comprehend the audience, supply them with a lot of information, and assess the worth of each piece of material sent. We hope that the lessons learned and trends identified in this study will help you as we move deeper into 2021 and beyond so that you may improve the effectiveness of your content marketing initiatives. The pandemic's continuing effects imply that this industry will simply have to as the year progresses, so any steps you can take to pinpoint problem areas or even to have a better grasp of your rivals' actions may be vital. Companies frequently make the error of thinking that posting any (bad) content is preferable to posting nothing at all when they present continuously through internet media.

Suddenly posting unfavorable, unimportant, or embarrassing content might damage your reputation and cost you, key supporters. Future repercussions for further investigation on creative and original methods to hold the viewer's attention. When the invention develops further and the consumer becomes more knowledgeable, the advertiser who can picture the container will wish to win over the customer's attention.

This tactic aids associations in gaining authenticity and partner support by encouraging transient trust and minimizing harm when it becomes obvious. Additionally, we make a contribution by illuminating how the effect of disguise tactics varies based on the particular strategy and stage of implementation (on the sending and identification). It typically has positive effects as long as a cover approach is applied. Nonetheless, the kill mechanism safeguards the relationship from negative outcomes in any circumstance when it is understood. This review expands our knowledge of the sharing economy organizations' use of alternative strategies to accomplish their objectives. (2018); Pelzer et al. 2019). Uzunca et al. The only content that should ever be hidden is that which is beneficial for customers.

Content marketing and camouflaging marketing are two key strategies used by businesses to reach their target audience and increase sales. In this chapter, we explore the concept of assenting strategies, where businesses use a combination of content marketing and camouflaging marketing to create a positive image for their brand while also increasing sales.

Content Marketing and Camouflaging Marketing

Content marketing involves creating and sharing valuable content to attract and retain a clearly defined audience, with the ultimate goal of driving profitable customer action. This could be in the form of blog posts, videos, podcasts, or social media content, and is designed to educate and inform customers about a business's products or services.

Camouflaging marketing, on the other hand, involves blending marketing messages with non-promotional content to make them less intrusive and more appealing to consumers. This strategy is often used in native advertising, where sponsored content is seamlessly integrated into a website or social media platform, making it more likely that consumers will engage with it.

Assenting Strategies

Assenting strategies involve combining content marketing and camouflaging marketing to create a positive image for a brand while also increasing sales. This involves creating valuable content that educates and informs customers about a product or service, while also integrating marketing messages in a subtle and non-intrusive way.

Key Takeaways and Implications for Businesses

Businesses can benefit from using assenting strategies by creating content that is both informative and engaging, while also promoting their products or services in a non-intrusive way. This can lead to increased brand awareness, customer loyalty, and sales.

However, businesses need to be careful not to overdo it with their marketing messages, as this can quickly turn off customers and lead to a negative image for the brand. They also need to ensure that their content is of high quality and relevant to their target audience, as this will help to establish them as a thought leader in their industry.

Future Research Directions for Content Marketing and Camouflaging Marketing

As the world of marketing continues to evolve, there are likely to be many new developments in the area of content marketing and camouflaging marketing. One area of future research could focus on the effectiveness of different types of content in engaging customers and driving sales.

Another area of research could look at how businesses can use data analytics to track the effectiveness of their marketing campaigns and make adjustments in real-time to optimize their results.

Recommendations for Businesses Looking to Implement Assenting Content Marketing With Camouflaging Marketing

For businesses looking to implement assenting strategies, it is important to start with a clear understanding of their target audience and their needs. They should then create high-quality content that is relevant and engaging, and integrate marketing messages in a subtle and non-intrusive way.

Businesses should also be prepared to invest in data analytics tools to track the effectiveness of their campaigns and make adjustments as needed. Finally, they should be patient and persistent, as building a positive brand image and increasing sales takes time and effort.

Assenting strategies that combine content marketing and camouflaging marketing can be highly effective in creating a positive brand image and driving sales. However, businesses need to be careful not to overdo it with their marketing messages and ensure that their content is of high quality and relevant to their target audience.

As the world of marketing continues to evolve, there are likely to be many new developments in the area of content marketing and camouflaging marketing. Businesses that stay up to date with these trends and are willing to adapt their strategies as needed are likely to be the most successful in the long run.

TEACHING NOTE

Synopsis

Content marketing an eye opener to various customers and prospecting consumers to give them the viewpoint of understanding and knowledge. Consumers are educated due to the awareness of digital media and easy access of it. In today's era this digital platform is also talking an advantage in camouflaging the content as per their viewpoint which needs to be put at forefront. Today shopper's various reports show that these associations are vulnerable to acts of neglect and may take on substitute freak procedures like disguise. The purpose of this chapter is to explore the reason and objective of camouflaging the content and brainwashing consumers in the manner like marketers are wishing to prove nationally and globally. This research makes salient contributions by integrating various portals of digital marketing with the concept of camouflaging and through which channel consumers interest gets hamper. Every organization should use digital platform with their uniqueness intact that it should not be driven to another meaning of message. Digital Marketing is a spokesperson which is one way so it should be guided and directed with objectivity.

CASE OBJECTIVES

- To make students aware about the need of Content Marketing.
- To explain the requirement of correct content while sharing on web.
- To help students understand the strategies in safeguarding their content of not being int camouflaging and understand the disadvantages of the same.
- To explain students the organic traffic and conversions can be increased on web page without content camouflaging.
- To help students gain knowledge of the strategic actions for building relationship with business and customers.
- Helping the students in creating a sense of community around your brand.

POSITION IN THE COURSE

This example can be used for management courses at the undergraduate and graduate levels as well as for any businessman-specific sessions. This instance can be applied to undergraduate students around the third semester because by then they would have had a solid foundation in digital Marketing areas. If the postgraduate student is studying digital marketing, this scenario can be applied to the first semester. This can be used for a 90-minute session as part of a course relating to digital marketing or content creation.

SUGGESTED PRE-READINGS

The following pre-readings might be given to students to help them gain a basic understanding of startup expansion finance and the possibilities available for it.

PRE-READING MATERIAL

- https://www.mgb2b.com/blog/marketing-in-camouflage-native-advertising-for-manufacturers/
- https://contentmarketinginstitute.com/what-is-content-marketing/
- https://www.forbes.com/sites/forbescoachescouncil/2021/02/18/four-reasons-why-content-marketing-is-hard/?sh=38a054a16864
- https://zenmedia.com/blog/21-common-questions-about-content-marketing-answered/
- https://india.oup.com/productPage/5591038/7421214/9780199469550

TEACHING PLAN

In the beginning, the case could be given to the class as pre-reading along with other resources pertinent to the lesson being taught.

By posting the following question on the board and asking the class for a show of hands, the instructor might begin the lesson by conducting a brief survey of the participants.

SUGGESTED TIME PLAN

Exhibit 1 offers a recommended strategy that instructors can utilize to run the 90-minute case study programme.

Table 1. Suggested time plan

Exhibit 1: Suggested Time Plan	
Content Marketing and its usage	10 minutes
Split Class into 5 groups – allocate one question to each group to brainstorm	5 minutes
Group Analysis	15 minutes
Discussion on Need and Camouflaging Content Marketing	10 minutes
Advantages and Disadvantages of the Camouflaging Content Marketing	15 minutes
How to Monitor Camouflaging	15 minutes
Future challenges to expect	10 minutes
Wrap-up	Wrap-up
Source: Author's Analysis	

What Precisely Is Content Marketing?

Traditional marketing is turned on its head by content marketing. The requirements of the customer come first, not the demands of the business and its goods or services. The purpose of content marketing is to build trusting relationships with customers by giving them useful, really helpful material for free. This will eventually encourage them to make a purchase. Over the past several years, the significance of content in an online marketing plan has skyrocketed. Digital marketing is all about using online platforms to advertise brands. It uses a number of different strategies, such as SEO, SEM, link building, email marketing, PPC, affiliate marketing, etc.

Today's consumers favor more contact and less disruption. Digital advertising is still the greatest strategy to attract organic traffic, engage customers, and increase sales. The changing consumer behavior brought on by technological advancements makes the work tough as well. We have put up the most comprehensive collection of interview questions for digital marketing to make things simple for you. They are appropriate for organizations of all sizes and across all important industries. You are not far from your ideal work with the help of the digital marketing interview questions and answers at your disposal.

SUGGESTED QUESTIONS FOR DISCUSSION

The following series of questions can then be used by the instructor to facilitate class discussion on the case. If necessary, the instructor can additionally provide one question to each of the five groups, divide the class into those groups, and ask the groups to come up with a solution. The remaining students can then hear each group's analysis. Based on the answers provided below, the instructor can then conclude the lesson and recap any points that were missed. If the instructor chooses to adopt this method, a sample lesson plan with suggested timelines is also included toward the end of this teaching note.

Q. What various forms of digital marketing are there?
various facets of digital marketing

- Search Engine Optimization (SEO)
- Search Engine Marketing (SEM)
- Content Marketing
- Email Marketing
- Social Media Marketing
- E-commerce Marketing

Q2. What are the best strategies for boosting website traffic?
The most well-liked and efficient methods of boosting website traffic are:

- paid search
- display advertising
- content marketing
- creating catchy headlines
- and SEO activities.

- Targeting long-tail keywords
- guest blogging
- Looking for referral traffic
- posting content on LinkedIn
- internal linking
- email marketing are all examples of content optimization

Q3. What are the online marketing's restrictions?

Strenuous Competition Online marketing has been a popular strategy for most firms because it is convenient and affordable. Therefore, in the face of such fierce competition, it is difficult to stand apart.

It might become too much: It's simple to become overwhelmed and confused because there is a deluge of information, data, and tools. To make sense of it all, you need a lot of practise and experience.

Analytics are only as useful as their user: There is analytics for everything, but using raw data requires understanding how to read and use it. Sometimes it might be deceptive, and you could get caught up in it. pursuing pointless KPIs and wasting money where it shouldn't be Internal linking and email marketing.

Q4. Content marketing: What is it?

Information marketing is a tactical strategy that focuses on producing and disseminating pertinent, worthwhile, and consistent content in order to draw in and hold on to a target audience and encourage profitable consumer action. The main justifications for businesses using content marketing are:

- Higher sales
- Cost savings
- Better, more devoted customers

Q5. Why is digital marketing more popular than traditional marketing?

The following are the reasons why online marketing is preferable to offline marketing:

Information is immediately available online, allowing you to reach a broader audience and expand regionally with ease. You can interact with clients more easily and quickly. There is better tracking.

Q6. Make a distinction between marketing context and content.

The answer is that the work's content refers to the information available to the audience while the context refers to the placing of the content, storyline, or purpose that benefits the audience.

Q7. What metrics would you use to evaluate the success of your content marketing? Can you give some instances of effective content you have used?

Only half the battle is won when the world becomes aware of what you have to say. Candidates must be able to monitor social media shares and evaluate the success of each piece of content they produce using Google Analytics.Candidates for content production must be able to define "success." If they utilise phrases like "traffic," "repeat visits," "retweeting," "liking," and "SEO" in their comments, that's a solid sign that they understand what you're saying. It's also much better if they provide particular instances of their own successes in these areas.

Q8. What essential information must be contained in a content brief?

The most important component of a content brief is the outline. The brief needs to be explicit where headings should be placed and what keywords should be targeted. To the extent that the brief permits, the writer is free to include other ideas and thoughts. On the other hand, content briefs are always able to offer the fundamentals and particular instances of their own achievements in such sectors.

Q9. What is the way you approach content strategy? What should you watch out for and in what order?

How the material should be written depends on the message it is trying to convey, the audience it is intended for, and how it will be interpreted.Look for a variety of editorial experience in your interview candidates, such as creative, newsroom, and branded content. Smart content strategists are aware that diverse writing styles are required for various reasons. Watch out for their ideation process as they polish, disseminate, and package the content to reach their target audience and meet their objectives.

Q 10 What do you think the voice of our company is? What kind of voice would you use?

The communication from your company strikes a friendly, informed professional tone. As a result, it's crucial to include helpful details and a few technical terms, but make sure to define them frequently throughout your blog entries.

Candidates that can recognise the interview tone your company is going for are more likely to have done their study on your company's brand story and prepared for the interview. Since this example shows how to write brand messages, look for the keywords that you associate with your company. Strong candidates will also be aware that your target audience will anticipate a particular tone and voice.

Q11. The Process of Content Marketing

Businesses may communicate with (and go where) their prospects through the use of content marketing. Getting in front of your target audience and publishing interesting material helps you become more visible and develop connections with people who might become new clients. And even if they don't, your level of awareness has still grown. And that is advantageous. However, with so many online platforms available, your company can concentrate on those that are most frequently used by its target market.

However, there's more!

There are various groups of people you could wish to interact with your brand with in addition to your target demographic. Bloggers, for instance, might write on your content. If those blogs have a sizable audience, they might provide your company more exposure.

Q 12. Do I Actually Need a Content Marketing Strategy?

"A plan for creating an audience by writing, maintaining, and disseminating regular and consistent material that educates, entertains, or inspires to turn strangers into fans and fans into clients," according to Demian Farnworth of Copyblogger.com. Your company can be putting out material every day through blogs, videos, digital and print newsletters, and periodicals. This makes up a sizable portion of your company's material. And there can be a lot of it or not enough.Additionally, you want the content you produce to be pertinent to and appropriate for your business. If you want to be sure that your material is reaching its intended audience, you can't depend on UPS. Making a content marketing strategy is necessary if you want to be strategic with your content marketing.

REFERENCES

Buller, D. B., & Burgoon, J. K. (1996). Interpersonal deception theory. *Communication Theory*, *6*(3), 203–242. doi:10.1111/j.1468-2885.1996.tb00127.x

Elsbach, K. D., & Sutton, R. I. (1992). Acquiring organizational legitimacy through illegitimate actions: A marriage of institutional and impression management theories. *Academy of Management Journal*, *35*(4), 699–738. doi:10.2307/256313

Fichman, M., & Levinthal, D. A. (1991). Honeymoons and the liability of adolescence: A new perspective on duration dependence in social and organizational relationships. *Academy of Management Review*, *16*(2), 442–468. doi:10.2307/258870

Hotten, R. (2015, December 15). *Volkswagen: The scandal explained.* BBC. https://www. bbc.com/news/business-34324772

Milligan, E. (2020 September 15). Uber Tried to Conceal Driver Photo Fraud, London Cabbies Say. *Bloomberg*, https://www.bloombergquint.com/business/uber-tried-to-conceal-driver-photo-fraud-black-cab-drivers-say

Pache, A. C., & Santos, F. (2013). Inside the hybrid organization: Selective coupling as a response to competing institutional logics. *Academy of Management Journal*, *56*(4), 972–1001. doi:10.5465/amj.2011.0405

Srikant, C. D. (2019). Impression management strategies to gain regulatory approval. *Journal of Business Research, 105*, 136–153. https://doi.org/.jbusres.2019.08.006 doi:10.1016/j

Uber to 'hide' surge pricing notification. (2016, June 24). BBC. https://www.bbc.com/ news/technology-36619414

Wang, T., Wezel, F. C., & Forgues, B. (2016). Protecting market identity: When and how do organizations respond to consumers' devaluations? *Academy of Management Journal*, *59*(1), 135–162. doi:10.5465/amj.2014.0205

Weick, K. E. (1976). Educational Organizations as Loosely Coupled Systems. *Administrative Science Quarterly*, *21*(1), 1. doi:10.2307/2391875

Wong, J. (2017, November 22). Uber Concealed Massive Hack That Exposed Data of 57m Users and Drivers. *The Guardian*. https://www.theguardian.com/technology/2017/ nov/21/uber-data-hack-cyber-attack

Chapter 9
Fortune Investments and Assets:
Cognitive Biases, Investor Behavior, and the COVID-19 Pandemic

Stutee Mohanty
KIIT University, India

Suresh Kumar Sahoo
Sri Sri University, India

EXECUTIVE SUMMARY

This case study highlights a few prominent cognitive biases influencing investor behavior in India during the COVID-19 pandemic. Financial decisions of an investor are affected by cognitive factors and not just knowledge. Decision-making is not always necessarily rational by nature. Investors are inclined towards irrational decision making quite frequently due to the impact of various cognitive factors. Moreover, the ongoing COVID-19 pandemic has made situations around us extremely precarious. Every business segment has been affected by it, including financial markets. This case study emphasizes significant cognitive biases faced by Stella while investing her and her clients' hard-earned money in the Indian capital markets and expanding her business during COVID-19. She had numerous thoughts and questions in her mind while going through the investment and expansion process ranging from investment amount and options available at her disposal to the level of risk and return involved in each of them. Such apprehensions are also faced by several other investors in India and the world.

INTRODUCTION

It was a rainy evening of 2020 and Stella was planning her investments and taxation sitting in front of her laptop with her excel sheet open on the bed in her bedroom. It involved her hard-earned money including all the huge bonuses and incentives she had to her credit after slogging day in and day out for the past 5 years in the cut-throat corporate sector. Any wrong decision taken by her would result in massive

DOI: 10.4018/978-1-6684-8488-3.ch009

losses and bad tax payments. On the contrary, prudent decisions would lead to drastic increase in her net worth and proper tax planning. She had all the possible investment options written on the excel sheet opened on her laptop screen and was trying to pick the best ones for herself along with deciding on the share of the entire amount she would put in each of them. She had a variety of thoughts and questions in her mind, confirming all the data to checking out the latest market trends to sticking to her knowledge and awareness of the capital markets, she was doing it all. There was complete chaos in her mind. After weighing the advantages and disadvantages of every option available to her, she had to take an instant decision and start moving forward before it was too late.

Why Investment and Investor Behaviour?

Stella D'Souza graduated with an MBA-Finance degree from a Tier-1 B-school in India and like any other individual from a middle-class Indian family, accepted employment offer by a renowned MNC in Bangalore city. After earning for a while, she realized the significance and importance of investment in order to allow her wealth to grow and create a corpus for her old age (post-retirement life). She enrolled into various investment courses and started mastering the financial concept of investment. Soon, she was able to create a strong theoretical knowledge base for herself and also had serious discussions about it with her CA. But when the time came for her to plan her tax and investments, she came across various thoughts and questions ranging from investment amount to investment avenues to the fear of losses and taking wrong decisions as it involved her savings and bonuses that she had earned after putting loads of diligent and sincere efforts in the corporate sector in India.

She also had to focus on her personal life being a quintessential young Indian girl. Her parents wanted her to get married to a well settled boy from a decent family and were hunting for prospective grooms for her. She also wanted to contribute financially towards her wedding expenses and support her parents as she was a single-child, her father was a simple retired government employee, and her mother a traditional Indian housewife. She was also vary of the kind of family she would get married into in near future and if she will have to take up certain more financial liabilities then. Being the only earning member of her family currently, money was her top priority and she could not afford to lose any by making lame decisions.

At the same time, she knows how important investment and financial management is for a professional like her who is not lucky enough like her father to be eligible for the retirement pension scheme by the Indian government. Moreover, if her investments click then, she can take up investment as a career sometime in future and earn a lot more than what she does now by working in the Indian corporate.

Decision -making is not always rational and straight forward as it seems. Therefore, she concluded only having theoretical finance knowledge did not solve the purpose for her. It involves both traditional theoretical finance and cognitive factors that has resulted in the evolution of a new stream of finance called Behavioural Finance which studies the behaviour of an investor while making financial decisions.

Investment in India. Why Is India an Upcoming Economic Powerhouse?

India has a fair share of the world economy and hence the capital markets or the share markets of India form a considerable portion of the world economy. The capital market is vital to the financial system. Fund raisers, fund providers, intermediaries, organizations/FIIs like BSE, NSE, CSDL, NSDL, LIC, etc, and market regulators are the major constituents of the Indian capital markets. The total value of

Indian capital markets is estimated to be around USD3.5 trillion as of August, 2022. Organizations/FIIs are the largest investors in the Indian capital markets with an investment of over USD99 million. LIC is the largest FII with investment worth USD6.68 billion in 2022. India also has many individual professional investors who have been consistently named among the richest in the world by renowned business magazines like Forbes, Times, etc. A few prominent Indian investors are Radhakrishnan Damani (USD21.45 billion), Rakesh Jhunjhunwala (USD 18.55 billion), Mukul Aggarwal (USD317.32 million), etc. Youth in India are also taking up investment seriously and if possible are also planning to make it their profession. It can be noted that brokerages like Zerodha, Upstox and AngelOne, and traditional players like HDFC Securities, ICICI Securities, Geojit, etc more than doubled their number of customers since the Covid-19 pandemic. 70% of their new customers are first-time investors and under the age of 30. The user base of BSE doubled to 80 million between May 2020 to September 2021. According to a Nov 2021 survey backed by various brokerage firms, 81% respondents were investing their money in capital markets and mutual funds apart from staying focused on savings and long-term growth and returns. Financial literacy has steeply increased in due course of time which has resulted in rapid growth of number of investors majorly constituting of growth. With 75% of the respondents being below the age of 34 years and 76% being first-time investors, it can be concluded that the new generation of Indians are keen on investment and its various aspects.

The Birth of Fortune Investments and Assets

After Stella realized the existence and significance of behavioural or cognitive biases in the decision-making process of investors, she discussed about it with her CA and her parents. They then, decided to explore this fascinating aspect of finance and investments. Stella had always made it a point in life to pursue things that intrigued her and caught the whim of her imagination as a whole irrespective of how unconventional the idea was. She immediately knew that this was her calling.

While returning back home the other day, she happened to get into the bank that was on her regular office-home route to meet her best friend who was retail banker by profession. She suddenly stumbled upon the fixed deposit counter at the bank and found it almost empty. While talking to her bestie, she discussed about her idea and asked regarding the empty counter. Upon which her bestie replied that people now a days are concerned about high returns and growth for which they are into capital markets and investments. So, fixed deposit and other conventional saving avenues are no longer an option for them. This made Stella even more curious and she made up her mind to explore investment and its traditional and behavioural theories not as tax saving or wealth maximization means but as a profession in near future and assist people in realizing their financial goals in life. Therefore, she decided on naming her business venture "Fortune Investments and Assets".

Competition in the Indian Investment Market

Though the investment market in India is risky, volatile, and highly regulated, numerous new players have entered into the market with new age financial products. In addition, novel financial models and technology using AI have been an area of interest for many into investments particularly, Gen X. Indian capital markets can be among the top 3 in the world in future with the kind of growth and enthusiasm it is witnessing (Rakesh Jhunjhunwala, 2017).

An impressive increase in domestic investments has been the catalyst behind the globally appreciated Indian growth story. While India has the 6th largest capital markets and the 5th largest economy in the world, the percentage of investors with respect to total population is 5.5% (77 million Indians are investors) by August 2022, still lower than other major world economies like USA (45.2%), China, Japan, Germany, UK, etc. As per predictions by the International Monetary Fund (IMF) and World Bank (WB), Indian economy grew at 7% in 2022 and will continue to grow at the same rate with India overtaking Japan as the 3rd largest economy in the world in 2028. Indian capital markets also grew at a rate of 13.5% in 2022 and will continue to grow at the same rate with India moving to the 3rd spot globally. Therefore, the investment market in India is experiencing rapid growth in case of established companies and start-ups who are able to achieve their funding and incubation targets. Many players have been in this market since 2008. For eg: Groww, Fidelity, Oswal, etc. Fortune Investments and Assets had to compete with these star firms with added novelty to it in order to differentiate itself from the rest of the lot.

Beginning of Fortune Investments and Assets

The first concern for Stella was gathering minimum funds required to be able to start her investment firm. She had her savings but putting them all into the venture was not an option as she had her own personal liabilities. So, she decided to put a part of her savings into the venture and borrow money from family and friends. Her father, uncles, and aunts mostly being retirees had their own limitations but still lent Stella a considerable amount to rent out an office space at the posh Koramangala area of Bangalore city and get its interiors done. With her part of the funds, Stella hired a business manager and a few employees to manage her clients and office. She then thought it was a good idea to talk to her bestie as she was a banker and had ultra-high net worth individuals as her clients. Stella spoke to her and offered her stake in Fortune in return. Her bestie agreed and spoke to few of her close clients on her behalf. One of them, Mr. Kamal Gowda, who was a multi-billionaire businessman and an angel investor agreed to fund the seed capital for Fortune. He met Stella and was extremely impressed by her business ideas and enthusiasm. He offered USD5 million as seed capital which was huge for Stella and Fortune. Stella had an elaborate discussion with her CA. She even gave a serious thought to all the cognitive biases she had learnt about. It was important for she could not afford to lose Mr. Gowda's money, his association, and business. Mr. Gowda as her business investor positioned Fortune in the market and got her many new high-profile clients. Fortune Assets and Investments started growing and Stella decided to set up another office in Mumbai, the financial capital of South Asia, in 2019. This rapid business expansion gave her satisfaction and anxiety at the same time. The thoughts which she initially had in her mind while investing her own hard-earned money became more pervasive. They started haunting her day and night as Fortune now involved not just her hard-earned money but her clients' too. Moreover, Fortune's failure meant her career being over and Mr. Gowda's reputation being jeopardized.

Expanding Fortune Pan-India, Cognitive Biases Experienced, and the Advent of the COVID-19 Pandemic

Stella was confident that if they do not have at least 1,000 clients in total with 500 ultra-high net worth clients and investments worth USD100 million then, Fortune cannot be a success. Now, the firm had 400 clients with 100 of them being ultra-high net worth clients. Stella had the challenge to achieve the determined target. She also had plans to open offices in other Indian metropolis like Delhi, Hyderabad,

Chennai, Ahmedabad, and Kolkata. Once, the scope of the business covered all the Tier-1 cities in the country, she would then focus on upcoming Tier-2 cities like Chandigarh, Bhubaneswar, Indore, Jaipur, Surat, Baroda, etc. Competition was even fierce in the BFSI sector. Fortune had to compete with not just start ups like itself but established players like ICICI Securities, Hdfc Securities, SBI Securities, etc. Under this situation, it became inevitable for Fortune to retain its current market share as well as expand it. However, the expansion comes with additional CapEx investment to ensure that the scaling up remains smooth. Stella knew that she had to build a robust and smooth system to ensure that all the business units and processes are in place. She was also aware that investment start-ups like Groww, Stok, etc that have been operating prior to Fortune are not yet profitable despite massive funding and novel technology. She had to be extremely meticulous while preparing her business expansion plan.

To add to her contingencies and anxiety that she already had was the advent pf Covid-19 pandemic in India in January 2020. Human life was significantly disturbed by the outbreak of the highly infectious Covid-19 pandemic. Social distancing, self-isolation, shutting down of institutions and establishments, restricting modes of transport, and nation-wide lockdowns were adapted as measure to combat the pandemic. This had a long-lasting impact on economic activity around the globe. The first COVID-19 positive case in India was registered on 30th January 2020 and then there was continuous increase in number of cases across the country. The Government of India declared a three weeklong country-wide lockdown to restrict the number of cases due to the contagious nature of the virus on 25th March,2020. Educational institutions, offices, public and tourist places, public utilities, religious places, and non-essential businesses and services were instructed to remain shut during the specified time period. Transportation was also restricted. The lockdown was further extended in a phased manner and continued till 31st May and then, services were restored in steadily. This caused economic slowdown in the country and resulted in millions of lay-offs, and businesses were worst hit. The Covid-19 economic slowdown and subsequent recession can be compared with the liquidity crisis of 2008 (Kenourgios et al. 2011; Bekiros, 2014; Luchtenberg & Vu, 2015; Yarovaya et al., 2016). The COVID-19 pandemic has triggered systematic risk and its impact on financial transactions demands extensive study. The five unique stages of global economic and financial crisis: 1) the beginning of the subprime mortgage disaster; 2) the expansion of credit risk with mounting losses of financial institutions; 3) liquidity crunch; 4) the commodity price bubble; and 5) the ultimate freeze of credit markets (Orlweski, 2008). Extensive literature is available to study the causes and consequences of the financial crisis on housing and securities markets, corporate investment decisions, financial institutions, bank lending, financial regulations and institutional investors. Significant research attention has also been paid to the effects of the COVID-19 pandemic on gold prices, crude oil prices, cryptocurrencies and market indices. However, the influence of the COVID-19 on individual investor behaviour is an area that remains relatively under-examined. At the time of crisis, investors are susceptible to sensational and surprising news (Dzielinski, 2011). An information overload may hinder intelligent decision-making and curb individual investor trading activity during a crisis (Agnew and Szykman, 2005).

Future Prospects and Challenges for Fortune

With an elaborate business expansion plan and various other opportunities available, it is always prudent to base one's plan for the future on the situation and challenges a business is facing or is being forecasted to come across in near future (Dickson et.al, 2020). Stella had ambitious expansion plans and vision for Fortune. She wanted Fortune to penetrate large and medium sized markets across India, get latest and unique technology and products into the business, and make a mark in the field of investments as an investor and entrepreneur.

Covid-19 pandemic was a challenge for all kinds of business in India and the world with Fortune being no exception. But cognitive biases resulting in irrational financial decision making was a bigger and more complex challenge. She had to decode the biases affecting her financial decisions in particular and her clients or potential investors in general to be able to make a solid business plan for Fortune's bright future. She had to take all her stakeholders into confidence in the process too for she is even answerable to them while accurately reporting the details of her business.

Cognitive Biases Pursued by Stella

Stella prepared a questionnaire consisting of all possible questions on cognitive biases influencing investor behaviour using a 5-point Lickert scale where 0 represented the least and 5 the most. She filled it up and circulated it among clients, other investors, family and friends to which she got an overwhelming response. She then used various statistical tools to boil down to a few specific cognitive biases significantly affecting investors' decision-making process.

TEACHING NOTES

Synopsis

Fortune was a start-up that was established in the year 2018 by Stella D'Souza in Bangalore, India. Stella realized the importance of financial literacy and investments. She made it a point to educate herself regarding it and plan her tax and retirement corpus accordingly. Soon, she came across various thoughts and biases while investing her hard-earned money and ascertained that theoretical finance is not enough to make prudent financial decisions. Behavioural finance plays an equally important role in the process. She also decided to start Fortune Assets and Investments, her business venture through which she could educate people on investments and help them make a fortune out of their income by making wise financial decisions and enhancing their financial literacy. She pooled in money from her savings, friends, and family to set up the first office in Bangalore and hire a business manager. She then got Mr. Gowda on board who helped her with funds and clients. Stella set up another office in Mumbai, hired more employees, made further plans of business expansion for Fortune and was determined to build a robust system to put each of the processes and business units in place. As her business was expanding her anxiety was even increasing day by day as enormous amount of money and her reputation were at stake. Fortune's failure would break her career and sabotage Mr. Gowda's credibility in the society. She had also left her stable corporate job for the sake of this business venture and had additional responsibilities at home. To add to her anxiety, came the Covid-19 pandemic that changed the entire societal and economic dynamics in India and the world. This case study discusses the influence of cognitive factors on investors' financial behaviour.

Case Objectives

- To help students understand the concept of various cognitive biases.
- To explain the significance of Behavioural Finance in decision making among investors.
- To understand the various challenges faced by investors and entrepreneurs while making investments and business expansions.
- To help students gain insights of strategies that can be framed by start-up founders considering the various socio-economic situations like Covid-19 and cognitive biases.

Position in the Course

This case can be studied by under-graduate (final semester) and post-graduate students (second semester). It can also be used in programmes conducted for investors and entrepreneurs.

Suggested Pre-Readings

Students can read the following articles to get some understanding of different types of cognitive biases, their influence on investors' behaviour, and the concept of Behavioural Finance.

- Shah, S. F., Alshurideh, M., Dmour, A., & Al-Dmour, R. (2021). *Understanding the Influences of Cognitive Biases on Financial Decision Making During Normal and COVID-19 Pandemic Situation in the United Arab Emirates*. 10.1007/978-3-030-67151-8_15.
- Mohanty, Patnaik, Satpathy, & Sahoo. (2022). A Study on Cognitive Factors Affecting Decision-Making of Investors during Covid-19. *Universal Journal of Accounting and Finance, 10*(3), 635-642. DOI: 10.13189/ujaf.2022.100301
- Chang, C.-H. (2008). The impact of behavioral pitfalls on investors' decisions: The disposition effect in the Taiwanese warrant market. *Social Behavior and Personality: An International Journal, 36*(5), 617-634.
- Chaudhary. (2013). Impact of behavioral finance in investment decisions and strategies–a fresh approach. *International Journal of Management Research and Business Strategy, 2*(2), 85-92.
- Speidell. (2009). Investing in the unknown and the unknowable—Behavioral finance in frontier markets. *The Journal of Behavioral Finance, 10*(1), 1-8.

Teaching Plan

The case can be presented in the class along with other suggested materials relevant to the subject that will be explained subsequently. In the class, a quick survey of the class members can be conducted on the following questions and the responses can be recorded.

Suggested Teaching Plan

The below plan, Exhibit 1, can be used by the trainer to conduct a 90 minutes class on this case study.

Table 1. Suggested time plan

Exhibit 1: Suggested Time Plan	
Initial Survey – Influence of cognitive factors on investors' behaviour during Covid-19	10 minutes
Split Class into 5 groups – allocate one question to each group to brainstorm	5 minutes
Group Analysis	15 minutes
Discussion on Statistical Analysis	10 minutes
How does situation enhance cognitive bias and impact business strategy	10 minutes
Concept of various cognitive biases	10 minutes
Need of Behavioral Finance	10 minutes
Future challenges to expect	10 minutes
Wrap-up	10 minutes
Source: Author's Analysis	

Question: Should Stella and other investors take cognitive biases and COVID-19 pandemic seriously and make financial decisions and business expansion plans accordingly? Raise your hands if you feel 'Yes'.

The trainer can explain the need to understand the concept of cognitive factors and Covid-19 pandemic for financial decision-making and business expansion plans as follows:

Need for Behavioural Finance

Investors scout for opportunities in various sectors to construct optimal portfolios. Therefore, they tend to be careful and invest in a planned manner to earn decent profits in competitive markets. Their behavior towards investment is either rational or irrational, depending on the school of thought followed. Financial theories cannot explain investors' aberrations when making investment decisions (Chang et.al.,2008). Hence, equal attention may be paid to behavioral finance. Behavioral finance is a sub-vertical of behavioral economics which explains that psychological biases and factors affect the financial decision-making of investors and analysts. Moreover, these factors and biases may result in the extensive impact on all kinds of market abnormalities, particularly in the stock market, like drastic fluctuations in stock prices. As Behavioural Finance is an inalienable part of investment and its decision-making process, the Securities and Exchange Board of India (SEBI) has a distinct Behavioural Finance team. Cognitive biases have a profound impact on financial behavior and decisions (Chaudhary.,2013). Hence, this study attempts to explore cognitive biases and financial decisions within the limits of Covid-19.

Fortunately, Stella discovered the world of Behavioural Finance and cognitive biases at a very early stage in her life and career. She had the benefit of time and could explore the entire field to be able to educate herself, her family, friends, and clients regarding it. Secondly, Austrian school of strategy postulates that innovation is the right strategy in the context of growing in an uncertain market (Jacobson, 1992). There is a high potential for service and technology innovation in the context of Fortune during the Covid-19. The implementation of service and technology innovation can help new ventures to gain profitable market share in the dynamic yet uncertain business environment amidst the pandemic. Thirdly, by investing in adaptive capabilities, new ventures can compete with existing players and protect themselves against future losses due to external environment changes. With this theoretical background, it is evident that Stella must continue with her expansion journey. In the process, she should also be aware of the challenges mentioned above while expanding Fortune operations.

Suggested Questions for Discussion

The instructor can then use the following set of questions to discuss on the case in the classroom. If required, the instructor can also divide the classroom into five groups, give one question to each group, and have the groups find a solution to the question assigned. Each group can then present their analysis to the rest of the class. The instructor can then wrap up the session based on the answers given below to present any missed-out points. A sample teaching plan with suggested timelines is also shown towards the end of this teaching note if the instructor wants to use this approach.

Q- What statistical methods can be used to identify significant cognitive biases and their impact on Stella and other investors' financial behaviour during Covid-19?

A- *Stella should study all the aspects of Behavioural Finance and cognitive biases sincerely. This won't only help educate her in the field of investments and expand her business but also educate her clients, family, and friends through her knowledge and research.*

Statistical methods that can be used to identify significant cognitive biases and their impact on Stella and other investors' financial behaviour during Covid-19 are:

- **Factor analysis**
- **Reliability test**
- Co-relation
- Multiple Regression

Q- What are the advantages and disadvantages of Behavioural Finance?
A- The advantages that arise because of using Behavioural Finance to make investment decisions are:

- **Wealth Is a Decision-Making Function:** A lot of investors are skeptical about making wealth in capital markets as they lack financial literacy and required qualifications. Many of them do not belong to finance and economics background and happen to be doctors, engineers who are very highly skilled with respect to their own line of work. Therefore, making investment decisions is not a choice for them. Behavioral finance focuses on success that comes from emotional management in the capital markets rather than having traditional financial knowledge. This is why even financial analysts are generally not very successful in capital markets but relatively unskilled investors make more money.
- **Theory vs. Application:** Traditional finance deals with the theoretical view of stock market operations. People trained in traditional finance can analyze data on the basis of mathematical models

and predict markets to function accordingly. But, as a matter of fact, markets are not always efficient contrary to the efficient market hypothesis that rules all the mathematical models. This results in market participants and investors behaving irrationally to a certain extent and subsequently, inefficiency is relevant in the market. Study of behavioral finance enables investors to highlight other investors' irrationality and to avoid mistakes while investing.

- **Asset Bubbles Description:** Traditional finance does not explain asset bubbles concept. If at all efficient market hypothesis is correct always, then why irrationality is witnessed in investor behaviour? Behavioral finance focuses on the fact this disparity and tries to fill up the gap. This gives rise to asset bubble by giving way to herd behaviour among investors.
- **Creates Trading Opportunities:** If the study of Behavioural Finance is not made common among investors, they will follow the accepted market conventions and make mistakes. Investors with knowledge of behavioral finance are able to segregate the truly catastrophic events from overreactions in the market. Therefore, investors are able to identify buying and selling opportunities in the market and create more wealth for themselves.
- **Creation of Patterns:** Study of behavioral finance helps market participants to maintain certain predictable patterns as they are driven by emotions. Behavioral investors often use technical analysis and methodologies to identify these patterns. Once the patterns re-iterate themselves, investors capitalize on them and create wealth.
- **Helps Understand the Concept of Time Horizon:** Behavioural Finance explains that investors behave as per the situation they are put into. A young person takes higher and more frequent risks than an older person. While, older people have a selling tendency once the stock prices drop.

Some of the main limitations are as follows:

- **Alternatives Are Not Available:** Behavioral finance is fills up the gap left behind by traditional finance. It addresses the irrationality in investors' behaviour that is often witnessed in the capital markets. But, it does not give a solution to the irrationality among investors. Behavioural Finance theories are not well developed in this sense. Hence, Behavioural Finance is not reliable.
    - **Confidence Is Reduced:** Another prominent issue in case of Behavioural Finance is that it is responsible for reducing confidence of market participants. This happens as investors start questioning themselves at every step. Every bit of knowledge and belief appears as a bias to them. Hence, they lack confidence.
- **Contradictory Inferences:** Behavioural finance makes contradictory inferences and conclusions very often. Using one Behavioural Finance theory one can conclude that the investors have a risk aversion tendency while another theory can prove them to be overconfident. This aspect of Behavioural Finance confuses researchers, analysts, and investors in the capital markets.
- **Not Relevant to Institutional Investors:** Cognitive factors studied in Behavioural Finance are only limited to individual investors and not applicable on their institutional counterparts. Therefore, they cannot be completely applied on capital markets as a whole for institutional investors constitute majority of the capital market participants.
- **Does Not Consider Social Status:** Behavioural Finance does not explain the social status of investors based on which they behave and invest. Certain investments are made by investors to enhance their social status. Eg: Gold, Real Estate, Diamond and precious stones,etc.

- **Does Not Value Emotions:** Behavioural Finance does not consider human emotions the way they should be and declares them as cognitive biases. Emotions are useful at times as they bring solution the chaos in the capital markets and human mind. Investors should realize that emotions are important and should use them wisely while making investments.

Q-What are the most common cognitive biases Stella would face while investing and expanding her business during Covid-19?

A-The most common cognitive biases Stella would face while investing and expanding her business during Covid-19 are:

1. Confirmation bias

Confirmation bias refers to the tendency of a human being to search for information that reassures an already given conclusion or hypothesis. Confirmation bias generally leads to wrong decisions as data available at the disposal of an investor may not always complement a foreseen situation. This can lead to false reassurance that data can always predict the trend or pattern followed by stock prices in the capital markets.

2. Hindsight bias

Hindsight bias is a human tendency that considers positive milestone events in the past as predictable and negative milestone as not predictable. Investors often follow capital markets milestones, both positive and negative, to make investment decisions in the process and they turn out to be wrong then they blame past vents or capital market anomalies.

3. Anchoring bias

Anchoring bias refers to the human tendency of making an anchor the basis of all the future investment decisions. This anchor can be anything- any past event or new piece of information, etc. Many a times, past experiences or events or any new piece of information leads to aberration in investors' behaviour and faulty decision-making as capital markets are unpredictable. Therefore, past events do not necessarily repeat themselves and new information does not always complement the situation in near future.

4. Recency bias

Recency bias occurs when investors change their initial beliefs and make subsequent decisions based on new information at their disposal. This is the change in the financial behavior and decisions of an investor when the initial belief is changed by new information. Recency bias attracts investors' attention to the latest information. The sequential presentation of information leads to recency bias among investors and affects their financial decisions. Investors also showcase changes in behavior and financial decisions based on the training and knowledge they obtain. Behavioral changes have been observed in knowledgeable and trained investors. It exists in financial markets and is highly influential on investors' decision-making processes. It has a substantial impact on investors' financial decision-making processes.

5. Familiarity bias

Investors exhibit familiarity bias when they choose stocks of acquainted companies. It exists among investors and affects their financial decisions when buying stocks in the market. It is prevalent among investors and influences their financial decision-making processes, as evidence indicates that familiar investments are preferred by them. Geographical location and gender also lead to familiarity bias and its impact on investors' financial decisions. It is highest in the USA and lowest in Asia. Researchers found financial decision familiarity bias among American investors and U. S-grown companies. The researchers identified that familiarity bias significantly affects investors' financial decisions in Egyptian markets. Familiarity bias has a negligible impact on the decision-making process of investors in European capital markets. Familiarity bias has a substantial impact on the financial behavior and decisions of investors in the US and Canadian capital markets. Familiarity bias is found among employees in the financial service sector and positively affects their investment decisions. Familiarity bias leads to employees prioritizing their own company or sector while making financial decisions.

6. Overconfidence bias

Overconfidence bias is a tendency because of which investors are overconfident with regard to certain data based on which they make investment decisions and do not re-affirm it. It has a significant effect on investors' financial decisions but is limited by hindsight bias, moderated by financial literacy and mediated by risk perception. Overtrading and overconfidence are based on geography and determine investor behavior and financial decisions in U.S., Abu Dhabi, and Indian capital markets. It also affects investors' financial decisions both positively and negatively based on their market situation.

Q-How can Stella deal with Covid-19 economic crisis situation?
A-The general is to delay expansion plans in case of adversity until the situation normalizes; deducting unnecessary expenditures that can be done anytime in future like R&D, client and employee entertainment, marketing, and employee training; freezing new hiring; and reducing headcounts. But these attempts are not always good enough for the business as it may be hit hard. Keeping calm and framing novel strategies can help in better business expansion and investment in near future. Managers can benefit from and even plan for growth in this mercurial environment using the following methodologies:

1. Study success cases.

There is exemplary growth and prosperity that is witnessed after a recession which is mostly short-lived. For example: WW II was followed by the fastest global economic growth in the history of modern times. The world economy also experienced similar trends after the OPEC oil embargo recession (1973 to 1975), the energy crisis recession (1981 to 1982), the Gulf War recession (1990 to 1991), the dotcom bust (2000 to 2002), and the Great Recession (2008 to 2009). The economic and financial expansion after each of these recessions have been recorded as milestones in world modern history.

Recessions allow us the chance to recognize winners and separate them from the rest of the lot. It is like separating wheat from chaff or clear the flour using a sieve. For example: the dotcom boom saw a massive number of companies going IPO and most of them were new-age companies with novel ideas like Shaadi.com, Pets.com, etc. These business entities were expanding while implementing new entrepreneurial ideas and experimenting. A record number of companies were listed at the stock exchange and went IPO, to the tune of 7,400, by 1997. The dotcom boom also resulted in the bankruptcies and de-listings of many business firms at the stock exchange for they were not able to cope up with new technologies and market trends, and the ones that were able to overcome it are today the largest companies on earth that have created massive wealth for themselves and their investors in the past century (for example, Facebook, Apple, Amazon, Netflix, Nvidia, Google, and Microsoft).So, despite cognitive challenges and Covid-19 pandemic, Stella should not give up on her business expansion and investment plans. If she strategizes her moves well, then she can emerge as a winner and take Fortune to new heights when compared to her peers. Intensive case study and success stories are the points from which she can begin with.

2. Expand while competitors are cutting back.

When during recession, all her competitors are cutting down on business plans and costs, Stella can focus on business expansion and strategies by incorporating new resources into the business. One of the most prominent resources is talent that is widely available in the market due to job cuts and hiring freeze by competitors. With deduction in R&D and new projects, reduce headcounts, and cut down employee salaries and bonuses and as declining stock prices pull stock options under the water, talent in the market look for stable jobs with cash rich companies over start-ups and fin-techs. Stella can also focus on creating assets for Fortune by buying failed businesses and other assets at auctions where they are sold at dirt cheap rates. For example: During the liquidity crisis of 2008, prominent technology firms created a lot of assets. Moreover, as competitors reduce their customer service, Stella can also focus on acquiring their dissatisfied customers and increase Fortune's market share.

3. Accelerate digital transformation.

The reduction in the stock prices of digitally enabled firms does not mean digital revolution has ended. Proper digital strategies incorporated with business processes enabled many corporates to run their operations the way they did in pre-Covid-19 times. Well established digital strategies come with advantages like being well documented, improved visibility of resources that results in better resource management, enhanced flexibility and organization agility, lower costs, smoother supply chain management, better customer experience, improved productivity, faster product development, and superior human resource planning. Decline in the stock prices of digital companies does not mean these advantages are mitigated. Hence, digital transformation should not be overlooked and should be strategized over to act as catalyst in business expansion and investments. With lockdowns and social distancing Covid-19 pandemic threw challenges that could only be solved through digital transformation. For example: Retail companies are facing tough challenges like supply chain issues with decrease in revenue and increase in costs due to Covid-19. Digital transformation may either reduce issues being faced by companies or eliminate them completely. For instance, AI can help retail firms in identifying shopping patterns, understanding buying behaviors, adjusting promotions and special offers, personalizing product recommendations, tweaking prices if needed, and balancing supply with fluctuating demand and customer tastes and preferences.

4. By studying investor behaviour.

An intensive study of Behavioural Finance would help Stella get acquainted with investors' behaviour in India during Covid-19 Pandemic. This even includes herself, her clients, and potential clients. She can even conduct a demographic analysis of her current and potential clients, and other investors for factors like age, gender, income, qualification, etc also play a major role in cognitive biases influencing investor behaviour.

What Happened?

Stella studied Behavioural Finance and mastered the concepts of cognitive biases and their influence on investors decision making. She trained herself accordingly and also focused on new age technologies, digitization, and hiring best talent in the market, Covid-19 scenario and its impact on the Indian economy and business operations, and made plans for the expansion of Fortune.

REFERENCES

Ahmad, M., & Shah, S Z A. (2020). Overconfidence heuristic-driven bias in investment decision-making and performance: mediating effects of risk perception and moderating effects of financial literacy. *Journal of Economic and Administrative Sciences*.

Alvia, L., & Sulistiawan, S. (2010). The examination of recency and knowledge effect in investment decision making: An experimental study. *Indonesian Journal of Accounting Research*, *13*(1), 45–58.

Aprayuda R, Misra F, Kartika R. (2021). Does the Order of Information Affect Investors and Investment Decisions? *Experimental Investigation, Journal of Accounting and Investment, 22*(1).

Baack, D. W., Dow, D., Parente, R., & Bacon, D. R. (2015). Confirmation bias in individual-level perceptions of psychic distance: An experimental investigation. *Journal of International Business Studies*, *46*(8), 938–959. doi:10.1057/jibs.2015.19

Baker, H. K., & Nofsinger, J. R. (2002). Psychological biases of investors. *Financial Services Review*, *11*(2), 97.

Baker, H. K., & Ricciardi, V. (2014). How biases affect investor behavior. *The European Financial Review*, 7–10.

BansalT. (2020). Behavioral finance and COVID-19: cognitive errors that determine the financial future. SSRN. doi:10.2139/ssrn.3595749

Bashir, T., Mehmood, F., & Khan, A. (2019). *Comforting Investments are Rarely Profitable: Impediments in Investor Decision Making*. Global Social Sciences Review.

Bashir, T., Rasheed, S., Raftar, S., & Fatima, S., & Maqsood, S. (2013). Impact of behavioral biases on investor decision making: Male vs female. *Journal of Business and Management*, *10*(3), 60–68.

BatesA. N. (2020). Investor Behavior in the Midst of a Global Pandemic. SSRN.

Cao, H. H., Han, B., Hirshleifer, S., & Zhang, H. H. (2011). Fear of the unknown: Familiarity and economic decisions. *Review of Finance, 15*(1), 173–206. doi:10.1093/rof/rfp023

Chang, C.-H. (2008). The impact of behavioral pitfalls on investors' decisions: The disposition effect in the Taiwanese warrant market. *Social Behavior and Personality, 36*(5), 617–634. doi:10.2224bp.2008.36.5.617

Chaudhary, A. K. (2013). Impact of behavioral finance in investment decisions and strategies–a fresh approach. *International Journal of Management Research and Business Strategy, 2*(2), 85-92.

Chen, M., Cheng, H., Du, Y., Xu, M., Jiang, W., & Wang, C. (2021). *Two Wrongs Don't Make a Right: Combating Confirmation Bias in Learning with Label Noise*. Academic Press.

Corzo, T., Prat, M., & Vaquero, E. (2014). Vaquero E, Behavioral Finance in Joseph de la Vega's Confusion de Confusiones. *Journal of Behavioral Finance, 15*(4), 341–350. doi:10.1080/15427560.2014.968722

Čuláková, T., Kotrus, P., Uhlírová, A., & Jirásek, M. (2017). *The overconfidence bias and CEO: A literature overview*. Academic Press.

Dilla, W., & Steinbart, P. J. (2005). Relative Weighting of Common and Unique Balanced Scorecard Measures by Knowledgeable Decision Makers. *Behavioral Research in Accounting, 17*(1), 43–53. doi:10.2308/bria.2005.17.1.43

Faisal, S., Shurideh, A., Dmour, A. S., & Al-Dmour, R. (2021). *Understanding the Influences of Cognitive Biases on Financial Decision Making During Normal and COVID-19 Pandemic Situation in the United Arab Emirates*. Academic Press.

Hartono, J. (2004). The recency effect of accounting information. *Gadjah Mada International Journal of Business, 6*(1), 85–116. doi:10.22146/gamaijb.5536

Henseler, J., Ringle, C. M., & Sarstedt, M. (2015). A new criterion for assessing discriminant validity in variance-based structural equation modeling. *Journal of the Academy of Marketing Science, 43*(1), 115–135. doi:10.100711747-014-0403-8

Hogarth, R. M., & Einhorn, H. J. (1992). Order effects in belief updating: The belief-adjustment model. *Cognitive Psychology, 24*(1), 1–55. doi:10.1016/0010-0285(92)90002-J

Huang, H. H., Hsu, J., & Ku, C.-Y. (2012). Understanding the role of computer-mediated counter-argument in countering confirmation bias. *Decision Support Systems, 53*(3), 438–447. doi:10.1016/j.dss.2012.03.009

Kafayat, A. (2014). Interrelationship of biases: effect investment decisions ultimately. *Theoretical and Applied Economics, Asociatia Generala a Economistilor din Romania-AGER, 6*(595), 85-110.

Kalm, K., & Norris, D. (2018). Visual recency bias is explained by a mixture model of internal representations. *Journal of Vision (Charlottesville, Va.), 18*(7), 1. doi:10.1167/18.7.1 PMID:29971347

Kwatra. (2020). Behavioral Finance and Stock Performance: Biases Influencing the Market. *IOSR Journal of Humanities And Social Science, 25*(7), 66-69.

Lathe, A. S., Jain, S., & Anand, S. (2020). An Empirical Examination of the Impact of Locus of Control on Investor Behavioral Biases. *International Journal of Management, 11*(1), 98–107.

Levy, D. S., Frethey-Bentham, C., & Cheung, W. K. S. (2020). Asymmetric framing effects and market familiarity: Experimental evidence from the real estate market. *Journal of Property Research*, *37*(1), 85–104. doi:10.1080/09599916.2020.1713858

Luu, T. B. (2014). Behavior Pattern of Individual Investors in Stock Market. *International Journal of Business and Management*, *9*(1), 1–16.

McAndrews. (2017). *How Familiarity Bias May Impact Your Investment Decision-Making*. WrapManager.

Metawa, N., Hassan, M. K., Metawa, S., & Safa, M. F. (2019). Impact of behavioral factors on investors' financial decisions: case of the Egyptian stock market. *International Journal of Islamic and Middle Eastern Finance and Management*.

Nasution, S. (2017). Effect of Evidence Order, the Cognitive Style and Personality of the Revision Process Confidence. *Accounting National Symposium X*.

Nelson, J. A. (2014). The power of stereotyping and confirmation bias to overwhelm accurate assessment: The case of economics, gender, and risk aversion. *Journal of Economic Methodology*, *21*(3), 211–231. doi:10.1080/1350178X.2014.939691

Nickerson, R. S. (1998). Confirmation Bias: A Ubiquitous Phenomenon in Many Guises. *Review of General Psychology*, *2*(2), 175–220. doi:10.1037/1089-2680.2.2.175

Onsomu, Z. N. (2014). The impact of Behavioral biases on investor decisions in Kenya: Male vs Female. *Impact Journals*, *2*(6), 87–92.

Park, J., Konana, P., Gu, B., Kumar, A., & Raghunathan, R. (2010). Confirmation bias, overconfidence, and investment performance: Evidence from stock message boards. *McCombs Research Paper Series, 7*(10).

Patni, I., & Choubey, S. (2019). Behavioral Traits and Investment Decisions: An Empirical Study on Executives of Financial Service Sector. *International Journal of Recent Technology and Engineering, 7*.

Putri, M. D. P. W., Xu, C., & Akwetteh, L. N. (2020). Financial Behavior during COVID-19: Cognitive Errors That Can Define Financial Future. *Open Journal of Social Sciences*, *8*(10), 259–269. doi:10.4236/jss.2020.810017

Qadri, S. U., & Shabbir, M. (2004). An empirical study of overconfidence and illusion of control biases Impact on investor's decision making: An evidence from ISE. *European Journal of Business and Management*, *6*(14), 38–44.

Qasim, M., Hussain, R., Mehboob, I., & Arsha, M. (2017). Impact of herding behavior and overconfidence bias on investors' decision-making in Pakistan. *Accounting*, 81-90.

Rangaswamy, U. M. (2021). Chai Thela: The Might "Tea" Problem of Start-up Expansion. *South Asian Journal of Management*, *28*(1).

Sadi, R., Asl, H. G., Rostami, M. R., Gholipour, A., & Gholipour, F. (2011). Behavioral finance: The explanation of investors' personality and perceptual biases effects on financial decisions. *International Journal of Economics and Finance*, *3*(5), 234–241. doi:10.5539/ijef.v3n5p234

Speidell, L. S. (2009). Investing in the unknown and the unknowable—Behavioral finance in frontier markets. *Journal of Behavioral Finance*, *10*(1), 1–8. doi:10.1080/15427560902719323

Trehan, T., & Sinha, A. K. (2021). A study of confirmation bias among online investors in virtual communities. *International Journal of Electronic Finance*, *10*(3), 159–179. doi:10.1504/IJEF.2021.115647

Von Bergen, C W., & Bressler. (2018). Confirmation bias in entrepreneurship. *Journal of Management Policy and Practice*, *19*(3), 74–84.

Vries, A. D., Erasmus, P. D., & Gerber, C. (2017). The familiar versus the unfamiliar: Familiarity bias amongst individual investors. *Acta Commercii*, *17*(1), 1–10. doi:10.4102/ac.v17i1.366

Zahera, S. A., & Bansal, R. (2018). Do investors exhibit behavioral biases in investment decision making? A systematic review. *Qualitative Research in Financial Markets, 10*(2).

Zaleskiewicz, T., Gasiorowska, A., Stasiuk, K., Maksymiuk, R., & Bar-Tal, Y. (2017). Lay evaluation of financial experts: The action advice effect and confirmation bias. *Frontiers in Psychology*, *7*, 1476. PMID:27729892

Chapter 10
MobiKwik: Dealing With the Fallout From an Alleged Data Breach and Its Repercussions on Its Proposed IPO

Rajeev Sengupta
https://orcid.org/0000-0001-7451-239X
Dr. Vishwanath Karad MIT World Peace University, India

Ameya Anil Patil
Dr. Vishwanath Karad MIT World Peace University, India

Monica Apte
Dr. Vishwanath Karad MIT World Peace University, India

Sushil Nirbhavane
Dr. Vishwanath Karad MIT World Peace University, India

EXECUTIVE SUMMARY

Bipin Preet Singh and Upasana Taku, the power couple of the FinTech world, had sought to differentiate their wallet company by turning it into a microloan disbursement platform. Simultaneously, they had been extending the number of physical stores that accept MobiKwik payments. Mobikwik's image suffered a big blow in February 2021 when it was reported to have compromised the KYC details of over 3.5 million users, in addition to making personal details of 100 million phone users public, which landed the startup on the radar of the regulator Reserve Bank of India following an RTI (Right to Information Act 2005) petition. This also had an impact on its future IPO. The markets had not been receptive to FinTechs accessing capital markets, and its competitor company Paytm's IPO was a disaster. Crises planning and associated risk management was vital for MobiKwik. Was the response to the crises appropriate and effective? Bipin and Upasana were dealing with issues impacting their brand reputation and a possible fallout and impact on their upcoming IPO.

DOI: 10.4018/978-1-6684-8488-3.ch010

Bipin Preet Singh and Upasana Taku, the power couple of the Fintech[2] world had sought to differentiate their wallet company by turning it into a microloan disbursement platform. Simultaneously, they had been extending the number of physical stores that accept MobiKwik payments. There was already an agreement with leading retailers, as well as nearly 10,000 physical retail outlets. MobiKwik had granted shops access to its patent-pending Power Wallet functionality.

Mobikwik's image suffered a big blow in February 2021 when it was reported to have reportedly compromised the KYC[3] details of over 3.5 million users, in addition to making personal details of 100 million phone users public, which landed the startup on the radar of the regulator –Reserve Bank of India following an RTI[4] (Right to Information Act 2005) petition. This also had an impact on its future IPO. The markets had not been receptive to Fintechs accessing capital markets and its competitor company Paytm's[5] IPO was a disaster. Crises planning and associated risk management was vital for MobiKwik. Was the response to the crises appropriate and effective? Did they need to have a media action plan to allay and assuade apprehensions of the stakeholders? Bipin and Upasana were dealing with issues impacting their brand reputation and a possible fallout and impact on their upcoming IPO.

INTRODUCTION

The Digital Payments Ecosystem in India had seen a significant increase in traction, particularly in recent years. This could be attributed to the introduction of innovations such as UPI[6]. Indian Government's demonetization exercise of 2016 provided a major fillip to digital payments. India had seen a sharp increase in digital payments. Transactions rose thanks to many digital payment solutions, including UPI and Aadhaar[7]-enabled Payment Systems(AePS), from Rs 23.4 billion in 2019 to Rs 46.7 billion in July 2022. The payments ecosystem in India had changed as a result of advancements in payments infrastructure, changes in information and communications technology, a flexible regulatory framework, a supportive political climate, and a growing emphasis on customer-centricity. The subsequent growth was accelerated by the COVID 2019 pandemic and the new societal norms associated with the same wherein digital transactions increased as individuals switched to contactless payment options. Physical PoS[8] and QR[9] acceptance locations for digital payments in the country were on the rise. The payments industry's expansion had been the obvious outcome of this scenario. With the Indian government's push for better infrastructure, there had been a steady increase in procurement of POS devices. Growing Indian digital population is a harbinger of growth for the digital payments industry. The Indian Government's aim towards digital economy was also in accordance with its objectives to tackle black money and corruption in the country. In the Budget Speech, 2017, Finance Minister Arun Jaitley[10] had stated:

Dealing in cash currency had led to a lot of aberrations in terms of tax non-compliance, currency being used for collateral purposes like crime, escaping the tax net and not getting into the banking system.

LITERATURE REVIEW

We first look at the demonetization of Indian banknotes in 2016 as an external shock that encouraged people to move to digital payments. In an unplanned move on November 8, 2016, the Indian government demonetized the two biggest denomination banknotes in use (INR 500 and INR 1,000). This left the economy with a cash shortage. Overnight, 86% of the currency in use was deemed to be unreliable. Due to this, there were significantly more digital payments made using both cards and e-wallets (Agarwal et al., 2018a). Users of mobile phones can deposit, transfer, and withdraw money using mobile money without having a bank account. This differs from mobile banking, which enables consumers to access and manage their online banking accounts using their mobile devices. Telecommunications providers offer mobile banking, which enables users to pay with their SIM card directly. (Suri, 2017). The ability to use big data analytics and unstructured data to better forecast loan behaviour is one of the benefits of FinTech lenders. These details include "mobile footprints," which refer to the online habits of the households as observed through their mobile devices. Agarwal et al. (2020) found that the mobile footprint of an individual surpasses traditional credit bureau ratings in forecasting loan approvals and defaults using data from one of the largest FinTech lenders in India. utilising extensive digital data on the applicant's social connections or the kinds of programmes they utilise. Startups fail due to the longer time required to achieve a profitable position, high initial investment costs, a lack of understanding of the Indian consumer market, and a lack of understanding of logistics (Velayanikal, 2016)[10a].

Asides the numerous benefits bestowed by the tech revolution in the Fintech space, it has been fraught with its issues concerning data security and confidentiality. In public relations and other related periodicals, there seems to be little scientific research on data breach and cyber crisis management challenges. According to recent requests for study, the majority of studies come from publications relating to legal or technological issues. However, others may argue that the few studies discovered in journals related to communication imply there is some sign of interest in data breach research. Furthermore, there is a dearth of academic studies on data breaches in journals of public relations and other communications-related fields, according to the public relations research stream. While earlier studies (Kelly, 2005; Ramakrishna, 2012) tended to concentrate more on the legal or technological aspects of data breaches, little is known about how news media, as an intermediary public, interpret and report data breaches differently from corporate perspectives in determining the primary cause of the crisis. The definitions of a data breach, its detrimental effects on a firm experiencing a breach crisis, and acceptable templates for notifying customers about the data breach are all demonstrated by prior data breach studies. However, there is very little research on data breaches in the context of PR and crisis communication. This can further emphasize the need for a study of these issues, particularly from the standpoint of crisis response management.

MOBIKWIK – The Fintech Player

MobiKwik, headquartered in Gurgaon, was founded in 2009 as a mobile wallet company by the founders Bipin Preet Singh, Chandana Joshi and Upasana Taku. The company was in the business of Fintech and one of the major mobile wallets and Buy Now Pay Later (BNPL)[10] player in India. The company basically allowed a user to load money in a mobile wallet and make payments through this wallet, in a single-click.

Promoters of Mobikwik: Bipin Preet Singh, Upasana Rupkrishan Taku, Koshur Family Trust and Narinder Singh Family Trust.

The wallet could be used for online shopping, shopping at physical retail stores, food delivery, gas stations and pharmacies. The platform also supported peer-to-peer payments. As a digital payment company, MobiKwik had played an important role to address the credit requirements of the rapidly increasing online shoppers in India.

Competition Analysis

From 180 million in Fiscal 2018 to over 250 million in Fiscal 2021, India's online transacting users had increased at a CAGR of approximately 15%. However, as of March 31, 2021, India had only 30-35 million unique credit card users, resulting in a low credit card penetration of 3.5%. Furthermore, the online BNPL market in India has grown rapidly, reaching US$ 3-3.5 billion in disbursals in Fiscal 2021 and is expected to grow to US$ 45-50 billion by Fiscal 2026, driven by user growth.

Table 1. Competition analysis

S.No	Player	Company	Features, Charges, and AMC	Rating (Playstore)-2021
1	Google Play(G-Pay)	Google	Connects with Bank a/c, strong brand recall.	4.2/5
2	PhonePe	Flipkart	Over 100 mn downloads and strong brand recall.	4.3/5
3	Dhani	Indiabulls Ventures Limited	From the Indiabulls group	3.8/5
5	Paytm	One97 Communications	No onetime or recurring charges	4.6/5
6	MobiKwik	One MobiKwik Systems Private Limited	No wallet to wallet charges, 3.45% on bank transfers	3.9/5
7	Yono (by SBI)	State Bank of India	Strong brand name, Rs 1-2/transaction	3.4/5
9	HDFC PayZapp	HDFC Bank	Strong brand name,	3.9/5
10	Amazon Pay	Amazon	Late entrant but strong brand in BNPL. 1.95% per transaction	4.3/5
11	Freecharge	Snapdeal	5 mn userbase	4.3/5
12	AirtelMoney	Airtel	Telecom promoter.	4.1/5

Source: https://pmjandhanyojana.co.in/list-e-wallet-companies-india/

MobiKwik revenue stream

Like the other mobile wallet-based digital payments company, MobiKwik's business was based on P2P[11] transactions conducted through its app.

The company derived revenues through the commissions earned on each transaction, partnerships with businesses and the appropriate advertisements on its app. Additionally, the company also earned fee-based revenue via cross-selling of some financial products such as insurance and mutual fund.The founders and the leadership team had expanded the business exponentially and the company had over 3 million e-commerce, physical retail, and biller partners along with more than 101 million Registered Users. In FY 2021, the company's revenue crossed $ 40 billion (See Exhibit 1 and 2).

MobiKwik's funding:

A strong forward looking business model had helped the company to consistently raise huge funds since its inception. MobiKwik, till date, had accumulated funding of more than $ 200mn. On 12th October, 2021, it was was declared a unicorn12 after the end of the sale of the secondary ESOP round

.MobiKwik declared its intentions to get listed on the Indian stock exchanges . Accordingly, it even filed a DRHP13 with SEBI14, the Indian capital market regulator. The objectives behind IPO were two-fold, viz. repayment of company's debt and secondly, address the organic as well as inorganic growth initiatives. However, around this time, another fintech unicorn in digital payments, Paytm came up with its IPO. Paytm had a disastrous debut on stock markets and was on a falling spree thereafter. This news led to further re-thinking of MobiKwik IPO (See Exhibit 3)

The Crisis:

Early in March 2021, Internet Security Researcher Rajashekhar Rajaharia (Rajaharia) discovered the data leak. The researcher tweeted[15] on March 4, 2021, that a MobiKwik server had exposed data on 110 million Indians, including critical information. In a series of tweets, the researcher identified MobiKwik and added that the company's data had been compromised since January 2021. Rajaharia communicated with Jordandaven, a hacker[16], over Discorde on February 25, 2021. "The hacker omitted to mention the company's name. The hacker hid the identity of the company that had been compromised because he wanted to get rewarded. Later, he started sharing information as proof of the breach in a group he had founded on Discord. I assumed it belonged to MobiKwik based on his sample data" said Rajaharia.

MobiKwik, however, issued its first formal comment on March 4, 2021, rejecting the data leak and asserting that it was a regulated organisation that took the protection of its data very seriously and was completely compliant with all relevant data security legislation. The business said that it was looking into the data leak and that it was absolutely feasible for any user to have posted their information to several platforms. The company claims that it is false to imply that MobiKwik or any other known source was used to obtain the data that was made public on the dark web [17].

In addition, the business alleged that Rajaharia had damaged its reputation by fabricating a cybersecurity18 incident in order to garner media attention. "Over the past week, a media-obsessed so-called security researcher has regularly submitted fabricated files while frantically attempting to gain media attention, squandering valuable time from our organisation. We reviewed his claims in-depth and found no security flaws, the business said. According to reports, Rajaharia's Twitter account was suspended and only unlocked once he removed the alleged data breach tweet from MobiKwik. The business even threatened legal action against the researcher because it believed he was attempting to damage its reputation for personal gain. One section of MobiKwik's note sticks out since it tends to imply that consumers were partially at fault. "Some users claim that their information is accessible on the dark web. While we look into this, it's quite possible that a single individual posted information to several other platforms. Therefore, it is false to imply that MobiKwik or any other known source was used to obtain the data available on the dark web, according to the disclaimer (see Exhibit 6).

The allegations of a data breach at Mobikwik made by Rajaharia were, however, corroborated by other researchers. Elliot Alderson, a French security researcher, revealed screenshots of the MobiKwik breach on Twitter (Alderson). The "biggest KYC data dump in history," he referred to it as. The reported leak was also corroborated by independent Indian researcher Avinash Jain, who said, "Users' personal information may be viewed in plain text and is stored unsecurely on their systems. The attacker appears to have gained access to their cloud infrastructure and been able to access the data stores where this information was kept.

On March 29, 2021, the hacker proposed deleting all the data in exchange for MobiKwik officially acknowledging the data breach. He insisted that they had no other intentions with the money other than to receive it from the business.

In a new comment on Raid Forum[19] on 30th Mar'21, the hacker claimed that he had destroyed all data freely and had not stolen any money. "I've done this deletion myself and no foul play here. Now all of your data is secure with MobiKwik and no one misuse it except of course MobiKwik for targeted ads or call which everyone does anyway. We just don't want to see a company dig themselves deeper and bury themselves in. Guess we all learned some useful life lessons during this past couple of days. Adios," he posted.

The hacker said that his purpose was not to harm the company before its IPO, albeit he did not specify why he gave up his data. Prior to September 2021, MobiKwik planned to go public and hoped to raise between \$200 million and \$250 million. Some analysts claim that the data leak had major repercussions for both the corporation and its customers. According to them, the information exposed could be exploited for online crimes such as impersonation, bullying, targeted spam and phishing attempts, and more. The corporation tried to blame consumers instead of accepting responsibility for the leak, but experts pointed out that individuals had no control over data held on the server-side. Users were exposed because MobiKwik refused to accept any accountability. According to some cybersecurity experts, customers whose data was purportedly compromised had little choice except to change the passwords for all of their bank accounts or enable two-factor authentication in order to access their accounts. "Up to 100 Mn Mobikwik users have had their data leaked, but the IPO-bound fintech company has buried its head in the sand with denials. Besides ridiculing independent security researchers, Mobikwik CEO also shifted the blame on users, saying they could have themselves leaked the data. Like Mobikwik, Indian startups have a woeful track record in dealing with major cybersecurity incidents and this needs to change if India is to capitalise on the tech revolution"[12] said Nikhil Subramaniam, Senior Editor at Inc42 Media, an Indian media platform.

Numerous organisations asked CERT-In[20] to look into the situation after the data release. The CERT-In concluded that MobiKwik had committed a data breach throughout the course of its investigation, but the firm refuted the claims. Mobikwik acknowledged that a payment link created using their platform has been connected to an unlawful attempt to access its user-facing application programming interface. Mobikwik, however, asserted that the attempt had been thwarted. But CERT-In didn't change its mind. After that, CERT-In was instructed by the Reserve Bank of India (RBI)[21] to carry out a forensic data security audit and submit a report. It stated that MobiKwik would be subject to fines if any security flaws were discovered on its end. In this situation, the RBI had the right to fine a provider of payment systems a minimum of Rs 500,000. Rajaharia was also supported by the Internet Freedom Federation (IFF), which intervened and called for a policy change that would give legal protection to cyber security researchers who were threatened with legal action by businesses impacted by data leaks. In comparison to the first quarter of 2019, data breaches in India grew by 37% in 2020, with a minimum total cost of Rs. 140 million. The data protection laws

Data privacy laws govern how a person's personal information is acquired, managed, utilized, processed, and disseminated. Except in certain circumstances, federal laws in the United States do nothing to safeguard their citizens against the misuse of their data. Although the United States safeguards its citizens' data from misuse by companies and corporations to some extent, it also has some of the world's most intrusive monitoring laws. However, in India there was currently no explicit regulation governing data collection, storage, mining, and protection i.e data protection law had not seen the light of day as of 2021.

Founder's dilemma:

The company was one of the top providers in the digital payments industry and was in business expansion with the digital India transition. The company's brand image and client loyalty were at risk as a result of the data breach22 disaster (see Exhibit 7). Its IPO had to be postponed due to the data-breach issue and because of the adverse market conditions for tech companies, when it needed capital to explore both organic and inorganic growth prospects in the fast-changing fintech market. Should Bipin and Upasana continue to defend their stand on the breach? How should they allay the apprehensions of the stakeholders of the company? Should they adopt the Corporate Governance norm as was applicable to listed companies? What are the options available with Bipin and Upasana to ensure their proposed IPO receives the successful response from the market. Can they get this data breach behind them for good? These were some of the questions confronting the Founders alongwith the think tank at MobiKwik.

Questions:

1. Crises and communication are two sides of the same coin. Discuss the communication strategy adopted by MobiKwik post the alleged data breach? Critically evaluate MobiKwik's approach in the data breach episode.
2. What measures the company should take to ensure its brand image and customer trust remained intact?
3. How should MobiKwik plan its IPO in the wake of the debacle of Paytm IPO? Outline in light of the financials given in the case and the DRHP of MobiKwik.
4. Why are Personal Data Protection laws important and what should be the penal clauses for violation?

A data breach is a security violation, in which sensitive, protected or confidential data is copied, transmitted, viewed, stolen, altered or used by an individual unauthorized to do so.

https://www.trendmicro.com/vinfo/us/security/definition/data-breach

Exhibit 1: About MobiKwik
Exhibit 2: Leadership Team at MobiKwik and their compensation
Exhibit 3: Performance of Paytm IPO on NSE
Exhibit 4: MobiKwik User Growth (2016 to 2020)
Exhibit 5-Key Financial Highlights of MobiKwik as of FY 2020
Exhibit 6: Screenshots of MobiKwik's Data Leak Posted on the Dark Web
Exhibit 7: Some Major Data Breaches in India (2021)

SYNOPSIS

Bipin Preet Singh and Upasana Taku, the power couple of the Fintech world had sought to differentiate their wallet company by turning it into a microloan disbursement platform. Simultaneously, they had been extending the number of physical stores that accept MobiKwik payments. There was already an agreement with leading retailers, as well as nearly 10,000 physical retail outlets. MobiKwik had granted shops access to its patent-pending Power Wallet functionality.

Figure 1. About Mobikwik
Source: https://startuptalky.com/mobikwik/

Startup Name	MobiKwik
Headquarters	Gurgaon
Origin Country	India
Industry	Digital Wallet, Fintech
Founders	Bipin Preet Singh, Upasana Taku and Chandan Joshi
Founded	2009
Revenue	$39.98 million (Rs 302.25 in FY21)
Valuation	$1 billion+ (October 2021)
Total Funding	~ $213.94 Mn (August 2022)
Parent Organization	One MobiKwik Systems Private Limited
Website	mobikwik.com

Figure 2. Leadership team at Mobikwik and their compensation
Source: https://inc42.com/features/org-chart-the-people-with-power-at-ipo-bound-mobikwik/

Figure 3. Performance of Paytm IPO on NSE
Source: Trading View

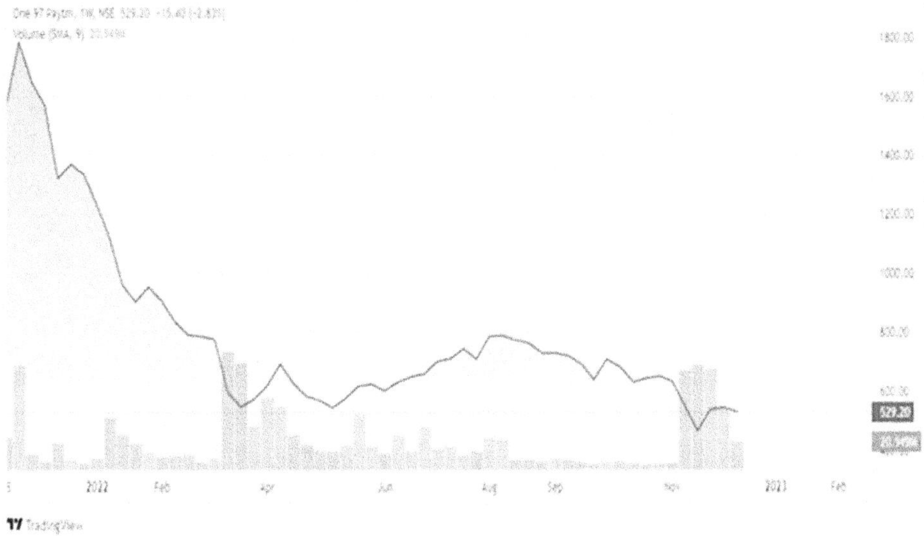

Table 2. Mobikwik user growth (2016-2020)

Year	No. of Users
2016	55 million
2017	107 million
2018	110 million
2019	100 million
2020	120 million

Compiled from various sources

Table 3. Key Financial highlights of MobiKwik as of FY 2020

Particulars	Amount (in Indian Rs)	Y-o-Y Growth (in %)
Net Revenue	3.79 billion	134
Consumer Payments Revenue	2.30 billion	159
Fintech Net Revenue	0.91 billion	216
Payment Gateway	1.90 billion	188
Revenue per Employee	13.00 million	195

Source: https://blog.mobikwik.com/mobikwik-annual-report-fy2020/

Figure 4. Screenshots of MobiKwik's data leak posted on the dark web

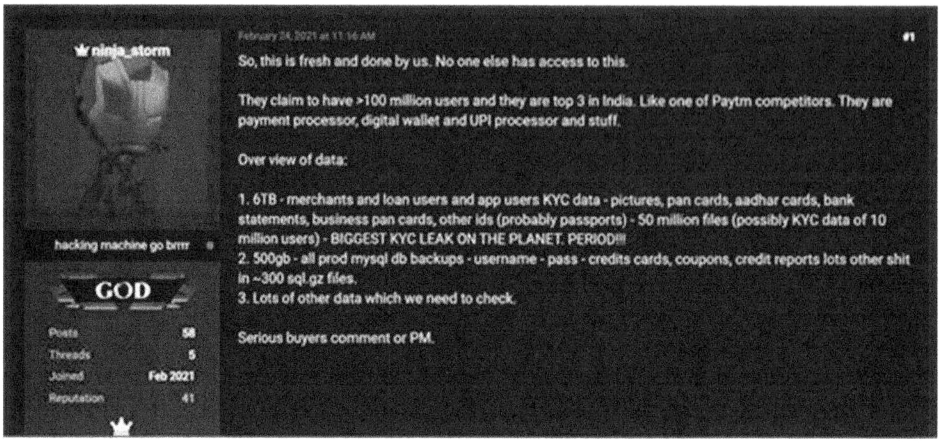

Figure 5. Screenshots of MobiKwik's data leak posted on the dark web
Source: https://thehackernews.com/2021/03/mobikwik-suffers-major-breach-kyc-data.html

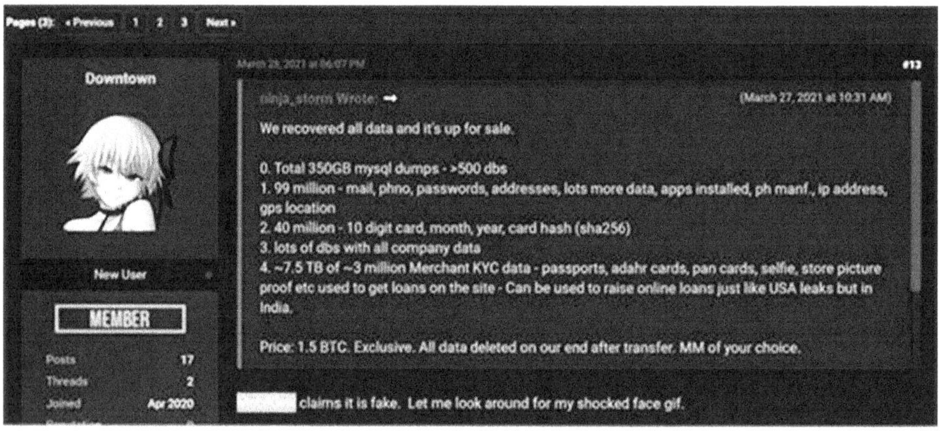

Table 4. Some major data breaches in India (2021)

Data Fiduciary	Size of Breach	Kind of Data Breached
Dominos India (April 2021)	Data related to 180 million orders placed with Domino's India	Name, Email, Mobile No., No. of orders, amount spent, GPS location
Upstox (April 2021)	KYC data of 2.5 million Upstox customers	Name, Mobile No. Email, PAN, Aadhaar, Bank account number
MobiKwik (March 2021)	Data of 100 million Indian MobiKwik users	KYC, passport, email ID, phone no., Aadhar
Facebook (April 2021)	Data of 6 million Indian Facebook users	Phone no., FB ID, location, past locations, birthdate, email, relationship status
Air India (February 2021)	As per Air India, data of 4.5 million customers globally was leaked	Name, DoB, Contact Information, Passport, Ticket, Credit Card Data
BigBasket (November 2021)	Data of 20 million + Indian BigBasket Users	Email, names, birthdates, phone no., IP, password hashes

Source: https://www.91mobiles.com/hub/5-major-data-breaches-india-2021/

Figure 6. Tweet
Source: Bipin Preet Singh on Twitter: "A note to our users. https://t.co/J3WRM0Ko8v" / Twitter

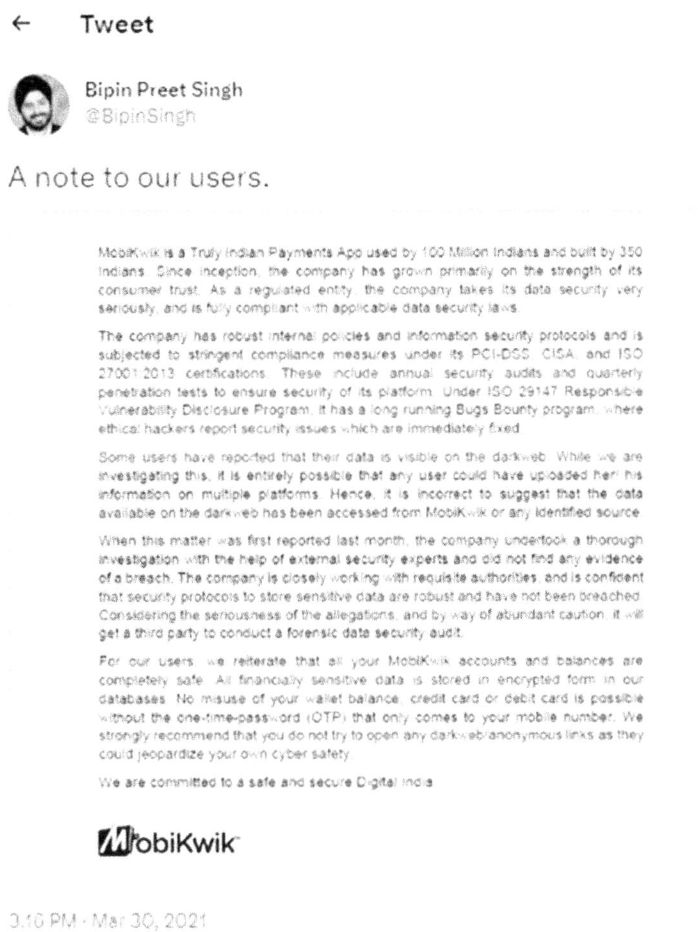
← Tweet

Bipin Preet Singh
@BipinSingh

A note to our users.

MobiKwik is a Truly Indian Payments App used by 100 Million Indians and built by 350 Indians. Since inception, the company has grown primarily on the strength of its consumer trust. As a regulated entity, the company takes its data security very seriously, and is fully compliant with applicable data security laws.

The company has robust internal policies and information security protocols and is subjected to stringent compliance measures under its PCI-DSS, CISA, and ISO 27001:2013 certifications. These include annual security audits and quarterly penetration tests to ensure security of its platform. Under ISO 29147 Responsible Vulnerability Disclosure Program, it has a long running Bugs Bounty program, where ethical hackers report security issues which are immediately fixed.

Some users have reported that their data is visible on the darkweb. While we are investigating this, it is entirely possible that any user could have uploaded her/ his information on multiple platforms. Hence, it is incorrect to suggest that the data available on the darkweb has been accessed from MobiKwik or any identified source.

When this matter was first reported last month, the company undertook a thorough investigation with the help of external security experts and did not find any evidence of a breach. The company is closely working with requisite authorities, and is confident that security protocols to store sensitive data are robust and have not been breached. Considering the seriousness of the allegations, and by way of abundant caution, it will get a third party to conduct a forensic date security audit.

For our users, we reiterate that all your MobiKwik accounts and balances are completely safe. All financially sensitive data is stored in encrypted form in our databases. No misuse of your wallet balance, credit card or debit card is possible without the one-time-password (OTP) that only comes to your mobile number. We strongly recommend that you do not try to open any darkweb/anonymous links as they could jeopardize your own cyber safety.

We are committed to a safe and secure Digital India.

MobiKwik

3:10 PM · Mar 30, 2021

Mobikwik's image suffered a big blow in February 2021 when it was reported to have reportedly compromised the KYC details of over 3.5 million users, in addition to making personal details of 100 million phone users public, which landed the startup on the radar of the RBI following an RTI petition. This also had an impact on its future IPO. Bipin and Upasana were dealing with a crisis that was affecting the brand they had developed, and they were unsure about the timing of their IPO now that Paytm's IPO had received a tepid response from the market.

LEARNING OBJECTIVE

The purpose of this case is to highlight issues that entrepreneurs face in their startup journey, like attracting customers, investors, organizational crisis and the need to make changes in business strategy. It also highlights the importance of ethical issues for decision-making. Thus, after going through this case, the students should be able to:

- Understand the issues and challenges faced during crises and possible ethical ways to overcome.
- Corporate Governance
- Tapping the capital market.

IMMEDIATE ISSUES

- Crises Management-alleged data breach
- Communication to the stakeholders and with authorities.
- Timing of IPO and its management

BASIC ISSUES

- Managing Organisational Crises
- Retaining Investors' Confidence
- Regulatory compliance
- Corporate Governance

POSITION IN COURSE

This case is meant for students studying entrepreneurship, business communication and strategic management/leadership in senior graduate and graduate-level management programs. This case can be used in courses on start-up, entrepreneurship, business communication and marketing of fintech services to discuss the strategies of distribution in a fintech environment. Since the case has an interdisciplinary flavour, instructors may augment the teaching note with course-specific material of their own to enrich the teaching and learning experience.

TEACHING PLAN

Students should be well-prepared for the class by going through the case and other readings on cash burn, runway, decision-making, turnaround strategies and important parts of startup leadership. This case shows that MobiKwik had been going through a crisis leading to erosion of trust and its repercussion on its IPO. The instructor might start the conversation by giving a general overview of Mobikwik and its place in fintech space in India. Then, the participants who are taking part can talk as to why MobiKwik was facing challenges. Students might be asked to talk about the Promoters leadership qualities, strengths and weaknesses, and how they should address the issues.

This case is suitable for a 90 min class, based on time allocations as given below:

Table 5. Topic/activity durations

Topic/Activity	Time (Min)
Reading of the case and question, supporting material	....
Discussion about MobiKwik(company background, change in management, the position of the protagonist in the company, etc.)	10 Minutes
Discussion about challenges faced by Bipin and Upasana	5 Minutes
Discussion about question 1	10 Minutes
Discussion about question 2	10 Minutes
Discussion about question 3	20 Minutes
Discussion about question 4	10 Minutes
Discussion about question 5	10 Minutes
Wrap-up of the case	15 Minutes

RELEVANT READINGS AND VIDEO CONTENTS FOR STUDENTS TO PREPARE BEFORE CLASS

1. DRHP-Mobikwik: https://www.sebi.gov.in/filings/public-issues/jul-2021/one-mobikwik-systems-limited_51019.html
2. Marsen, S. (2020). Navigating Crisis: The Role of Communication in Organizational Crisis. *International Journal of Business Communication, 57*(2), 163–175. https://doi.org/10.1177/2329488419882981
3. Crisis Communications Messaging Best Practices: https://www.youtube.com/watch?v=i2tehRamG7Y
4. Privacy and data protection: https://www.youtube.com/watch?v=ZNEPaGFApX4
5. Kaplan, Y. (2021). Good Corporate Governance Policies and Disclosure Mechanisms in Startup Companies. *U. Miami Bus. L. Rev., 29*, 31.
6. Tybout, A., & Roehm, M. (2009). Let the response fit the scandal. *Harvard Business Review, 87*(12), 82-88.
7. Youngblood, S. (2010). Ongoing Crisis Communication: Planning, Managing, And Responding, (Coombs, W. T.) and Handbook Of Risk And Crisis Communication (Heath, R. L. And O'Hair, H. D., Eds.) [Book Reviews]. *IEEE Transactions on Professional Communication, 53*(2), 174-178.
8. Brown, H. S. (2016). After the data breach: Managing the crisis and mitigating the impact. *Journal of Business Continuity & Emergency Planning, 9*(4), 317-328.

Assignment Questions

Q1. Crises and communication are two sides of the same coin. Discuss the communication strategy adopted by MobiKwik post the alleged data breach? Critically evaluate MobiKwik's approach in the data breach episode

Q2. What measures the company should take to ensure its brand image and customer trust remained intact?

Q3. How should MobiKwik plan its IPO in the wake of the debacle of Paytm IPO? Outline in light of the financials given in the case and the DRHP of MobiKwik.

Q4. Why are Personal Data Protection laws important and what should be the penal clauses for violation?

Q5. How should a fintech firm like MobiKwik embrace corporate governance laws?

CASE ANALYSIS/DISCUSSION

Q1. Crises and communication are two sides of the same coin. Discuss the communication strategy adopted by MobiKwik post the alleged data breach? Critically evaluate MobiKwik's approach in the data breach episode.

Ans. *Organizational Crisis*

An organizational crisis is a short-term, undesirable critical situation in a corporation that challenges its continuity, growth, and existence[22]. It has the potential to decrease revenue and income and leads to negative profitability[23]. It can also result in a decrease in market share and sales. Crises and communication are indeed closely linked, and effective communication during a crisis can be critical in managing its impact. The alleged data breach incident involving Indian fintech company MobiKwik provides an interesting case study in crisis communication.

MobiKwik is a digital wallet and payment service provider with over 120 million users in India. In March 2021, news reports emerged claiming that MobiKwik had suffered a major data breach, with sensitive data of millions of users allegedly being leaked online. The company initially denied the reports, but later acknowledged the breach and claimed that only a small amount of non-sensitive data had been compromised. MobiKwik was swift in its rebuttal of all allegations made by the Internet Security Researcher Rajashekhar Rajaharia. The company sent its response by the way of tweet on 4th Mar'2021 rejecting the data leak and asserting that it was a regulated organisation that took the protection of its data very seriously and was completely compliant with all relevant data security legislation. On March 29, 2021, the alleged hacker proposed deleting all the data in exchange for MobiKwik officially acknowledging the data breach. The next day, on 30th Mar'21 there is a change of heart and in a new comment on Raid Forum, the hacker claimed that he had destroyed all data freely and had not stolen any money. The Hacker maintained that he had no intention to harm the upcoming IPO of MobiKwik.

Coincidently, Bipin Preet Singh, Founder & CEO in his tweet on 30th Mar'21 completely defended the internal processes of MobiKwik and its compliance to national and international standards. He maintained that they were looking into the data leak and that it was absolutely feasible for any user to have posted their information to several platforms.

In terms of communication strategy, MobiKwik initially adopted a defensive approach, denying the reports and questioning the credibility of the sources. However, as the incident gained wider attention and the company faced criticism from users and the media, it shifted to a more proactive approach, acknowledging the breach and issuing a statement outlining the steps it had taken to address the issue.

In terms of communication strategy, MobiKwik initially adopted a defensive approach, denying the reports and questioning the credibility of the sources. However, as the incident gained wider attention and the company faced criticism from users and the media, it shifted to a more proactive approach, acknowledging the breach and issuing a statement outlining the steps it had taken to address the issue.

MobiKwik also set up a dedicated webpage with information about the incident, including a timeline of events, a FAQ section, and a statement from the company's CEO. The webpage also provided users with instructions on how to secure their accounts and suggested that they change their passwords.

While MobiKwik's communication strategy can be seen as a step in the right direction, there are also several criticisms that can be made of their approach

Critically evaluating MobiKwik's approach, there are some positives and negatives:

Positives:

1. **Timely Response:** MobiKwik responded quickly to the crisis by issuing public statements and notifying customers of the breach. This was important in establishing trust and transparency with its stakeholders.
2. **Reassurance of Customer Data:** MobiKwik's messaging focused on reassuring its customers that their financial data was safe and that the company had taken steps to ensure the security of its systems. This was an important step in mitigating the potential damage to the company's reputation.
3. **Engagement With External Security Experts:** The company's decision to engage external security experts to investigate the breach was a positive step in demonstrating its commitment to resolving the issue.

Negatives:

1. **Lack of Clarity:** MobiKwik's initial statement lacked clarity on the extent and nature of the breach, which led to confusion and speculation among stakeholders.
2. **Delayed Disclosure:** MobiKwik had reportedly known about the breach since February 2021 but only disclosed it in March. This delay may have eroded some of the trust that customers and other stakeholders had in the company.
3. **Inconsistent Messaging:** MobiKwik's messaging was inconsistent at times, with some statements contradicting others. This lack of consistency may have caused further confusion and uncertainty among stakeholders.

In conclusion, MobiKwik's communication strategy in response to the alleged data breach had some positives, such as timely response and reassurance of customer data, but also had some negatives, such as a lack of clarity and inconsistent messaging. The company could have improved its approach by providing clearer and more consistent messaging, disclosing the breach in a timely manner, and demonstrating a stronger commitment to resolving the issue.

Q2. What measures the company should take to ensure its brand image and customer trust remained intact?

Ans. MobiKwik should take several measures to ensure its brand image and customer trust remain intact post the data breach episode in India. Here are some of the steps the company can take:

1. **Strengthen Security Measures:** MobiKwik should review and strengthen its security measures to prevent similar incidents from happening in the future. This could include improving encryption, implementing multi-factor authentication, and conducting regular security audits.
2. **Conduct an Independent Review:** MobiKwik should commission an independent review of its security systems and procedures to identify any weaknesses and make recommendations for improvement. This would demonstrate the company's commitment to transparency and accountability.

3. **Communicate Regularly:** MobiKwik should continue to communicate regularly with its customers and other stakeholders to provide updates on the incident and the steps being taken to address it. This would help to maintain transparency and rebuild trust.
4. **Educate Customers:** MobiKwik should educate its customers on the steps they can take to protect themselves from cyber threats, such as using strong passwords and being vigilant for suspicious activity. This would help to improve customer awareness and prevent similar incidents from happening in the future.
5. **Collaborate With Industry Stakeholders:** MobiKwik should collaborate with industry stakeholders, such as cybersecurity experts and regulators, to address the issue and prevent similar incidents from happening in the future. This could involve sharing best practices and collaborating on initiatives to improve cybersecurity across the industry.

Overall, MobiKwik should take a proactive approach to address the data breach episode and rebuild customer trust. By strengthening its security systems, disclosing information transparently, compensating affected customers, enhancing customer support, and collaborating with industry stakeholders, the company can demonstrate its commitment to addressing the issue and ensuring the security of its customers' data.

Q3. How should MobiKwik plan its IPO in the wake of the debacle of Paytm IPO? Outline in light of the financials given in the case and the DRHP of MobiKwik.

Ans. Planning an IPO can be a complex process, and MobiKwik should take several factors into consideration to ensure the success of its IPO in the wake of the Paytm IPO debacle. Here are some steps MobiKwik can take:

Conduct a thorough analysis of its financials: MobiKwik should conduct a thorough analysis of its financials to ensure that its financial performance meets the expectations of investors. The company should ensure that its financial statements are accurate and transparent, and it should provide detailed information on its revenue streams, expenses, and profitability.

Focus on investor education and engagement: MobiKwik should focus on educating potential investors about its business model and growth prospects. The company should engage with investors through roadshows, investor presentations, and other communication channels to build investor confidence.

Highlight its competitive advantages: MobiKwik should highlight its competitive advantages, such as its strong market position in the Indian digital payments market and its innovative product offerings. The company should also provide details on its growth strategy, including plans to expand its customer base and enter new markets.

Address concerns around cybersecurity: In the wake of the data breach episode, MobiKwik should address concerns around cybersecurity and demonstrate that it has taken steps to strengthen its security systems. The company should provide details on its security measures and its collaboration with industry stakeholders to prevent similar incidents from happening in the future.

Price the IPO appropriately: MobiKwik should price its IPO appropriately to attract investors while also reflecting the company's valuation and growth prospects. The company should work with its underwriters to determine the appropriate price range for the IPO based on market conditions and investor demand.

Overall, MobiKwik should take a cautious and transparent approach to its IPO planning, focusing on building investor confidence through education, engagement, and clear communication around its financial performance, growth prospects, competitive advantages, and cybersecurity measures. By addressing concerns around these areas and pricing the IPO appropriately, the company can increase its chances of a successful IPO in the wake of the Paytm IPO debacle.

Q4. Why are Personal Data Protection laws important and what should be the penal clauses for violation?
Ans: Personal Data Protection laws are important for several reasons:

Protecting Privacy: Personal Data Protection laws protect individuals' right to privacy by regulating the collection, use, storage, and sharing of their personal data.

1. **Preventing Misuse:** These laws prevent companies and organizations from misusing individuals' personal data for commercial or other purposes without their consent.
2. **Increasing Transparency:** Personal Data Protection laws require companies and organizations to be transparent about how they collect and use individuals' personal data, thereby increasing transparency and accountability.
3. **Building Trust:** By protecting individuals' personal data, Personal Data Protection laws help build trust between individuals and the companies and organizations that collect and use their data.
4. Penalties for violation of Personal Data Protection laws vary depending on the jurisdiction, but typically include fines and other legal remedies. In some cases, criminal penalties may also be imposed. Penalties may be based on the severity of the violation, the type of data involved, and the number of individuals affected. Some common penalties for violating Personal Data Protection laws includes:
5. **Fines:** Companies or organizations that violate Personal Data Protection laws may be fined a certain amount per violation, which can add up quickly if many individuals' data has been compromised.
6. **Legal Remedies:** Individuals affected by a violation of Personal Data Protection laws may be entitled to sue for damages or other legal remedies.
7. **Suspension or Revocation of License:** In some cases, companies or organizations that violate Personal Data Protection laws may have their licenses suspended or revoked.
8. **Criminal Penalties:** In extreme cases, individuals or companies that violate Personal Data Protection laws may face criminal penalties, including fines and imprisonment.

Overall, the penalties for violating Personal Data Protection laws are intended to serve as a deterrent to prevent companies and organizations from misusing individuals' personal data and to ensure that they take appropriate steps to protect that data.

Q5. How should a fintech firm like MobiKwik embrace corporate governance laws?

Fintech players, like any other business, should embrace corporate governance norms to ensure that their operations are ethical, transparent, and in compliance with applicable laws and regulations. Here are some steps that a fintech player can take to embrace corporate governance norms:

1. **Establish a Strong Board of Directors:** The board of directors should have a diverse set of skills and experience, and be responsible for overseeing the company's strategy and risk management. They should also have a clear understanding of the company's mission, values, and culture.

2. **Develop Policies and Procedures:** The company should develop policies and procedures that govern its operations, such as code of conduct, risk management policies, and anti-bribery and anti-corruption policies. These policies should be communicated to employees and stakeholders, and reviewed regularly.
3. **Implement Strong Internal Controls:** The company should have internal controls in place to ensure that its operations are conducted in compliance with applicable laws and regulations. These controls should be designed to prevent fraud, errors, and other irregularities.
4. **Establish an Independent Audit Function:** The company should establish an independent audit function to review its financial statements and ensure that they are accurate and comply with accounting standards.
5. **Foster a Culture of Compliance:** The company should foster a culture of compliance throughout the organization, by promoting ethical behavior, providing training on compliance issues, and encouraging employees to report any concerns or violations.
6. **Engage With Stakeholders:** The company should engage with stakeholders, such as customers, investors, and regulators, to understand their needs and concerns, and to build trust and credibility.

By embracing these corporate governance norms, a fintech player can build a strong foundation for sustainable growth and success, while also ensuring that its operations are conducted in an ethical and transparent manner.

REFERENCES

Agarwal, S., Alok, S., Ghosh, P., & Gupta, S. (2020). *Fintech and credit scoring for the millennials: evidence using mobile and social footprints*. Manuscript.

Agarwal, S., Basu, D., Ghosh, P., Pareek, B., & Zhang, J. (2018a). *Demonetization and digitization*. Manuscript. doi:10.2139srn.3197990

Grover, P., Kar, A. K., & Ilavarasan, P. V. (2017). Understanding nature of social media usage by mobile wallets service providers–an exploration through SPIN framework. *Procedia Computer Science*, *122*, 292–299. doi:10.1016/j.procs.2017.11.372

Kapoor, A., Sindwani, R., & Goel, M. (2020). Mobile wallets: Theoretical and empirical analysis. *Global Business Review*. Advance online publication. doi:10.1177/0972150920961254

Leong, L. Y., Hew, T. S., Ooi, K. B., & Wei, J. (2020). Predicting mobile wallet resistance: A two-staged structural equation modeling-artificial neural network approach. *International Journal of Information Management*, *51*, 102047. doi:10.1016/j.ijinfomgt.2019.102047

Panagariya, A. (2022). Digital revolution, financial infrastructure and entrepreneurship: The case of India. *Asia and the Global Economy*, *2*(2), 100027. doi:10.1016/j.aglobe.2022.100027

Ramakrishna, A. (2012). An exploratory analysis of data breaches from 2005-2011: Trends and insights. *Journal of Information Privacy & Security*, *8*(2), 33–56. doi:10.1080/15536548.2012.10845654

Rana, N. P., Luthra, S., & Rao, H. R. (2022). Assessing challenges to the mobile wallet usage in India: an interpretive structural modelling approach. *Information Technology & People*. doi:10.1108/ITP-07-2021-0535

Rangaswamy & Shanka. (2021). The Migh "Tea" Problem of Start-up Expansion. *South Asian Journal of Management, 28*(1), 171-190.

Salampasis, D., & Mention, A. L. (2018). FinTech: Harnessing innovation for financial inclusion. In Handbook of Blockchain, Digital Finance, and Inclusion, Volume 2 (pp. 451-461). Academic Press. doi:10.1016/B978-0-12-812282-2.00018-8

Saluja, S. (2022). *Identity theft fraud-major loophole for FinTech industry in India*. doi:10.1108/JFC-08-2022-0211

Shaw, B., & Kesharwani, A. (2019). Moderating effect of smartphone addiction on mobile wallet payment adoption. *Journal of Internet Commerce*, *18*(3), 291–309. doi:10.1080/15332861.2019.1620045

Shekhar, S., Manoharan, B., & Rakshit, K. (2020). Going cashless: Change in institutional logic and consumption practices in the face of institutional disruption. *Journal of Business Research*, *114*, 60–79. doi:10.1016/j.jbusres.2020.04.010

Suri, T. (2017). Mobile money. *Annual Review of Economics*, *9*(1), 497–520. doi:10.1146/annurev-economics-063016-103638

ENDNOTES

1 An initial public offering (IPO) refers to the process of offering shares of a private corporation to the public in a new stock issuance for the first time.
https://www.investopedia.com/terms/i/ipo.asp

2 Fintech refers to the integration of technology into offerings by financial services companies in order to improve their use and delivery to consumers https://www.investopedia.com/terms/f/fintech.asp

3 Know Your Customer (KYC) standards are designed to protect financial institutions against fraud, corruption, money laundering and terrorist financing.
https://www.swift.com/your-needs/financial-crime-cyber-security/know-your-customer-kyc/meaning-kyc

4 · RTI Act 2005 The Right to Information is an act of the Parliament of India which sets out the rules and procedures regarding citizens' right to information https://rtionline.gov.in/

5 Paytm is an Indian digital payments and financial services company, based in Noida.
https://paytm.com/

6 UPI -Unified Payments Interface (UPI) is a system that powers multiple bank accounts into a single mobile application (of any participating bank)
https://www.npci.org.in/what-we-do/upi/product-overview

7 Aadhaar is a 12-digit unique identity number that can be obtained voluntarily by the ... functioning of the UIDAI https://uidai.gov.in/

8 The point of sale or point of purchase is the time and place at which a retail transaction is completed. https://www.investopedia.com/terms/p/point-of-sale.asp

9 A QR code (an initialism for quick response code) is a type of matrix barcode (or two-dimensional barcode) invented in 1994 by Japanese company Denso Wave.
https://en.wikipedia.org/wiki/QR_code

10 BNPL Buy Now, Pay Later (BNPL) is a type of short-term financing that allows consumers to make purchases and pay for them at a future date, often interest-free
https://www.investopedia.com/buy-now-pay-later-5182291

10a Rangaswamy, Uma ShankaChai Thela: The Migh "Tea" Problem of Start-up Expansion, South Asian Journal of Management. Jan-Mar2021, Vol. 28 Issue 1, p171-190. 20p

11 Peer-to-peer payments, or P2P payments, let you send money directly to another person
https://www.nerdwallet.com/article/banking/p2p-payment-systems

12 Unicorn- A Unicorn Company or startup is a private company with a valuation of $ 1Bn
https://www.cbinsights.com/research-unicorn-companies

13 DRHP, a legal preliminary prospectus, serves as a crucial communication link between the company and its investors and stakeholders.
https://www.business-standard.com/about/what-is-draft-red-herring-prospectus

14 SEBI- The Securities and Exchange Board of India is the regulatory body for securities and commodity market in India under the ownership of Ministry of Finance within the Government of India.
https://www.sebi.gov.in/

15 Tweet- to post a short message using the Twitter social networking service
https://www.techtarget.com/whatis/definition/tweet

16 Hacker A hacker is a person who breaks into a computer system. The reasons for hacking can be many: installing malware, stealing or destroying data,
https://www.cisco.com/c/en/us/products/security/what-is-a-hacker.html

17 The dark web refers to encrypted online content that is not indexed by conventional search engines.
https://www.investopedia.com/terms/d/dark-web.asp

18 Cybersecurity is the protection of internet-connected systems such as hardware, software and data from cyberthreats.
https://www.techtarget.com/searchsecurity/definition/cybersecurity

19 RaidForums is a well-known dark web forum that gained media attention from its high-profile mega leaks.
https://webz.io/blog/dark-web/the-top-5-dark-web-forums/

20 The Indian Computer Emergency Response Team (CERT-In) is an office within the Ministry of Electronics and Information Technology of the Government of India. It is the nodal agency to deal with cyber security threats like hacking and phishing. It strengthens security-related defense of the Indian Internet domain.

21 The Reserve Bank of India (RBI) is the central bank of India that monitors the Indian banking system and is also responsible for the issue and supply of the Indian rupee.

22 Dubrovski (2004b; cf. Barnett and Pratt 2000).

23 Hambrick and D'Aveni (1988).

Chapter 11
Motivational Leadership and Mukesh Ambani: A Case Study

Bhanwar S. Rathore
Mody University of Science and Technology, India

Sunita Verma
Mody University of Science and Technology, India

EXECUTIVE SUMMARY

Motivational leaders who consider not only company development but also societal and national development as a whole are needed in the current tumultuous climate. Motivational leaders see the best in their employees and also facilitate society's efforts to breed compassionate and transformational leaders for inclusive growth. This case study highlights the major motivational leadership style adopted by Reliance Industries Limited (RIL) chairman Mukesh Ambani at different stages of his business deployment. Through his tactics and wisdom, he has not only changed the complete face of Indian industries but also helped society stand up during the pandemic. This case discusses four motivational leadership approaches, i.e., compassionate leadership, inclusive leadership, transformational leadership, and value-based leadership. A motivational leader understands that people and society are the sources of all progress and innovation and thus the key to success in the future. This case study may be used in MDPs, FDPs, and academic programmes to highlight the value of motivational leadership.

INTRODUCTION

"To make Reliance the world's most healthy company, protecting, promoting, enhancing employee health and wellbeing; providing outstanding health services and operating an exemplary HSE management system in all sites, services, and offices of the enterprise, improving productivity and reducing health care costs; and with our results, inspiring our customers and partners", is an endorsement of healthy workplace strategy at the highest level." – Mukesh Ambani, Chairman, and Managing Director, Reliance Industries Limited, in 2022

DOI: 10.4018/978-1-6684-8488-3.ch011

The eagerly anticipated Forbes Billionaires 2022 list highlighted that list of the world's wealthiest people was affected by the crisis in Russia and Ukraine, the coronavirus outbreak, and weak market conditions.

With a net worth of $100.1 billion, Mukesh Ambani, chairman of Reliance Industries Limited (RIL), is the only Indian to make it to the coveted top 10 list and is placed 10th richest on Forbes' list of billionaires for 2022. Reliance Industries, a $74 billion corporation with holdings in petroleum, oil and gas, telecommunication, and merchandising, is run by him as chairman and CEO. He is unquestionably among the most prosperous businesspeople in the history of commerce. Thanks to his tactics and vision, he has dramatically transformed the appearance of Indian industries and improved the nation's economy.

He is the sort of person who has big ideas. He has a gift for predicting the future. He is aware of the strategy that will support future business growth for the organisation. He is able to predict a company's potential and its survival span.

Mr. Mukesh Ambani supervised the construction of the largest grassroots petroleum refinery in the world at Jamnagar in Gujarat in the late 1990s and integrated it with petroleum, a sea port, and related infrastructure and also supervised the construction of a second refinery in Jamnagar. Along with developing Reliance's infrastructure, he oversaw the installation of a multi-format, organised retail network over all of India. Reliance Retail is currently India's biggest organised retailer. He has accomplished world firsts in client acquisition for Jio, Reliance's digital services endeavour. With end-to-end solutions that address the full value chain across a variety of digital services in crucial sectors of the public interest, including as entertainment, healthcare, security, and financial services, he directed and developed one of the largest 4G broadband wireless networks in the world.

Mr. Mukesh Ambani is a member of "The Foundation Board of the World Economic Forum" and a chosen foreign member of the prestigious "American National Academy of Engineering". He is a member of the global advisory council for Bank of America.

LEADERSHIP

In the past 15 years, a new category of leadership theory, instead referred to as "compassionate," transformational," "inclusive," and "value-based," has emerged in organizational works (Bass, 1985; Bennis & Nanus, 1985; Burns, 1978; Conger & Kanungo, 1987; House, 1977; Tichy & Devanna, 1986).

Beyond management is leadership. The goal of management is to accomplish tasks by utilizing organizational resources as well as the formal procedures and rules that are in place. On the other side, leadership occasionally entails implementing novel ideas and improvements that may not be well-liked by everyone. Depending on the leader's use of authority and the level of latitude granted to subordinates, a variety of techniques for facilitating change within an organization can be identified.

An authoritarian strategy entails a leader making choices alone and instructing followers on how to behave. A consultative strategy entails speaking with the individuals who will be affected by a decision, possibly soliciting their opinions and suggestions, and also alerting them of any changes that are likely to occur.

Giving people the opportunity to participate in decision-making, potentially through cooperation, is a democratic approach. The leader's task is to facilitate the formation of teamwork structures and to motivate the teams to assume accountability for decision-making.

The consultative and democratic techniques are more motivating because the leader is giving staff greater accountability, which encourages them to feel involved. Employees are much more likely to take ownership of the effort and be committed to making sure that it works in practice when they are involved in decision-making.

COMPASSIONATE LEADERSHIP

Among many leadership styles, one that has started to receive considerable attention in the business world and has been suitably amplified by the disastrous impact of COVID-19 is compassionate leadership. Compassionate leadership is viewed as a leader who embodies an act of love, care, and selflessness and enables a caring and supportive organization (Oruh et al., 2021). Compassionate leadership is an interpersonal process involving noticing, feeling, sense-making, and acting by the giver in a way that alleviates the suffering of the receiver (Banker and Bhal 2018).

To inspire and influence team members, friends, and family members so they can in turn inspire and influence others is the practice of compassionate leadership. Additionally, such leadership places a priority on an organization's workforce for its overall development.

With a pandemic spreading across the globe, unemployment at depression levels, and civil and political turmoil from Mumbai to New Delhi to Kolkata, it appears as though the world as we know it is in danger. Jobs are being lost as economies collapse. It is more important than ever for leaders to show compassion.

The pandemic has caused many people to lose friends and family members on a global scale. The team members at RIL benefited from the leadership's support system and a common forum for discussing losses and issues relating to both work and personal lives.

RIL, under the leadership of Mr. Mukesh Amabani, introduced a program – WE CARE as a common, unifying thread that runs through everything. Through this RIL has attached the highest importance to Employee Care.

Reliance supported the grieving families of coworkers who had passed away. Following is how RIL unveiled the Reliance Family Support and Welfare Scheme:

1. For a period of five years, Reliance will continue to pay the candidate the last drawn monthly salary.
2. For all children, Reliance will cover 100% of their tuition costs, housing costs, and book costs up to a bachelor's degree at any Indian institution.
3. Until the children have earned a bachelor's degree, Reliance will pay 100% of the premium for hospitalization coverage for the spouse, parents, and children.
4. All employees who personally or through their families have been impacted by COVID-19 are eligible to take advantage of the special COVID-Leave for the entire time they need to recover emotionally and physically.

Mr. Mukesh Ambani sent a message on 03 June 2021 to all RIL employees – "Dear colleague, even though these times may seem very bleak, always remember that you are not alone and the entire institution of Reliance stands with each one of you and your family. We have come together thus far precisely on the strength of our solidarity as One Team and with the Ownership Mindset that we will keep fighting this adversity until we win. Let us not give up on that fighting spirit, because surely there are better days ahead for all of us. Until that time comes, we pray that our bereaving families find the strength they need to cope with their loss. And let us continue to support each other and remain optimistic about the future."

Reliance Industries Limited (RIL), stepped into oxygen supply under the direction of Mukesh Ambani. They are now, however, supplying enormous quantities of these from their Jamnagar Petroleum Plant. According to the report's description of its pandemic response, frontline workers and vulnerable communities received more than 8.5 crore free meals. During the second wave, Reliance produced 1,000 tonnes of oxygen per day and gave it gratis to the states for more than 1 lakh patients. Additionally, it built a hospital with 2,000 beds for Covid care.

According to the Fortune Global 500 list of the "World's Largest Corporations," RIL is among the top 100 profitable businesses. In the years FY2021-22, RIL invested 1186 crores in CSR initiatives in India. Over the past five years, the Company has consistently spent the most on corporate social responsibility.

Mr. Mukesh Ambani drove on the following missions.

- Mission Oxygen (Production and distribution of medical oxygen)
- Mission COVID Infra (Building new hospitals, adding beds, etc.)
- Mission Anna Seva (Distributing food to the needy)
- Mission Employee Care (Care & concern for Reliance Family)
- Mission Vaccine Suraksha (Vaccination drive across the organization).

INCLUSIVE LEADERSHIP

Leadership means inclusiveness and reaching out, not dominance and power.—Sadhguru (Jaggi Vasudev).

Sabharwal (2014) empirically explained diversity alone could not lead to the effectiveness of organizational performance. However, diversity, along with inclusion is more beneficial for the enhancement of performance in the workplace. Also, among leadership styles, the inclusive leadership style emphasizes being people-oriented (Liu et al., 2017), fairness, and justice (Liu et al., 2016).

Leadership with a focus on supporting employees as group members by ensuring justice and equity and providing shared decision-making opportunities, while encouraging diverse contributions (Randel et al., 2018).

Industrial townships, as proposed by Mr. Mukesh Ambani, are consistent with inclusive leadership. The townships at Reliance's entities foster the ideas of inclusivity and unity through community living, where the top management shares housing with the working staff and has access to the same amenities as schools, colleges, hospitals, and other establishments. As cultural and regional barriers dissolve, modern leadership should place a premium on inclusivity in order to foster a climate of equity and equality.

Through its four main pillars of work, including rural transformation, health, education, disaster response, and sports for development initiatives, Reliance undertook a number of initiatives in FY 2021–2022.

People from different nationalities, cultures, genders, ages, abilities, and experiences make up the Reliance family, and they all work together to create a welcoming work environment where everyone has the chance to contribute, participate, and advance.

Reliance has developed a policy to prevent sexual harassment in the workplace under the direction of Mr. Mukesh Ambani. This complies with existing legal requirements, including the 2013 Sexual Harassment of Women at Work (Prevention, Prohibition, and Redressal) Act. Employees at Reliance can call the on-campus helpline in case of an emergency while on the job. On-demand, self-defense classes for female coworkers are occasionally organized in cooperation with the security team.

A variety of initiatives have been developed by RIL to promote gender inclusion and make the workplace more productive for women. Reliance provides working mothers and expectant mothers with benefits like special leaves, help, designated parking, and a new mothers' Employee Resource Group to help them successfully balance work and life. People from various backgrounds, genders, cultures, and abilities work at Reliance and contribute to an inclusive workplace by being themselves.

TRANSFORMATIONAL LEADERSHIP

A management philosophy known as transformational leadership empowers and motivates staff to innovate and create new strategies for a company's growth and success. Transformational leaders generally tend to show four main characteristics: charisma, inspirational leadership, intellectual stimulation, and the consideration of the needs of followers (Dubinsky et al., 1995.

Tepper (2018) shown that team members behave well when managed by transformational leaders, particularly when they encounter most formidable distress at work.

The Leadership at Reliance comprises young, dynamic professionals with a wealth of expertise between them. They are all "open-door" leaders, accessible and communicative, who reinforce and drive Reliance's Vision and DNA down the line and inspire their teams to always look at out-of-the-box solutions and excellence in all their actions.

In the 1990s and 2000s, when oil was a goldmine, Mukesh Ambani operated his oil company. However, during the 2000s, "Data" has emerged as the new gold mine, and Ambani has turned his business into one that is data-driven. In 2007, he shifted directions and established his new business, Jio. But back then, he was aware that data was the new oil. He began working on 4G LTE technology, where data is crucial. In his organisation, voice calls were being transmitted through data rather than through traditional telephony technologies.

India's drive for digital transformation has benefited from Jio, the telecom behemoth Mukesh Ambani's RIL created in 2016. Ambani said that Jio constructed a future-proof 4G network in just three years as opposed to 25 years for India's 2G network. "Today, India consumes more than 6 exabytes of data each month—more than 30 times what it did during the Jio era, which was just four years ago. In just four years, we went from being 155th in the world to being first in mobile data usage, according to Mukesh Ambani. Jio Platforms, the digital solutions division of RIL, has a growing portfolio of over 20 start-ups with notable capabilities in fields like cloud and edge computing, big data analytics, artificial intelligence and machine learning, blockchain, augmented reality and virtual reality, and the internet of things. "

Reliance Retail announced in January 2022 that it had led a $240 million fundraising round in the Bengaluru-based startup Dunzo and currently holds a 25.8% stake in it. This marks the entry of the oil-to-technology behemoth into the ultra-fast commerce market.

Mr. Mukesh is gung-ho about his investments in 5G and retail, which in India is growing rapidly and is expected to touch $1.3 trillion by 2025. He is already ahead of even international behemoths. As with 5G, with the world looking forward to doing business with non-China-based companies, RIL is expected to hit pay dirt.

Reliance is being refocused by Ambani on renewable energy. Over the next 10 to 15 years, the firm will invest $80 billion in renewable energy and construct a new facility next to its refinery. "Over the next 12 months, our investments across the Green Energy value chain will gradually start going live, scaling up over the next couple of years. This new growth engine holds great promise to outshine all our existing growth engines in just 5-7 years," Mukesh Ambani said in a statement to shareholders in its annual report for the year ended 31 March 2022.

VALUE-BASED LEADERSHIP

The shared ideas and presumptions of the leader and the team form the foundation of values-based leadership, which are both a leadership style and a philosophy. Teams have stronger alignment and gain from higher productivity because they share a set of values.

Strong Principles + Belief in People = Strong Leadership

A great leader must be able to alter others' attitudes or behaviors since the purpose of leadership is to bring value to others and influence is the true test of leadership (Reese, 2017). Responsible leadership (example: Tirmizi 2018), mindful leadership (e.g., Mackey et al. 2020), and sustainability leadership (e.g., Bendell and Little 2015) are other emerging leadership theory initiatives that are values-driven.

Mr. Mukesh Ambani is practicing responsible leadership, conscious leadership, and sustainability leadership, which could be made out from the vision statement of the RIL.

Vision: To build a global enterprise for all our stakeholders, and a great future for our country, to give millions of young Indians the power to shape their destiny, and the means to realize their full potential…

Values and Behaviors at RIL

"We aim to conduct our businesses ethically and in a manner that is respectful to all. We achieve this by aligning our goals with our six core values."

Ownership Mindset: We believe the success and reputation of the company are paramount. Having an ownership mindset is fundamental to our existence. It creates a sense of inspiration and purpose. It enables accountability and accomplishment. It ensures our strong commitment to the highest standards of safety and environment.

Customer Value: We believe the customer is the reason for our existence and the only guarantee of our future. Everything that we do must delight our customers, each time and always.

Respect: We believe that without respecting all our stakeholders there can be no Reliance. We acknowledge that there may be a difference in perspectives but there must always be respect.

Integrity: Upholding our reputation is paramount as we are judged by how we act. We are committed to being truthful in all our actions. We strive to be honest and forthright with one another and with all our stakeholders. We respect the world in which we operate. It begins with compliance with laws and regulations. We hold ourselves to the highest ethical standards and behave in ways that earn the trust of others.

One Team: Whatever the strength of the individual, we will accomplish more together. We put the team ahead of our success and commit to building its capability. We trust each other to deliver on our respective obligations.

Excellence: We are committed to excellence, in spirit and action. We believe everything that we do and everything we think can always get better. We see all of our activities in terms of our higher purpose and ideals, which drives our quest for excellence always.

In the case of Jio, Mukesh Ambani has been acting as a good value-based leader who is running one of the largest empires of Reliance Groups by creating a wider pool of jobs that requires technical knowledge and envisages in itself the concept of a welfare state.

He is providing training to the subordinates so that they can update themselves with the changing scenario of the technological environment. Making them well versed with the technology, not only the employees but also, people of all ages of life, now are learning to use digital technologies. The management of Jio is quite talented, based on experience, learning, and the ability to foresee the future, which is truly supported by a visionary leader as stated by Kautilya. Arthsahstra focuses on the use of opportunistic tactics to grow and expand, which can be seen very clearly in Jio's strategy as it was launched at a time when no player in the market was even thinking of giving free 3G data.

MOMENTOUS LEADERSHIP TRANSITION

On December 29, 2021, Mr. Mukesh Ambani made a statement regarding the leadership transition at his energy-to-retail conglomerate, stating that he wanted the process to be sped up with elders, including him, ceding to the younger generation.

Achieving big dreams and impossible-looking goals is all about getting the right people and the right leadership. Reliance is now in the process of effecting a momentous leadership transition.

"From seniors belonging to my generation to the next generation of young leaders... I would like the process to be accelerated. All Seniors—myself included—should now yield to the highly competent, extremely committed, and incredibly promising young leadership talent at Reliance," said Mr. Mukesh Ambani.

Reliance now has three business sectors: the energy sector, which includes oil refineries in Jamnagar, Gujarat, petrochemical plants, and new energy factories; the retail sector, which consists of physical stores and an online e-commerce unit under the name JioMart; and the telecom and digital sectors, which are housed under the name Jio.

As RIL enters the second half of the golden decade, the future of the company looks brighter to me than ever before. I can confidently make two predictions. First, India will become one of the top three economies in the world. Second, Reliance will become one of the strongest and most reputed Indian multinational companies in the world," he said.

"Now, Reliance is poised to become a global leader in clean and green energy and materials," he said. "This transformation of our oldest business will provide us the largest growth engine for Reliance and yet another opportunity for many of you to do things that will be first in the world." With a presence in both online and physical store formats, Reliance Retail has revolutionized organized retail in India.

CONCLUSION

Motivational leadership could be defined by compassion, inclusion, transformation, value, and vision. Motivational leaders make decisions, set clear goals, show compassion, and provide their teams with inclusive empowerment and value-based tools to achieve success. Motivational leaders not only see the best in their employees but also facilitate society to breed compassionate and transformational leaders for inclusive growth.

The power of the leader is very important in motivating others. There are several sources of power i.e. personal power, legitimate power, expert power, and political power.

Motivational leadership involves striking the right balance between these four sources of power, and using them when appropriate. Mr Mukesh Ambani has used these powers appropriately at different stages of his business deployment.

Finding the perfect balance between these four sources of power and utilising them as necessary are key components of motivational leadership. At various points throughout the development of his firm, Mr. Mukesh Ambani has utilised these powers appropriately.

Exhibit 1

Figure 1. Leadership styles year wise growth

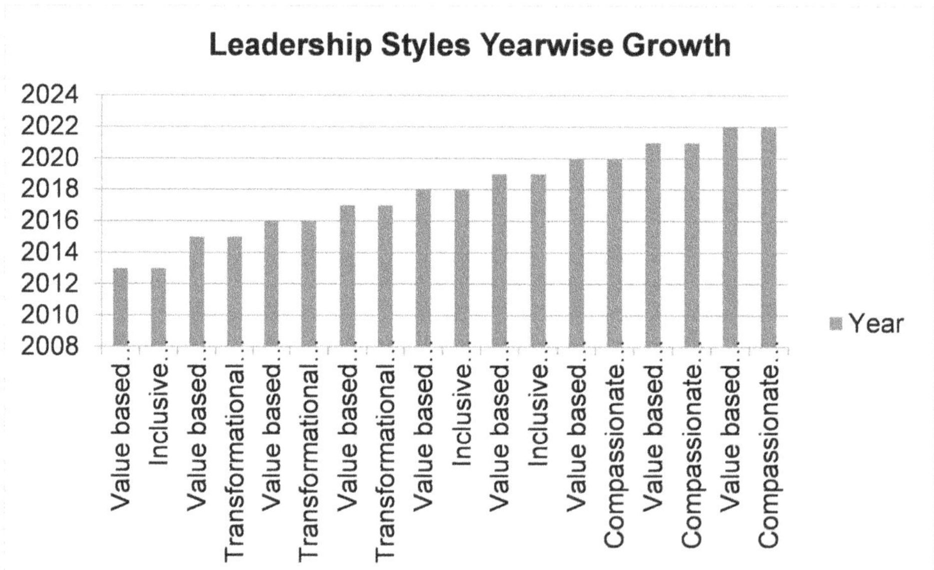

Exhibit 2

Figure 2. Wealth History: Hover to reveal net worth by year

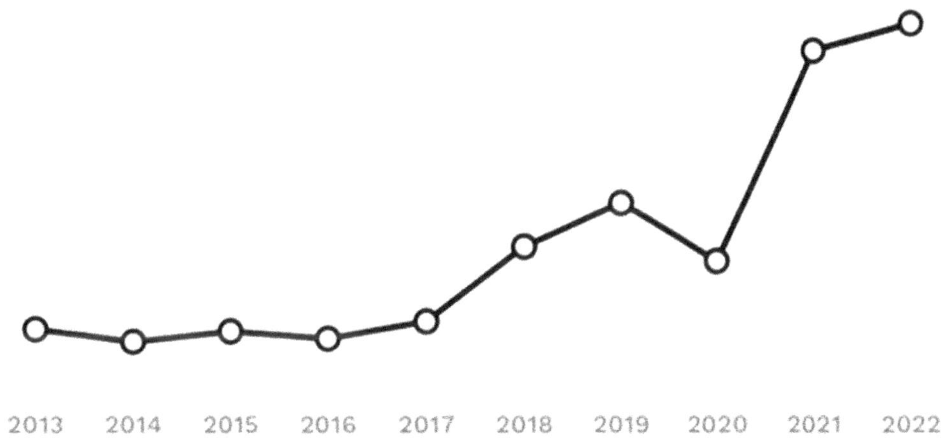

Exhibit 3

Figure 3. CSR spend

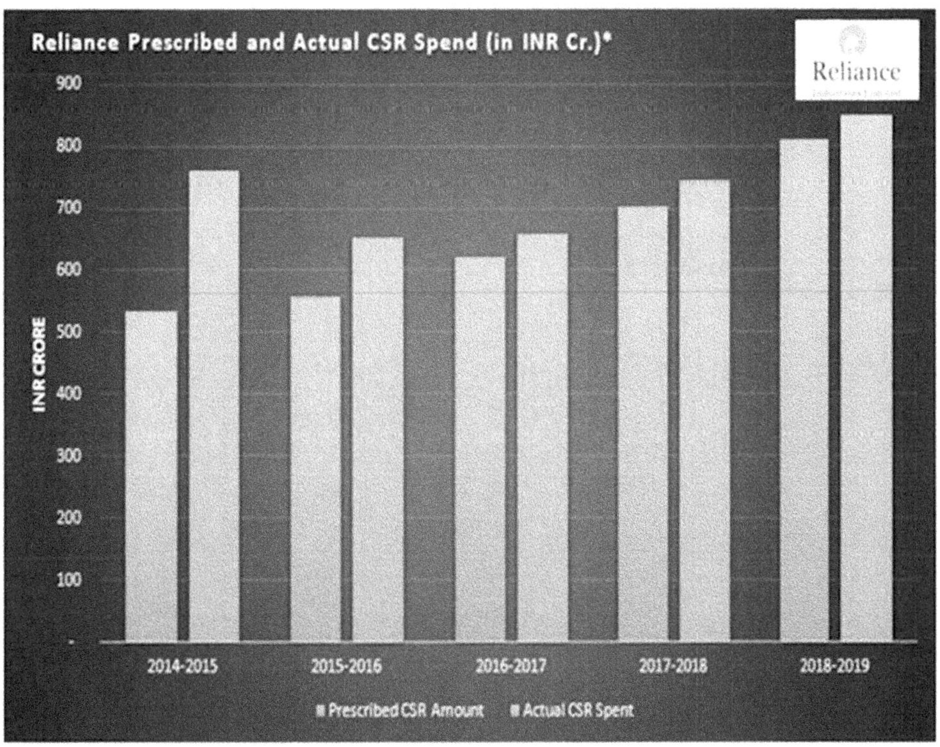

Exhibit 4

Figure 4. Gender inclusion at RIL

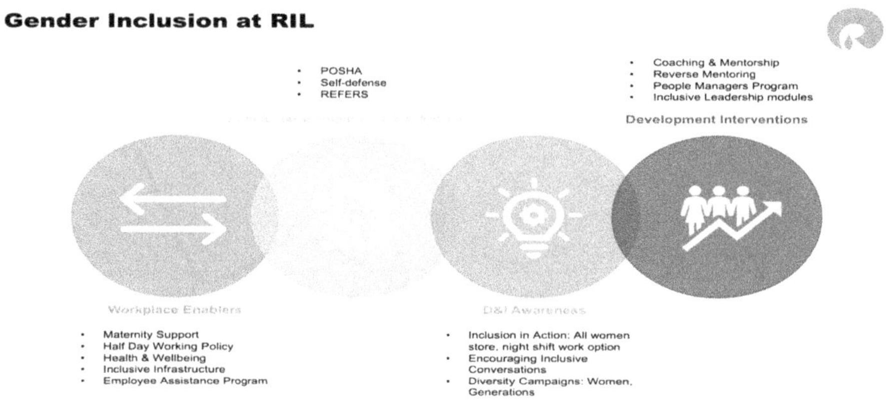

Exhibit 5

Figure 5. Overall gender inclusion

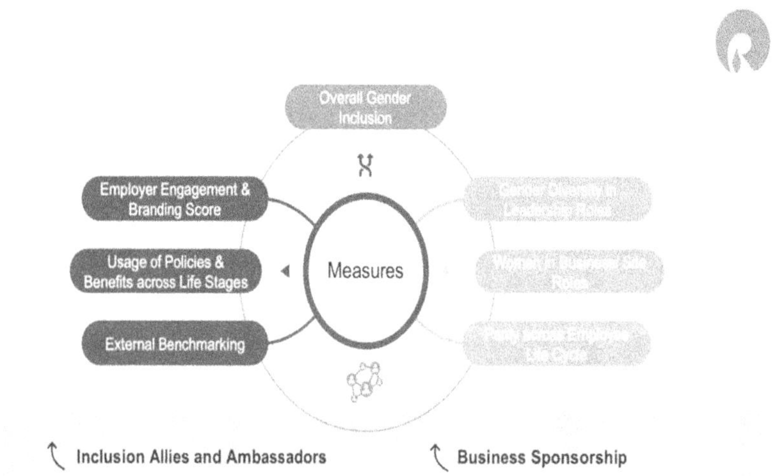

Exhibit 6

Entrepreneurial Characteristics (Interview by CNBC-TV18)

Nine rules to success in Mr. Mukesh Ambani's words:

Be Courageous

The first lesson is courage. Nobody has ever achieved anything big in business or any walk of life without courage. Of course, whenever you do anything big you do feel a little scared but you have got to conquer fear to discover the hidden hero within you. With courage, self-belief, and a can-do spirit, you can overcome any adversity.

Find and Solve Problems

The second piece that I learned is that as an entrepreneur, it's very important to find a problem that you want to solve and that you are passionate about. I was blessed to have professor Sharma at the University Department of Chemical Technology (UDCT) (now Institute of Chemical Technology (ICT)). He would always say I am not going to give you a list of problems and then you can go and work on anything, you find a problem and then I will grade you on the quality of the problem that you, find, and then I will grade you on the quality of solution that you do. So the same rules apply to an entrepreneur that it's not solving problems, it is first finding problems. Once you find the problem, then you solve it.

Work Hard

Put on your running shoes, but remember that personal and professional success is not a sprint but a marathon. We are lucky to be living in a dynamic world where anything is possible but it is important to remember there are no overnight successes you will need to be dedicated, single-minded and there is no substitute for hard work. Also, remember that this marathon of life is not a rat race, it is important to achieve our goals but not at any cost.

Serve a Higher Purpose

My father (Dhirubhai Ambani) started RIL with $100. When I joined RIL in 1980, the market value of the company was $30 million or $40 million and in 30 years, the opportunities that were provided by this country have enabled us to create wealth for India. My father was a big believer that any business that has the sole purpose of making money is not worth doing, it must serve a larger societal purpose. RIL raised all its money from capital markets and individual small shareholders, so we have created a million millionaires just by investing in RIL out of ordinary Indians and that is the process of creating wealth for the country. Once you create opportunity wealth comes.

Accept Failure

Failures are normal. With all the success that one sees, people even in my case don't see how many times I have failed before I succeed, they are just a step before you succeed. So never get disheartened by failures learn from them but never give up.

Ignore the Naysayers

Keep your headphones on, fill your ears and minds with melodies of optimism, and turn out the critics and the cynics, the naysayers - people who say this cannot be done and treat them as noise cancellation. Dance to your music and take some risks in life because it is often the risk taker who changes the course of history, who innovates, who creates something the world desperately needs and contributes to the well-being of millions of lives.

Feel Empathy

Empathy means caring and sharing with every human being in our organization and the world at large, the more we care the higher we grow as human beings. I understand empathy as 'Dil Ki Daulat', it is the wealth of your heart, the more you spend it on others the more wealthy you become.

Make Memories

I think this whole business of making memories - it is such a simple statement but I think it's profound in saying that and particularly now after papa, the only thing that we have of him are his memories and they are very dear to us. Nita used to always say this, that every moment is important and that's what life is all about and I understand what she's saying.

Always Be an Optimist

An entrepreneur is always positive, he's an optimist. There are lots of cynics, and lots of negative people around but an entrepreneur spreads the positive energy that's really what I have learned.

TEACHING NOTE

Synopsis

Compassion, inclusiveness, transformation, value, and vision can all be used to illustrate motivational leadership. Motivational leaders make decisions, establish clear goals, exhibit compassion, and give their teams the tools they need to succeed by empowering everyone and upholding core values. Motivational leaders encourage society to produce caring and transformative leaders for inclusive progress in addition to seeing the best in their workforce.

With a net worth of $100.1 billion, Mukesh Ambani, chairman of Reliance Industries Limited (RIL), is the only Indian to make it to the coveted top 10 list and is placed 10th richest on Forbes' list of billionaires for 2022. Unquestionably, Mr. Ambani is one of the most prosperous entrepreneurs in the history of commerce. He has changed the whole face of Indian industry via his strategies and intelligence, and he also helped society in surviving the pandemic.

By fostering a larger pool of occupations that demand technological expertise and inherently embrace the idea of a welfare state, Mr. Mukesh Ambani has been operating as a good value-based leader while managing one of the largest empires of Reliance Groups. Due to the pandemic, many individuals worldwide have lost friends and relatives.

Reliance Industries Limited (RIL), under the leadership of Mr. Mukesh Amabani, introduced a program – WE CARE as a common, unifying thread that runs through everything. Through this RIL has attached the highest importance to Employee Care.

Having the right people and the right leadership is essential for achieving condescending ideas and seemingly insurmountable objectives. Reliance, under the leadership of Mukesh Ambani, is now implementing a significant leadership turnover.

A motivating leader is aware that society and its members are the sources of all advancement and innovation and, thus, the secret to future success.

Position in Course

This case can be used in PGDM and MBA programs level in courses including organizational behavior, strategic HRM, and change management covering topic leadership, HR planning, and OD interventions.

Learning Objectives

After studying this case, students will be able to:

- Understand the responsibilities and core values of effective leadership
- Learn the role of motivational leadership in business decision-making, social development, and the development of a nation.
- Emulate the motivational leadership characteristics of motivational leaders to develop leadership qualities for self, organization, and social development.

Assignment Questions

1. Why has Mukesh Ambani been so economically successful?
2. Which of those leadership approaches practiced by Mr. Mukesh Ambani leads to motivational leadership?
3. What are the signature traits that inclusive leaders share?

Teaching Plan

A 90-minute class is suggested for the scenario. For there to be a fruitful discussion, the students must have read the case beforehand and done their own analysis.

Table 1. Discussion point durations

Discussion Point	Time (Minutes)
Introduction	10
Assignment question 1	20
Assignment question 2	20
Assignment question 3	20
Conclusion	20

Suggested Supplementary Readings

- BrianA.Hatcher,MantraofHinduHumanism`TheCosmosisOneFamily'(VasudhaivaKutumbakam), Contributions to Indian Sociology 1994 28:149, DOI: 10.1177/006996694028001006.
- Juliet Bourke and Andrea Titus, The Key to Inclusive Leadership, HBR Digital Article, March 06, 2020.
- Timothy Judge and David Wagner, Making Sense of Motivational leadership: The Trail from transformational Leaders to Motivated Followers, Journal of Leadership and Organizational Studies, 2006, Vol. 13, No. 1.

Analysis

1. Why has Mukesh Ambani been so economically successful?

Mr. Mukesh Ambani believes that professional human resource management is required to strike a balance between employees' needs, organizational requirements, and capabilities and the significance of quality human resources for the development of the business and the country as a whole.

He is a visionary type of human who makes future predictions that can help company to gain success in the future. He understands that diverse workforce in the Reliance family seeks for a comprehensive workplace environment where each one is provided with an opportunity to participate, contribute, and grow. People from all backgrounds, genders, ethnicities, and abilities therefore contribute to an inclusive workplace at Reliance by coming as themselves to work. Also, he comprehends the sustainability of a company and its potential, which is not based on its present promises but on what it promises in the future.

Mr. Mukesh is enthusiastic about his investments in 5G and retail, which is estimated to reach $1.3 trillion by 2025 and is growing quickly in India. Even giants of the world have already backed him. Similar to 5G, RIL is projected to prosper as more non-Chinese businesses do business globally. (see Exhibit 1).

Mukesh Ambani said in a statement to shareholders in its annual report for the year ended 31 March 2022. "Just as India has the world's most affordable wireless broadband today, we will have the world's most affordable green energy within this decade."

Mr. Ambani is a value-based leader who expands the pool of occupations that demand technical expertise and envisions the idea of a welfare state in himself. In addition to the employees, he is also teaching people from all walks of life how to use digital technologies. He is giving his subordinates training so they can keep up with the changing technical world and become knowledgeable about it.

Mr. Mukesh Ambani has been so economically successful because he adopted a motivational leadership style with compassion, inclusion, transformation, value, and vision. He makes decisions, sets clear goals, shows compassion, and provides his teams with inclusive empowerment and value-based tools to achieve success. He not only sees the best in his employees but also facilitates society's breeding of compassionate and transformational leaders for inclusive growth (see Exhibit 3).

2. Which of those leadership approaches practiced by Mr. Mukesh Ambani leads to motivational leadership?

Mr. Mukesh Ambani practiced the following leadership approaches, which lead to motivational leadership:

Compassionate leadership is the act of inspiring and influencing team members, friends, and family with compassion so that they might in turn inspire and influence others is known as. Mr. Mukesh Amabani, introduced a program – WE CARE as a common, unifying thread that runs through everything. Through this RIL has attached the highest importance to Employee Care.

Leadership that is inclusive emphasizes inclusivity and outreach rather than domination and strength. Om Sarve Bhavantu Sukhinah, Sarve Santu Niraamayah, Sarve Bhadraanni Pashyantu, and Maa Kashcid-Duhkha-Bhaag-Bhavet are the most well-known Shanti Mantras. It also emphasizes the idea of inclusivity and unity by implying, "May All be Happy, May All be Free from Illness, May All See what is Auspicious, May no one Suffer." Industrial townships, as proposed by Mr. Mukesh Ambani, are consistent with these principles. The townships at Reliance's companies foster the ideas of inclusivity and unity through community living, where the top management shares housing with the working employees and has access to the same amenities as schools, universities, hospitals, and other establishments.

Transformational leaders believe in agility. Mr. Mukesh Ambani is a visionary. He can think of the future; the unknown. He understands the sustainability of a company and it is potential not based on its present promises but on what it promises in the future. He is ahead of even international behemoths. As with 5G, with the world looking forward to doing business with non-China-based companies, RIL is expected to hit pay dirt. "Over the next 12 months, our investments across the Green Energy value chain will gradually start going live, scaling up over the next couple of years. This new growth engine holds great promise to outshine all our existing growth engines in just 5-7 years," Mukesh Ambani said in a statement to shareholders in its annual report for the year ended 31 March 2022. "Just as India has the world's most affordable wireless broadband today, we will have the world's most affordable green energy within this decade."

Values-based leadership is a leadership philosophy and style that is built on the team's and the leader's common assumptions and beliefs. Teams have stronger alignment and gain from higher productivity because they share a set of values.

Vision: To build a global enterprise for all our stakeholders, and a great future for our country, to give millions of young Indians the power to shape their destiny, and the means to realize their full potential. Mr. Mukesh Ambani has been acting as a good value-based leader who created a wider pool of jobs that requires technical knowledge and envisages in itself the concept of a welfare state.

Momentous leadership transition: On December 29, 2021, Mr. Mukesh Ambani made a statement regarding the leadership transition at his energy-to-retail conglomerate, stating that he wanted the process to be sped up with elders, including him, ceding to the younger generation. "From seniors belonging to my generation to the next generation of young leaders... I would like the process to be accelerated. All Seniors—myself included—should now yield to the highly competent, extremely committed, and incredibly promising young leadership talent at Reliance," said Mr. Mukesh Ambani.

3. What are the signature traits that inclusive leaders share?

Given this equation, inclusive leadership is developing as a distinctive and essential skill that enables organizations to adjust to varied clients, markets, ideas, and people. According to the study, published on HBR.org (March 6, 2020), inclusive leaders exhibit a group of six distinguishing characteristics:

1. **Visible Commitment:** They prioritize diversity and inclusion personally, challenge the status quo, hold others accountable, and exhibit a genuine dedication to diversity.
2. **Humility:** They take responsibility for their mistakes, have modesty about their skills, and allow others to contribute.
3. **Awareness of Bias:** They actively work to ensure a meritocracy and exhibit awareness of their own blind spots as well as systemic issues.
4. **Curiosity About Others:** They listen without passing judgment, show a genuine interest in others, have an open mind, and work hard to understand those around them.
5. **Cultural Intelligence:** They are sensitive to the cultural differences of others and take appropriate action.
6. **Effective Collaboration:** They place a strong emphasis on team cohesiveness while also taking psychological safety and variety of thought into consideration.

The class discussion could also cover issues such as:

I. Motivational leadership not only builds the business organization but also the nation.
II. India's philosophy of the world is one family — Vasudhaiva Kutumbakam.

REFERENCES

9 Rules to Success from India's Richest Man Mukesh Ambani. (2019). www.cnbctv18.com

After revenues, Reliance Retail is now biggest in categories too. (2015). www.business-standard.com

Anand, S. (2014). *RelianceFreshDirect.com to deliver fresh groceries in Mumbai.* economictimes.indiatimes.com

Bailey, R. (2014). *RIL plans to launch Jio with 2,000 Digital Xpress Mini outlets.* economictimes.indiatimes.com

Banker, D. V., & Bhal, K. T. (2018). Understanding compassion from practicing managers' perspective: Vicious and virtuous forces in business organizations. *Global Business Review*, *20*(6), 1–17. doi:10.1177/0972150917749279

Bass, B. M. (1985). *Leadership and performance beyond expectations. New York, NY: The Free Press.*

Bennis, W., & Nanus, B. (1985). Leaders: The strategies for taking charge. Harper & Row.

Burns, J. M. (1978). *Leadership*. Harper & Row.

Conger, J. A., & Kanungo, R. A. (1987). Towards a behavioral theory of charismatic leadership in organizational settings. *Academy of Management Review*, *12*(4), 637–647. doi:10.2307/258069

Dubinsky, A. J., Yammarino, F. J., & Jolson, M. A. (1995). An examination of linkages between personal, characteristics and dimension of transformational leadership. *Journal of Business and Psychology*, *9*(3), 315–335. doi:10.1007/BF02230972

FE Online. (2020, Oct. 8). *Mukesh Ambani roots for India to become a global leader, says Jio conceived to enable this journey*. Author.

Ganguly. (2019). *Reliance e-commerce venture to be fueled by $1.4 Bn West Bengal investment.* inc42.com

Hougaard, R., Carter, J., & Hobson, N. (2020). *Compassionate Leadership Is Necessary-but Not Sufficient.* www.hbr.org

House, R. J. (1977). A 1976 theory of charismatic leadership. In J. G. Hunt & L. L. Larson (Eds.), *Leadership: The cutting edge*. Southern Illinois University Press.

It is not just about micro-inequities, it is about inclusion: Seema Nair, Reliance Industries Limited. (n.d.). www.peoplematters.in

Jaiwar, P. (2019). *Mukesh Ambani vs Jeff Bezos vs Jack Ma – The Bulls of Indian e-commerce! Reliance Industries' massive leap of faith.* www.zeebiz.com

Kumar, A. (2013). *Mukesh tops retailer list, too*. www.business-standard.com

Kumar, M. (2016). *Reliance Retail shuts 20 stores, to launch Reliance Smart*. FashionUnited.

Liu, B., Qi, L., & Xu, L. A. (2017). Cross-level impact study of inclusive leadership on employee feedback-seeking behavior. *Journal of Management*, *14*, 677–685. doi:10.3969/j.issn.1672-884x.2017.05.005

Liu, Y., Zhu, W., & Zhao, S. M. (2016). Research on the influence of inclusive leadership on the relationship of the employment relationship and employees' active behavior. *Manag. Rep.*, *10*, 1482–1489.

Mackey, J., McIntosh, S., & Phipps, C. (2020). *Conscious leadership: elevating humanity through business*. Penguin.

Message from our Chairman and RF Founder-Chairperson to the Reliance Family: WE CARE: Honouring the promise of 'One Reliance Family. (2021, June 3). www.ril.com

Mile, R. (n.d.). *World's Billionaires' List – The Richest in 2022.* www.forbes.com/billionaires

Mitter. (2018). *Mukesh Ambani rides on Jio success to become Asia's richest man, surpasses Alibaba founder Jack Ma*. yourstory.com

Mukerjee, W. (2019, Jan. 26). *Reliance Retail to open grocery stores in tier III, IV towns*. economictimes.indiatimes.com

Mukherjee, A. (2018). *Amazon's real rival in India isn't Walmart, it's Reliance.* www.livemint.com

Mukherjee, A. (2019). *Jeff Bezos vs Mukesh Ambani is the bout that had to happen.* economictimes.indiatimes.com

Oruh, E. S., Mordi, C., Dibia, C. H., & Ajonbadi, H. A. (2021). Exploring compassionate managerial leadership style in reducing employee stress level during COVID-19 crisis: The case of Nigeria. *Employee Relations*, *43*(6), 1362–1381. doi:10.1108/ER-06-2020-0302

Our Values & Behaviours. (n.d.). www.ril.com

Raghavendra Kamath, K. (2013). *Few RIL retail arms still making losses*. www.business-standard.com

Randel, A. E., Galvin, B. M., Shore, L. M., Ehrhart, K. H., Chung, B. G., Dean, M. A. U., & Kedharnath, U. (2018). Inclusive leadership: Realizing positive outcomes through belongingness and being valued for uniqueness. *Human Resource Management Review*, *28*(2), 190–203. doi:10.1016/j.hrmr.2017.07.002

Rasul & Chakravarty. (2016). *Reliance Industries plan fashion e-commerce site AJIO.com under Jio brand.* economictimes.indiatimes.com

Reese, S. R. (2017). *Leadership Core Values and Beliefs are Keys to Greatness.* Center for Management and Organization Effectiveness. Available at: https://cmoe.com/blog/great-leaders-have-specific-beliefs-and-core-values

Reliance announces e-commerce foray plans; to challenge Amazon, Flipkart. (2019). www.adgully.com

Reliance in process of momentous leadership transition says Mukesh Ambani. (2021). www.indiatoday.in

Reliance Industries adds 2.32 lakh new jobs in FY22, retail business top recruiter. (2022). www.livemint.com

Reliance Industries to raise $ 750 mn overseas. (2015). www.business-standard.com

Reliance Retail leaps to 94th spot on Deloitte's top retailers' list. (2019). www.economictimes. indiatimes.com

Reliance Retail to launch B2B e-marketplace. (2015). www.business-standard.com

Sabharwal, M. (2014). Is diversity management sufficient? Lead to further performance. *Public Personnel Management*, *43*(2), 1–21. doi:10.1177/0091026014522202

Sharma. (2018). *Soon Reliance Jio might charge its users for JioTV and JioCinema Applications.* telecomtalk.info

Singh, S. (2016a). *Reliance Jio 4G: Data plans, prices, how it is different and everything else you need to know.* www. indiatoday.in

Singh, S. (2016b). *Reliance Jio: Free calls forever, Rs 50 for 1GB data, free to try until Dec 2016.* www. indiatoday.in

Tepper, B. D., Dimotakis, N., Lambert, L. S., Koopman, J., Matta, F. K., Man Park, H., & Goo, W. (2018). Examining follower responses to transformational leadership from a dynamic, person-environment fit perspective. *Academy of Management Journal*, *61*(4), 1343–1368. doi:10.5465/amj.2014.0163

Thacker, H. (2022). *The Definitive CSR Report of Reliance Industries Ltd. The CSR Journal.*

Tichy, N. M., & Devanna, M. A. (1986). *The transformational leader*. Wiley.

Tirmizi, S. A. (2018). An integrative Framework for responsible Leadership Practice. In *In Enacting values-based change* (pp. 123–136). Palgrave Macmillan. doi:10.1007/978-3-319-69590-7_9

Chapter 12
People Management in an Indian IT Services Company During COVID-19: A Case Analysis

Navreet Kaur
Chitkara Business School, Chitkara University, India

EXECUTIVE SUMMARY

The case revolves around the reactionary measures taken by an Indian IT services company based in Pune in an attempt to stay afloat during the COVID-19 pandemic. The case, in particular, brings to light the effect of the employee-related managerial decisions on their well-being and work involvement amidst the unprecedented health crisis. The pronounced role of leadership, decision making, communication, conflict management, employee perceptions, and HR policies is well brought out in the narrative. Apart from the key takeaways, the readers are provoked to analyze the case and deliberate on novel ways to manage a business within India's unique socio-economic scenario. The in-depth account acquires significance in the light of rapid digital transformation due to the pandemic and its impact on business and management. It paves the way for empirical research on the newer constructs in the areas of organizational behavior and has implications for human resource policies in the VUCA environment.

INTRODUCTION

"Like Abraham Lincoln, I am a firm believer in the people. If given the truth, they can be depended upon to meet any national crisis. The great point is to bring them the real facts." – Douglas MacArthur

Shivraj Shekhar, the Chairman of IndoGlobal IT Remedies Pvt. Ltd. sat in his Pune home office. It was the 12th of June, 2020 and he was reflecting on the unprecedented damage caused by the pandemic. The issue on his mind was the reactionary measures taken, so far, by the company in response to Covid-19, their ramifications, and the future course of action. He regretted the short-sightedness of

DOI: 10.4018/978-1-6684-8488-3.ch012

the company leadership in handling the employees during the first wave of the pandemic, the serious mistakes committed in dealing with the emergency and the inability to devise flexible HR policies. Amidst the sensitive scenario, it was crucial to take decisions that could help business stay afloat. His mind was in a brainstorming mode trying to come up with ideas of how to manage the various resources in the company – both tangible and intangible. Instant decisions were the need of the hour. It was time to respond with agility to this volatile, uncertain, complex and ambiguous situation.

Background Information

1. Healthcare IT Industry in India

A knowledge-based economy is characterised by the use of information technology in various business domains and health services is no exception. Hospitals in India either have an in-house IT department or have outsourced IT services such as computerization of medical records, networking of various departments in a hospital, and providing of tele-medicine services. This has resulted in a symbiotic relationship between different levels of health care. The primary and secondary level hospitals can have a direct access to the Super Speciality Hospitals resulting in collaboration. This new organisation model in a HealthTech company provides an atmosphere conducive to patient health resulting in a win-win situation.

With the changing ecosystem of the healthcare industry, its IT requirements are radically different from the past. The emergence of corporate hospitals on a larger scale is relatively a recent development which has led to greater professionalism. With privatisation, modern management models are being applied to most healthcare institutions, with a few exceptions. Today, resources and manpower are being strategically utilized; patient convenience and experience is in the forefront along with the use of analytics not only for reporting purposes but for all aspects of patient care and hospital functioning. The existence of different categories of hospitals throws light on the complex Indian hospital landscape. The primary and secondary hospitals are still working on the traditional health services model. Technology in health care is primarily associated with super speciality and multi speciality hospitals and also tertiary care hospitals which work on the dictum "Expert Care for Everything".

Health-tech market in India has seen a considerable expansion since the onset of the pandemic. Teleconsultations, digital wellness and health tracking, e-diagnostics, e-pharmacy etc. started witnessing a sharp rise with more and more people seeking remote healthcare solutions. The onset of Covid-19 resulted in an unprecedented need for IT solutions in all the four kinds of patient care viz. acute, chronic, preventive, and predictive; the focus on acute health being more salient (Sharma, 2023).

2. Challenges Specific to Healthcare IT Industry in India (Sharma, 2023):
    i. Inaccessible and insufficient quality care in the backward areas is a roadblock to the application of IT in hospitals. Healthcare can be facilitated through IT only in major Indian cites where specialist doctors are available.
    ii. Application of IT remains uneven because of incomplete, fragmented and contradictory information on patient care and medical procedures.
    iii. Handling complete, updated and accurate patient records through a database is not easy because of a resource crunch.

Nonetheless with the help of IT, patient care has improved drastically (Salam & Bajaba, 2021). In IT enabled hospitals:

i. The quality of service is better because of efficiency in terms of reach and delivery of service.
ii. Structured data is made available through integrated electronic medical records which help in trend analysis and in identifying disease outbreaks.
iii. Electronic patient record documenting each patient's blood group, known allergies etc. prevents manual errors.
iv. IT facilitates remote diagnosis of patients. As a result, people in rural areas can also have access to consultation from speciality doctors.
v. Electronic Customer Relationship Management (CRM) aids in tracking patient loyalty, satisfaction and grievances.
vi. Patients can move seamlessly across different geographical locations.
vii. IT provides accounting framework thus enabling billing, inventory management, store management, laboratory management, etc.

The present case study brings to the forefront the challenges in people management in an IT support company providing essential services to hospitals during the pandemic. The case also highlights the inability of the management in handling human resources in a crisis situation and suggests remedies thereof.

THE COMPANY: INDOGLOBAL IT REMEDIES PVT. LTD.

IT solutions being the need of the hour, the company was set up way back in 2010. From a humble start-up to a growing giant of a company, the business had come a long way. The company offered essential services in the form of IT solutions to the healthcare sector and had partnerships with other IT enterprises. It succeeded in maintaining a stable market share amidst considerable competition and had started expanding in the Asian continent only recently. Shivraj had visualized the company to expand to Europe by the year 2025. Covid-19 was a bolt from the blue that not only hit the nation's economic roots but also its social framework (N. Kaur, 2020).

With over 30,000 employees and regional centres in different Indian states, the Health Tech company strived to offer world-class software solutions to both public and private sector hospitals. Its motto being "building digitally healthy societies", IndoGlobal addressed both the software and services needs of healthcare facilities and broadly offered two kinds of key job roles viz. that of a software engineer and of a call centre employee.

The IT professionals within the organization helped maintain digital infrastructure and provide troubleshooting assistance to technology consumers in the health care industry (Pradhan et al., 2022). Besides, there were data management professionals who designed hospital-specific structured database systems, created data-loss contingency plans and analytics of gathered data. These Electronic Health Records (EHRs) were used by health care professionals and also patients to store, share, and analyze health information. IT consultants worked with health care groups to solve business problems related to technology.

IndoGlobal IT Remedies had a pivotal role to play during the pandemic for two reasons viz.

1. The increasing need for remote health care or telehealth. Hospitals had outsourced the task of organizing virtual visits which allow the patient to see a health care provider, mental health counsellor or a nurse via online video or phone chats.
2. The company had a tie up with the National Health Ministry for developing a digital service in the form of a mobile app named 'Sanjeevani' which could tell the user the risk of getting Covid-19, identify symptoms, and provide updates on local and national Covid-19 cases. The ultimate purpose of this app was to spread awareness of Covid-19 and to connect essential Covid-19-related health services to citizens.

The tasks performed by the call centre representative included handling many inbound and outbound calls from and to patients and health care providers and administrators; identifying the needs of customers, resolving issues, and providing solutions; up-selling software products wherever possible; and abiding by the customer service script provided by the company for uniformity. The aim of the medical call centre was also to provide other patient support services such as referrals, admissions and discharges, prescriptions, scheduling, etc.

THE COMPANY'S RESPONSE TO COVID-19

Early March: When Covid-19 was declared a pandemic, the first directive issued by the CEO was that it is imperative for employees to be present in the office as a mark of support to the frontline employees and also to maintain group morale. The instructions showed his apprehensions towards online work and his general resistance to change (N. Kaur, 2021).

Employees showed frustration and anger towards the announcement along with heightened safety concerns. Some voiced their worries as regards the irresponsible, unethical and callous attitude of the management. Being onsite was pointless in the wake of the virus spreading and WHO guidelines on the severity of Covid-19 and social distancing. A compromise on health was not possible. An employee interview revealed how a discontented employee went to the vice president's office and gave a resignation which was not accepted. The employee was asked to re-think over the weekend. However, on the same day when he reached home, he received an email that his resignation has been accepted.

Late March: Covid cases continued to increase but government's instructions on shutting down of private enterprises were unclear and varied considerably from state to state. The CEO issued another set of instructions saying that there would be no layoffs for the next 2 months and that all employees will receive 3 weeks of paid time off to deal with Covid related circumstances. If employees desired to work from home, they were heavily encouraged to use their PTO, otherwise they should report to their offices. Employees were told that they would be updated regularly on the guidelines but this did not happen.

By April, 2020, it was found that over 10,000 employees in different regional centres have contracted the virus. 65% of call centre employees were still required to be in the office and 10% were fired despite the promise of 'no layoffs'. The situation became further grim with the passing away of 120 employees. Amidst the mismanagement the company started making efforts to control further damage. A 10% hike in pay on returning to normalcy was decided upon along with medical aid to the employees and their dependents. However, workers were sceptical about the new HR policies.

SUGGESTED PRE-READS

Kaur, N. (2020). The global impact of economic, psychosocial and geopolitical changes in the context of Covid-19: An analytical review. *Journal of Advanced Research in Dynamical and Control Systems, 12*(SP7), 1954-1960. https://doi.org/10.5373/JARDCS/V12SP7/20202310

Kaur, N. (2021). Digitalization and work behaviour: A paradigm shift. In A. Singh (Ed.), *Big data analytics for improved accuracy, efficiency, and decision making in digital marketing* (pp. 102-123). IGI Global. https://doi.org/10.4018/978-1-7998-7231-3.ch008

Salam, M.A. & Bajaba, S. (2021). The role of transformative healthcare technology on quality of life during the COVID-19 pandemic. *Journal of Enabling Technologies, 15*(2), 87-107. https://doi.org/10.1108/JET-12-2020-0054

TEACHING NOTE

Synopsis of the Case

In the first phase of COVID-19, the management of IndoGlobal IT Remedies Pvt. Ltd. took some injudicious decisions which led to employee discontent and unrest. Shivraj Shekhar, the Chairman of the company, was much perturbed by the narrow, unimaginative approach of the CEO in handling a crisis situation. In order to maintain the company performance, he began thinking of how to respond in the future. The case is about how the company which provides essential services in the health care sector needs to revamp its HR policies, restructure itself, and more importantly, modify its leadership style.

Target Group

The case study is a generic one meant to be discussed with students of business administration, both undergraduate and postgraduate. It can be specifically incorporated in the courses on Organizational Behaviour and Human Resource Management. It will be useful in helping students gain conceptual clarity and get acquainted with contemporary challenges in people management. The complete case discussion is for 120 minutes.

Case Objectives

1. To make students understand the challenges in people management during a crisis situation.
2. To appreciate the crucial role of leadership and communication during a catastrophe.
3. To understand employee grievances and realize the necessity of devising new HR policies that keep the employees engaged in difficult times.
4. To understand the significance of strategic changes in business in the Covid-19 era.

Teaching Strategy (Rangaswamy, 2021)

The case study along with relevant pre-reads will be shared with the class prior to the class discussion. A discussion on geo-political and socio-economic changes related to Covid-19 would serve as a prelude to actual case analysis. The duration of the activity would be 120 minutes and the time plan will be as follows:

Table 1. Initial discussion durations

Initial Discussion	20 minutes
Class to be split into 5 groups and one question allocated to each group for brainstorming	5 minutes
Group Analysis Question 1 (key issues)	15 minutes
Group Analysis Question 2 (leadership)	15 minutes
Group Analysis Question 3 (communication)	15 minutes
Group Analysis Question 4 (HR policies)	15 minutes
Group Analysis Question 5 (restructuring)	15 minutes
Wrap up (consolidation of learning at the end of the case session)	20 minutes

Source: Author

Questions for Discussion

1. What are the key people management issues in the case?
2. What kind of company leadership should have been effective in the event of a global disaster like the pandemic?
3. How can the company reduce errors in the process of communication?
4. Should HR policies be reframed in a crisis like this? If so, how?
5. How crucial is organizational restructuring in an unprecedented scenario like this?

Probable Answers to Case Questions

Question 1: What are the key people management issues in the case?

Probable Answer:

An analysis of the aforementioned timeline of events brought out the following underlying issues:

1. Leadership style.
2. Inadequate communication resulting in lack of transparency and consequent breach of trust of employees by the management.
3. HR policies and employee scepticism surrounding these.
4. Organizational restructuring, work re-arrangements, and process improvement (Jaiswal & Arun, 2022).

Based on the case study and pre-reads, the views of Group 1 on each of the above issues will form the basis of discussion.

Question 2: What kind of company leadership should have been effective in the event of a global disaster like the pandemic?

Probable Answer:

A perusal of the case indicates leadership ineffectiveness within the company both at the CEO and HR levels resulting in a serious effect on employee engagement and consequent revenue generation. An analysis of the issue reveals the significance of cultural relativity in regard to leadership. Indian management is traditionally 'paternalistic' and thus marked by command and control, excessive supervision and micro-management which negatively impact employee performance, particularly in a crisis situation. Also, in the virtual workplace, a supervisor's ability to exercise micromanagement is almost impossible.

To handle a remote workplace, it was crucial for the CEO to display an empathetic mode of leadership which is at the very core of 'androgynous leadership' (N. Kaur & Parihar, 2022). 'Androgyny' refers to psychological gender as opposed to biological gender. It is a blend of male and female characteristics at a psychological level. An androgynous person, whether a male or female, will present a confluence of masculine and feminine behavioural traits and will be goal-oriented or relationship-oriented depending on the situation. An androgynous male leader, for instance, would be high on assertiveness, risk-taking and task-orientation and also on compassion, nurturance, expressiveness, sensitivity, concern for others and attention to detail. Such individuals are emotionally balanced and adaptive and succeed both personally and professionally. They are flexible with an ability to switch roles and hence, function effectively in the VUCA environment. Androgynous leaders can provide their employees with an environment that is conducive to their well-being.

In a time of crisis, managerial leaders need to re-align their skills and capabilities to enable people to adapt to the new normal. In order to prevent further damage at the workplace due to the Covid-19 calamity, the leadership of IndoGlobal IT Remedies Pvt. Ltd. must focus on developing a network of teams, maintaining a flexible hierarchy, exhibiting informed optimism, making information-based decisions, and showing the human side through empathy.

Question 3: How can the company reduce errors in the process of communication?

Probable Answer:

Communication is the most important factor in successfully leading people through changes. It can be seen in the case that communication was intimidating, scarce and lacking in transparency. The authorities did not abide by what was promised which resulted in a breach of trust. In the future, a demonstration of purpose behind any piece of communication would make the process rational and non-threatening. Communicating a reason behind a decision would make the management trustworthy thus reducing the antagonism of employees.

To rebuild employee relations, the company could set up two-way communication channels, a 'Tell & Listen' portal, for instance. Table Top Workshops (TTX) involving a simulated disaster-preparedness activity could be set up and cross-functional teams formed to bring in a sense of collective ambition. Virtual Town Hall Meetings can be a regular feature for company updates and also for building team spirit. Information should be clearly transmitted to customers and other stakeholders. Instead of taking on a strong stance while ignoring employee concerns, it is reasonable to write a weekly email providing a company-wide update.

A "3 Cs approach" can enable employee engagement in a virtual scenario viz. Care, Culture, and Community. Care is possible through frequent manager check-ins in this stressful time to instil in the employees a sense of inclusion and belongingness. Culture can be created by building learning agility in the employees through opportunities for re-skilling so that they remain productive and relevant, and also by employee sentiment analysis and a positive virtual onboarding experience. A community feeling can be instilled by enabling workers join interest groups, share their daily stresses and Covid stories enabling them to build resilience and feel a sense of bonding and psychological safety.

Question 4: Should HR policies be reframed in a crisis like this? If so how?

Probable Answer:

In general employee needs must be balanced with business needs. Cost-saving initiatives should be planned and managed. Strategic responses must be decided upon after critically evaluating the situations. The HR policies must be revamped and reframed keeping telework in mind (Azizi et al., 2021). A task force, responsible for writing new policies keeping in view future unprecedented events, must be created. Following aspects are important in this regard:

1. The HR department must refrain from downsizing; instead more IT professionals should be hired for troubleshooting.
2. New joiners must experience adequate organizational, job, and human induction. This can be made possible through effective induction software.
3. Questions on compensation, benefits and appraisal bonus should not generate anxiety and insecurity among employees.
4. Since work will extend beyond office hours, there will be a blurring of spatial and temporal differences between work and home. Hence, management will have to ensure a work-life balance to the extent possible. For example, monitoring or too much surveillance should be avoided as it erodes trust in the organization and also generates anxiety resulting in errors at work.
5. Virtual fun evenings can be organized once in a week for one hour to counter the effects of social isolation and generate positive employee attitudes and mental well-being. Medical aid must be provided to employees and their families. A quarantine centre can be made inside the premises of the company in various states.
6. Key performance indicators must be based on productivity and quality both. Appraisal politics should be discouraged and holistic assessment of performance which includes behavioural indices and not just number of hours worked should be ensured.
7. Training and development programs will have to be redesigned in the wake of organizational restructuring due to pandemic-induced remote work.
8. A resource centre must be set up for employees to seek information and guidance along with crisis task forces well equipped to handle changes.

Question 5: How crucial is organizational restructuring in an unprecedented scenario like this?

Probable answer:

Organizational design must stay aligned with two-pronged organizational strategy of customer service and employee well-being (Sulaiman et al., 2020). A decentralized structure that could foster creativity would be workable. Restructuring of the organizational design in a catastrophe is crucial to organizational survival. Following are the areas of concern:

1. Job descriptions will have to be revised owing to a paradigm shift in the method of dong work. Changes in job design would mean adapting jobs to meet new standards and expectations.
2. Re-engineering would be required because of some processes becoming irrelevant and burdensome.
3. Performance management must continue to track important metrics such as sales and project completions etc.
4. A significant HR function associated with organizational restructuring is training and development particularly of the frontline call centre employees who handle both hospital specific and patient related issues. Virtual call centres would require different kind of skills and it is imperative in the pandemic scenario that every interaction with the patient is healing so that he is set on a positive path. The company has numerous challenges to face in this regard:
    i. To get a huge call centre workforce to work remotely from home. The process could be made easier by using cloud-based software.
    ii. Handling the burden on contact centres and keeping its customer service workforce safe.
    iii. Reducing customer wait times and managing customer frustration.
    iv. Deflecting or redistributing contact volumes to control average wait times.
    v. Automating quickly and enhancing digital channels.
    vi. Managing workforce if physical work locations are no longer viable.
    vii. Offering the same level of customer support and workforce productivity when agents work from home.
    viii. Maintaining the trust of both workforce and customers.
    ix. Training call centre employees on both technical skills and soft skills.
    x. Protecting a workforce in a high-risk environment.

Health care centres are lifelines to improve patient health. During Covid-19, customer service and outreach is an essential service. Given the rapid spread of Covid-19, many organizations faced difficulties in transitioning from a traditional call centre to a virtual one. Many firms struggled to ship the required hardware and software to their agents' location to enable them to begin working remotely. In a virtual health care centre, risks of execution failure are higher than normal. But an adequately trained workforce can effectively respond to the immediate needs created by Covid-19 which in turn can bring the company a long-term benefit in terms of increased customer brand perception and loyalty (Kumar et al., 2021).

To summarize, the company leadership must stay ethical and dedicated and strive to bring constructive changes in technology, structure and people management in an adverse environment. In certain states like Maharashtra which were under complete lockdown, managing the servers amidst technical glitches and power failures is an enormous task for workers. Hence, state-specific strategies should be formulated and implemented given the country's unique socio-economic scenario, uneven development, diversity, and health care issues. From a wider perspective, companies need to analyze the current landscape, look at challenges and upcoming trends, consult key practitioners from outside the company, and adopt a proactive approach.

Conclusion: The global COVID-19 pandemic has led to serious psychological and economic complexities for people all over the globe. The role of HR professionals had assumed a greater significance in the light of unprecedented changes within and outside the organization. The case study in question is about three major challenges which required strategic changes in the way the workforce was to be handled. The below mentioned challenges (Harte, 2020) demanded an overhauling of organizational policies that would have implications for government regulations during the health crisis:

i. **Communication:** For their faster adaptation, a quicker formal communication with the employees was required due to continual changes in government directives and regulations by health authorities. The higher authorities were expected to connect to the staff on a regular basis to reassure that they are being looked after. A virtual informal platform could be created where employees can chat with each other and feel de-stressed in the distressing time.
ii. **Trust:** Companies should show transparency to gain trust of the employees, more so due to remote work. This was possible if managers openly discussed about work priorities and attainable targets asking employees to voice barriers preventing the execution of their work. KPI metrics should be reported weekly by each team to the CEO who must behave more like a coach than an evaluator for effective performance management.
iii. **Rapid Policy Change:** Due to volatile changes in the situation, every company policy needed to be updated by integrating COVID-19 clauses and with respect to new government guidelines. Online webinars by different companies could provide the HR department with benchmarks necessary to get through the business disruption. Company regulations were to be participatively set by allowing employees autonomy. Employees would then perceive organizational justice leading to organizational commitment, reduced turnover intentions and employee engagement (Aggarwal et al., 2022).

EXPERIENCE OF USING THE CASE

Includes feedback on how the case has worked in different classes and the issues on which students have tended to focus. This can be useful for other teachers preparing to teach the case.

REFERENCES

Aggarwal, A., Jaisinghani, D., & Nobi, K. (2022). Effect of organizational justice and support on organizational commitment and employee turnover intentions: The mediating role of employee engagement. *International Journal of Quality and Service Sciences*, *14*(4), 525–554. doi:10.1108/IJQSS-08-2021-0112

Azizi, M. R., Atlasi, R., Ziapour, A., Abbas, J., & Naemi, R. (2021). Innovative human resource management strategies during the COVID-19 pandemic: A systematic narrative review approach. *Heliyon*, 7(6), e07233. doi:10.1016/j.heliyon.2021.e07233 PMID:34124399

Harte, A. (2020, April 2). 3 HR automation challenges during the Covid-19 pandemic. *FlowForma*. https://www.flowforma.com/blog/3-challenges-faced-by-human-resources-during-the-covid-19-pandemic

Jaiswal, A., & Arun, C. J. (2022). *Working from home during COVID-19 and its impact on Indian employees' stress and creativity*. Asian Business and Management. doi:10.105741291-022-00202-5

Kaur, N., & Parihar, A. (2022). Hybrid Model of Work and Employee Attitudes: Challenges to HR Leadership in the Context of Indian Organizations. *NeuroQuantology : An Interdisciplinary Journal of Neuroscience and Quantum Physics*, *20*(10), 5656–5667. https://doi.org/NQ.2022.20.10.NQ55565

Kumar, N. S., Kapoor, S., & Gupta, S.K. (2021). Impact of Covid-19 on the future of HR in India's service sector. *Turkish Journal of Physiotherapy and Rehabilitation, 32*(3), 34941-34949. https://www.researchgate.net/publication/357738038_Impact_of_Covid-19_on_the_future_of_HR_in_India's_service_sector

MacArthur, D. (1944, April 14). Getting facts to the people. *Tuscaloosa (AL) News*. https://www.barrypopik.com/index.php/new_york_city/entry/i_am_a_firm_believer_in_the_people_if_given_the_truth_they_can_meet_any_nat

Pradhan, K., John, P., & Sandhu, N. (2021). AI in healthcare. *Journal of Hospital Management and Health Policy*, *5*, 1–10. doi:10.21037/jhmhp-20-126

Rangaswamy, U. S. (2021). Chai Thela: The Migh"Tea" problem of start-up expansion. *South Asian Journal of Management*, *28*(1), 171–190.

Sharma, A. S. (2023). Healthcare IT in India. *Asian Hospital & Healthcare Management*. https://www.asianhhm.com/information-technology/ajaysharma-interview

Sulaiman, M. A. B. A., Ahmed, M. N., & Shabbir, M. S. (2020). Covid-19 challenges and human resource management in organized retail operations. *Utopía y Praxis Latinoamericana*, *25*(12), 81–92. doi:10.5281/zenodo.4280092

Chapter 13
Leadership Succession Challenges and Issues in Social Enterprise

Muklesh Kumar Tiwari
Chandigarh University, India

Tarun Kumar Sharma
Dalmia Cement Bharat Ltd., New Delhi, India

EXECUTIVE SUMMARY

Every organisation has leadership succession issues. This is more challenging in social entrepreneurship. This case addresses leadership succession issues in social enterprise. Social entrepreneur Padmshree Phoolbasan Bai Yadav fought poverty and empowered rural women. Her 2 million rurally disadvantaged and uneducated women's network earned 40 crore rupees through social business until 2018. She concentrated on education, health, hygiene, fighting addiction, and independent jobs. She designed a four-layer framework to fulfil these societal tasks. She worried about replacing leaders at each level. As she sought leadership succession, she stressed that a leader should shun politics, work from the heart, not be arrogant or self-driven, and be willing to give her life to society. Her successor and leadership transitions scared her.

BACKGROUND

Phulbasan was born into a rural household that was so poor that her parents were unable to feed her every day. She had to start working at the age of seven due to her tremendous poverty, yet she was still able to finish seventh grade. She married at the age of 10 in Sukuldaihan, Rajnandgaon (Chhattisgarh), a neighbouring hamlet (Annexure 1). She was sent to her husband's home after four years of marriage in accordance with the *Gauna*[1] (social rite). Her in-law's family's only source of income was cow grazing, which was insufficient for their ability to support themselves.

DOI: 10.4018/978-1-6684-8488-3.ch013

Phulbasan's husband was a herder who was also uneducated. She also engaged in the same occupation, but the revenues were insufficient for them to afford enough food each day. They lived in a modest cabin on the village's outskirts as their place of residence. She had five children when she was twenty years old and was unable to provide for their needs in terms of housing, food, education, and clothing. Cattle grazing in the village and gathering cow dung to bake cakes from, which she sold, were her main sources of revenue. She was not receiving enough money from her job to provide for her family.

She was a mother of five children and was constantly depressed since she was unable to give her kids food, an education, and other necessities. Because no one in the hamlet provided them with food, her children often went the whole day without eating. She was preparing meals for them after coming back from cattle grazing. It was a challenging period for her as a mother; she frequently considered suicide, but she always had the idea that "God gave this life to achieve something, not to commit suicide" cross her thoughts. She believed that her situation was not unique to her and that it affected many women in her village's community at the time of her poverty and misery. She made the decision one day to help economically independent, impoverished, and illiterate women escape poverty.

The Journey of Social Entrepreneurship

Phulbasan began promoting the economic independence of women in her community in the year 2000 and tried to advance society so that other women would not experience the same issue she did. She highlighted the main issues plaguing society as being poor financial standing, a lack of a reliable source of income, low levels of education among women, and a lack of resources available to the underprivileged. She began her social entrepreneurial adventure by encouraging the economically underprivileged and lower class ladies of Sukuldaihan village to create their own businesses. She urged them to recognise their rights, pursue education, and achieve financial independence. She initially believed that the poor would be exploited by society if they were not financially independent, and that poverty was the main factor in exploitation. She first began assisting ladies in the community who shared her position in education and cleanliness. She faced fierce opposition from every quarter of the town, but she was determined to transform society, so she kept her spirits up and organised a group of women to do the task. Phulbasan began promoting the economic independence of women in her community in the year 2000 and tried to advance society so that other women would not experience the same issue she did. She highlighted the main issues plaguing society: poor financial standing, a lack of a reliable source of income, low levels of education among women, and a lack of resources available to the underprivileged. She began her social entrepreneurial adventure by encouraging the economically underprivileged and lower-class ladies of Sukulbihan village to create their businesses. She urged them to recognise their rights, pursue education, and achieve financial independence. She initially believed that the poor would be exploited by society if they were not financially independent, and that poverty was the main factor in exploitation. She first began assisting ladies in the community who shared her position in the areas of education and cleanliness. She faced fierce opposition from every quarter of the town, but she was determined to transform society, so she kept her spirits up and organised a group of women to do the task.

She took part in bidding for a *Bazar Theka*[2] (market contract) into a *gram panchayat*[3] under the auspices of the women's society (the first women's society) to become financially independent. The community received the contract. She encountered several issues, some of which were life-threatening, from groups who had before been her competitors in the market to her group. This job was primarily male-dominated. She encountered difficulties in the early stages of her profession, including threats to her life, vandalism, and social exclusion. They went to the district collector (DM)[4]Dinesh Shrivastava, who recognised her efforts and offered to aid and advise them on how to deal with the issues.

He proposed that they establish a women's self-help organisation so that the government could assist them. In her hamlet of Sukulbihan, she founded the "Pragya women Self Help Group" (WSHG), which she renamed Maa Bamleshwari Janhit Kare Samiti in honour of Goddess Durga in 2012. A local village hat awarded the tax collecting contract to this WSLG. All of the group members were greatly inspired by this victory. The WSHG-awarded position was mostly seen as male-dominant, demanding, and difficult, particularly for women. She struggled in the early stages of her project with threats, vandalism, and social backlash, but her perseverance helped her reach the goal. Her team was successful on their first attempt. She gained more fame and acceptability in society due to her accomplishment.

By utilising the government's women's empowerment programme in 2001, Phoolbasan initially established the "Women Self Help Group" (WSHG) "Pragya" in the hamlet and began the battle for women's rights. She pushed women to make little saves, which had huge results quickly. Poor women were motivated to establish unorthodox professions by Phulbasan. Out of her 12000 groups, 18 are engaged in mine contracts, 129 in fishing, 432 in agriculture, 215 in catering, 339 in vegetable growing, and 276 in operating fair price stores, in addition to animal husbandry and the making of bricks and roof tiles (Annexure 2). Her village's women are no longer repressed and powerless. Phoolbasan picked up cycling and has encouraged more than 4000 ladies to do the same. She makes sure that women take part in the *Gram Sabhas* and contribute to the village's growth.

Once the organisation was established, they began engaging in various activities in the village, many of which were dominated by males in the community. Examples include running women's sewing centres and implementing village sanitation and cleaning programmes. Soon, the organisation ramps up its efforts by carrying out a variety of tasks, such as organising health camps, blood donation drives, providing nourishing food, promoting vitamin use, taking precautions for pregnant women, performing general health checks on women in the village, etc. Her contributions to society were received with great enthusiasm.

The district's women SHGs were engaged in a variety of income-generating activities, including *Bazar Theka*[5] (market contract), operating fair price ration shops[6], setting up mines, operating general/provision stores, fishing, horticulture, animal husbandry, poultry farming, agricultural works and produces, gathering-buying and selling of forest products, vegetable vending, operating cottage industries, operating hotels, grocery and cloth shops, etc.

The Success and Recognition

One of Chhattisgarh's poorer districts in terms of economic health, Rajnandgaon received a considerable economic boost. (Census Data: 1991, 2001, 2011 - for financial status, males and women, income, etc.) All facets of society recognised and valued Phulbasan's contributions. She and her team began receiving several honours from various platforms. Phulbasan received the "Padam Shree," the fourth-highest civilian honour in India, in 2010 (Annexure 3).

Challenges

The initiative that Pragya launched in 2001—later renaming it Maa Bamleshwari Janhit Kare Samiti, after Goddess Durga—has grown to include 12143 SHGs across all villages and taluka in the state of Chhattisgarh. All of the villages in the Rajnadgaon district employ two lakh women. In 2021, all SHGs operating in the Rajnandgoan area had integrated the economically disadvantaged poor into society. A catalyst for social change among the uneducated and underprivileged women of the Rajnandgaon district, she created women's SHGs and gave them the power to aid the weak and underprivileged.

Phoolbasan concentrated her efforts on five key areas: society's de-addiction efforts, education, health, cleanliness, and self-employment. She developed a four-layer framework to carry out these general activities for society members at the *village level-→Cluster level →Block level → and District level* society members. She was worried about how each level's leaders will be replaced. She emphasised that a leader should stay away from political activities, work from the heart, not be egotistical, self-driven, and especially eager to give her life to society, as she is searching for leadership succession. She was concerned about her own successor as well as leadership succession at many levels.

"In my 18 years of social transformation I got many people who have wished to work for the social transformation but the commitment, perseverance and time requires so high that people left association after some time." – Phoolbasan

ADDITIONAL READING

Austin, J., Stevenson, H., & Wei-Skillern, J. (2006). Social and Commercial Entrepreneurship: Same, Different, or Both? *Entrepreneurship Theory and Practice*, *30*(1), 1–22. doi:10.1111/j.1540-6520.2006.00107.x

Cho, A. H. (2006). Politics, Values and Social Entrepreneurship: A Critical Appraisal. In J. Mair, J. Robinson, & K. Hockerts (Eds.), *Social Entrepreneurship* (pp. 34–56). doi:10.1057/9780230625655_4

Mair, J., & Marti, I. (2006). Social Entrepreneurship Research: A Source of Explanation,BPrediction, and Delight. *Journal of World Business*, *41*(1), 36–44. doi:10.1016/j.jwb.2005.09.002

ENDNOTES

1. Gauna is a ceremony in Northern and Central part of India where after several years of marriage the bride is gone to the groom's house for consummation pf the marriage.
2. In India there is revenue collection system from shops in the market; and govt. awards revenue collection through private parties /society through open tender process.
3. In India the local self-governance by villages through elected local government named Gram Panchayat.
4. Collector was the highest administrative authority in the district as per Govt. of India.

5 In Chhattisgarh state rural market viz. weekly market and vegetable markets are allowed to run on government land and against that government collects very minimal taxes from the shoppers.

6 In India for poor family essential food items viz. rice, wheat, pulses, oil and sugar etc. are distributed in Public distribution system (PDS) by the government and shops are government licenced shops where foods and other items are priced by the government.

7 This award was honoured by either President of India or Vice President of India.

8 Bihan – Sun Rising/ Morning

9 https://www.wcd.nic.in/pressrel.htm

10 www.msdstrust.org/Profile-of-awardees.pdf

11 http://www.godfreyphillips.com/bravery-awards

12 https://www.sitaramjindalfoundation.org/

13 http://www.dbindiaprideawards.com/winners/winners-2012-13/

Table 1. Annexure 1 (activities performed)

Income generating activities	Bazar Theka (market contract), fair price *ration* shops, contract of mines, general/provision stores, fisheries,horticulture, animal husbandry, Poultry farming, Agricultural works & produces, collecting- buy & sale of forest products,vegetable vending, running cottage industries, running hotels, grocery and cloth shops etc
Rural development	Women Self Help Group(WSHG) and encourage small saving among woman
Cleanliness programme in the Villages	Village Cleanliness Campaign through awareness programme towards cleanliness
Blood donation	Organized health camp and blood donation camp
Adopted children	Adopted 2800 children through WSHG in the district(Rajnandgaon)
Woman's active Participation in Gram Sabha	More than 75% women attend Gram Sabha and now they are showing interest towards constructive & developmental works in the village.

ANNEXURE 1

1. Image attached separately

ANNEXURE 2: ACTIVITIES PERFORMED

ANNEXURE 3: SELECTED AWARDS HONORED TO PHULBASAN

TEACHING NOTES

Learning Objectives

- To understand the dynamics and challenges of a social enterprise
- To recognize the challenges of long-term sustainability for a social enterprise
- To assess strategic leadership and the application of strategic management concepts in a social enterprise

Course Positioning

This case is intended to be taught in an undergraduate or graduate course on entrepreneurship, particularly in a class on social entrepreneurship, in a strategic management course in a discussion of strategic leadership or in a human resources management course in a session on succession planning.

Table 2. Awards

Sr. No	Year	Awards	Cause	Remarks
1	2001,2002 and 2003	Maa Bamleshwari	Exemplary contribution in social upliftment of women, & developing awareness among them,	District Administration (Rajnandgaon)
2	2004-05	Mini Mata	Social contribution	Chhattisgarh State
3	2004-05	NABARD National (New Delhi)	Organize Women and Encouraging small savings	NABARD(National Board of Agriculture and Rural Development, New Delhi) and Raipur (Chhattisgarh)
4	2006-07	Union Bank Trophy	Women empowerment	Union Bank of India
5	2008	Jamuna Lal Bajaj[7]	Social Contribution and women development	JamunaLal Bajaj foundation,Mumbai
6	2009	Bihan[8]	Women empowerment	ZEE 24 Ghante (Television news channel)
7	2009	Stree Sakti Award[9]	Social development	Government of India
8	2009	Sadguru Gyannanad[10]	Excellence in Social development	Chennai
9	2011	Amodani Award (National)[11]	Significant contribution in women development	Godfrey Phillips Bravery New Delhi
10	2012	Padamshree	Social and Women Development	Government of India
11	2012	RastriyaEktaSamman (National)		Unity Confrenece New Delhi 2012.
12	2012	SP Jindal[12]	Women development	Sitaram Jindal Foundation, New Delhi
13	2012-13	National Pride[13]	Social Change Agent	DainikBhaskar Group (MP)
14	2013	Life Time Achievement		Union Bank of India

TEACHING PLAN

Pre-Class Preparation

The following questions will help to understand the whole issue and makeup learnners mind to participate in in-class discussions:-

Q1. Origins of the Word Entrepreneur.

Being an entrepreneur is often thought of as establishing a business, but this is a very loose use of a phrase with a long history and many deeper connotations. Beginning in the 17th and 18th centuries, French economics is where the word "entrepreneur" first appeared. It signifies someone who "under-takes" a substantial endeavour or activity, not an "undertaker" in the sense of a funeral director. More precisely, it started to be used to designate the risk-takers who sparked economic development by coming up with new and improved methods of doing things. The French economist Jean Baptiste Say is generally credited with giving the phrase this specific meaning. Say stated in a piece he wrote at the beginning of the 19th century that "the entrepreneur shifts economic resources out of an area of lower and into an area of higher productivity and greater yield." Entrepreneurs produce worth.

In the 20th century, Joseph Schumpeter was the economist most closely associated with the term. He described entrepreneurs as the innovators who drive capitalism's "creative-destructive" process. He says, "The function of entrepreneurs is to reform or revolutionise the production pattern." They can do this in many ways: "by exploiting an invention or, more generally, an untried technological possibility for producing a new commodity or producing an old one in a new way, by opening up a new source of supply of materials or a new outlet for products, by reorganising an industry and so on." Schumpeter's entrepreneurs are the change agents in the economy. They move the economy forward by serving new markets or creating new ways of doing things.

Indeed, many of the entrepreneurs Say and Schumpeter have in mind serve their function by starting new, profit-seeking business ventures, but creating a business is different from the essence of entrepreneurship. Though other economists may have used the term with various nuances, the Say-Schumpeter tradition that identifies entrepreneurs as the catalysts and innovators behind economic progress has served as the foundation for the contemporary use of this concept.

Q2. Current Theories of Entrepreneurship.

Contemporary writers in management and business have presented a wide range of theories of entrepreneurship. Many leading thinkers remain faithful to the Say-Schumpeter tradition while offering variations on the theme. For instance, in his attempt to understand what is unique about entrepreneurs, Peter Drucker starts with Say's definition but amplifies it to focus on opportunity. Drucker does not require entrepreneurs to cause change but sees them as exploiting the opportunities that change (in technology, consumer preferences, social norms, etc.) creates. He says, "This defines entrepreneur and entrepreneurship. The entrepreneur always searches for change, responds to it, and exploits it as an opportunity." The notion of "opportunity" has become central to many current definitions of entrepreneurship. It is how today's management theorists capture Say's notion of shifting resources to areas of higher yield. An opportunity, presumably, means an opportunity to create value in this way. Entrepreneurs have a mindset that sees the possibilities rather than the problems created by change.

For Drucker, starting a business is neither necessary nor sufficient for entrepreneurship. He explicitly comments, "Not every new small business is entrepreneurial or represents entrepreneurship." He cites the example of a "husband and wife who open another delicatessen store or another Mexican restaurant in the American suburb" as a case in point. There is nothing incredibly innovative or change-oriented in this. The same would be true of new not-for-profit organisations. Not every new organisation would be entrepreneurial. Drucker also makes it clear that entrepreneurship does not require a profit motive. Early in his book on Innovation and Entrepreneurship, Drucker asserts, "No better text for a History of Entrepreneurship could be found than the creation of the modern university, and especially the modern American university." He then explains what a significant innovation this was at the time. Later in the book, he devotes a chapter to entrepreneurship in public service institutions.

Howard Stevenson, a leading theorist of entrepreneurship at Harvard Business School, added an element of resourcefulness to the opportunity-oriented definition based on research he conducted to determine what distinguishes entrepreneurial management from more common forms of "administrative" management. After identifying several dimensions of difference, he suggests defining the heart of entrepreneurial leadership as "the pursuit of opportunity without regard to resources currently controlled." He found that entrepreneurs see and pursue opportunities that elude administrative managers; they do not allow their initial resource endowments to limit their options. To borrow a metaphor from Elizabeth Barrett Browning, their reach exceeds their grasp. Entrepreneurs mobilise the resources of others to achieve their entrepreneurial objectives. Administrators allow their existing resources and job descriptions to constrain their visions and actions. Once again, we have a definition of entrepreneurship that is not limited to business start-ups.

Q3. Differences between Business and Social Entrepreneurs.

The ideas of Say, Schumpeter, Drucker, and Stevenson are attractive because they can be as easily applied in the social sector as in the business sector. They describe a mindset and a kind of behaviour that can be manifest anywhere. This is an advantage in a world where sector boundaries are blurring. We should build our understanding of social entrepreneurship on this strong tradition of entrepreneurship theory and research. Social entrepreneurs are one species in the genus entrepreneur. They are entrepreneurs with a social mission. However, because of this mission, they face some distinctive challenges; any definition should reflect this.

For social entrepreneurs, the social mission is explicit and central. This affects how social entrepreneurs perceive and assess opportunities. Mission-related impact becomes the main criterion, not wealth creation. Wealth is just a means to an end for social entrepreneurs. With business entrepreneurs, wealth creation is a way of measuring value creation. This is because business entrepreneurs are subject to market discipline, which determines whether they create value. They tend to be driven out of business if they do not shift resources to more economically productive uses.

Markets are not perfect, but over the long haul, they work reasonably well as a test of private value creation, precisely the result of value for customers willing and able to pay. An entrepreneurs ability to attract resources (capital, labour, equipment, etc.) in a competitive marketplace indicates that the venture represents a more productive use of these resources than the alternatives it is competing against. The logic is simple. Entrepreneurs who can pay the most for resources are typically the ones who can put the resources to higher-valued uses, as determined in the marketplace. Value is created in business when customers are willing to pay more than it costs to produce the goods or services sold. The profit (revenue minus costs) that a venture generates is a reasonably good indicator of the value it has created. Suppose an entrepreneur cannot convince enough customers to pay a fair price to generate a profit. In that case, this strongly indicates that low value is being developed to justify this use of resources. A re-deployment of the resources happens naturally because firms that fail to make value cannot purchase sufficient resources or raise capital. As a result, they go out of business. Firms that create the most economic value have the cash to attract the necessary growth resources.

Markets do not work as well for social entrepreneurs. In particular, markets do not value social improvements, public goods and harms, and benefits for people who cannot afford to pay. These elements are often essential to social entrepreneurship. That is what makes it social entrepreneurship. As a result, it is much harder to determine whether a social entrepreneur is creating sufficient social value to justify the resources used in completing that value. The survival or growth of a social enterprise is not proof of its efficiency or effectiveness in improving social conditions. It is only a weak indicator, at best.

Social entrepreneurs operate in markets, but these markets often need to provide the proper discipline. Many social-purpose organisations charge fees for some of their services. They also compete for donations, volunteers, and other kinds of support. But the field of these "markets" is frequently not closely aligned with the social entrepreneur's mission. It depends on who is paying the fees or providing the resources, their motivations, and how well they can assess the social value created by the venture. It is inherently difficult to measure social value creation. How much social value is created by reducing pollution in a given stream, saving the spotted owl, or providing companionship to older people? The calculations are not only hard but also contentious. Even when improvements can be measured, attributing them to a specific intervention is often difficult. Are the lower crime rates in an area due to the Block Watch, new policing techniques, or just a better economy? Even when improvements can be measured and attributed to a given intervention, social entrepreneurs often cannot economically capture the value they have created to pay for the resources they use. Whom do they charge for cleaning the stream or running the Block Watch? How do they get everyone who benefits to pay? Social entrepreneurs rely on subsidies, donations, and volunteers to offset this value-capture problem, but this further muddies the waters of market discipline. The ability to attract these philanthropic resources may provide some indication of value creation in the eyes of the resource providers, but it is not a very reliable indicator. The psychic income people get from giving or volunteering is likely to be only loosely connected with actual social impact if it is connected at all.

Q4. Defining Social Entrepreneurship.

Any definition of social entrepreneurship should reflect the need for a substitute for the market discipline that works for business entrepreneurs. However, we cannot assume that market discipline will automatically weed out social ventures that do not effectively and efficiently utilise resources. The following definition combines an emphasis on discipline and accountability with the notions of value creation taken from Say, innovation and change agents from Schumpeter, the pursuit of opportunity from Drucker, and resourcefulness from Stevenson. In brief, this definition can be stated as follows:

Social entrepreneurs play the role of change agents in the social sector by:

- Adopting a mission to create and sustain social value (not just private value),
- Recognising and relentlessly pursuing new opportunities to serve that mission,
- Engaging in a process of continuous innovation, adaptation, and learning,
- Acting boldly without being limited by resources currently in hand, and
- Exhibiting heightened accountability to the constituencies served and for the outcomes created.

This is an "idealised" definition. Social sector leaders will exemplify these characteristics in different ways and to different degrees. The closer a person gets to satisfying all these conditions, the more that person fits the social entrepreneur model. Those who are more innovative and create more significant social improvements will naturally be seen as more entrepreneurial. Those who are genuinely Schumpeterian will reform or revolutionise their industries. Each element in this brief definition deserves some further elaboration. Let's consider each one in turn.

Change agents in the social sector: Social entrepreneurs are reformers and revolutionaries, as described by Schumpeter, but with a social mission. They make fundamental changes in how things are done in the social sector. Their visions are bold. They attack the underlying causes of problems rather than simply treating symptoms. They often reduce needs rather than just meeting them. They seek to create systemic changes and sustainable improvements. Though they may act locally, their actions have the potential to stimulate global improvements in their chosen arenas, whether that is education, health care, economic development, the environment, the arts, or any other social field.

Adopting a mission to create and sustain social value is the core of what distinguishes social entrepreneurs from business entrepreneurs, even socially responsible businesses. For a social entrepreneur, the social mission is fundamental. This mission of social improvement must be addressed to create private benefits (financial returns or consumption benefits) for individuals. Making a profit, building wealth, or serving customers' desires may be part of the model, but these are means to a social end, not the end itself. Profit is not the gauge of value creation or customer satisfaction; social impact is the gauge. Social entrepreneurs look for a long-term social return on investment. Social entrepreneurs want more than a quick hit; they want to create lasting improvements. They think about sustaining the impact.

Recognising and relentlessly pursuing new opportunities: Where others see problems, social entrepreneurs see opportunity. They are not simply driven by the perception of a social need or their compassion; instead, they have a vision of achieving improvement and are determined to make their vision work. They are persistent. The models they develop and their approaches can, and often do, change as the entrepreneurs learn about what works and does not. The critical element is persistence and willingness to make adjustments as one goes. Rather than giving up when an obstacle is encountered, entrepreneurs ask, "How can we surmount this obstacle? How can we make this work?"

Engaging in continuous innovation, adaptation, and learning: Entrepreneurs are innovative. They break new ground, develop new models, and pioneer new approaches. However, as Schumpeter notes, innovation can take many forms. It does not require inventing something wholly new; it can simply involve applying an existing idea in a new way or to a unique situation. Entrepreneurs need not be inventors. They merely need to be creative in using what others have invented. Their innovations may appear in how they structure their core programs, assemble resources, and fund their work. On the funding side, social entrepreneurs look for innovative ways to ensure that their ventures will have access to help as long as they create social value. This willingness to innovate is part of the modus operandi of entrepreneurs. It is not just a one-time burst of creativity. It is a continuous process of exploring, learning, and improving. Of course, with innovation comes uncertainty and risk of failure. Entrepreneurs tend to have a high tolerance for ambiguity and learn how to manage risks for themselves and others. They treat the failure of a project as a learning experience, not a personal tragedy.

Acting boldly without being limited by resources currently in hand: Social entrepreneurs do not let their limited resources keep them from pursuing their visions. They are skilled at doing more with less and at attracting resources from others. They use scarce resources efficiently and leverage their limited resources by drawing in partners and collaborating with others. They explore all resource options, from pure philanthropy to the commercial methods of the business sector. Sector norms or traditions do not bind them. They develop resource strategies likely to support and reinforce their social missions. They take calculated risks and manage the downside to reduce the harm resulting from the failure. They understand the risk tolerances of their stakeholders and use this to spread the risk to those who are better prepared to accept it.

Exhibiting a heightened sense of accountability to the constituencies served and for the outcomes created: Because market discipline does not automatically weed out inefficient or ineffective social ventures, social entrepreneurs ensure they create value. This means they seek a sound understanding of the constituencies they serve. They ensure they have correctly assessed the needs and values of the people they intend to do and the communities in which they operate. In some cases, this requires close connections with those communities. They understand the expectations and values of their "investors," including anyone who invests money, time, and expertise to help them. They seek to provide real social improvements to their beneficiaries and their communities and attractive (social and financial) returns to their investors. Creating a fit

between investor values and community needs is integral to the challenge. When feasible, social entrepreneurs create market-like feedback mechanisms to reinforce this accountability. They assess their progress in terms of social, financial, and managerial outcomes, not simply their size, outputs, or processes. They use this information to make course corrections as needed.

Q5. Social Entrepreneurs: A Rare Breed.

Social entrepreneurship describes a set of unusual behaviours. These behaviours should be encouraged and rewarded in those with the capabilities and temperament for this work. We could use many more of them. Should everyone aspire to be a social entrepreneur? No. Only some social sector leaders are well suited to being entrepreneurial. The same is true in business. Only some business leaders are entrepreneurs in the sense that Say, Schumpeter, Drucker, and Stevenson had in mind. While we might wish for more entrepreneurial behaviour in both sectors, society needs different leadership types and styles. Social entrepreneurs are one particular breed of leader and should be recognised as such. This definition preserves their distinctive status and assures that social entrepreneurship is not treated lightly. We need social entrepreneurs to help us find new avenues toward social improvement as we enter the next century.

Pre-Class Readings

- J. Gregory Dees, "The Meaning of 'Social Entrepreneurship,'" Comments and suggestions contributed from the Social Entrepreneurship Founders Working Group, Center for the Advancement of Social Entrepreneurship, Fuqua School of Business, Duke University, Durham, NC, 1998, www.caseatduke.org/documents/dees_sedef.pdf.
- Janelle A. Kerlin, "Social Enterprise in the United States and Europe: Understanding and Learning from the Differences," Voluntas: International Journal of Voluntary and Nonprofit Organizations, 2006, 17(3), pp. 246–262.
- Roger L. Martin and Sally Osberg, "Social Entrepreneurship: The Case for Definition," Stanford Social Innovation Review, 2007, 5(2), pp. 28–39.

Total Time for Class Discussion

The following discussion times are based on a 90-minute class:

(A) Social entrepreneurship and its nuances: 20 minutes

In the context of business, the term "social entrepreneurship" refers to the process of establishing and operating a company with the primary aim of accomplishing a social or environmental purpose, as opposed to strictly profit-driven one. Commonly, the domains in which social entrepreneurs operate are ones in which traditional firms and government organisations are still grappling with how to successfully solve social or environmental issues.

The concept of social entrepreneurship involves a broad variety of activities, including the creation of novel goods and services as well as the provision of education and training to members of underprivileged communities. Entrepreneurs in the social sector may pursue careers in a variety of disciplines, including poverty reduction, environmental protection, education, and healthcare, amongst others.

The priority of social effect over financial gain is one of the most distinguishing characteristics of social entrepreneurship. While it is true that the primary goal of social entrepreneurs is to make a profit and keep their businesses afloat, they also have a secondary goal of effecting constructive social change. since a result, social entrepreneurs need a special set of talents in addition to a mindset that is distinct from that of regular commercial entrepreneurs, since they must strike a balance between fulfilling their social goal and maintaining their financial viability.

The focus placed on working with other people and forming partnerships is another essential component of social entrepreneurship. In order to discover and put into action efficient solutions to social and environmental problems, social entrepreneurs frequently collaborate closely with local communities, non-profit organisations, government agencies, and other interested parties.

In conclusion, social entrepreneurship frequently requires a mindset that is open to taking chances and pursuing unusual avenues of inquiry. Social entrepreneurs typically have a profound sense of purpose and a strong desire to effect positive change in the world; also, they are open to new ideas and are prepared to experiment in order to attain their objectives.

Overall, social entrepreneurship may be understood as a dynamic and rapidly expanding movement that blends innovative business practises with a focus on improving society in order to build a better world.

(B) Types of social entrepreneurship: 15 minutes

Social entrepreneurship can take many forms, and there are several types of social entrepreneurship that can be identified. Some of the most common types include:

1. **Non-Profit Social Entrepreneurship:** Non-profit social entrepreneurship involves creating and running non-profit organizations with a social mission. These organizations may focus on a variety of social or environmental issues, such as poverty alleviation, education, healthcare, or environmental conservation.
2. **For-Profit Social Entrepreneurship:** For-profit social entrepreneurship involves creating and running businesses that prioritize social impact alongside financial sustainability. These businesses may be structured as social enterprises, benefit corporations, or other types of socially responsible companies.
3. **Cooperative Social Entrepreneurship:** Cooperative social entrepreneurship involves creating and running cooperatives, which are businesses owned and operated by their members. Cooperatives can be used to address a wide range of social and environmental issues, such as creating jobs for disadvantaged communities or providing access to affordable housing.

4. **Environmental Social Entrepreneurship:** Environmental social entrepreneurship involves creating and running businesses or organizations that focus on environmental sustainability. This can include developing sustainable technologies, promoting conservation, or addressing environmental challenges such as climate change.
5. **Community-Based Social Entrepreneurship:** Community-based social entrepreneurship involves creating and running businesses or organizations that are rooted in local communities. These businesses or organizations may be owned and operated by community members, and they may focus on addressing specific social or environmental challenges facing the community.
6. **Corporate Social Entrepreneurship:** Corporate social entrepreneurship involves creating and running social impact initiatives within larger corporations. This can include initiatives focused on sustainability, diversity and inclusion, or other social or environmental issues.

Each type of social entrepreneurship has its own unique characteristics and challenges, but all share a commitment to creating positive social change.

(C) Cooperative society and other non-profit organizational forms: 15 minutes

Cooperative societies are a form of non-profit organisation that are owned and democratically governed by its member-owners. Cooperative societies are also known as member-owned cooperatives. Cooperatives are organisations that are established with the purpose of catering to the requirements of their individual members. Cooperatives can be active in a diverse variety of industries, including agriculture, finance, healthcare, housing, and retail. Credit unions, housing cooperatives, and consumer cooperatives are a few examples of the type of organisation known as a cooperative. In addition to cooperatives, there are several other non-profit organizational forms, including:

1. **Non-Profit Corporations:** Non-profit corporations are formed for charitable, educational, religious, scientific, or other purposes that benefit the public. Non-profit corporations are owned by a board of directors, and they do not issue stock or pay dividends to shareholders.
2. **Foundations:** Foundations are non-profit organizations that provide funding and support for charitable, educational, scientific, or other purposes. Foundations are typically created by individuals or corporations and are governed by a board of directors.
3. **Charities:** Charities are non-profit organizations that are formed to provide charitable services or support to those in need. Charities are often funded through donations from individuals, corporations, and governments.
4. **Social Enterprises:** Social enterprises are businesses that are formed with a social or environmental mission, and that reinvest their profits to further that mission. Social enterprises can take many forms, including cooperatives, benefit corporations, and other types of socially responsible companies.

All of these non-profit organizational forms have different structures and characteristics, but they share a commitment to serving the public good. Non-profit organizations can play a vital role in addressing social and environmental challenges, and they can provide a valuable alternative to for-profit businesses in many sectors.

(D) Maa Bamleshwari Janhit Karya Samiti position: 5 minutes
(E) Leadership succession in social entrepreneurship: 10 Minutes

Leadership succession is a critical issue in social entrepreneurship, as the success of a social enterprise often depends on the effectiveness of its leadership. Effective leadership succession planning can help to ensure that the mission and values of the organization are preserved over time, and that the organization continues to make a positive impact on the world.

Here are some best practices for leadership succession in social entrepreneurship:

1. **Start Early:** Succession planning should start early, ideally several years before the current leader plans to step down. This allows for adequate time to identify potential successors, develop their skills and knowledge, and ensure a smooth transition of leadership.
2. **Identify Potential Successors:** Organizations should identify potential successors who share the same values and commitment to the social mission of the organization. This may involve looking within the organization or seeking out external candidates.
3. **Provide Mentorship and Development:** Potential successors should be provided with mentorship and development opportunities to help them build the skills and knowledge they will need to lead the organization effectively.
4. **Involve the Board:** The board of directors should be involved in the succession planning process, as they have a critical role in selecting and overseeing the new leader.
5. **Develop a Transition Plan:** A transition plan should be developed to ensure a smooth transfer of leadership. This may involve setting clear expectations and timelines for the transition, as well as ensuring that key stakeholders are informed and engaged.
6. **Communicate Openly:** Effective communication is essential during the succession process, both with internal stakeholders and external partners. Open and transparent communication can help to build trust and maintain support for the organization's mission and goals.

In summary, effective leadership succession planning is critical for the long-term success of social enterprises. By identifying potential successors early, providing mentorship and development, involving the board, developing a transition plan, and communicating openly, social entrepreneurs can ensure that their organizations continue to make a positive impact on the world for years to come.

(F) Evaluating the options: 15 minutes

Evaluating the options for leadership succession in social entrepreneurship involves a careful analysis of potential candidates and their fit with the organization's mission, values, and goals. Here are some factors to consider when evaluating potential successors:

1. **Skills and Experience:** The successor should possess the necessary skills and experience to effectively lead the organization. This may include experience in the relevant industry or sector, as well as leadership and management experience.

2. **Commitment to the Mission:** The successor should be committed to the social mission and values of the organization. This includes a deep understanding of the organization's purpose and goals, and a passion for making a positive impact on the world.
3. **Cultural Fit:** The successor should be a good cultural fit with the organization. This includes an alignment with the organization's values, as well as the ability to work collaboratively with staff, board members, and other stakeholders.
4. **Leadership Style:** The successor's leadership style should be compatible with the organization's culture and goals. This includes an ability to inspire and motivate staff, as well as a willingness to make difficult decisions when necessary.
5. **Communication Skills:** The successor should possess strong communication skills, including the ability to communicate the organization's mission and goals to external stakeholders, as well as to inspire and engage staff and board members.
6. **Financial Acumen:** The successor should possess financial acumen, including the ability to manage budgets, fundraising, and financial planning.
7. **Succession Planning Experience:** The successor should have experience in succession planning, including the ability to manage the transition of leadership effectively.

In addition to evaluating potential successors based on these factors, it may also be helpful to involve staff, board members, and other stakeholders in the decision-making process. This can help to build consensus around the new leadership and ensure that all stakeholders are supportive of the decision. Ultimately, the key to successful leadership succession in social entrepreneurship is to prioritize the organization's mission and values, and to select a leader who can effectively advance those goals over the long term.

(G) Key takeaways: 10 minutes.

Chapter 14
Strategic Alliance Between Toyota and Suzuki:
Is It a Win for Toyota or a Loss for Suzuki?

Ruhi Sarangal
Chitkara Business School, Chitkara University, India

Prashant Chauhan
Chitkara Business School, Chitkara University, India

Ashok Kumar
Department of Defense and Strategic Studies, Himachal Pradesh University, India

Aarti Dangwal
Chitkara Business School, Chitkara University, India

Devesh Bathla
Chitkara Business School, Chitkara University, India

Mankaj Mehta
Chitkara Business School, Chitkara University, India

EXECUTIVE SUMMARY

It was in the year 1977 in October that the Toyota Motor Corporation entered India. Toyota entered into a joint venture with the Kirloskar Group, therein establishing Toyota Kirloskar Motor Private Limited. Carving their place in the Indian automobile sector, Toyota has successfully carved its place known for their dependability and durability likewise as it was globally. In India, the cars like Corolla Altis sedan, Innova Crysta premium MPV, and the Fortuner premium SUV are one of the most popular models that run successfully. In addition to being the largest automobile manufacturer in the world, the Toyota camp has always been renowned for the cutting-edge technology and brilliant production practices it employs in its manufacturing operations. Toyota has always been a path finder propagating and manufacturing eco-friendly automobiles. Over the years Toyota has developed and mastered developing incredible and refined power plants, which empowers it to deliver tremendous power while minimising fuel consumption.

DOI: 10.4018/978-1-6684-8488-3.ch014

Dilemma/Issues: Challenge of Product Cannibalization for Suzuki as the launch of Hybrid Glanza leads to decrease in sales of original model Baleno which is Suzuki's Best seller car in Hatchback segment.
Name of the Organization: Maruti Suzuki and Toyota
Name of the Protagonist: Maruti Suzuki and Toyota

Toyota's coming to India:

It was in the year 1977 in October that the Toyota Motor Corporation entered India. Toyota entered into a joint venture with the Kirloskar group, therein establishing Toyota Kirloskar Motor Private Limited. Carving their place in Indian automobile sector, Toyota has successfully carved its place known for their dependability and durability like wise as it was globally. In India the cars like Corolla Altis sedan, Innova Crysta premium MPV, and the Fortuner premium SUV are one of the most popular models that run successfully. Toyota has a wide network spread over more than 300 dealers for sales and services catering to the users nationwide for new as well as existing customers. In addition to being the largest automobile manufacturer in the world, the Toyota camp has always been renowned for the cutting-edge technology and brilliant production practices it employs in its manufacturing operations. Toyota has always been a path founder propogating and manufacturing the eco-friendly automobiles. Over the years Toyota has developed and mastered developing incredible and refined power plants, which empowers it to deliver tremendous power while minimising fuel consumption.

TOYOTA'S INDIA BIG SMALL CHALLENGE

Toyota has been a synonym for the quality, premiumness and reliability when it comes to cars but it has failed to win the hearts of the Indians when it comes to the economy segment or the hatchback cars are concerned. Toyota has very limited to offer in the hatchback offers. In addition to it the Indian market is highly price sensitive and price driven in fact. The Toyota cars as compared to the counterparts are priced higher and are not perceived as affordable by the Indian consumers. The Japanese giant blames it on the Government's tax structure saying that despite the repeated demand of a viable Tax structure the government levies Heavy taxes which do not let them operate at the Economies of scale. According to industry executives and experts, these automakers face roadblocks due to a lack of knowledge of the Indian market and a mindset that isn't adapted to the local requirements.

"India is primarily a market for small cars" therein lie the true challenge for Toyota. Toyota's lack of knowledge when it comes to Indian market is another reason that is quoted by the various industry experts. "To be successful in any market, it is essential to understand the customer in order to create the right product lineup, effective channels to reach the customers, and an aspirational, relevant brand. The strategy that Toyota uses for Indian market is not sustainable the experts claim.

SUZUKI: INDIA'S LOVE AFFAIR WITH THE JAPANESE GIANT

The story of Maruti Suzuki dates back to the year 1981, when the Indian government laid foundation of the Maruti Udyog. In the following year 1982, India's Maruti merged with Japan's Suzuki to form well known Maruti Suzuki India Ltd as it is known today. His 1980s "Maruti car" became immensely popular and is still regarded as a classic.

After the country's economy liberalized after adoption of LPG in 1991, Maruti Suzuki remained as favorite of people and it was not at all surprising that it still remained as the market leader in the passenger car segment. Even lately, this giant automaker in India has been working on the launch of new models to expand its product line, adding various feathers to its cap. Currently, the Maruti Suzuki Swift is the most popular automobile in India.

In fact, Maruti Suzuki has a market share of approximately 50% in the local automobile industry, meaning it produces one out of every two new vehicles on our roads. Affordability is the Key for Suzuki's Success in India.it is a household name for cars in India. The brand Suzuki is synonym for Brand loyalty. the affordable price tag for Suzuki is not just restricted to the entry level cars. Even the mid segment and the high segment cars from the manufacturer are more cost effective and affordable than its competitor counter parts.

VERSATILITY IN THE SUZUKI'S STABLE

The versatility and the extensive range of portfolio that Suzuki offers to the customer is endless.it is highly unlikely that any other rival has such a portfolio to offer. From hatchbacks and sedans, to SUV's and MPV's there is literally nothing that the Japanese Giant does not offer.

To summarize we may suggest that although there are ample of automobile manufacturers actively present in the Indian markets that offer affordable-budget friendly cars, high end vehicles, Maruti Suzuki has always been a market leader and one of the most preferred option for the Indian customer.

THE TWO JAPANESE GIANTS COME TOGETHER AS ALLIES-THE NEW CHAPTER

Suzuki and Toyota announced on March 20, 2019, that they would begin specific considerations for joint product development and production collaboration. This would be accomplished by combining Toyota's strengths in electrification technologies and Suzuki's strengths in small vehicle technologies. The Toyota Glanza, which is effectively a Maruti Suzuki Baleno with a different name, is one of the products that have already been produced as a result of the partnership between Toyota and Suzuki. Maruti Suzuki will also supply Toyota with the Vitara Brezza, Ciaz, and Ertiga as part of the alliance. Toyota will supply Suzuki with its hybrid system. They will also work together on the development of a new Toyota C-segment MPV, which will be supplied to Suzuki as well. Toyota Motor Corporation and Suzuki Motor Corporation have been working together in India for two years.

Toyota Motor Corporation (Toyota) and Suzuki Motor Corporation (Suzuki) have reached a consensus upon the supply of the hybrid and other vehicles for the supply in Indian Market. To be Specific under which the Suzuki will provide Toyota with the various models like Baleno and Vitara Brezza, wherein Toyota will provide Suzuki with the Corolla model. The Details of the respective models, which include the details about supply start schedule, the total number of units supplied, specifications of the selected models, pricing etc was yet to be decided later. The vehicles will be sold in India by Toyota and Suzuki's respective supply channels utilising their respective sales networks.

As per the partnership between Toyota-Suzuki partnership, Toyota would provide hybrid technology to Maruti Suzuki. However, The Smart Hybrid Vehicle by Suzuki (SHVS) still remains the most commonly used technology for its vehicles.

Toyota brand is very is renowned not only in India but worldwide for its quality, durability, and dependability. Customers have the best of both worlds when it comes to Suzuki's reputation for reliability and familiarity as a result of its extensive network and its positioning as a value brand. As per the expert opinions, it may be too early to predict how this global partnership may fair its way into heart of Indian economy. however, given the significance of the Indian market to both automakers, TKM and Suzuki will be extremely cautious not to disrupt existing systems and a well-oiled business machine. The alliance, which includes equity investments in one another and rebranding of some of their most popular models, appears to have been successful in India thus far.

CROSS BADGED CARS FOR TOYOTA IN INDIA: ITS A WIN-WIN

Toyota has been a global leader in Car manufacturing globally but has admitted that it failed to make a mark in the Indian Car Market. Owing to different reasons due to which Toyota succeed in India especially in the Hatchback or the entry level segment. The high cost of manufacturing, un-favorable Tax Structure, Price sensitive Indian market are a few of them. The two Giants have come together to Offer Hybrid Cars to Indian consumers

Suzuki is the market leader in India when it comes to Cars. Its success has created History. It is not an overstatement to say that Suzuki has caught the beat of the Indian Customers when it comes to cars. It is well-known that Suzuki excels in the entry-level and economy class segment, whereas Toyota automobiles are renowned for their performance and luxury. Cross-branding in favour of Toyota will be limited to the entry-level and economy classes in this instance. When it comes to performance and luxury models for a customer, Toyota models will dominate. Suzuki is an expert manufacturer of compact and subcompact vehicles. In contrast, Toyota excels in electrification with its Hybrid and other electrified technologies. So far, the alliance has performed well in India, which is good news for the partners. Although the sales volume is not huge but the real benefits will pour in the long term as said by the company officials.

The Toyota Glanza is the first product from the recently formed partnership between Toyota and Suzuki. The Glanza is nothing but a re-badged Maruti Baleno that has been given a new front grille and, of course, new badges to look slightly different from the donor model. While the Glanza is still far from clocking the amazing sales numbers of the Baleno, it has pretty much managed to quickly find a sweet spot in the B2-segment of the Indian car market.

Basically, compared to the Maruti Baleno, the specifications remain totally unchanged. Even though the highly successful model Toyota Glanza is essentially a rebadged Maruti Baleno, it gets a better standard warranty. Compared to the 2-year/40,000 km standard warranty that's available on the Baleno, buyers of the Glanza benefit from a 3-year/unlimited km cover.

Toyota marked a 14% growth in sales in December 2020, in comparison to the same month the year before. The major contributing factor to this growth is the cooperation between Toyota and Maruti Suzuki.

The sales report for December 2020 shows that the Maruti-Suzuki sourced products accounted for more than 52% of Toyota's total sales. This is where Toyota has evidently benefitted from joining hands with Maruti Suzuki. The following table depicts the sales figures table no. 1.

Table 1. Car models

Models	Dec21	Dec20	Difference	Growth %
Toyota Glanza	2634	2102	532	25.31
Suzuki Baleno	9,931	17,872	7941	-44%

The data and the performance is very subjective here as the comparison between the two is not completely fair at this point of time as Baleno is in the market since 2015 and the Toyota Glanza is comparatively very new. It might be too early to conclude but the trend and the anticipation till now has clearly indicate that the hatchback from Toyota and Suzuki is more or less a success.

A SUCCESSFUL ALLIANCE: IS IT AS SUCCESS FOR SUZUKI?

Toyota is currently experiencing success in India for the first time thanks to its alliance with Suzuki, but Suzuki Baleno sales have declined since the launch of the Toyota Glanza in June. Baleno's monthly sales have decreased to 12,000 units per month from 15,000-16,000 units a year prior to the introduction of the Toyota Glanza. However, we can also say that the sales figure is impacted by the overall bump in the sales market; is it worth the risk for suzuki to ignore?

IS SUZUKI ABOUT TO WITNESS PRODUCT CANNIBALIZATION? THE DIFFICULT ROAD AHEAD

In India, cross-branding strategies between alliance partners in the automobile industry have never been profitable. Maruti has already sold 36,257 units to Toyota, which is significantly more than the 21,224 units sold to Toyota during the same period in 2020. The quantity has increased by just over 15 thousand units. Toyota's best-selling vehicles are the Glanza, Innova, Fortuner, and Urban Cruiser.

As a result of the introduction of the Toyota-badged premium hatchback, Maruti Suzuki Baleno sales have declined. All of these inputs raise the question of their immediate effect on Maruti Suzuki's sales. Glanza could result in a loss of customers for Maruti Suzuki, as there were no internal or external differences between the two models.

The fact that Maruti will share yet another blockbuster product with Toyota, the Vitara Brezza, is a source of concern for some brokerage firms. They want the company to provide significant design and product attribute differentiation to keep the two products distinct. As the company defends it by stating that Differentiation in design or features also means addition to the cost and India being a Highly Price sensitive market this move may backfire.

For Toyota the Glanza has been one of their best selling cars in India but owing to the launch of Glanza the Suzuki's best seller Baleno has decreased significantly. Is suzuki about to witness the Product Cannibalization.

WEARING A SAFETY BELT FOR SUZUKI: IT MIGHT BE A BUMPY RIDE AHEAD

It may be too early to act as the alliance has just taken off for both Toyota and Suzuki but the market outputs have put Suzuki at risk of Product Cannibalization if we talk about Baleno and Glanza specifically. Although the reason behind Baleno's compromised sales could be an overall slowdown in Economy but Glanza doing extremely well in the same segment may worry Suzuki in the long run.

The Prices and designs for both the variants are more or less the same, specifications are more or less the same but the Warranty offered for Glanza is better than for Baleno. This is one of the factors behind Glanza's success. To add to it the most of the customers who have brought Glanza are the first time customers. If the trend continues and Baleno sales decline should Suzuki consider price differentiation or Product differentiation as a breakthrough? Interestingly the alliance aims at collaborating and not competing and differentiation will defeat the purpose. It is for us to see over time what Suzuki chooses. The Japanese Giant may be falling prey to its own Alliance that was done for good.

Another prospect for Suzuki could be the marketing strategy that it chooses for branding of Suzuki Cars. Making the most of strategies like Make It Clear Why You're Better but that would in itself indicate that the Japanese giant is potentially scared of its own partner alliance. This again Defeats the purpose of the alliance if we remember what Suzuki said "Collaborate and not Compete".

As the Future for Suzuki and Toyota Alliance will unfold their performance it will be very interesting to see how Suzuki deals with the challenges that the alliance poses to Suzuki. The alliance is going great for the Toyota company but it seems otherwise for Suzuki. Suzuki has been the best seller car brand in India. Out of every two cars that one sees on Indian roads one belongs to Suzuki. The Hybrid variants were supposed to enhance their market performance and out put. Although the Alliance seems to be a success and both the companies are planning to launch many more hybrid cars in different segments but the Product Cannibalization challenge may soon be Suzuki's new nightmare.

TEACHING NOTES

The primary advantage of teaching case studies in the classroom is that it encourages student participation. It exposes the students to a real-world situation and helps them figure out the problems with the aid of examples. Students develop skills such as problem-solving and decision-making in complex situations. The use of role play could be a novel approach to the case study. It aids the students in assuming the roles of the case study's various characters so that they can truly comprehend the perspectives of the case characters. Additional examples of instructional experience include:

Students should be well-prepared for the class by going through the case and other readings on the various marketing strategies that brands use for their products. The strategic global alliance of Toyota with Suzuki will be thoroughly discussed including the products that they manufacture under their mutual agreement. The concept of Brand Cannibalization will also be very well introduced to the class with the help of this case quoting the market situation of Toyota and Suzuki.

Objectives of the Study

- To learn about the strategic alliance between Toyota and Suzuki in India
- To compare the individual performances of Toyota and Suzuki as compared to their hybrid cars launched under their alliance.
- To study and analyse the concept of brand cannibalization

Level of case difficulty – UG and PG
Course(s) in which the case can be used – BBA, B Com, and MBA

Questions

Question 1: What are the key strengths of Toyota Motors and Suzuki Motors individually?

Expected answer:

The company's assets indicate that it is capable of maintaining its position as one of the world's leading automakers. This component of the SWOT model identifies the internal strategic factors that serve as the organization's capabilities. These are Toyota's principal strengths:

- Strong brand identity
- Global supply network
- Rapid innovation capabilities

One of the strongest trademarks in the global automotive industry is Toyota. The company's global supply chain provides resilience and market-based risk mitigation. In addition, Toyota's organizational culture fosters rapid innovation, which is essential for sustaining a long-term competitive advantage. Toyota is widely recognized for its commitment to sustainability and environmental responsibility, pioneering the development of hybrid and electric vehicles. The company has also gained a reputation for its advanced safety features, consistently receiving high rating for crash test performance.

In addition to its strong engineering and design capabilities, Toyota has built a loyal customer base through its dedication to customer satisfaction and service. The company's focus on continuous improvement and innovation has resulted in a diverse range of vehicles, from compact cars to full sized trucks that meet the needs of consumers around the world.

Overall, Toyota's brand strengths lie in its reputation for quality, reliability, innovation sustainability and customer service. These factors have helped the company to establish a strong global presence and maintain its position as one of te worlds most respected and trusted automotive brands.

Suzuki motors is a Japanese multinational corporation that specializes in manufacturing automobiles, motorcycles, marine engines, the company has a strong presence in India, where it is known as Maruti Suzuki India Limited. Ever since its entry into the Indian market in 1983, Maruti has become a household name, with a market share of over 50% in the passenger car segment. The company has consistently delivered high-quality affordable cars that cater to the needs of the Indian customer.

Suzuki's success in India can be attributed to its focus on innovation, quality, and customer satisfaction. The company has also invested heavily in local manufacturing, creating jobs and contributing to the Indian economy. Overall, Suzuki motors has established itself as a key player in the Indian automobile industry with a reputation for reliability and customer- centricity.

Question 2: Why could Toyota not perform well in the Indian market?

Expected Answer:

There are several reasons why Toyota had to struggle in the Indian market:

Competition: The Indian markets is highly competitive with many established players and new entrants vying for the market share. Toyota faces tough competition from both domestic and international automakers including Maruti Suzuki, Hyundai, Tata motors and Honda.

Price Sensitivity: India is a price sensitive market and buyers are highly focused on getting value for money. Toyota's cars tend to be more expensive than the other brands making them less attractive to the price sensitive buyers.

Brand Perception: Toyota is generally perceived as a premium brand in India, which can make it harder to penetrate the mass market. Many buyers in India prefer to purchase cares from local manufacturers which are seen as more affordable and better suited to the Indian markets.

Limited Product Portfolio: Toyota has a limited product portfolio in India compared to other automakers. This means that they are unable to cater to the needs of all buyers limiting their market share.

Lack of Localization: Toyota has been criticized for not localizing its products sufficiently for the Indian market. This has led to higher costs and less appeal to price sensitive buyers.

Overall a combination of intense competition price sensitivity brand perception, limited product portfolio and lack of localization have all contributed to Toyota's struggles in the Indian market.

Question 3. Why did Suzuki and Toyota enter into alliance in India?

Expected answer:

Toyota and Suzuki entered into alliance in India in 2017 with the aim of jointly developing new cars and technologies and sharing production facilities. The alliance was formed to leverage the strengths of both the companies and help them overcome challenges such as rising costs, stricter emissions regulations and intense competition in the Indian market.

Specially, the alliance aimed to:

Develop New Models and Share Technology: Toyota and Suzuki agreed to collaborate on the development of new vehicles, including electric cars and compact models suitable for the Indian market. This would allow both companies to share costs and leverage their strengths in different areas of expertise.

Share Production Facilities: Toyota agreed to Suzuki models at its plant in Bidadi, Karnataka while Suzuki agreed to produce Toyota models at its plant in Gujarat. This would help both companies improve their production efficiency and reduced costs.

Expand Their Market Presence: By working together, Toyota and Suzuki hoped to expand their market share in India where they faced tough competition from both domestic and international car manufacturers.

Overall, the alliance between Toyota and Suzuki in india was a strategic move to address the challenges of the automative industry and leverage the strengths of both companies to increase their competitiveness in the market.

Suzuki and Toyota entered into a partnership in 2019 with the aim of developing new technology and sharing their respective strengths to produce more efficient and affordable vehicles. The partnership between the two companies was seen as a way for Suzuki to gain access to Toyota's hybrid and electrification technology while Toyota would benefit from Suzuki's expertise in making compact cars for emerging markets.

However, one of the challenges faced by Suzuki due to the alliance with Toyota is brand cannibalization. Brand cannibalization occurs when two or more brands from the same company or partnership compete against each other causing a loss in market share and revenue for both brands.

In this case, Toyota and Suzuki offer similar vehicles in the same segments such as small cars, compact SUVs, and hatchbacks. This overlap in the product portfolio could lead to confusion among customers, who might find it difficult to choose between two brands. Additionally, Toyota has a stronger brand image in many markets, which could lead to customer choosing Toyota over Suzuki even though the two companies are now partners.

Another challenge is risk of diluting Suzuki's brand identity. Suzuki has built a reputation for offering affordable, practical, and reliable vehicles, particularly in emerging markets. However, the alliance with Toyota could potentially change the way Suzuki is perceived by consumers, particularly if Toyota's more premium brand image begins to overshadow Suzuki's brand identity.

To mitigate these challenges, both the companies will need to carefully manage their product portfolios and marketing strategies. They will need to ensure that their respective brands continue to appeal to their target markets, and that there is a clear differentiate between the two brands. This could involve offering different features or price points, or targeting different customer segments.

Overall, while the partnership between Suzuki and Toyota has the potential to bring many benefits to both companies, they will need to be careful to avoid brand cannibalization and ensure that their respective brands continue to thrive in highly competitive automotive market.

REFERENCES

Economic Times. (2022, January 19). *Toyota-Suzuki alliance scales up in India with shared platforms, tech, products.* Retrieved March 3, 2023, from https://economictimes.indiatimes.com/industry/auto/cars-uvs/toyota-suzuki-alliance-scales-up-in-india-with-shared-platforms-tech-products/articleshow/89043745.cms

Mint. (2021, February 17). *Toyota-Suzuki alliance expands in India with two new models.* Retrieved March 3, 2023, from https://www.livemint.com/companies/news/toyota-suzuki-alliance-expands-in-india-with-two-new-models-11613667886734.html

Mohanty, D. (2020). Toyota-Suzuki alliance in India: Strategic choices and performance outcomes. *Journal of Business Research*, *110*, 297–306. doi:10.1016/j.jbusres.2019.12.044

Chapter 15
The Fall of Yes Bank

Ruhi Sarangal
Chitkara Business School, Chitkara University, India

Maninder Kaur
University Business School, Punjab University, India

Ashok Kumar
Department of Defense and Strategic Studies, Himachal Pradesh University, India

EXECUTIVE SUMMARY

This case study focuses on a major challenge faced by Yes Bank as a result of increasing NPAs, a 30-day moratorium imposed by the RBI on its operations, and withdrawal limits of Rs. 50,000 from their accounts. This situation downgraded the value of the bank and built a bad image among its customers. Yes Bank was the UPI companion for almost 20 apps, according to the National Payments Corporation of India (NPCI). However, as a result of its failure, Yes Bank has suspended most of its UPI accounts. Now the government is trying to fix the problem and looking into what went wrong at Yes Bank. Altman's Z-Score, developed by American professor Edward Altman in 1968, is a numerical measurement that can be used to predict the chances of bankruptcy, and after calculating the z-score, it is possible to conclude that Yes Bank is still safe from going bankrupt.

INTRODUCTION

Rana Kapoor, co-founder of Yes Bank, was arrested on Saturday, March 7, 2020, two days after the collapse of the Yes bank. The Directorate of Enforcement arrested him on suspicion of money laundering and for the disbursement of 4300 crores in loans to corporate entities that had allegedly turned NPAs. According to an Indian Express report, nearly Rs 34,000 crores was sanctioned by Yes Bank against 44 companies, including its top ten defaulters by Rana Kapoor.

These defaulters include the Anil Ambani Group, Essel, Dewan Housing Finance Limited, Cox & King, Radius Developer Omkar Group, and others. The names of the companies and the respective loans given to these defaulters are given in the below table no. 1.

DOI: 10.4018/978-1-6684-8488-3.ch015

Table 1. Companies and loan amounts

Company	Loan Amount (Rs. In Crores)
Reliance (ADAG)	12800
Essel	8400
DHFL	4375
ILFS	2500
Jet airways	1100
Kerkar Groups	1000
Omkar Realtors & Developers	2710
Radius Developers	1200
CG Power	500

Source: Economic Times

Some other big defaulters include Jet Airways, Cox & Kings and Go Travels, Bharat Infra, McLeod Russell Assam Tea, and many more. The list of companies to whom Yes Bank gave loans, such as infrastructure, real estate, and the financial sector, and their bad loan-paying capacity reflect the bank's vulnerability to the most stressed banks. Even Ranveet Gill (Yes Bank's reappointed MD and CEO) confirmed that the bank had granted a large amount of loans to many corporate entities that were experiencing stress and liquidity problems.

Yes Bank flourished in the market until 2017, but its NPA hoarded due to bad loans. This fiasco leads to uprising NPA's. According to the RBI, YES Bank's NPAs were seven times the true reported amount in their reporting account books in 2020. After this news, the stock market plummets drastically. To prevent the further downfall of Yes Bank, the RBI joined Yes Bank and its management. Still, the bank has been distressed by the NPA problem.

YES BANK FAILURE

The NPA problem is directed to vast trouble because companies such as Jet Airways, Cox & King, CCD, Essel, DHFL, and others had no strategy for repaying their outstanding amounts to the bank and were not secure in their reserves. The amount owed by Yes Bank increased from INR 55,000 crores in FY14 to INR 2.41 trillion during FY19.

Yes Bank was put on moratorium by the regulatory body and India's Central Bank, RBI, on March 5, 2020. As per these guidelines, the people who have an account at Yes Bank were allowed to withdraw only INR 50,000, and this was persistent until April 3, 2020. The government imposes a 30-day moratorium on its operations and limits withdrawals to 50,000 from their accounts, except for emergencies such as medical expenses, higher education expenses, and marriage outlays This crisis devaluated the value of the bank and created a bad image among customers. Several fintech firms, such as Phone Pay and Bharat Pay, which exclusively relied on Yes Bank for their UPI-based dealings, were caught off guard, with millions of their consumers witnessing disruptions in their services during the period of the moratorium. Let's have a look at the table of gross NPA, net NPA, and return on assets, which is given below in table no. 2.

Table 2. NPA ratios

NPA Ratios	Mar'21	Mar'20	Mar'19	Mar'18	Mar'17
Gross NPA	28,609.53	32,877.59	7,882.56	2,626.80	2,018.56
Net NPA	9,813.36	8,623.78	4,484.85	1,312.75	1,072.27
Gross NPA	15.41%	16.80%	3.22%	1.28%	1.52%
Net NPA	5.88%	5.03%	1.86%	0.64%	0.81%
Return on Assets	-5.70%	-5.10%	0.50%	1.60%	1.80%

Source: moneycontrol.com

Because of the increase in NPAs, the stock price took a dive and now hovers around 3.5% of the all-time high price of Rs 383.25 on the BSE. The bank's market share price in 2020 is Rs. 13.45.

Altman's Z-Score and the Insolvency Position of Yes Bank

Altman's Z-Score, developed by American Professor Edward Altman in 1968, is a numerical measurement that can be used to predict the chances of bankruptcy. This model is used to determine the bankruptcy potential of firm. This model cannot be used to identify the bankruptcy of banks. For that, there is need to use Altman's customized model for banks.

Z-Score Estimation for Non-Manufacture and Emerging Markets

Altman Z-Score (non-manufacturers) = (6.56 x A) + (3.26 x B) + (6.72 x C) + (1.05 x D)

Altman Z-Score (emerging markets) = 3.25 + (6.56 x A) + (3.26 x B) + (6.72 x C) + (1.05 x D)

Where

- **A** = Working Capital / Total Assets
- **B** = Retained Earnings / Total Assets
- **C** = Earnings Before Interest and Taxes / Total Assets
- **D** = Book Value of Equity / Total Liabilities

Zones of Discriminations

In 2020, the current assets and liabilities of Yes Bank were Rs. 212903.01 cr. and Rs. 16946.18 cr., respectively. The total value of assets and liabilities was Rs. 240,880.74 crore. The book value of equity was Rs. 21726.29 crore, while borrowing and liabilities were Rs. 219,102 crore and Rs. 17,036 crores, respectively. EBIT in 2020 was Rs. 31193.89 crore.

Table 3. Altman Z-score bench mark

Altman Z-Score Benchmark			
Situation	**Z Score**	**Indicator**	**Remark**
1	Less than 1.1	Distress	High probability of distress
2	Among 1.1 and 2.6	Grey Zone	Difficult to predict
3	2.6 and Above	Safe zone	Non-bankrupt considered as 'Safe"

Source: Altman et al. (1995)

GROUNDS FOR THE PROBLEMS AT YES BANK

One of the major issues in the Yes Bank crisis is the outflow of liquidity. The money deposited by customers is the backbone of any financial institution or bank. If there is a bad rumor, it can have an impact on the money deposited. The RBI put Yes Bank under the moratorium after knowing that it was unable to raise capital to handle potential losses. Yes Bank's board was superseded by the RBI, which limits withdrawals to Rs 50,000 per account. The total liability of the Yes Banks as of 2021 is 2.57 lakh crore, compared to 2.15 lakh crore in 2017. When one of the founders of Yes Bank, Mr. Ashok Kapur, died in the Mumbai attack on November 26, his wife dreamed of including her daughter on the board of directors but was opposed by the wife of Mr. Rana Kapur.

Sound governance is indispensable for the growth and survival of any organization, which is where Yes Bank was lacking, resulting in the former deputy governor of RBI Mr. R. Gandhi included in the Yes Bank board of directors. At Yes Bank, corporate customers outnumber retail customers, unfortunately, most of the corporate customers of Yes Bank are defaulters and not able to repay debts, resulting in increased NPA. The gross and net NPAs have risen to 15.41% and 5.88%, respectively, in 2021, from 1.52% and.81% in 2017.

YES BANK

The banking industry is an economic sector at the forefront of every country's economy. If there is a collapse at a bank, the whole economy will be affected. For instance, during the global financial crisis in 2008, there was a severe economic crisis. It began with the housing market bubble. Dealing with people or organisations that were unable to repay loans and defaulted on payments necessitates a government bailout. Yes Bank found itself in a similar situation after lending 34,000 crores to fraudsters.

Yes Bank Ltd. has a complete spectrum of customer-focused corporate banking services, including specialised corporate finance, working capital finance, risk management services, security investment, liquidity management solutions, etc. It has around 420 ATMs across India and two National Operating Centers in Gurugram and Mumbai. The bank also owns an across-the-board network of over 331 branches across 200 cities.

Rana Kapoor and Ashok Kapur both established Yes Bank in 2004, which is an Indian private bank headquartered in Mumbai. Yes Bank as a private limited company includes corporate finance, business finance, corporate and institutional banking, retail banking, and investment banking. Yes Bank has shares listed on the NSE and the BSE, and its bonds are also listed on the London Stock Exchange. Yes Bank listed itself on the stock exchange of India in June 2005 at an issue price of Rs. 35 and a face value of Rs. 10.

HISTORY OF YES BANK

Yes Bank, India's fourth-largest bank, was established on November 21, 2013, by Rana Kapoor and Ashok Kapur. Since its beginning, it has been a full-service commercial bank, but the certificate of commencement was received by the bank in 2004. Yes Bank issued its shares on the stock exchange for the first time in June 2005 and came up with the public issue. Yes Bank begged India's best bank award, the Financial Express Award, in 2006. The Agriculture Insurance Company of India (AIC) joined hands with Yes Bank in 2007. Yes Bank got a rating from CARE and CRISIL for its numerous long-term debt programmes in September 2014. It was Yes Bank, the foremost bank in India, that obtained funding through the Co-Lending Portfolio Program, managed by IFC. Yes Bank was the first bank to avail itself of the loan, through IFC's loan facility.

On July 27, 2016, the Securities and Exchange Board of India (SEBI) gave clearance to Yes Bank to launch its mutual funds, set up an asset management company to manage these funds, and establish a trustee company. Yes Bank made its place in the 30-share S&P BSE Sensex.

RBI, the Central Bank, and the regulatory authority of India declared that, with the help of Yes Bank's depositors, participants, and customers, it would restructure its management by superseding and replacing its board and levying a 30-day moratorium on all its operations and activities on March 5, 2020.

YES BANK ACHIEVEMENT

Yes Bank is the 4th largest bank, and 35% of all UPI transactions were done through Yes Bank. Phone Pay, Swiggy, Flipkart, and many more were the partner of Yes Bank for PUI transactions. In 2005, Rana Kapoor, Founder, MD & CEO of the Yes Bank earned Start-up Entrepreneur of the year 2005. In October 2017, Yes Bank founded Yes Pay (digital wallet) with Bharat Interface for Money and Unified Payments Interface. A memorandum of understanding was signed between YES Bank and the government of India on 3rd Nov 2017 to give ₹1,000 crore financing for the project of processing. In 2018, Yes Bank Received SEBI approval to launch Mutual Fund Business. In June 2021, the bank got permission from the panel to raise 10,000 crores by the issue of debt securities.

THE DOWNGRADE OF YES BANK

On March 6, 2020, Yes Bank's rating was degraded to a "D" rating on another side. Moody's also downgraded the rating to 'Caa3.". On March 8, 2020, the Directorate of Enforcement apprehended Rana Kapoor for suspicious activities such as giving loans to fraudsters and money laundering. Yes Bank Ltd. was fined 25 crores by the Securities and Exchange Board of India (SEBI) in April 2021 for fraudulently marketing certain risky bonds without the required cautions and risk estimates.

STRATEGIES AND PLANS BY THE GOVERNMENT TO RESCUE YES BANK

- The former CEO of SBI Bank, Prashant Kumar, was appointed as the CEO and MD of Yes Bank with the hope of rescuing the
- On March 13, 2020, the Reconstruction Scheme for Yes Bank was approved by the Union Cabinet. During this reconstruction, seven investors invested 12,000 crores in Yes Bank, and these investors include SBI, HDFC Bank, Axis Bank, ICICI Bank, Rakesh Jhunjhunwala, Kotak Mahindra Bank, Radhakishan Damani, and Azim Premji
- To support Yes Bank, the RBI has recently opened an emergency line of credit of around Rs 60,000 crore to ease the liquidity crisis of the bank, enabling the bank to pay back its depositors.
- On March 5, 2020, the RBI revealed that, for the welfare of its customers, participants, and depositors, it would replace Yes Bank's board and take the Yes Bank management under its control.
- On January 15, 2022, the RBI declared that it has initiated the process for partner selection for its asset reconstruction company and is seeking Rs 12,000 crore from potential investors to partner with its asset reconstruction.
- The government imposed a 30-day moratorium on its functions, and customers of the bank were allowed to withdraw only up to Rs 50,000 from their accounts except for emergencies, like medical troubles, higher education expenses, and marriage. Nirmala Sitharaman, the finance minister, declared that SBI will take a 49% stake in Yes Bank, and it is a remarkable turnaround plan.

ICICI-VIDEOCON SCAM AND YES BANK SCAM

Chandra Kocher, the former ICICI Bank CEO, and her spouse, Deepak Kochhar, charged in the ICICI-Videocon case, were apprehended by the Directorate of Electorate in the alleged money laundering scam in September 2020. It was a quick exchange deal between the Videocon group and Deepak Kochhar. Deepak Kochhar sanctioned a loan of Rs 18750 crores to the leader of Videocon, Venugopal Dhoot, and the State Bank of India (SBI) led a consortium in 2012. This deal was a hidden one between Videocon's promoter, Venugopal Dhoot, and Chanda Kochhar's husband.

An investigation found Chandra Kochhar to be at fault for failing to disclose her husband's business relationship with the Videocon group. According to allegations, the loans became part of the bank's non-performing assets in 2012, leaving the bank owing Rs 1,730 crore. The CBI holds the inquiry for the breach of the bank's principles, ethics, and policies.

This question was raised by a fiasco at one of India's biggest banks about the policies of corporate administration. To some extent, the ICICI case was similar to the Yes Bank money laundering case. These kinds of failures emphasize the requirement for strict regulators to keep an eye on the stringent surveillance of the functions of corporate boards.

CONCLUSION

In India, for UPI transactions, Yes Bank is the leader. Yes Bank accounted for 40% of UPI dealings in January 2020, helping with 514 million transactions.

Yes Bank was the UPI companion for almost 20 apps, according to the National Payments Corporation of India (NPCI). However, as a result of its failure, Yes Bank has suspended most of its UPI accounts. Now the government is trying to fix the problem and looking into what went wrong at Yes Bank. Every bank needs to adhere to government rules, but it has been noticed that Yes Bank has a culture of weak compliance. The bank NPA had proven its risky credit decisions. The cleaning up of the Yes Bank has started after appointing the new CEO, Prashant Kumar. With a sense of urgency, the RBI is following the due process of law.

TEACHING NOTES

Synopsis

Yes Bank's NPA is seven times greater than the amount reported in their reporting books, according to the RBI. The Yes Bank NPA in 2021 was 15.41% compared to 1.52% in 2017, so we can say it is ten times more than it was in 2017. According to a report, Yes Bank approved Rs 34,000 crores for 44 of its top ten defaulters by Rana Kapoor.

These defaulters include Anil Ambani Group, Essel, and DHFL. Other big defaulters include Jet Airways, Cox & Kings, CCD, IL&FL, Go Travel, Bharat Infra, McLeod Russell Assam Tea, and many more. Yes Bank is the 4th largest bank, and 35% of all UPI transactions were done through it. PhonePe, Swiggy, Flipkart, and many more were the partners of Yes Bank for PUI transactions. Yes, the bank's market share for UPI transactions was nearly 39%, or it processed 39% of all UPI transactions. The government imposes a 30-day moratorium on its operations and a restricted limit on withdrawing only up to Rs. 50,000 from their accounts except for emergencies, like medical emergencies, higher education costs, and marriage expenses. This situation downgraded the value of the bank and created a bad image among its customers.

Yes Bank flourished in the market until 2017, but its NPA was hoarded due to bad loans. The NPA revolts as a result of this shambles. According to the RBI, Yes Bank's NPAs are seven times the true reported amount in their reporting account books. After this news, the stock market plummets drastically. To prevent the further downfall of the RBI joined Yes Bank and its management. Still, the bank has been distressed by the NPA problem.

Objectives of the Study

- To find out the insolvency position of the company.
- To compare the Yes Bank crisis with other similar types of collapse.
- To study the major reasons that led to the crisis of yes bank.
- To examine how to fall in profits leads to a change in investors' behavior and results in a decline in stock price.

Level of case difficulty – UG and PG
Course(s) in which the case can be used – BBA, B Com, and MBA

Details of experience of a teaching case

The primary benefit of teaching case studies in the classroom is that students can actively participate in the class. It exposes the students to a real-world situation and helps them figure out the problems with the help of examples. Students develop various skills like problem solving, making decisions in complex situations, etc. Role play could be an innovative approach for the case study. It helps the students play the roles of different characters, which are mentioned in the case study, so that they can really understand the perspectives of the case characters. Some other examples of teaching experience:

- Students were keen to know if Yes Bank transfers all its NPAs to an asset reconstruction company in such a case, which will pay the bad debts. They are interested in how the Asset Reconstruction Company works. Asset Reconstruction Company is a financial institution that purchases bad debts from banks at a mutually agreed price and then recovers the debts by itself. The CEO of Yes Bank, Prashan Kumar, said when they would transfer gross NPAs to the Asset Reconstruction Company, the NPA ratio would plunge below 2 percent from around 14 percent in 2022.
- Students are also interested in knowing who owns Asset Reconstruction Company. The base bidder for bad loans worth Rs 48,000 crore at Yes Bank is JC Flowers. The Altman Z Score method and its calculation attract students a lot. This calculation will help them learn how to calculate working capital, retain earnings, EBIT, and many other ratios.

We have provided below a breakdown of the teaching structure that links the analysis back to the learning objectives and supporting background reading.

1. To find out the insolvency position of the company: To find out the solvency position of the company, students can use Altman's Z-Score, developed in 1968 by an American professor, Edward Altman, and the balance sheets and profit and loss account of Yes Bank. Earnings before interest and taxes (EBIT) is an indicator of the company's profitability. EBIT can be calculated as revenue minus expenses excluding tax and interest, whereas values for all these can be taken from the profit and loss account. Assets, liabilities, and working capital can be calculated from balance sheets.
2. To compare the Yes Bank crisis with other similar types of collapse: To contrast the Yes Bank with another similar type of bank, the case includes the ICICI Bank Scam and the Videocon Scam. Students can compare both scams and figure out which of theses two is considerably worse.
3. To study the major reasons that led to the crisis at Yes Bank, students can go through the whole case and find out which main reasons were actually responsible for the collapse of Yes Bank. All the main reasons, that contributed to Yes Bank's collapse are mentioned indirectly in the case study.
4. How to deal with the NPS problem: As declared by Prashant Kumar, CEO of the Yes Bank, as soon as possible, they will set up an asset reconstruction company and transfer all the NPAs into that ARC. Strategies and plans by the government to rescue Yes Bank in this case can help the students understand how the government and Yes Bank management can rescue the bank.
5. To examine how a fall in profits leads to a change in investors' behaviour and results in a decline in stock price, The chart of Yes Bank's stock price in 2020 is given in the case study. Students can see how, as Yes Bank's profit decreased, so did its stock price.

Questions

1. How can we find out the insolvency position with the help of finding out the zone in which the bank actually exists?

Expected answer:

We have a Z score formula, which we can use to calculate the insolvency position of the bank or any other non-manufacturing unit. The model is given below:

Z-score estimation for non-manufacture & emerging markets

Altman Z-Score (non-manufacturers) = (6.56 x A) + (3.26 x B) + (6.72 x C) + (1.05 x D)

Where

- **A** = Working Capital / Total Assets
- **B** = Retained Earnings / Total Assets
- **C** = Earnings Before Interest and Taxes / Total Assets
- **D** = Book Value of Equity / Total Liabilities

Zones of Discriminations

Table 4. Altman Z-score benchmark

Altman Z-Score Benchmark			
Situation	**Z Score**	**Indicator**	**Remark**
1	Less than 1.1	Distress	High probability of distress
2	Among 1.1 and 2.6	Grey Zone	Difficult to predict
3	2.6 and Above	Safe zone	Non-bankrupt considered as 'Safe"

Source: Altman et al. (1995)

- **A** = Working Capital / Total Assets

A = 195956.83/240,880.74

A = .8135

Note: -

Working Capital = Current Assets-Current Liabilities

Working Capital = 212903.01-16946.18

Working Capital = 195956.83

Working Capital / Total Assets

- **B** = Retained Earnings / Total Assets

B = 0/240,880.74

B = 0

- **C** = Earnings Before Interest and Taxes / Total Assets

C = 22778.89/240,880.74

C = .094

- **D** = Book Value of Equity / Total Liabilities

D = 21726.29/240,880.74

D = .090

Altman Z-Score (non-manufacturers) = (6.56 x .8135) + (3.26 x 0) + (6.72 x .094) + (1.05 x .090)

Altman Z-Score (non-manufacturers) = 5.33 + 0 + .635 + .95

Altman Z-Score (non-manufacturers) = 6.91

We can see the Z-score is higher than 2.6, which means Yes Bank is still in a safe zone.

2. How do you compare the ICICI Bank case with the Yes Bank case?

Expected answer:
ICICI Bank is the 3rd largest private bank, whereas Yes Bank is the 7th largest bank in India in 2021. Yes Bank's case is considerably worse than the ICICI Bank-Videocon case. The money laundering amount involved in the Yes Bank case was around Rs 34,000 crore, whereas in the ICICI Bank-Videocon case it was Rs 1730 crore. In the YES Bank case, it was a large-scale misappropriation of money compared to the ICICI Bank-Videocon case. In the Yes Bank case, the CEO, the promoter, and the top executives were all hand in glove, whereas in the ICICI Bank-Videocon case only Chanda Kochhar and Deepak Kochhar were involved. In the case of YES Bank, the entire system was the culprit. There is no comparison between the ICICI Bank scam and the Yes Bank scam.

3. What do you believe are the major reasons for the downfall or problems at Yes Bank?

Expected answer:

Yes Bank is the leading commercial bank in India's banking sector. During the year 2020, Yes Bank faced a hard situation. On March 5, 2020, the RBI imposed a 30-day moratorium on Yes Bank and appointed Prashant Kumar as administrator. The following factors may have contributed to the failure of Yes Bank:

Worsening Financial Situation

Yes Bank's financial situation has steadily deteriorated over the last few years. The bank's total unsettled loans rose to Rs 2.24 lakh crore in the quarter under evaluation, down 6.3 percent year on year. Negative working capital, negative retained earnings, and a huge amount of non-performing assets are reasons for our worsening financial position.

A Hefty Amount of Withdrawals/Outflow of Liquidity

On the one side, the credit amount was swelling at an extraordinary speed, whereas on the other side, withdrawals were also increasing. The bank has witnessed the withdrawal of deposits from consumers. The bread and butter for the banks are deposits. Customers' panic causes banks to run out of money rather than actual insolvency.

Inadequate Governance/Governance Issues

Although Yes Bank is a private sector bank, it has experienced a number of supremacy issues in recent years, which has resulted in this crisis. For example, the bank's unpublicized NPAs turned in Rs 3,277 crore in 2018-19, and in January 2020, Uttam Prakash Agarwal, an independent director, quit Yes Bank. When one of the founders of Yes Bank, Mr. Ashok Kapur, died in the Mumbai attack on November 26, his wife dreamed of including her daughter on the board of directors but was opposed by the wife of Mr. Rana Kapur. Sound governance is indispensable for the growth and survival of any organization, which is where Yes Bank was lacking, resulting in the former deputy governor of RBI Mr. R. Gandhi included in the Yes Bank board of directors.

Announcement of Moratorium

The crisis at Yes Bank was handled by different authorities, such as Firstly The RBI announced a cessation for 30 days in the case of Yes Bank in March 2020. Secondly, the SBI (State Bank of India) will buy a 49% stake in Yes Bank, as stated by finance minister Nirmala Sitharaman.

Retail Customers are More as Compare to Retail Customers

At Yes Bank, corporate customers outnumber retail customers, unfortunately, most of the corporate customers of Yes Bank are defaulters and not able to repay debts, resulting in increased NPA.

4. How do we get rid of NPAs?

Expected answer:

Yes, the bank can reduce its NPA because the main reason for its crisis is its NPA. If Yes Bank intends to bring down its NPAs through recoveries and upgrades, it will take a long time. In this situation, it can sell its NPAs. Prashant Kumar, CEO of the bank, hopes to set up an asset reconstruction company to sell their bad loans.

1. By improving the quality of its assets
2. Reduce the provision of bad debts

5. How RBI can save yes bank?

Expected answer:

According to Section 17 of the RBI Act 1934, the CB (central bank) must provide liquidity support to money lenders in the form of loans and advances in exchange for collateral such as stocks or funds, and securities (other than fixed assets). In this situation, a specific trustee is permitted to place money in trust with an Act of Parliament.

Yes Bank has received a Rs 60,000 crore lifeline from the Reserve Bank of India in order to meet the needs of its depositors. The (CB) central bank has extended the main thing, which is liquidity support, to the Yes Bank besides the collateral security submitted in the forms of stocks, funds, and securities. There is an urgent need to set up the Asset Reconstruction Company so that Yes Bank can transfer its NPA to ARC and easily start from scratch with no huge NPA. If Yes bank intends to bring down its NPAs through recoveries and upgrades, but it will take a long time. In this situation, they can sell their NPAs, and the best way to sell NPAs is ARC.

RBI can give financial aid and take a stake in Yes Bank to save it. Even the Indian Finance Minister, Mrs. Nirmala Sitharaman, declared that the SBI would have 49% of the Yes Bank, and it is a remarkable turnaround plan of the government.

6. Why do Yes Bank depositors suffer?

Expected answer:

The Yes Bank crisis has sent a freighting wave across local markets and households where individuals have accounts with the bank. Several people are dependent on this bank, and many more big organisations like Zomato used to accept all the online payments from this bank. Many people used to get their salaries and pay EMI transactions through this bank, and due to the crisis at Yes Bank, many depositors and account holders suffered a lot. Later on, the government assured us there was no need to panic as the Reserve Bank of India would come up with a useful idea for the bank's recovery.

7. Is your money safe at Yes Bank?

Expected answer:

It is very controversial whether depositors' money is safe or not at Yes Bank. We know India is a developing country, while the banking sector is at the forefront of the Indian economy. If there is a collapse at the bank, the whole economy will be affected. The government cannot afford such a disastrous loss. "We have to ensure that the customers' interests are primarily protected," said Finance Minister Nirmala Sitharaman.

8. Did it justify using taxpayers' money to save banks like Yes Bank?

Expected answer:

No, it is not justified to use the taxpayer's money to save banks like Yes Bank because such an environment will provide fertile ground for rogue bankers and unlawful borrowers that could result in large non-performing assets. But on the other side, if the government does not intervene and bail out the bank, it can lead to an economic collapse on a large scale. How the government has tackled the problem and infused a huge amount of money is praiseworthy. To protect the bank, the government declared SBI would take a 49% stake in Yes Bank.

REFERENCES

Akhtar, S., Alam, M., & Khan, M. M. (2021). YES Bank Fiasco: Arrogance or Negligence. *Emerging Economies Cases Journal*, *3*(2), 95–102. doi:10.1177/25166042211061003

Chotalia, P. (2012). Evaluation of financial health of sampled private sector banks with Altman Z-score model. *Circulation in more than 85 countries, 7.*

Dutta, B. (2022, September 5). *Business standard.* https://www.business-standard.com/article/finance/yes-bank-plans-to-invest-up-to-rs-350-crore-for-20-stake-in-jc-flowers-arc-122071801173_1.html

Manikandan, A. (2020, March 7). *The Economic Times.* https://economictimes.indiatimes.com/industry/banking/finance/banking/digital-payments-hit-cos-tap-alternatives/articleshow/74520306.cms

Singh, S. (2020, September 4). *The Indian Express.* https://indianexpress.com/article/business/banking-and-finance/yes-bank-crisis-rana-kapoor-arrested-bad-loans-6307485/

Chapter 16
Bikaner as a City of Happiness:
A Peep Into the Cultural and Historic Evolution of an Unorganized Initiative to Develop a Happy City

Trilok Kumar Jain
Suresh Gyan Vihar University, India

Neeraj Anand
Chitkara Business School, Chitkara University, India

EXECUTIVE SUMMARY

This is a case study on the relevance of the culture and heritage of a city to overall happiness and comfort of the citizens. India ranks at 136 in the World Happiness Ranking as per 10th World Happiness Report 2022. A happy city is a city that focuses on building infrastructure for get-togethers, interactions, parties, and socializing of the residents. This case study takes a look at the evolution of culture of Bikaner city and identifies key elements of this culture. It is located in Thar Desert and has extreme climatic conditions. It has geographical disadvantage but has many distinct advantages also. The city has been able to maintain its unique identity and culture despite the changes and pandemic the world has undergone over the decades. This city has been able to preserve its heritage and its deeply rooted traditional values. The authors have highlighted unique cultural characteristics of the city and also raised some concerns to be addressed to develop it as a preferred destination while developing it as modern city of happiness. The case study leaves many questions to ponder.

WHAT MAKES A CITY HAPPY AND SMART?

A smart city is one which has adopted the latest technology in urban management. This makes the city an advanced city because all the amenities are technologically accessible such as digital payments etc. Plenty of wi-fi hubs enable people to use the internet and technology very easily and connect with the resources of the city. Smart cities offer residents all the modern amenities with ease of access – infra-

DOI: 10.4018/978-1-6684-8488-3.ch016

structure, transport and telecom connectivity etc. India ranks at 136 in the World Happiness Ranking as per 10th World Happiness Report 2022. A happy city is a city which focuses on building infrastructure for get-together, interaction, parties and socializing of the residents. Happy cities are known for creating warmth and excellent hospitality in the city with plenty of celebration points and plenty of traditions for promoting mingling of the local residents such as Picnic spots (*Goth*), sand dunes, historical monuments, lily pond (Public Park), Bawri (Shivbari) and ancient temples- Shivbari, Laxmi Narayan temple, Bhandasar Jain temple, Garh Ganesh, Nagnechi etc. Traditions like Wearing Safa (turban), Pataa culture (elderly people sitting on a cot in the street side in the city), eating together in the smaller groups in one thali (plate) in weddings and social gatherings, playing Holi in the city with paint and water, offering fodder to cows and roti to dogs, food grain to pigeons, going for morning walk in the city/Vradh Jan Path, temples; chewing supari (*kircha*) and consuming paan etc. Most of the residents staying outside Bikaner visit the city during weddings and social gatherings, they prefer this city as the wedding place even if they have been staying in other states for more than 50 years.

Every city is a living organization because it has some traditions, common values, cultural roots and some common beliefs. This is a study of a cultural city, which has existed for over 500 years carrying a set of beliefs and values. This city is often termed a "Big Village" because many people confuse the values of this city with those of rural societies. However, this city has its own identity and it has been able to maintain its unique characteristics in spite of the challenges of modern society.

Culture and values are based on the common beliefs and mindset of the people. What most people assume to be common beliefs become the center of a cultural backbone.

While most cities are striving for becoming smart cities, Bikaner continues to remain a "Happy City" - the city remains glued to its old forte - being happy, complacent and remaining attached to joy and happiness. There is a lack of ambition among common people, but this is a merit here because people are content with what they have. People give higher weightage to happiness, their family members and therefore, they devote more time towards spiritual activities, family get-togethers and community meetings in comparison to professional or occupational goals.

EVOLUTION OF BIKANER CITY

Bikaner was established in 1488 and it is located on Western Rajasthan (bordering to Pakistan). This city is located in the Thar Desert area and therefore water scarcity has always affected this city. The population of Bikaner is approximately 8 Lakhs. Being a border city, it has always faced challenges relating to infrastructure. It's connected with Delhi through rail with the distance of 463 km and well connected through National Highway with Jaipur, NCR, Gujarat via Jodhpur. Industries could not be developed due to lack of infrastructure and political will. Still, we may witness limited industries in the field of wool processing, insulators, carpet, edible oil and other industries. The desert climate is its strength as well as weakness. Being a dry climate, this city has the best environment for food production such as lintel, bajra etc. This city has grabbed this opportunity and has become the largest food item producing city of India. Well-known brands of Bhujia (namkeen) such as Bikanerwala, Bikaji, Haldiram, BC, Milan etc. have originated from this city. The city has been producing almost 80% of the country's Gypsum and POP (Plaster of Paris) requirements. The city has huge milk production and is known as 'Denmark of Rajasthan'. The city has been known for its crafts including paintings, Usta art, miniature painting, manihari jewelry, jadau, bandhej, doria and The city is also known for its unique culture, heritage and values. Lack of water is a major problem in agriculture. Wherever, Indira Gandhi Canal water is available - there is abundant crop, but its coverage is limited to few places only. Handmade carpets by prisoners are well known throughout the country.

When you visit the Barah Guwad, (where traditional Bikaner is still alive), you find a very big Kadhav (pan). The story says that the earlier Kings of Bikaner used to offer free food to the people by cooking food in that Pan. The story says that the kings of Bikaner displayed a visionary approach to development. King Ganga Singh developed the Gang Canal to bring water to this city. He established Railway Workshop, Veterinary College and Veterinary Hospital. Rail coach is displayed in Lalgarh palace, which was the initiative of King Ganga Singh only. He started coal mining and tried to attract the best human resources - engineers and veterinary doctors to this city. Due to his efforts, Dr. Sivakamu joined and settled down in Bikaner as a renowned Veterinary doctor. The king established one of the finest libraries of the country at that time. The people of Bikaner established twenty private libraries at that time, which enabled the development of the literary environment. Lot of research work has been carried out by Indian and foreign researchers on the heritage and culture of this city. Great Italian scholar Mr. Tessitory devoted his life to understanding the literature and culture of Bikaner.

The Characteristics of the City of Bikaner

History of Bikaner: Bikaner has a long history. The modern city came into existence about 500 years back. But earlier this city was called "Jangal Pradesh" and has a very long history - dating back to saint Kapil. This is the region where local residents given preference to relationship building and nurturing the relationships. This is evident in the old structure of the city. In every mohalla (every ward), we find one community centre, one Paata and one common resource centre. There used to be one community library also in the mohallas earlier. The remnants of this unique cultural practice is visible even today. This city has been able to maintain its unique system of cultural cohesion due to its unique cultural and traditional values. This city is best known for 'Communal harmony', not a single incident of riots or conversion of religion has been reported since independence of the country or earlier.

a) **Pata:** Pata is a wooden platform in every mohalla. The system of urban management can be seen here. People are able to handle their issues through participative management. Pata, which is a platform for discussion and management of mohalla (mohalla is similar to ward). The people of a mohalla will discuss all the aspects relating to that mohalla on the paata. Everyone is equal on Pata. One mohalla may have between 50 to 300 homes, and all these people are tied together in the form of "Bhaipo" – bhaipo means the people living in a mohalla are like brothers. They may be from any caste, but they are all brothers because they are living in that village. They celebrate festivals together and discuss all matters relating to their mohalla in their mohalla panchayat.

b) **A City of Festivals:** The city is addicted to festivals so much that when it is the festival time, everyone is part of the festival. People celebrate different festivals with fervour and joy. Gangour festival is one such festival, when all the women of the city are fully involved in the celebration. The foundation day of this city 'Akshya Tritya' is celebrated very well with kite flying and other rituals every year.

c) **A City of Heritage:** The city has the pride of having over 1000 *Havelies* - which denotes its rich heritage. These havelies are old houses built in red stones. The city has been able to preserve its culture and values by preserving and protecting its heritage. Junagarh and Lalgarh Palace are well known and a lot of foreigners visit these historical places. It is surrounded by Kolayat, Husangsar, Deshnok, Neyveli Lignite Plant, Plan; Punrasar, Gajner Wildlife Century etc. these can further promote Bikaner as a tourism destination.

d) **Goth:** 'Goth' denotes a type of party. When the people of a ward (mohalla) want to celebrate a party, they announce a Goth and all the residents of that mohalla join to celebrate a Goth. It is not just a party, but a spiritual meeting. The meeting starts with prayers in some temples followed by some get-together, plays and joy. At the end there is prasadi or food distribution which is managed by people together. They call it prasadi because it was offered to God and later on distributed among all as God's blessings. All the expenses are shared by the people equally. The frequency of Goth is often once a month. Generally it is organized on some hoiliday or on some Sunday so that everyone can participate in the celebration.

e) **Jeeman:** Jeeman is also a type of party. Bikaner is a city of celebration. People are well connected to their families and also to their mohalla. Whenever they have any occasion to celebrate, they organize a 'Jeeman'. This is a type of party, where people join together and every aspect of the party is managed by the people collectively.

f) **Mohalla Panchayat:** Traditionally every mohalla had a panchayat bhawan, common resources for celebration, paata, reading room, library etc. These common resources allowed people to grow together in the form of a well managed urban centre. However, these practices are now disappearing due to spread of modern institutions, which are replacing the traditional institutions

g) **Traditional Systems of Education, Health-Care, and Community Care:** The city has nurtured traditional systems of education, health-care and community care for many a generation. Even before the spread of modern educational institutions, there was 'Marza' a type of Gurukul - a traditional educational system. Mohta trust has been running its Ayurvedic centre and producing ayurvedic medicines for decades. Shiv Shakti Malham (Gel) is well known for curing burn cases.

h) **City of Jaagan (Ratri Jagaran):** Jaagan or Ratri Jagaran is a whole night prayer - where a group of people start chanting prayers and continue throughout the night. Bikaner is a city of temples, and often there is some Ratri Jagaran in some or other temple - where people spend whole night chanting prayers and bhajans.

i) **Jatra:** Jatra means walking to some holy place - there are plenty of holy places near Bikaner - i.e. Deshnok Karni Mata Temple, Salasar Hanuman Temple, Punrasar Hanuman temple, Runicha Ramdev Temple etc. People walk down to these temples during Jatra. They enjoy their journey in which they walk and engage themselves in spiritual discourse and Bhajans. Hundreds of businessmen carry such Jatra annually, closing their shops or making alternative arrangements.

j) **A City of Taste:** The city may be called a city of taste - because it is known for tasty Bhujia, Rasgulla, Gondpak and other sweets, Papad, Namkeen and Supari. There are various food joints in the city catering to the traditional food and other varieties. There are different food items in different seasons. Some sweets are available during winter only, while some other sweets are available during summers. People generally prefer sweets rich in pure ghee and oil. Traditional recipe 'Daal Baati and Churma' is popular worldwide. 'Sangri' herb is the delicacy recipe served during weddings and social gatherings etc. Aloe Vera (Guar Patha) is commonly used as a vegetable in meals, helping to control blood pressure and diabetes etc. The traditional sweets of this city include Feeni, Ghewar, Pandhari, Gajak, Tilpapdi, Motichoor, Motipak, Katli and many other sweets, which are prepared as per seasons and as per climate conditions. Sweets like Ghewar are prepared at the time of winter, while there are some sweets which are prepared during summer.

k) **Spiritual Confluence:** This is the city where Muslim scholars speak Urdu Ramayan and create a spiritual confluence. This city has always created a great spiritual confluence. Great scholars like Ramsukh Das ji, Samvit Somgiri ji etc. have continued the great traditions of Maharshi Kapil. Ramsukhdasji, Samvit Somgiri ji, Acharya Tulsi, Acharya Mahapgragya, and Acharya Mahashraman have significantly contributed to the spiritual values of the city. The city is surrounded by plenty of "Teerth '' – which are world famous. Some of these teerth are: -

   a. Karni Mata Dham, Deshnok
   b. Salasar Dham
   c. Punrasar Dham
   d. Shakti Peeth (Acharya Tulsi Samadhi Sthal)
   e. Kolayat (Kapil Muni samadhi)
   f. Muktidham Mukam
   g. Katariasar
   h. Jamsar
   i. Runicha (Ramdev Temple)
   j. Kodamdesar
   k. Sardarshahar (Acharya Mahapragya samadhi sthal)
   l. Sagar (samadhi of Kings of Bikaner)
   m. Toliasar Bherun ji

Jaatra (Pad-yatra) & Teerthyatra are always the most devoted approach towards holiness. People walk to offer their prayers at their Teerth. Approximately one million people do teerthyatra of Ramdev Temple in Roonicha. Approximately the same number of people do teerthyatra of Karni Mata Temple in Deshnok. Swastik is considered a very holy symbol in Indian culture. Bikaner has the world's largest Swastik spread out in a vast area, which is visible from the sky.

l) **Hathai:** Hathai means when people sit together and discuss the issues of day to day matters. People in Bikaner enjoy talking to each other for a long time. This is called Hathai. They sit down on "paata" and start Hathai. However, with the arrival of the digital revolution, hathai is now disappearing. People are now busy in whatsapp or social media chats.

m) **City of Camels and Animals:** Bikaner has always nourished camels, cows, horses, goats and other pet animals. The city has a national research Centre on camels namely CRI (Camel Research Institute) and National Research Centre on Equines. The city is known for its annual camel festival, which is held in the second week of January every year. Tourists from all over the world come here to participate in the Camel Festival and enjoy camel rides. The city has a very large population of Rathi Cow (Rathi Cow is considered a very good cow due to A2 Milk). The city has huge Gochar Land, which is managed by the people of the city. People do protect and preserve "Bad-peepal parikrama" in Gochar Land thereby managing age-old tradition of protecting the Peepal (Ficus religiosa) Tree and Banyan Tree.

n) **Padhaaro Saa:** In Bikaner, it is a culture to add suffix "Saa" with every name. If your name is Amol, people will call you Amol Saa. This is a tradition. "Saa" means very high respect. The people offer respect by adding Saa as suffix with every name. Tourists, visitors and Teerthyatri find it exhilarating to see "Padharo Saa"written for them. This is just a method of welcoming visitors. It is commonly written on the entrance gate of hotels and restaurants etc.

The above discussion can lead someone to conclude that people are happy and everything is good in this city. But this is not true. There are many issues, which remain unaddressed. Culture has its impact on the residents, their philosophy and their institutions. People are driven by an "affiliation motive" and that has resulted in their reduced aggressiveness towards their demands and towards their rights as citizens. The administration and local political leaders take them for granted and ignore their problems. The result of this culture is an apathetic approach in bureaucracy and administration towards the general public. The lack of required "achievement motive" and "power motive" is probably responsible for lack of public protests in spite of very poor local administration, and in spite of very poor cleanliness and urban governance.

Ways and Means of Preservation of Culture

With the passage of time, the city has tried to preserve its unique culture and identity. All the festivals are celebrated with traditional fervour and zeal. Except Covid19, there was no barrier and these festivals were never interrupted. These festivals have always been organized with community participation.

Current Debate

The new generation is migrating out of this city. The new generation is giving more importance to economic prosperity and therefore this city looks like a place for rest and recharge. The new generation thinks that the culture of this city is not appropriate for the present-day context. However, the old generation continues to enjoy the culture and heritage. Tradition of Joint families is also withering away and heading towards nuclear families. Residents have been moving out of the old city to the modern and posh colonies; outskirts for better facilities and standard of living.

Lack of Modern Amenities

Bikaner has not yet been identified as a spiritual city or as a smart city. There is a lack of modern amenities. There is one public library, which is in a dilapidated condition. There are many private libraries, but they are not given support by the government. There is no public transport system by the government. There is no space for parking of vehicles near important markets or important tourist destinations. Heritage walk was started, but due to lack of proper government support, it did sustain. There is no cleanliness in the city and therefore there are huge piles of waste all around. A few NGOs are trying to spread cleanliness and a few government vehicles do make loud noises about Swachh Bharat - but there is no change in the overall dirt and waste spread all around.

Major Problems of the City

Bikaner is located in the Thar Desert. The Thar desert is spreading continuously. The city experiences extreme climates. It is one of the coldest regions (among plains) during winter and it is also the hottest region during summers. It is very difficult to grow trees in this region due to adverse climate and lack of adequate rainfall. Thus the city continues to face the challenges of desert regions.

The city has a beautiful pond just opposite the palace – Sursagar. The local municipality allowed the drainage water to be put in the pond and the pond became a dirty pond. It became a garbage collection point. It started smelling badly. Once Sursagar was considered the biggest problem. The bureaucracy and political leadership didn't take much lead. The people of the city started organizing discussions and they prepared suggestions and forwarded a plan to the government. Ultimately one government accepted the proposal and decided to clean this putrid pond. The initiative by the common people helped in raising the administration to action.

Kotegate is considered as the hub of this city. There is a railway crossing near Kotegate. It is a matter of disappointment that there is no under or over bridge at this railway crossing. Local residents have been raising this issue for an under bridge - but due to some constraints, there is no action so far.

Air connectivity is still a major issue. Though the city is well connected through road and rail to Delhi/NCR, Punjab, Haryana and other states yet it lacks a proper airport. Naal airstrip is being used for operating certain flights to Delhi and Jaipur etc. and this city is connected with the rest of the world through these cities.

Currently, the city is lacking in state of the art infrastructure for cleanliness and modern amenities. There is not even a single pink toilet in the city. Ideally every government hospital and every government institution should establish a Pink Toilet. However, the local bodies in the city consider it unnecessary. They are apathetic towards the need of the hour. When the researcher contacted a few government organizations including hospitals about their plan for establishment of public toilets and pink toilets, their replies were shocking. They said that it is not their responsibility. Is there any possibility of transforming public institutions towards public welfare?

Challenges of the Future

Modernity is spreading fast and the city is losing its traditional values and culture. The age-old practices and festivals are disappearing now. These eroding values are creating a vacuum. The traditional community care is now disappearing. The spiritual environment is now disappearing. Modern internet revolution is bringing new forms of crime. The youth are getting addicted to the internet. The old people are finding it difficult to find someone to talk to. Cyber-crimes are increasing. The government schools and government hospitals are not able to function at their best due to rising population and these things are causing stress and anxiety among people, who have to rush to Jaipur for any small health-care issue. The traditional culture of tolerance has resulted in tolerance of inefficient and corrupt government institutions and this has resulted in overall poor urban governance. Political interests dominate decision making and the city lacks vision-based planning. Cities like Jodhpur and Ajmer have improved substantially, but Bikaner has never been able to get any good political leader as its patron. Though this city has produced many great leaders like Dr. B D Kalla but the city itself has never got the kind of treatment that it deserved. The city has produced many entrepreneurs like Radhakishan Dammani, H.C. Nahata, Shiv Ratan Agarwal etc. but the city is lacking in industrialization. The government didn't approve the proposal of establishing a Food Park in Bikaner, which has been its demand for a long time. The city also deserves a Heritage Corridor to display its paintings, meenakari, Jadau and other handicrafts and crafts. There are a large number of products of this city, which need to be given "Geographically Indicated Goods" under Indian Patent Act but there is lack of concerted planning and support for such initiative is not evident.

Sustaining Happiness?

Sustaining the happiness of this city is a major challenge now. If good health-care and education is not available, how can citizens sustain happiness? The culture and traditions cannot help the residents in maintaining happiness for a long time. The age-old values will help the city, but there is a need for government actions for creating a good, clean, healthy and prosperous city. There is not even one pink toilet in this city. There is complete apathy in the bureaucracy towards common facilities for the common people. This lack of support for the common people is visible in its poor infrastructure. The happiness of this city is disappearing. This city has a large number of heritage venues and heritage hotels; however, it has not been able to achieve any tourism destination tag till date, there is a need of modern infrastructure support to enable this city to emerge as a good tourist destination.

Questions for Discussions?

1. In the present-day context where competition and growth are the most important characteristics, do you still believe that this city should continue its culture?
2. How should this city adopt new technologies in developing and promoting its identity and a preferred tourism destination? Suggest a roadmap and vision for this city.
3. Is happiness more important than economic prosperity? Discuss various factors to create more job opportunities, promote startup culture and Prepare a roadmap for Bikaner city.

Teaching Note

Prior to discussion on this case, the teacher should introduce the concept of theory of culture development. The teacher should also discuss the theory of participative approach to urban management and governance. The teacher should also introduce the concept of a happy and smart city. This case study presents the cultural practices of a traditional city from western Rajasthan (India). The cultural values of happiness and joy are very important and they should be given importance, but it is equally important to give importance to modern technologies, urban governance and development. This case study should be discussed by the participants and road-map should be developed. The participants may be able to arrive at a roadmap which brings balance between competing goals. The participants may be able to create a path which may bring collaboration between competing issues i.e. cooptition. The issues relating to human motivation and cultural issues are such which give better understanding when discussed in a group.

Another important issue is how to promote Bikaner City as the Tourism Destination, how digital and smart infrastructure can support the administrators to bring this heritage city on the World Map. What demographic and psychographic variables could be considered significant for this purpose.

Migrating from Bikaner to other cities and metro cities is also on the rise. Participants may discuss pros and cons of migration from the city. What could be the role of administrators, senior citizens, educational institutions, NGOs, Entrepreneurs and intellectuals to prevent migration and create more job opportunities and startups in the city.

REFERENCES

Aggarwal, A., Lim, W. M., Jaisinghani, D., & Nobi, K. (2022). Driving service-oriented organizational citizenship behavior through error management culture. *Service Industries Journal*, 1–40. doi:10.1080/02642069.2022.2147160

Aggarwal, A., Sadhna, P., Gupta, S., Mittal, A., & Rastogi, S. (2022). Gen Z entering the workforce: Restructuring HR policies and practices for fostering the task performance and organizational commitment. *Journal of Public Affairs*, *22*(3), e2535. doi:10.1002/pa.2535

Anthopoulos, L. G. (2015). Understanding the smart city domain: A literature review. *Transforming city governments for successful smart cities*, 9-21.

Haque, A. B., Bhushan, B., & Dhiman, G. (2022). Conceptualizing smart city applications: Requirements, architecture, security issues, and emerging trends. *Expert Systems: International Journal of Knowledge Engineering and Neural Networks*, *39*(5), e12753. doi:10.1111/exsy.12753

JainE.JainT. K. (2019). Rainwater Harvesting–The Case Study Related to India's Thar Desert. Available at SSRN 3327743. doi:10.2139/ssrn.3327743

JainT. K. (2019). Concept of Happy City: The Smart Cities of the Future. Available at SSRN 3314531. doi:10.2139/ssrn.3314531

JainT. K. (2019). Smart Cities and Happy Cities in India–A Review Paper. Available at SSRN 3367763. doi:10.2139/ssrn.3367763

Mirzaei, S., & Zangiabadi, A. (2021). Studying and Complying Dimensions, Indicators and Variables Related to a Happy City. *International Review for Spatial Planning and Sustainable Development*, *9*(2), 94–111. doi:10.14246/irspsda.9.2_94

Shaheen, L., & Ibrahim, M. A. A. (2021). Smart happy city. *WIT Transactions on Ecology and the Environment*, *253*, 527–537.

Chapter 17
How India Is Able to Control Inflation During the Russia–Ukraine War

Abhishek Anand
Chitkara Business School, Chitkara University, India

Sarparaj Ramanand Sagar
Tilka Manjhi Bhagalpur University, India

Chandan Kumar
Tilka Manjhi Bhagalpur University, India

EXECUTIVE SUMMARY

The case study focusses upon the control of inflation in India during the time of higher inflation rates globally. Post pandemic and Russia-Ukraine war have had a great negative impact on ongoing slow growth of the economies globally. All the economies all over the world are facing economic instability, having higher inflation and increasing unemployment in the economy. The study discusses the policy regarding crude oil, which is a major contributor in Consumer Price Index for inflation, increase in exports of agricultural products, and gains in trade from the trade of fertilizers. The case will try to study the impact of Russia-Ukraine war on the economy in context of India, draw attention towards the situation faced by the countries after the sanctions on Russia implemented by them. How the countries globally are facing energy security and India through its policy is importing many of the commodities at discounted prices compared to prices in the international market.

DOI: 10.4018/978-1-6684-8488-3.ch017

INTRODUCTION

The outbreak of war situation is always very crucial for the world not only in the political and economic sense but also in the aspect of human lives. The hit of the pandemic coronavirus on global economic activity is not over yet. Countries are struggling to gain momentum and stability in productivity and economic activities yet to recover the losses; the Russia- Ukraine war broke.

The global connect today is so strongly interlinked that a country like Russia being an economic power, its decisions certainly hamper the economies globally. The war being inhuman can never be supported and advised in any situation. Along with the loss of lives and inhumanity, it also impacts trade (export/ import), GDP, economic imbalances, inflation, and scarcity of goods and hits strongly each sector of the economy globally.

The case will try to study the effect of the war between Russia and Ukraine on the economy in the context of India. The case will draw attention to the situation when the European countries were facing inflation along with the job cuts; how India was able to reduce its ever-increasing inflation rate which continued since the impact of COVID-19. The case discusses the policy adopted by the Indian government during the war period, foreign policies, foreign trade, and the results which helped India to control inflation and managed for itself energy security.

As the war between Russia and Ukraine started, economists and experts believed that there will be a very severe impact on the world economy. Coupled with the post-COVID-19 and high prices of crude oil, the development and recovery of the economies in the world presented a challenge.

IMPACT DUE TO SANCTIONS ON RUSSIA

The invasion of Russia on Ukraine led to many economic sanctions on Russia by the countries like U.S.A., European nations, Canada, and other international organizations in order to limit Russia's access to money. Sanctions are basically the penalties that are imposed on any country when they break any international law. Some of the sanctions or penalties being imposed on Russia are- the removal from the system of Swift which would delay the payments of exports of gas and oil to Russia by banning banks of Russia from the International financial managing system. to other nations, a ban on oil, and refined oil, freezing of plans of gas pipelines by Germany, stopping of coal imports by European Union, etc.

This has shocked the global economy which is struggling yet to recover from the pandemic. The sanctions being imposed have disrupted the global supply chain which has led to slow economic growth and high commodity prices all over the world, leading to high inflation rates all over the world. IMF forecasts that there will be a slowdown of growth in the economy from 6.0 percent in 2021 to 3.2 percent and 2.7 percent in the year 2022 and 2023 respectively. Traditionally European Union has been Russia's strongest economic partner are now facing the greatest economic disruption. It is because European countries are majorly dependent on their energy requirements and the imports from Russia in crude and natural gas.

The sanction and ns have also disrupted the global market of grain and fertilizers. Russia is the largest exporter of wheat in the world and has a major share in the global export of fertilizers. However, the import and export of agricultural trade are being exempted from the financial sanctions being imposed on Russia, in view of the global food security.

The sanctions imposed have led to an increase in the trade relations between Russia and other countries of the world. Russia's exports now to Brazil, China, India, and Turkey have increased by 50 percent from February 2022. We will be basically analyzing the impact in the Indian context.

IMPACT OF RUSSIA SANCTIONS ON EUROPE

Sanctions being imposed on Russia have impacted Russia, but also have caused a challenge and negative impact causing strain on Europe and the West. There are many threats which are being faced by Europe by imposing sanctions on Russia such as-

1. **Higher Rate of Inflation From Rising Energy Prices:** The sanctions imposed on Russia will bring down the imports from Russia. Russia has been traditionally the largest source of imports of oil and gas to Europe which accounted for about 40 percent of the total demand. Oil exports from Russia are the biggest source of revenue for it as it accounted for about 10 percent of the total global trade of 5 million barrels per day. Europe has been dependent on oil imports from Russia buying around 50 to 60 million tons per year from Russia. This will cause a decline in the imports of oil and will cause inflationary pressures in the economy as there will be a shortage of supply.
2. **Threat of Running Out of Gas:** In 2021, Russia's supply of gas to European countries accounted for 40 percent of its natural gas demand. In particular, Eastern Europe and Germany are dependent on imports from Russia. The sanctions would have a severe impact on the economy of Europe and particularly Germany as many of the manufacturing industries rely on natural gas. The impact on the German manufacturing sector is so severe that 16 percent of the firms are reducing or stopping their production due to the threat of a shortage of natural gas. The sanctions on Russia would bring down the German GDP by 4.8 percent according to the estimates of the IMF. From the figure, we can see that traditionally and according to the data of 2021 by IEA, European countries have been the major importers of Russian gas and are almost dependent on imports from Russia, on which Germany was the majorly dependent. Germany imported around 56.2 percent of its total demand which is a very large share. Italy was also importing its major share of imports from Russia which accounted for about 29.2 percent of total demand.
3. **Risk of Recession:** The imposition of export sanctions on Russia for the components which are technological-based will hit Western firms that are the supplier of these goods, but as the share of exports from the European Union to Russia is very small it will not have a major loss to the Russian economy. Similarly, there has been a loss in assets due to Western firms withdrawing from the nation, however total financial assets in Russia accounted for only 1.2 percent of total external assets of the euro in 2022. In Q1 2022, they stood at €385, down 12% from 2022.

INDIA AND RUSSIA TRADE RELATIONS

India and Russia traditionally have been sharing economic and political bonds with each other in many sectors. According to Indian former Foreign Secretary Rajan Mathai, India, and Russia's partnership is comprised of five major components which are namely- political, defense, nuclear energy, anti-terrorism cooperation, and exploration of outer space. There has been bilateral trade between India and Russia which includes key value chain sectors such as – metals, fertilizers, chemicals, automobiles, etc. the bilateral trade has been India and Russia stood at $1.5 billion in 2022 which has increased to over $11 billion in 2012 and have now increased up to $27 billion in 2022.

Figure 1. Share of gas imports from russia
Source: IEA, Estimates from 2021

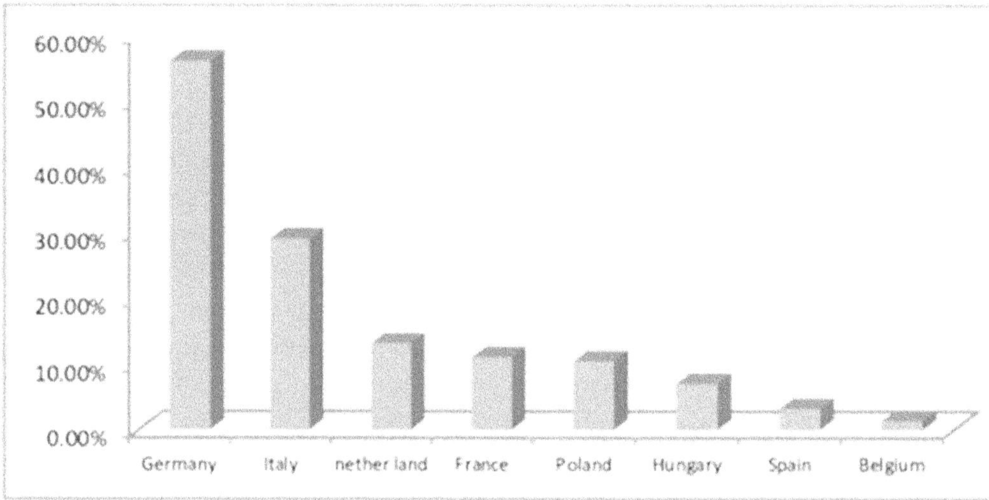

CRUDE OIL MARKET

For the development and growth of any country energy is a basic need. Industrial development, electricity, transportation, or any other thing can't be thought of without the sufficient availability of energy. Russia is the major exporter of oil and natural gas in the market. The availability of these resources is limited and not available in all countries. India for its energy requirements is dependent on imports of crude oil of nearly 85 percent of its total requirements. There has been a paradigm shift in the oil market due to sanctions being imposed on Russia, and Russia fulfilled most of the energy demand of Europe before the sanctions were imposed.

The demand for oil globally is set to contract by 110 kb/d (thousand barrels per day) during the fourth quarter of 2022 which is set to about 100.8 mb/d (million barrels per day). The reason behind this is due to the use of gasoline in place of oil by many countries according to the experts as the Western countries after the sanctions are trying to shift to alternative sources of energy as they are facing an energy crisis. There has been however an increasing trend in the global market as there has been an increase of 2.3 mb/d (million barrels per day) in total oil demand growth which now accounts for 140 mb/d for 2022. The global supply of oil decreased by 190 kb/d in November 2022 to 101.7 mb/d. the reason behind this is that the OPEC + countries have decreased the global supply of crude oil. The drop has been realized in the world more due to sanctions being imposed on Russia and the price cap effect being imposed by G7 countries at $60.

However, the oil exports from Russia have increased by 270 kb/d to 8.1 mb/d which is the highest since April 2022 due to an increase in direct exports by 300 kb/d to 1.1 mb/d. exports to India have reached a record highest of 1.3 mb/d. however, the revenue generated has decreased due to discounted prices being offered to the countries importing oil from Russia by $0.7 billion to $15.8 billion.

Taking into consideration the prices after the sanctions on Russia, ICE Brent futures were around $80, MEYMEX WTI slumped to $71 and Russia after the sanctions being imposed on it, allowed the third-party buyer and other countries to buy it at a discounted price. The price of Urals fell nearly $30 to $43 in December 2022.

Figure 2. Oil price changes
Source: Bloomberg, ICE, Argus Media

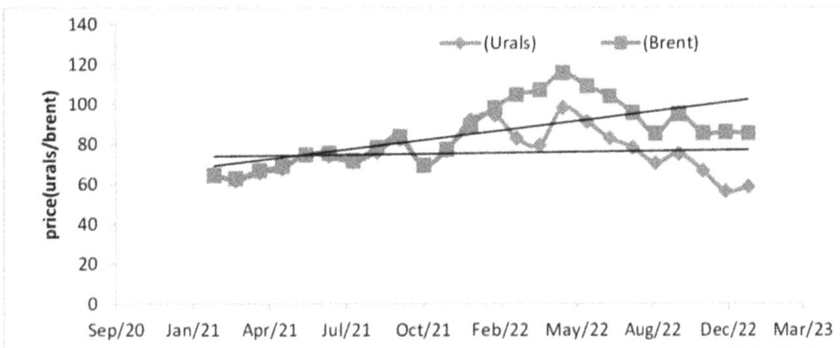

Crude Oil and India

Experts during the month of March and April 2022 predicted that the increasing oil prices will directly impact the economy and the nation will face inflationary pressures. This is also evident from the current scenario of rising inflation globally. Oil is the basis for inflation in many countries and a source of energy for any economy. The higher prices will lead to demand-pull inflation due to a shortage of supply because of the sanctions on Russian exports. Thus, it will impact severely economic progress and market development.

Experts advised that India should work on and improve the energy security situation by improving domestic production, calibrating global energy diplomacy, and import substitution. Modern energy supply at an affordable price is necessary to fuel industrial growth and socio-economic development. Atmnirbhar Bharat goals would also can't be achieved without energy security. Considering the situation, India adopted the policy to continue the import of crude oil from Russia in spite of the sanctions on it.

India is the third largest importer of crude oil and 85 percent of its requirement is fulfilled by imports. Before the invasion of Russia Ukraine, the total share of crude oil imports of India from Russia was 0.2 percent. The United Arab Emirates and Iraq were the major suppliers of crude oil to India.

Due to sanctions imposed on Russia, the Russian export of crude oil and natural gas decreased majorly as the major importing countries have banned imports from Russia. India despite the criticism adopted the policy to continue the trade relations with Russia, despite the sanctions imposed by the USA, Europe, and major world economies. The reason behind is also said that the developed countries who have imposed sanctions can manage the alternative source of energy, but India being a developing economy can't switch to any alternative energy source, and having a high population will not be able to sustain the energy crisis. In turn, India received crude oil at discounted price from Russia of about $30 per barrel which has led to saving more than 40,000 crores. Russia is selling to India crude oil even lower than that of the price cap being imposed and declared by G7 nations of $60 per barrel making imports from Russia the most attractive.

According to Vertexa, "Russia has likely offered its crude at an attractive discount to Indian refiners, which has surpassed China as the largest importer of Indian crude". The result of heavy discounts per barrel is that India is importing more than 1 billion barrels of crude oil per day from Russia. If we take reference from Bloomberg data, India is buying Russian oil 33 times higher compared to a year earlier.

The figure shows how the import of crude oil from Russia has increased on a monthly basis in India. Since, March, 2022 it can be seen that the imports have increased substantially which is due to the discounts being offered to India by Russia of about 7 to 10 percent. India which was importing 68,600 barrels of crude oil per day from Russia has now increased in November to more than 9 lakh barrels in November 2022 and by December 2022 have crossed 1 million barrels per day.

Figure 3. Oil imports of India from Russia
Source: Vertexa Limited

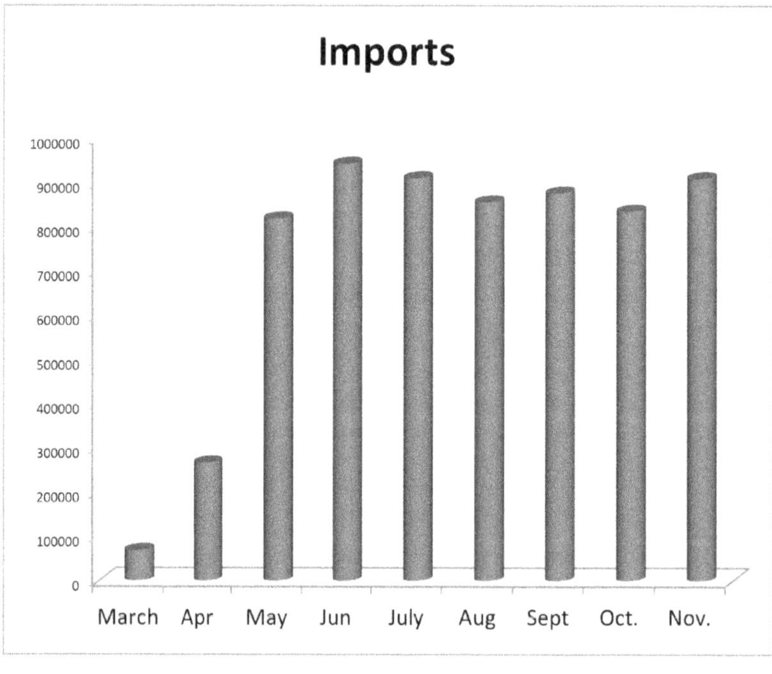

Impact of Oil Prices on Inflation

Crude oil is an important input that contributes to the rise in the prices of the economy. If the oil prices are high, it leads to a higher rate of inflation in the economy as each commodity transportation, agriculture, etc., all depends upon the crude oil prices in the economy. Therefore, the prices of crude oil directly or indirectly impact the input cost of any commodity.

Adverse impact on Fiscal deficit: India is importing about 1.5 billion barrels of crude oil per year, and 85 percent of the total country's requirement is fulfilled by imports from the oil-producing nations. If there is an increase in the prices of global crude oil prices the government expenditure will increase due to high prices on imports. This will cause an adverse impact on the fiscal deficit of the country.

Impact on Rupee: the rupee will further depreciate due to the high prices of crude oil. The reason behind this is the supply of money will increase in the exchange market due to which the currency will depreciate in comparison to other currencies.

Global Agricultural Market

Since the invasion of Russia on the Ukraine, and the sanctions being imposed on Russia, there have been many economic and food security issues around the globe. In almost all countries it has been experienced that there is high Domestic food price inflation and the global economy is projected to grow by 1.7 percent and 2.7 percent in the year 2023 and 2024 respectively according to the World Bank. There have been also obstacles being created globally due to high prices of fertilizers in many middle and low- income countries

Coffee, cotton and cocoa are included in the export index; however, maize, wheat and rice are included in the cereal index.

The data on food price inflation for the time period of September to December 2022 according to the International Monetary Fund shows that almost all low and middle-income countries were facing high inflation. The data shows that 94.1 percent, 92.9 percent and 89 percent of low-income countries, lower-middle-income countries and upper-middle-income countries respectively are experiencing inflation which is in double digits or more than 5 percent. In the context of countries with high income, about 87.3 [percent of the countries are facing high food inflation. Countries like Africa, South Asia, Latin America, Europe and Central Asia are affected the most. In 91 percent of the 160 countries, the real food inflation has exceeded the overall inflation which is measured as a change in the overall CPI the year after year.

On the basis of a report released by the International Monetary Fund in the month of December 2022, food prices globally are expected to remain high due to the factors such as – war, weather events and high energy costs. Food insecurity can be witnessed all over the world due to high food prices. There are several reasons which led to the increase in food prices globally between April 2022 and May 2022 which are as follows:

- Rise in global food prices due to low interest.
- Food trade restrictions and sanctions.
- Increased production cost due to high energy prices.
- Continuing bad weather due to La Naina.
- Diverting a few of the crops to biofuels instead of food.

The estimates of the IMF suggest that demand for food commodities will weaken and outweigh the constraints of supply if for the coming few quarters prices remain high. However, there is a downward pressure on the prices of food due to the rise in interest rates as it will discourage the holding of inventory and speculation for the future food markets. The rise in interest rate can also decrease economic activity by lowering the personal income of an individual.

Figure 4. Agricultural and cereal price trends (global trend)
Source: World Bank commodity price data

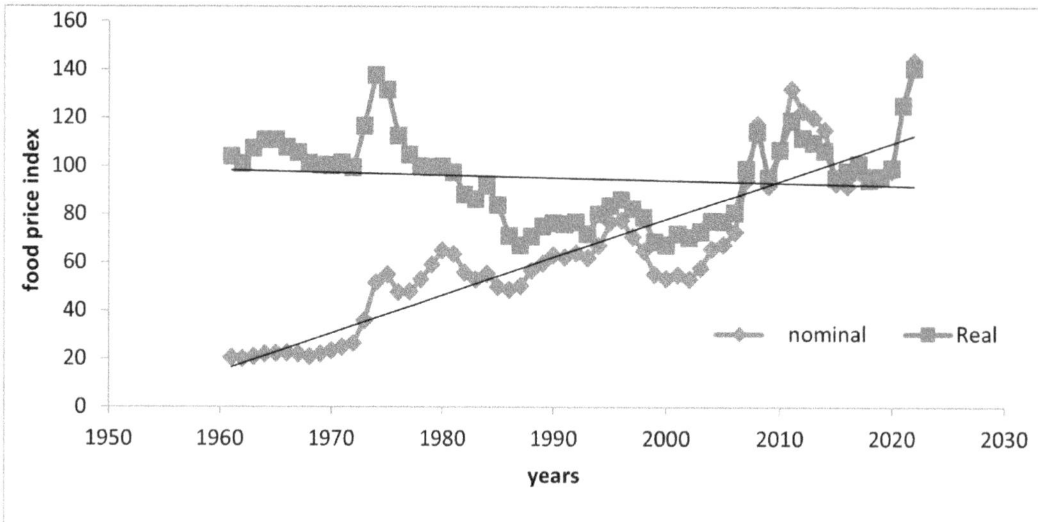

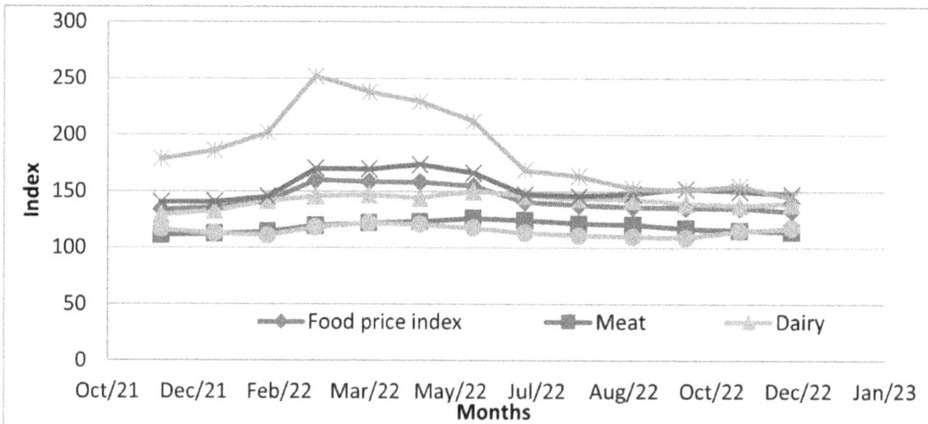

Rural Economy

Under the rural economy, we will be seeing the impact of the Russia- Ukraine war in the Indian context. What has been faced by the Indian economy, is basically the wheat and fertilizers in which Russia is having major global share in exports. This year in the financial year 2022, Indian exports of wheat have witnessed a rise due to the Russia- Ukraine war. The reason behind this is that Russia and Ukraine are the major producers and wheat exporters globally. Russia is the topmost and Ukraine is the fifth largest exporter of wheat globally and accounts for about 25 percent share of global wheat trade.

India adopted the policy on wheat on two fronts- the government increased the harvesting of wheat for domestic consumption and banned wheat export. The reason behind the ban according to the government was basically to manage overall food security in the country along with the help to be provided to the countries who are vulnerable to the food crisis. Prices of wheat globally have increased nearly double since Russia invaded Ukraine which has led to the steep shortage of wheat on the global market.

India's wheat export due to the crisis of food has increased by 116.7 percent in the financial year 2022. Exports of wheat by India in the first five months of the financial year 2022 are as below.

According to the data of the Ministry of Commerce and Industry, there was an increase of 25 percent in the export of processed food products and agricultural products during the time period of six months in the fiscal year. The export data published by APEDA (Agricultural and Processed Food Export Development Authority) shows an increase to USD 13.77 billion in April- September 2022 compared to exports in the same period during the last year which was USD 11.05 billion.

Table 1. Data on wheat exports

Month	2021	2022	Increase (%)
April	2,42,841.1	14,71,935	506.13%
May	4,08,975.5	10,79,117	163.86%
June	4,57,758.4	7,24,703.3	58.32%
July	3,75,442.7	4,34,221.4	31.64%
August	5,22,718	5,80,813.6	11.11%
total	20,07,736	43,40,791	116.7%

Source: Ministry of Commerce and Industry

Fertilizers

The main kinds of fertilizers such as ammonia, urea, and mono ammonium in Russia is having a major global share. Russia has exported 14 percent of urea and

mono ammonium along with the 22 percent of global exports in ammonia. Traditionally in India, inputs of fertilizers from China were having the largest share. However, the discount price offered by Russia of about $70 per tonne has made it the top export of fertilizers to India. Other countries import fertilizers at $1000 per tonne and the same is imported by India from Russia at $920- $925 per tonne. Indian import from Russia has increased by 371%. Import of fertilizers from Russia which accounts for about 6 percent in the 2021- 2022 financial year has jumped to 27 percent in the financial year 2022-2023 surpassing China as the biggest supplies to India.

Figure 5. Share of fertilizer imports by India
Source: Ministry of Commerce and Industry India

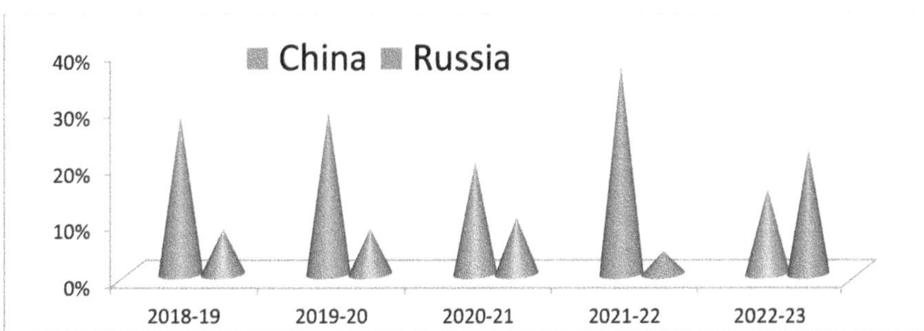

Inflation

Inflation is generally an economic phenomenon where prices of goods and services rise and the value of money decreases. It actually is an indicator of the decrease in purchasing power f the consumer in the economy. The rapid rate of inflation has adverse effects on the general population and can lead to a financial crisis. Monetary and fiscal measures are taken to curb inflation in the economy.

Since the pandemic, India along with other global economies are facing high inflation rates in their economy. The Russian invasion and sanctions on it have added to it being Russia a major economic power globally. However, the slowdown of inflationary pressures can be witnessed globally, India has controlled it under the allowed RBI band of 6 percent in the month of November 2022 and below 5 percent in December 2022. The WPI inflation (Wholesale Price Index) which was at its peak in June 2022 at 16.2 percent has been curbed by more than half and brought under control. For RBI and the government, there was a challenge of policy adoption whether to adopt the policy to boost economic growth (facing a slowdown since the pandemic) or to curb the rising inflation in the country.

In this context, RBI has taken monetary measures to control high inflation rates in the economy through changes in the interest rates and narrowing the money supply in the economy. The chart below shows the measures being taken by the central bank in the month of September in this regard.

Annual inflation of India's WPI has fallen now to 4.95 percent for the month of December 2022 against 16.2 percent in the month of June 2022. Annual CPI inflation has fallen to 5.72 percent in December 2022 from 50.88 percent in November 2022. It is the lowest rate of CPI inflation after the pandemic that it has come under the limit band of RBI, i.e., 2 percent to 6 percent.

Table 2. Change in rates by RBI

Policy Rates	August 2022	September 2022
Repo rate	5.40%	5.90%
SDF rate	5.15%	5.65%
MSF rate	5.65%	6.15%
Bank rate	5.65%	6.15%

Source: RBI Website

Table 3. CPI Inflation data

Year	Jan	Feb	Mar	Apr	May	Jun	Jul	Aug	Sep	Oct	Nov	Dec	Annual
2022	6.0%	6.1%	7.0%	7.8%	7.0%	7.0%	6.7%	7.0%	7.4%	6.8%	5.9%	5.7%	6.7%
2021	4.1%	5.0%	5.5%	4.2%	6.3%	6.3%	5.6%	5.3%	4.3%	4.5%	4.9%	5.7%	5.1%
2020	7.6%	6.6%	5.8%	7.2%	6.3%	6.2%	6.7%	6.7%	7.3%	7.6%	6.9%	4.6%	6.6%
2019	2.0%	2.6%	2.9%	3.0%	3.0%	3.2%	3.1%	3.3%	4.0%	4.6%	5.5%	7.4%	3.7%
2018	5.1%	4.4%	4.3%	4.6%	4.9%	4.9%	4.2%	3.7%	3.7%	3.4%	2.3%	2.1%	3.9%

Source: IMF blog

CONCLUSION

The case explains how the Indian economy is able to bring the inflation rate under control and has adopted the best policy for the purpose. Despite the sanctions on Russia, India continues to trade with Russia and was able to get the commodities at discounted prices. Crude oil and fertilizers which are the basic necessity for the Indian economy were imported from Russia in much larger quantities than before to get the benefit of the discounted prices being offered to the country. This led India to save more than 40, 000 crores making Russia the largest exporter to India in Crude oil and fertilizers surpassing other countries. The Indian policy of increasing wheat production and its increased prices have also helped India to generate revenue through exports. This year in five months of the financial year India was able to export more than 107 percent of last year's export done by India. The discounted crude oil and RBI monetary measures have helped India in bringing down the inflation of the country which was roaring since the pandemic. We can say Indian policies have helped to gain India in terms of trade and the right domestic measures have led India to control the rising prices in the economy when most of the countries are facing high inflationary pressures and rates.

Table 4. Suggested time plan

Suggested Time Plan	
Initial Survey- Whether India should have trade relations with Russia or not	10
Split the class into 5 groups and allocate one question to each group	5
Group Analysis	15
Should India continue doing trade with Russia or not	10
Discussion on the Importance of trade and trade bans	10
Strategies behind the trade sanctions by the nations	10
India's Strategy on the Russia-Ukraine War	10
Strategic approach towards international trade for developing and developed nations	10
Impact of global activities on the economic order of the country	10

Question: Should India continue trade relations with Russia amidst the Russia-Ukraine war?

The instructor, based on the responses can add to the need and strategy behind India's trade relations with Russia.

Every nation's sole motive is its development along with the welfare of society. International trade and relations have a very important role to play for any economy. No country is self-sufficient due to geographical, technical, capital, or other kind of barriers. This makes it necessary for a country to have economic relations with other countries and trade to meet the demands of the product which are not produced or available in their country. India is a developing country and due to several barriers, it is dependent on imports from other nations. Therefore, as a rational consumer, India will buy the necessary products from the country which provides the goods and services at the cheapest rate to fulfill the demand of the nation.

India and Russia traditionally have been sharing economic and political bonds with each other in many sectors. According to Indian former Foreign Secretary Rajan Mathai, India, and Russia's partnership is comprised of five major components which are namely- political, defense, nuclear energy, anti-terrorism cooperation, and exploration of outer space. There has been bilateral trade between India and Russia which includes key value chain sectors such as – metals, fertilizers, chemicals, automobiles, etc. the bilateral trade has been India and Russia stood at $1.5 billion in 2022 which has increased to over $11 billion in 2012 and have now increased up to $27 billion in 2022.

For the development and growth of any country energy is a basic need. Industrial development, electricity, transportation, or any other thing can't be thought of without the sufficient availability of energy. Russia is the major exporter of oil and natural gas in the market. The availability of these resources is limited and not available in all countries. India for its energy requirements is dependent on imports of crude oil of nearly 85 percent of its total requirements.

Experts during the month of March and April 2022 predicted that the increasing oil prices will directly impact the economy and the nation will face inflationary pressures. This is also evident from the current scenario of rising inflation globally. Oil is the basis for inflation in many countries and a source of energy for any economy. The higher prices will lead to demand-pull inflation due to a shortage of supply because of the sanctions on Russian exports. Thus, it will impact severely economic progress and market development. Therefore, in order to support economic development and meet the demand of the nation to avoid an energy crisis it is suggested to continue trade relations with Russia.

SUGGESTED QUESTIONS FOR DISCUSSION

Question 1: What is the importance of international trade and how does a trade ban/sanction impact any nation? Discuss.

At present, international trade seems to be beneficial from both economic and non-economic points of view. Any country can increase the level of welfare of the people of its country only when it produces goods and services at a low cost and imports indigenous goods and services which cost relatively more in that country. Produces and services in which it receives specialization, natural and technical facilities are sufficient in those countries, the rest of the goods and services which lack sufficient natural resources and techniques for production and which are relatively expensive to produce, imports such goods and services. At present, the WTO is promoting open trade through bilateral and multilateral agreements among the member countries. On the one hand, the open trade system paved the way for a global market for the countries of the world, on the other hand, it also developed competition in the global economy, due to which no one country can have a monopoly on any goods and services. Due to competition in the global economy, the countries of the world get the supply of goods and services at average cost or at low cost. Through international trade, exchange of currencies of different countries, free trade through bilateral and multilateral, etc. agreements, use of rare resources of the world, search for a better market for its product, search for raw materials and market for manufactured goods are available. This paves the way for the development of any country, whereas when trade is banned from any country or by any by global organizations, it creates a global impact in the international market, some countries gain and some countries suffer loss and the people of those countries face difficulties. When a country is banned in the international market, some countries gain and some countries face loss. At present, all the countries of the world are getting affected due to the ongoing war between Ukraine and Russia. While on the one hand, due to the oil crisis in European countries, along with rising inflation, Lack of agricultural products and food securities, etc. are facing a crisis, on the other hand, India is exporting oil to European countries by buying cheaper oil from Russia than the global market. On the other hand, in the case of food grains, the Government of India's export of wheat is exporting about 117 times more to European countries than in the year 2021. In the case of fertilizers, India imports the most from China, but in the war between Ukraine and Russia, India is importing cheap fertilizers from Russia, the quantity of which is more than the import of the former.

Question 2: Why and what are the strategies behind the trade sanctions imposed by the USA, European Countries, and Other Nations on Russia? Discuss.

The trade sanctions against Russia have been imposed due to the military aggression of Russia against Ukraine which started on 24th February 2022. The confrontation between Russia and NATO was not appropriate so, the Western countries instead turned to impose sanctions on economic grounds so as to hamper Russia's primary war machine.

There were several strategies being adopted by major global economies to hamper the Russian economy and punish. Sanctions are actually the penalties that are being imposed on any country by another country, so as to stop them from breaking international law and acting aggressively. Some of the strategies are as follows:

- Banning of imports of diamonds from Russia: the strategy behind banning of import of diamonds from Russia is that they earned more than 4 billion pounds in the year 2021 from diamond exports.
- Freezing of the assets of Russia's central bank in their countries to limit Russia's access to money. In this context, there has been the removal of Russian banks from international financial management.
- Trade sanctions on the import of coal, oil, and natural gas from Russia.

Question 3: What is behind India's strategic neutrality on Russia's invasion of Ukraine?

India is a developing country and shares a strong bond with Russia since the Soviet Union. Despite several criticisms from the USA and other Western nations, India continues to remain neutral and expand its trade relations with Russia. India and Russia traditionally have been sharing economic and political bonds with each other in many sectors. According to Indian former Foreign Secretary Rajan Mathai, India, and Russia's partnership is comprised of five major components which are namely- political, defense, nuclear energy, anti-terrorism cooperation, and exploration of outer space. There has been bilateral trade between India and Russia which includes key value chain sectors such as – metals, fertilizers, chemicals, automobiles, etc. the bilateral trade has been India and Russia stood at $1.5 billion in 2022 which has increased to over $11 billion in 2012 and have now increased up to $27 billion in 2022.

It is in favor of India in their perspective to continue importing from Russia cheap goods and services such as fertilizers and crude oils. India imports about 85 percent of its oil demand which shares a major portion of India's GDP. So, it plays an important role in deciding the costs of goods and services within the economy. India can't afford to stop having trade relations with Russia because being a developing nation it is not possible to shift to new alternative sources of energy or have crude oil, fertilizers, and other products at higher prices. It is in the interest of the residents of India and the economy to continue trading with Russia. Unlike developed nations, India is not in a position to purchase sources of energy at high prices or to invest in alternative sources of energy. Therefore, it can also lead to energy crisis.

Question 4: Can developed and developing countries have the same strategic approach toward international trade?

In the field of international trade, due to the difference between the needs of developed countries and developing countries and the availability of available natural, human capital, and technical resources, the requirements of both countries and the export and import of goods and services are different. On the one hand, where there is an abundance of capital in capitalist countries, there is an abundance of human resources in underdeveloped countries. Therefore, most capitalist countries produce capital goods in large quantities, while in underdeveloped countries due to the abundance of human resources, labor-intensive goods predominate. Many development models related to developed and underdeveloped countries have been developed by different economists. Harshman and Singer presented the model of development for underdeveloped countries, and then Harrod and Domar's development model was presented his model in the context of developed countries. In underdeveloped and developed countries, the necessary resources for development and other factors of development are also different. The availability of energy for development also affects development. In the event of an energy crisis among European countries, Russia can also adopt other measures of energy but depends on the supply of oil and other energy supplied by OPEC and Russia in underdeveloped countries. As it depends on the available resources, human capital, availability of capital and technology, and on the business conditions in different countries. Different types of challenges differ in developed countries and underdeveloped countries. So, from the above discussion, it is clear that there cannot be a single strategy and a similar development model for the development of developed and underdeveloped countries.

Question 5: Identify how global activities and international trade can impact the economic order of any country. Also, discuss the context of India.

Under globalization, the world has come under one umbrella. There are significant examples that show the linkage between the economies of the world. Any instability or activity in the major economies of the world impacts the global economy. International trade is very essential as it leads to fulfilling the demand in the economy for those products which are not available in their economy. Developing countries like India also follow the policy in international trade the idea of import substitution and export promotion. Import is always an expenditure and export is a revenue for any economy. Any global disorder /instability creates chaos and inflation globally. The study also suggests such examples which are witnessed after the war and due to the sanctions being imposed on Russia. Such as:

1. **Higher Rate of Inflation From Rising Energy Prices:** The sanctions imposed on Russia will bring down the imports from Russia. Russia has been traditionally the largest source of imports of oil and gas to Europe which accounted for about 40 percent of the total demand. Oil exports from Russia are the biggest source of revenue for it as it accounted for about 10 percent of the total global

trade of 5 million barrels per day. Europe has been dependent on oil imports from Russia buying around 50 to 60 million tons per year from Russia. This will cause a decline in the imports of oil and will cause inflationary pressures in the economy as there will be a shortage of supply.

2. **Threat of Running Out of Gas:** In 2021, Russia's supply of gas to European countries accounted for 40 percent of its natural gas demand. In particular, Eastern Europe and Germany are dependent on imports from Russia. The sanctions would have a severe impact on the economy of Europe and particularly Germany as many of the manufacturing industries rely on natural gas. The impact on the German manufacturing sector is so severe that 16 percent of the firms are reducing or stopping their production due to the threat of a shortage of natural gas. The sanctions on Russia would bring down the German GDP by 4.8 percent according to the estimates of the IMF. From the figure, we can see that traditionally and according to the data of 2021 by IEA, European countries have been the major importers of Russian gas and are almost dependent on imports from Russia, on which Germany was the majorly dependent. Germany imported around 56.2 percent of its total demand which is a very large share. Italy was also importing its major share of imports from Russia which accounted for about 29.2 percent of total demand.
3. **Risk of Recession:** The imposition of export sanctions on Russia for the components which are technological-based will hit Western firms that are the supplier of these goods, but as the share of exports from the European Union to Russia is very small it will not have a major loss to the Russian economy. Similarly, there has been a loss in assets due to Western firms withdrawing from the nation, however total financial assets in Russia accounted for only 1.2 percent of total external assets of the euro in 2022. In Q1 2022, they stood at €385, down 12% from 2022.
4. Since the invasion of Russia on Ukraine, and the sanctions being imposed on Russia, there have been many economic and food security issues around the globe. Domestic food price inflation has been high in almost all countries and according to World Bank, the global economy is projected to grow by 1.7 percent in 2023 and 2.7 percent in 2024. There have been also obstacles being created globally due to high prices of fertilizers in many middle and low- income countries.
5. Under the rural economy, we will be seeing the impact of the Russia-Ukraine war in the Indian context. What has been faced by the Indian economy, is basically the wheat and fertilizers in which Russia is having major global share in exports. This year in the financial year 2022, Indian exports of wheat have witnessed a rise due to the Russia- Ukraine war. The reason behind this is that Russia and Ukraine are the major producers and exporters of wheat globally. Russia is the topmost and Ukraine is the fifth largest exporter of wheat globally and accounts for about 25 percent share of global wheat trade.

REFERENCES

Bansal, A., Katoch, G., Arora, N., Sharma, A., Bhadula, R. C., & Agarwal, S. (2022, April). Big data analytics in the Indian banking sector: An empirical study. In *2022 2nd International Conference on Advance Computing and Innovative Technologies in Engineering (ICACITE)* (pp. 1624-1627). IEEE.

Dhiresh, & Abhishek, & Sagar. (2022). Analyzing the linkage between GDP, Energy Consumption and Carbon Emission: Evidence from major Economies. *The Indian Economic Journal*, *4*, 67.

Chapter 18
The Malaysian Cocoa Industry

Muhammad Sallehudin Ali
Universiti Teknologi MARA, Malaysia

Sehrish Tariq
Universiti Teknologi MARA, Malaysia

Selvakkumar K. N. Vaiappuri
Universiti Teknologi MARA, Malaysia

EXECUTIVE SUMMARY

Cacao has been cultivated in Malaysia for almost two centuries, with the first pods being discovered in a garden in Malacca in 1778. The arrival of the fruit on these beaches is generally dated to 1770, when it was introduced by sailors from Sri Lanka, then known as Ceylon. In 2021, the worldwide cocoa and chocolate industry was estimated to be worth 46.91 billion USD. The market is expected to increase at a compound annual growth rate (CAGR) of 4.98% between 2022 and 2029, from USD 48.29 billion to USD 67.88 billion. This chapter will be comprehensive about the cocoa industry. It will widely cover the history of cocoa, the types of cocoa, and an understanding of cocoa throughout the overview of the cocoa industry in the world. This case study concludes by discussing the issues and threat of the cocoa industry in Malaysia from the economic perspectives.

INTRODUCTION

Cacao has been cultivated in Malaysia for almost two centuries, with the first pods being discovered in a garden in Malacca in 1778. The arrival of the fruit on these beaches is generally dated to 1770, when it was introduced by sailors from Sri Lanka, then known as Ceylon (Malaysian Chocolate & Cacao Culture, 2022). We may safely assume that the initial source of the Sri Lankan pods was the Brazilian Amazon. Malacca had been established at the time by the Portuguese and the Dutch, but the Malay people were eventually able to reclaim the city thanks to a conflict with the Netherlands. Over the following 150 years under British rule, Malaysia would become a global leader in cocoa output and would stay in the top 10 for decades. This trend was significantly disrupted by World War II, but it was eventually resumed

DOI: 10.4018/978-1-6684-8488-3.ch018

because of growing demand from Europe. This had a disproportionately large effect on the Malaysian Borneo states of Sabah and Sarawak.

The industrial era led to fundamental changes in chocolate and cocoa, impacting everyone from growers to end consumers. The first chocolate factory started in 1780 in Barcelona, Spain, soon afterward, Germany and Switzerland continued the unrelenting march toward the complete industrialization of cocoa. The cocoa plant's original cultivars have changed throughout time. The spread of European colonialism in Africa coincided with the introduction of the cocoa tree to Europe. Successful cocoa planting in Sao Tome and Principe led to the development of plantations throughout Africa. South American output gradually declined throughout the industrial era despite having spread to new producing regions along the Amazon River, while a new cocoa empire rose to power in Africa. In fact, Africa has been the world's largest cocoa producer since the turn of the 20th century.

In the global market cocoa beans, whether shipped whole or broken, unroasted or roasted, had a total worth of 8.6 billion USD in 2017, regardless of their preparation. 5,6 The worldwide market for cocoa beans is anticipated to increase at a compound annual growth rate (CAGR) of 7.3% between 2019 and 2025, reaching USD 16.32 billion by the end of the forecast period. The retail market value of the chocolate business was estimated to be 106.19 billion U.S. dollars in 2017, and it is anticipated that this value would increase to 189.89 billion U.S. dollars by the year 2026. In 2017, the chocolate sector accounted for 43% of the total cocoa consumption (Vivek et al., 2019). In Malaysia, the cocoa sector accounted for a contribution of RM1.64 billion to the GDP in the year 2020 alone. In the first six months of 2021, the cocoa sector contributed to GDP totaling 0.85 billion RM. In the year 2021, the total area of coca plantations is 5,955 hectares, and they produce 361 tonnes of the drug (Ministry of Plantation Industries and Commodities (MPIC), 2022).

COCOA INDUSTRY

Scenario of Downstream in Cocoa in the Industry

In 2021, the worldwide cocoa and chocolate industry was estimated to be worth 46.91 billion USD. The market is expected to increase at a compound annual growth rate (CAGR) of 4.98% between 2022 and 2029, from USD 48.29 billion to USD 67.88 billion. Demand is lower than expected in all locations compared to pre-epidemic levels because of the unprecedented and overwhelming worldwide COVID-19 pandemic. The research shows that international sales fell by 2.75 percent worldwide in 2020 compared to 2019 (Fortune, 2022).

Due to the rising popularity of chocolate treats throughout the world, this sector is showing signs of steady expansion. Overall consumption of cocoa-based products has increased as the original share of worldwide grindings has risen significantly. The expansion of the global cocoa and chocolate business is aided by the introduction of novel products across a variety of culinary industries. The most popular flavors for new beverages, baked goods, and candies are still chocolate. In the food and drink industry, it has also remained a staple. This pattern in business is expected to stimulate future market expansion.

Market participants are anticipated to invest in the trend to make money as customer perceptions of the excellence (ingredient quality) of single-origin and bean-to-bar chocolates are predicted to grow. Due to the growing focus on the bean-to-bar concept in recent years, the demand for specialty chocolate products and preimmunized offers has increased significantly. The single-origin cocoa craze is still driving new product development and innovations (Fortune, 2022). The demand for premium cocoa powder, cocoa liquor, and cocoa butter has increased because of this. Chocolate producers are being encouraged to choose cocoa sustainability initiatives by customers' growing demand for goods made from verified and traceable cocoa. The world's largest sustainable commercial cocoa processing farm will be built in Indonesia thanks to a partnership between Olam Food Ingredients and Mondelez International, which was announced in April 2021. The farm will use cutting-edge farming techniques and encourage biodiversity and carbon capture. The three most well-known certifications for cocoa are UTZ certification, Rainforest Alliance certification, and Fair-Trade U.S. certification, and their use has skyrocketed recently.

Current Value of the Downstream Cocoa Industry

Growing cocoa's cultivation area is important, but finding new ways to utilize the beans and turn them into marketable, high-value goods is quite tough. Functional connectivity between upstream (on-farm) and downstream (in the marketplace) generates value in the plantation subsector (off-farm) (Y Hariyati, 2022). Thus, the competitiveness and income of the community cocoa agribusiness can be increased by increasing the value-added of cocoa from upstream to downstream, beginning with the farmers who grow cocoa and continuing through the processing of cocoa pods and marketing institutions who process cocoa beans to create final products that are then marketed to end consumers.

The value-added occurs during the post-harvest processing of agricultural goods, which raises the price of the original output. As a result of the expenses incurred in processing cocoa beans, it is anticipated that a new, more lucrative price for cocoa beans will emerge (Review, 2022). Upstream, cocoa beans may be grown, and afterward, in the value chain, cocoa beans can be processed into chocolate. Upstream cocoa bean processing is a post-harvest practice that takes place on the farm. Meanwhile, marketing agencies handle the cocoa bean processing operations in the downstream sector, resulting in semi-finished and completed goods.

One of the downstream operations performed to raise the value of cocoa beans so that it might influence improving farmers' incomes is the processing of cocoa beans via agroindustry activities (Review, 2022). When developed, the cocoa agro-industry has the potential to create several jobs, increase economic activity in the region, and add value to cocoa products at every stage of the supply chain. Producers are compelled to process cocoa beans so that they may fetch a better price on the market to mitigate the financial losses that result from the inferior quality and quality of the raw product.

To be addition, some issues may affect cocoa agro-industry operations and ultimately lower cocoa's value downstream. The primary issue is in Indonesian cocoa farmers do not engage in post-harvest management procedures like fermentation (Y Hariyati, 2022). If you want higher-quality cocoa beans, you need to ferment them. Second, the time-honored practice of drying in the sun is still used. How seeds are treated after harvest has a significant impact on their viability and quality. Optimal post-harvest care for cocoa may lengthen its shelf life and boost its value, both of which lower production costs. An extended storage time, as opposed to the immediate raw product sale, might boost a farmer's earnings.

Alternative to Ensure the Industry Is Still Relevant

There are several economic and environmental factors putting pressure on the cocoa sector as it tries to increase output to meet consumer demand to produce the product. However, numerous potential solutions can aid the future sustainability of vital parts of this business, hence raising the output of the final product. Additional biotechnology that stops short of genetic manipulation is one path toward a more secure future for cocoa. The absence of Genetically Modified Organism (GMO) cocoa seeds may be due to the risk associated with consumer adoption of a GMO cocoa product, despite the encouraging results in yield gains from genetic manipulation (Elizabeth Holloway, 2018). As a result, the mapped cacao genome is being used to direct selective breeding efforts, ensuring that supply meets demand, without the use of genetic manipulation.

Nestle's Darrel High said the company is working with farmers, communities, and local and international organizations to create and implement solutions to the many problems that cocoa farming communities face. Better farming is one of three areas where the Nestlé firm has made strides. There are better lifestyles to be had in places where child labour is being combated, women's rights are being strengthened, and educational opportunities are being expanded. Finally, make more of the superior chocolate that this process yields to meet demand further down the line (High, 2020).

In addition, the quality of the cocoa beans in the bags must be checked before the cocoa is sold using the appropriate equipment (moisture, knives for cut-test, weighing machine, etc.). This is one solution that will help guarantee that chocolate production remains relevant to meet the demand (FFC, 2022). This step is vital since it determines the quality and cost of the final product. At this point, the cocoa beans must meet the specifications mentioned in the contract, such as being correctly fermented and dried, odourless, and containing no more than the specified amount of slaty, flat, double, broken, mouldy, insect-damaged, foreign matter, and germinated beans.

ECONOMIC PERSPECTIVE

Global and Regional

A significant CAGR of 5.62% is predicted for the global cocoa and chocolate market in 2030. The global cocoa and chocolate market are expected to reach USD 70.21 billion by 2030, up from USD 49 billion in 2018, with a Compound Annual Growth Rate (CAGR) of 5.62% from 2019 to 2030. The market is primarily driven by consumers' growing knowledge of cocoa's health advantages. The growing popularity of chocolate among people of all ages worldwide has further fuelled the industry. Due to its high antioxidant content and health advantages, cocoa is likely to be widely used, which will be the primary growth driver of the global cocoa market. The increased demand for cocoa and chocolate in the confectionery, food and beverage, cosmetics, pharmaceutical, and other sectors is directly related to the rising consumption of chocolate. (Global Cocoa and Chocolate Market: Market Segments: By Cocoa Type; By Chocolate Type; By Application; By and Region – Analysis of Market Size, Share & Trends for 2014 – 2019 and Forecasts to 2030, May 2022)

The global cocoa and chocolate market is divided into five key regions based on regional research. These include the Middle East and North Africa (MENA), Asia-Pacific (APAC), Europe, North America, and Latin America. Europe maintained the biggest global cocoa and chocolate market share in 2018 and experienced 2.6% CAGR growth over the forecast period. Moreover, Europe is a mature market where the retail infrastructure has remained remarkably steady. This results from rising consumer goods and beverage consumption and the rising spending power of the local populace. However, the European region's available cocoa and the chocolate market have saturated during the past few years. The cocoa and chocolate industries in North America have made significant advancements that have raised public knowledge of the health advantages. (Global Cocoa and Chocolate Market: Market Segments: By Cocoa Type; By Chocolate Type; By Application; By and Region – Analysis of Market Size, Share & Trends for 2014 – 2019 and Forecasts to 2030, May 2022)

Although cocoa is a fundamental ingredient in many goods, it is mostly used in the chocolate industry. It achieved a retail value of USD 100 billion in 2021 and is anticipated to expand from 4.5% to 5.5% through 2027. (EMR, 2021; Grand View Research, 2020; imarc, 2021; Mordor Intelligence, 2021b; Research and Markets, 2020). 40 to 50 million people work for companies that depend on cocoa to create their final products. An estimated 5 to 6 million cocoa farmers support their lives, with 90% of them growing under 5 hectares (CocoaNet, 2022; Tridge, 2021). For instance, more than 40,000 people were employed by the American chocolate sector in 2022.

(EMR, 2021). Only 5% of the world's crop is produced by plantations greater than 40 hectares (Tridge, 2021). According to the Food and Agriculture Organization of the United Nations, cocoa cultivation increased from 12.10 million hectares in 2008 to 5.76 million ha in 2020. (FAO, 2012). Since 2008, production has increased dramatically, with a CAGR of 2.53% from 2008 to 2019, rising to 3.44% from 2014 to 2019. (Hameed et al., 2009)

On the other hand, according to the Ministry of Plantation Industry and Commodities, Malaysia cocoa-based products have expanded significantly in the global market, with a global market coverage of more than 100 locations. In 2020, exports of goods containing cocoa and those made from cocoa reached RM6.29 billion. The value of cocoa exports reached RM3.37 billion in the first half of 2021. With a contribution of 37.2%, cocoa fat remains the leading export product, followed by cocoa powder (23%) and dry cocoa bean re-exports (17.3%). In addition, 53 chocolate and confectionery businesses and 232 chocolate entrepreneurs are registered with the Malaysian Cocoa Board as of 2021. Until June 2021, the chocolate industry's net export was expected to generate RM0.49 billion. ((MPIC), 2022)

Trends

Market participants are anticipated to invest in the trend to make money as customer perceptions of the excellence (ingredient quality) of single-origin, and bean-to-bar chocolates are predicted to grow. Due to the growing emphasis on the bean-to-bar concept in recent years, the demand for specialty chocolate products and immunised offers has increased significantly. The single-origin cocoa craze is still driving new product development and innovations. The demand for premium cocoa powder, cocoa liquor, and cocoa butter has increased. Chocolate producers are encouraged to choose cocoa sustainability initiatives by customers' growing demand for goods made from verified and traceable cocoa. The world's largest sustainable commercial cocoa processing farm will be built in Indonesia thanks to a partnership between Olam Food Ingredients and Mondelez International, which was announced in April 2021. The farm will use cutting-edge farming techniques and encourage biodiversity and carbon capture. The three most well-known certifications for cocoa are UTZ certification, Rainforest Alliance certification, and Fair-Trade U.S. certification, and their use has skyrocketed recently. (Chocolate and Cocoa Market Size).

In terms of the global price of cocoa, the price went down the most in 2000, with only USD 903.91 per metric ton, and achieved the highest price in 2015, with USD 3135.17 per ton. Meanwhile, the latest price of cocoa is USD 2,364. The global cocoa and chocolate market is expected to reach USD 70. 21 billion by 2030, up from USD 49 billion in 2018. In addition, the market is primarily driven by consumers growing knowledge of cocoa's health advantages. Hence, the growing popularity of chocolate among people of all ages worldwide has further fuelled the industry. The global bean-to-bar chocolates market is predicted to grow rapidly over the next few years. Demand for specialty chocolate products and immunised offers has increased significantly, according to Euromonitor International's (EMR) research.

GLOBAL DEMAND FOR COCOA PRODUCTS

Cocoa Paste

Cocoa paste imports totalled $3.59 billion in 2020. (ITC, 2021). Imports totalled $2.53 billion in 2020. Between 2001 and 2018, imports of cocoa paste grew 5.6% annually. 2019 and 2020 cocoa paste imports were not recorded by official sources. In the next few years, cocoa paste demand will likely slow. Health-conscious consumers will reduce demand for desserts worldwide. 2021-2025 cocoa paste demand is expected to grow by 1% annually. Only nutritious and healthy products will see a 2% annual increase, but they are a diminutive portion of the market (Euromonitor Consulting, 2020).

Since 2015-2020, the majority of cocoa paste imports have come from Europe, followed by the Americas and Asia. Despite popular belief, Africa and Oceania do not contribute much to global cocoa paste production. In 2020, the EU imported 650k metric tonnes worth $2.40b. (ITC, 2021). Value CAGR was 1.5% and volume CAGR was 0.6% from 20152020. This means cocoa paste import prices rose during this time.

America imported the second-most cocoa paste in 2020. America imported 195,000 metric tonnes worth 0.63 billion USD (ITC, 2021). The volume and value of cocoa paste imports rose 11% annually. Asia imported 134,000 tonnes of cocoa paste worth 0.43 billion USD in 2020. (ITC, 2021). This region's imports fell. Imports fell by 2.4% and 5.6% between 2015 and 2020.

In 2020, Oceania imported 18,500 for a total value of 0.08 billion USD. To the tune of 0.04 billion USD, Africa bought 10,450 tonnes in 2015. (ITC, 2021). The amount of cocoa paste sent to Oceania and Africa decreased between 2015 and 2020. Both the quantity and value of imports into Oceania declined by 3.5% and 3.3% respectively. The continent of Africa had a drop of between 0.03 percent and 3.6 percent in its imports.

Cocoa Butter

Imports of cocoa butter rose from USD1.1 billion in 2001 to USD5.61 billion in 2011. (2020). From 2001 to 2020, imports rose ranging from 530,000 to 960,000 tonnes. (ITC, 2021). Between 2001 and 2020, cocoa butter imports grew 3.2% annually. In 2020, the true cost of cocoa butter imports was USD 0.69 billion less than in 2014. Even at the height of the pandemic, imports of this derivative didn't fall in 2020.

Cocoa butter will see increased use in baked goods, liqueurs, and chocolate during the next several years. Seventy-five percent of chocolate is cocoa butter. The remaining 25% consisted of assorted cookies, ice cream, cakes, desserts, alcoholic beverages, and other goods. In 2019, chocolate confectionery used 840,000 MT of cocoa butter, while cookies and ice creams consumed a combined 144,000 MT. In the same year, there were 47 and 21 tonnes of cakes and sweets, respectively (Euromonitor Consulting, 2020). From 2015-2020, the majority of cocoa butter was sent to Europe, followed by the United States and Asia. Few cocoa butter products are sent to these regions from Africa and Oceania. In 2020,

EU imports will total 639k metric tonnes, costing $4,080,000. (ITC, 2021). For the period of 2015– 2020, the CAGR in volume was 3.3% and the CAGR in value was 2.4%. America imported the second-most cocoa butter in 2020. America imported 142k tonnes of cocoa butter worth USD 834,000 (ITC, 2021). The Americas' cocoa butter imports increased in both quantity and value from 2015-2020. Oceania imported 23,000 tonnes of cocoa butter worth USD 129,000 in 2020, while Africa imported 8,000 tonnes worth USD 45,000. (ITC, 2021). Between 2015 and 2020, the demand for cocoa butter in Oceania increased. Oceania's import volume rose 2% year over year, but its value fell 0.8%. Africa's imports of this product fell by 0.4% and 2.2% between 2015 and 2020.

Cocoa Powder

From 2001 to 2020, imports of cocoa powder worldwide rose, however, their value varied. In 2011, the amount of cocoa powder imported worldwide increased from USD 0.53 billion to USD 2.47 billion in 2020. Inbound shipments of cocoa powder went up. by 4.9% every year from 2001 to 2019. The total value of cocoa powder imports in 2019 was USD 0.05 billion less than in 2018, both in nominal and real terms.

Demand for cocoa powder is predicted to increase by 2.3% per year, reaching $3.06 billion worldwide by 2027. Perhaps the demand for cocoa powder has increased because of its use in functional foods and drinks. Because of its high minerals like magnesium, copper, calcium, zinc, sodium, potassium, and phosphorus, and other nutrient content, cocoa powder is seeing a surge in demand from the pharmaceutical business (Reports and Data, 2020).

Between 2015 and 2020, the majority of cocoa powder imports went to Europe, followed by Asia and the United States. Contrarily, only small demand for cocoa powder is brought in from outside for consumption in Africa and Oceania. The European Union imported 362 metric tonnes of cocoa powder worth USD 1,000,000 in 2020. (ITC, 2021). From 2015 to 2020, the compound annual growth rate (CAGR) in value was 2%, while the CAGR in volume decreased to -0.5%.

The second largest demand for cocoa powder is from Asia. Asia imported 314 metric tonnes of cocoa powder worth USD 746,000 in 2020. (ITC, 2021). Asia's import volume and value grew by 8.6% and 7.2% between 2015 and 2020. America was the third-largest cocoa importer in 2020. America imported USD 213,000 worth of cocoa powder (ITC, 2021). Over 2015-2020, cocoa powder imports grew 3.4% in volume and 2.4% in value annually.

Oceania imported 20,000 metric tonnes of cocoa powder worth USD 51,000 in 2020, while Africa imported 59,000 tonnes worth USD 134,000 (ITC, 2021). Between 2015 and 2020, Oceania and Africa imported more cocoa powder. Oceania's import volume and value both rose by 1.4%. Imports of this commodity into Africa increased by 7.3% in volume and 7% in value throughout the period.

Chocolate

Chocolate imports throughout the world skyrocketed from USD 0.53 billion in 2001 to USD 2.47 billion in 2016. From 2001 to 2016, imports increased from 2.69 to 5.67 million tonnes. (ITC, 2021). Global chocolate imports grew 5.1% annually between 2001 and 2016.

Although import volumes are unavailable for several years (2011, 2013–2014, 2017–2020), import values do reveal a pattern. In the middle ground, competition is expected to increase in the worldwide chocolate industry. The popularity of organic and dark chocolates has helped strengthen the industry. (Mordor Intelligence, 2020b). From 2015 to 2020, the European Union has been the world's top importer of chocolate (finished goods), followed by the United States and Asia. Two of the world's poorest regions,

Africa and Oceania, are also relatively insignificant chocolate importers. In 2020, the EU imported 3.49 million tonnes worth USD 17.2 billion. (ITC, 2021). Volume CAGR was 2.4% and value CAGR was 3.6% from 2015-2020.

In the year 2020, the United States was the second-largest importer of chocolate in the world. The United States brought in 1.08 million metric tonnes, or $4.73 billion, of chocolate last year (ITC, 2021). From 2015 through 2020, chocolate imports into the Americas grew yearly by 0.2% in volume and 1.1% in value. In 2020, Asia will import cocoa butter worth $4.67 billion, or 0.97 million tonnes. (ITC, 2021). From 2015 to 2020, Asia cut down on chocolate imports. There was a 1.4% and 2.3% decline in Asia's chocolate imports between 2015 and 2020, respectively. In 2020, the Oceania region imported chocolate worth $0.63 billion (0.11 million metric tonnes), while Africa imported 0.15 million metric tonnes (worth $0.56 billion) (ITC, 2021). Oceania and Africa both bought less chocolate from abroad between 2015 and 2020. Imports to Oceania were down 0.02 percent from the previous month and 1.1% from the previous year. Between 2015 and 2020, imports of chocolate into Africa increased by 0.5% and 4.2%, respectively.

DOWNSTREAM PLAYERS IN COCOA INDUSTRY

Intermediaries

Intermediaries aggregate cocoa producers' smaller volumes into exportable amounts. They harvest cocoa beans from individual farmers or farmer cooperatives, either while they are still wet or after they have been fermented and dried. Collectors and aggregators are also intermediaries. In most cases, intermediaries don't actively export and don't have the necessary licences; instead, they sell to FBOs or exporters. Individually or as an agent for an exporter or processor, they can make purchases. "Middlemen" or agents work with subagents. Post-harvest processes like fermentation and drying may be performed by intermediaries, depending on their size, equipment capacity, cash flow, and supply chain position. In addition to the formal and bureaucratic FBO system, producers can also access credit through intermediaries. Most cocoa farmers in producing nations don't belong to a cooperative or association. In these countries, intermediaries are crucial. Local collectors may lower farmgate prices to ensure a steady supply of cocoa beans, according to Abdulsamade et al. (2015). In value chains in which small traditional producers are connected to the market through local merchants and where (price) differentiation or compensation is provided between various qualities, intermediation is more prevalent but not exclusive. In value chains, it's more common. In the same way as a cooperative, they purchase cocoa beans from growers and sell them further up the supply chain. In cocoa supply chains, where growers and cooperatives have more contact and quality requirements are mainly set and maintained, intermediaries are less common (CBI, 2018b). Even in well-organized cocoa value chains, such as the Dominican Republic's, intermediation is common (Dominican sector stakeholders & personal communication, 2021).

Chocolate Makers

Small chocolate marketplaces include bean-to-bar manufacturers and similar operations. Bean-tobar chocolate manufacturers use less than 200 metric tons of cacao per year to make chocolate. Compare this to chocolatiers, who use different chocolate to make truffles, bonbons, etc (C. Martin, 2017). According to the Fine Chocolate Industry Association, even the smallest chocolate makers are true artisans (FCIA). Authentic artisanal chocolate requires a trained chocolatier, an artisan. A company can't make "artisanal" chocolate without an actual artisan. Craft chocolatiers celebrate and welcome quality variations (Gordon, 2019).

Specialty chocolate manufacturers are buying more cocoa beans from farmers (or farmer groups and cooperatives). Direct trade in cocoa is growing, but it only accounts for a fraction of the market. Not all chocolate manufacturers can handle direct trading's logistics, paperwork, and upfront funding. In "direct trade," an importer acts as an intermediary between the farmer and the chocolate factory. Bean-to-bar manufacturers usually buy from cocoa bean importers who can ensure traceability and relay the origin story along the supply chain (CBI, 2020f). Although there are many small chocolate manufacturers, there are few importers who focus on specialty beans in small volumes. Twenty Degrees, a subsidiary of OLAM, and Cacao Latitudes, a subsidiary of ECOM, are two new specialty chocolate importers. This study found that direct trade between FBOs and producers was common when the bean-to-bar manufacturer was in the cocoa-producing country. Bean-to-bar manufacturers at the source target many consumers. The demand for luxury goods, like as excellent chocolates, is on the rise in cocoa-producing nations like Indonesia, Brazil, and Colombia. Bean-to-bar chocolate exports require warehousing/distribution in consumer markets and specialized transportation/storage (reefer containers or air freight). For a low-volume industry, competition from regional and national companies can be intense. When a bean-to-bar manufacturer in the country of origin wants to expand into international markets, they hire a sales representative or partner with a distributor with a large clientele base and a web of retail outlets.

Small chocolate factories that don't use cocoa beans need cocoa paste, cocoa butter, and covertures (industrial chocolate) (Ferro & Groothuis, 2021). Due to low volumes, consumers often deliver cocoa derivatives to end-users like chocolatiers and pastry chefs. Low volume and erratic customer orders strain marketing and distribution resources.

OTHER INDUSTRY THAT SUPPORTS COCOA INDUSTRY

Cosmetic Industry

Cosmetics include soap, shampoo, deodorant, toothpaste, and even perfumes and makeup (CBI, 2020h). Cocoa butter is the most frequently used cocoa by-product. Medium- and large-scale processors and manufacturers in Europe and other consuming markets refine and/or deodorize cocoa butter for cosmetics (Ferro & Groothuis, 2021). Natural cosmetics require deodorized cocoa butter, so some companies buy it directly from local processors. Few firms in cocoa-producing countries meet the technical standards for making deodorised cocoa butter for cosmetics, according to this study. Since most cosmetics firms only use a little amount of cocoa butter each year, they get it from companies that import various oils and fats, natural ingredients, and chemicals. Butter processing companies must also compete in the similar but distinct cocoa powder sector (Anonymous & personal communication, 2021).

Pharmaceutical Industry

The pharmaceutical industry deals with medicines and pharmaceuticals. Cocoa butter is the primary component of most pharmaceutical cocoa preparations. The pharmaceutical sector, like the cosmetics industry, typically acquires cocoa butter that has been processed in the consuming market due to the strict quality and safety criteria for components in the key consuming countries (European Commission, 2020).

Animal Feed Industry

Producing food for animals is known as the "animal feed" business. The use of cocoa by-products (pod husk, shell, and meal) as livestock food is restricted. Research on the effects of feeding cocoa by-products to ruminants has found that at concentrations more than 10–15%, growth, and reproductive indices suffer. Because of their high fiber content, cocoa by-products cannot be utilized as feed without the addition of enzymes (John Makinde et al., 2019). Symptoms include nausea, vomiting, fatigue, agitation, diarrhea, muscular tremors, ataxia, hematuria, tachycardia, and seizures. More investigation on the present and future of the animal feed business using cocoa waste is required.

SWOT Analysis

An organization's opportunities and threats, as well as its strengths, may be better understood via a SWOT analysis. Here we will examine SWOT analysis of the large-scale, organic, and artisanal chocolate industries.

Huge Quantities of Cocoa Manufacturers

Strengths:

- Producers throughout markets that have been liberalised make acquaintances with various purchasers so they have more ways to market their goods.
- Owners can make money by growing cocoa as well as other things as well.
- It was common practice for farmers to form cooperatives ("la minga" in Latin America, "work gang" in West Africa) to tend to the weeds and gather the produce from one another's plots.

Weaknesses:

- Not knowing what the customer wants in quality terms.
- Inadequate understanding of child slavery and other problems with conservation.
- Insufficient education or practical help to improve growth.

Opportunities:

- In the previous 60 years, cocoa's demand has increased by almost 400% due to the expansion of the cosmetics and confectionary markets (Beg et al, 2017).
- For instance, Ecuador's INIAP has created high-yielding cultivars with palatable tastes (Anonymous & personal communication, 2021).
- Many international companies are trying hard to get farmers in developing countries to grow more cocoa. These are needed to fulfil the increasing need for chocolate around the world (Beg et al, 2017).

Threats:

- Old cocoa plantations with fungus and infestation, poor farm management, deteriorating soil, and increasing pest and disease prevalence all contribute to low yields (GISCO, 2021). Infected trees won't be able to grow anymore, which will slow down supply.

- Deprivations: Children of farmers may have to help harvest, which gets in the way of their education.

Organic Cocoa Producers

Strengths:

- Less likely that the producer and his or her family will get drunk.
- Better understanding of how to make organic solid and liquid fertiliser and how to use it than a conventional cocoa farmer.
- Learn how to use or not use inorganic fertiliser, pesticides, and insecticides.

Weaknesses:

- Not enough is known about how beans can get contaminated (packaging, transportation, and beans crossing borders)
- Outdated farming methods, such not knowing how to manufacture organic immunity boosters to fight pests and diseases.

Opportunities:

- That producer may receive assistance from the cooperative, exporter, or customer with his or her Organic Production System.
- Low-technology solutions are available to increase soil health and climate and pest-resilient trees and crops which solid liquid organic fertilizer with microorganisms.
- Transparency organizations and purchasers pay a higher price for organic beans.

Threats:

- Agrochemicals in organic cocoa beans have raised concerns from a number of exporters and importers of organic cocoa.
- Beans may be illegally trafficked across borders and wind up in the supply chain for organic products because of the significant (farm-gate) price differences between adjacent nations.
- None accredited Minimum Residue Level (MRL) labs in producing nations.

Craft Chocolate Makers

Strengths:

- Craft chocolate manufacturers have a good traceability system that requires food safety and process details. The transparent supply chain for customers (Perez et al, 2020).
- Craft chocolate producers don't use any ingredients you can't pronounce, like wheat, milk, eggs, soy, or genetically modified organisms.
- Craft chocolate companies provide higher farmgate prices to farmers compared to other clients (Cadby, 2021).

Weaknesses:

- Low profitability is a result of high fixed costs (maintenance, depreciation of equipment), high costs of premium packaging materials and large margins kept by the distribution channel. (The Chocolate Journalist, 2018).
- Craft chocolate producers collaborating with chocolate manufacturers in origin nations confront shipping, communication, shelf life, and labelling challenges.

- Lending is unavailable to small companies because lack of operating capital and pre-financing using private money.

Opportunities:

- Authentic artisanal chocolate is "exciting" and "distinct." These additions increase its desirability (Brown et al., 2020).
- Pastry chefs are looking for couverture with more flavour and more of a backstory. Manufacturers of ice cream want flavours that are true to their ingredients. Cafes and businesses want to give clients higher-quality hot chocolates or handmade chocolate items.

Threats:

- Market saturation is increasing competition. Anyone can produce handmade chocolate because to minimal entrance hurdles.
- Oversupply has led to a competitive market (The Chocolate Journalist, 2018).
- Large companies imitate craft chocolate phrases and stories. Big manufacturers utilise words like "single origin", "bean to bar", and "craft/artisan" They're packing cocoa pods with agricultural stories. Customers who aren't well-informed could confuse mass-produced with artisanal chocolate.
- Fine cocoa production may decline. Due to comparable pricing, cocoa producers may not harvest good cocoa. If so, handmade chocolate's core component may be jeopardised.

CONCLUSION

In conclusion, the study is about determining how the cocoa industry is essential to the country. The worldwide cocoa and chocolate industry has become worthy because of the increase in the market CAGR by 2022. The cocoa industry has also shown a significant expansion, which is the increased origin share of worldwide grindings that has risen effectively. Also, chocolate producers have been encouraged to choose to sustain cocoa to grow the demand for verified and traceable cocoa. In Indonesia, they become the most extensive sustainable commercial cocoa processing farm by partnering with Olam Food Ingredients by promoting cutting-edge farming and encouraging biodiversity to their farm. However, downstream of the cocoa industry, the operation has raised the value of cocoa beans so that the process can improve the farmer's income via agroindustry activities. Developing the cocoa agro-industry can create jobs, enhance regional economic activity, and add value to cocoa products at every stage of the supply chain.

From an economic perspective, the global cocoa and chocolate market are significantly high because the market is being driven by consumers growing knowledge of cocoa's health advantages. As per regional research, the market has five key regions that make Europe become the most significant market share in the global cocoa and chocolate in 2018. Also, North America imports cocoa and cocoa products to make the market anticipated to grow. Which the consumption of dark chocolate in North America, the cocoa market is rising due to public awareness of cocoa's health advantages. As for the pricing of cocoa, the price does not change significantly. From March 2021 to March 2022, the price was equal to London's closing time. But, by situation between Russia and Ukraine has a detrimental influence on travel across Western Europe. It significantly affects the number of chocolate sales at airports, one of the primary places for chocolate sales. Other than that, the import and export of chocolate market expansion are still projected. But many countries, like the five largest chocolate exporters, make an average annual growth rate between 2021 and 2026. Germany has imported cocoa butter by 152 000 tonnes from cocoa-producing nations. As for the global demand for end products, cocoa paste is demanded by Europe, which has imported the most, followed by America and Asia. Africa and Oceania are minor cocoa paste producers. Besides that, the cocoa butter demand is led by Europe, which has imported the most cocoa butter, followed by America and Asia.

REFERENCES

Abdulsamad, A., Frederick, S., Guinn, A., & Gereffi, G. (2015). Pro-Poor Development and Power Asymmetries in Global Value Chains. *Duke Center on Globalization, Governance & Competitiveness*, (September), 83.

Agus, B. A. P., Mohamad, N. N., & Hussain, N. (2018). Composition of unfermented, unroasted, roasted cocoa beans and cocoa shells from Peninsular Malaysia Chocolate and Cocoa Market Size. In *Cocoa and Chocolate Market* (p. 180). Fortune Business Insight. Retrieved from https://www.fortunebusinessinsights.com/industry-reports/cocoa-and-chocolate-markethttps://www.fortunebusinessinsights.com/industry-reports/cocoa-and-chocolatemarket-100075100075

Beg, M. S., Ahmad, S., Jan, K., & Bashir, K. (2017). Status, supply chain and processing of cocoa A review. *Trends in Food Science & Technology*, *66*, 108–116. doi:10.1016/j.tifs.2017.06.007

Brown, A. L., Bakke, A. J., & Hopfer, H. (2020). Understanding American premium chocolate consumer perception of craft chocolate and desirable product attributes using focus groups and projective mapping. *PLoS ONE, 15*(11). doi:10.1371/journal.pone.0240177

Cacao, B. G. (2021, November 15). *Global Cocoa Market Study*. Retrieved from GAIA CACAO: https://www.gaiacacao.com/

Cadby, J. (2021). Can COVID-19 Melt the Craft Chocolate Industry? *Food Ethics*, *6*(2), 8. doi:10.100741055-021-00087-8 PMID:33937518

doi:10.1007/s41055-021-00087-8

CBI. (2018b). Multisectoral Value Chain Analysis: 'Connecting Central America.' In *Organización de las Naciones Unidas para la Alimentación y la Agricultura*. http://www.oie.sieca.int/documentos/ver/Multisectoral VCA CA – Final report. Pdf

CBI. (2020f, September). *Entering the European market for certified cocoa*. CBI Ministry of Foreign Affairs. https://www. cbi.eu/market-information/cocoa-cocoaproducts/certifiedcocoa/market-entry

CBI. (2021). *The European market potential for semi-finished cocoa products*. CBI Ministry of Foreign Affairs.

Chen, X., Jiang, K., Zhu, Y., Wang, X., & Yun, T. (2021). Individual tree crown segmentation directly from uav-borne lidar data using the pointnet of deep learning. *Forests*, *12*(2), 1–22. doi:10.3390/f12020131

Claw, J. (2022, June 27). *Malaysia Chocolate & Cacao Culture*. Retrieved from Dame caco: https://damecacao.com/malaysian-chocolate-cacao-culture/

Cocoa and Chocolate Market by Type. (2020, August). Retrieved from https://www.marketsandmarkets.com/Market-Reports/cocoa-chocolate-markethttps://www.marketsandmarkets.com/Market-Reports/cocoa-chocolate-market226179290.html226179290.html

Consulting, E. (2020). Reseña del Mercado de Cacao Mundial. EUROMONITOR).

Economy, F. (2022). *Focus Economy: Over the last month, cocoa prices have decreased, mostly because supply prospects are looking good. May saw a 3.8% decrease in cocoa prices from April, with the average price per metric tonne coming in at USD 2,364. Additionally, compared to the same month*. Author.

Elizabeth Holloway, K. A. (2018, May 30). Retrieved from Chocolate Challenges: The Social, Technological, and Environmental Issues Facing the Cocoa Industry. *Red Vere Media*. https://redvervemedia.com/chocolate-challenges-the-social-technological

FFC. (2022, January 10). *Federation of Cocoa Commerce*. Retrieved from Agricultural Practices: https://www.cocoafederation.com/education/agricultural-practices#Quality%20control

Fortune. (2022, April 18). Retrieved from Market Research Report: https://www.fortunebusinessinsights.com/industry-reports/cocoa-and-chocolate-

Fund, I. M. (2023, January 6). *International Monetary Fund*. Retrieved from Global price of Cocoa (PCOCOUSDM): https://fred.stlouisfed.org/series/PCOCOUSDM#0

Global Cocoa and Chocolate Market: Market Segments: By Cocoa Type; By Chocolate Type ; By Application ; By and Region – Analysis of Market Size, Share & Trends for 2014 – 2019 and Forecasts to 2030. (2022). Academic Press.

Gordon, C. (2019). What is Craft Chocolate? In *Dalloway Chocolate* (pp. 1–6). https://www.dalloway-chocolate.com/ blogs/news/what-is-craft-chocolate

Hariyati, W. E. (2022). Farmers' contributions in the establishment of value-added from holistic cocoa processing: A case study in Trenggalek Regency, East Java. *Earth and Environmental Science,* 8.

High, D. (2020, January 16). *Nestle*. Retrieved from Sustainable Cocoa: https://www.nestle.com/sustainability/sustainable-sourcing/cocoa

Hosnan, D. M. (2009, November 13). *Anim Agro Technology*. Retrieved from Cocoa Rehabilitation: http://animhosnan.blogspot.com/search?q=cocoa

Hütz-Adams, F., Huber, C., Knoke, I., Morazán, D. P., & Mürlebach, M. (2016). Strengthening the competitiveness of cocoa production and improving the income of cocoa producers in West and Central Africa. *Institut Für Ökonomie Und Ökumene, 49*(0), 156. Retrieved from https://suedwind-institut.de/files/Suedwind/Publikationen/2017/2017-06 strengthening the competitiveness of cocoa production and improving the income of cocoa producers in West and Central Africa.pdf

ICCO. (2022, October). *Market Report*. https://www.icco.org/wp-content/uploads/ICCOMonthlyCocoa-Market-Report-October-2022.pdf

Intelligence, M. (2020). *Chocolate Market (2021-2026) Industry Share, Size, Growth*. Retrieved from https://www.mordorintelli-gence.com/industry-reports/chocolate-market

Jiménez Tobón, C. S. (2015). Estado legal mundial del cadmio en cacao (Theobroma cacao): fantasía o realidad. *Producción + Limpia, 10*(1), 89–104. doi:10.22507/pml.v10n1a8

John Makinde, O., Okunade, S., Opoola, E., Sikiru, A. B., O. Ajide, S., & Elaigwu, S. (2019). *Exploration of Cocoa (Theobroma cacao) By-Products as Valuable Potential Resources in Livestock Feeds and Feeding Systems. Theobroma Cacao – Deploying Science for.* Academic Press.

Lim, G. Y. (2019). Barry Callebaut eyes India's fast-growing chocolate industry with new factory. *William Reed*. https://www.foodnavigator- asia.com/Article/2019/08/05/Barry-Callebaut-eyes-India-s-fast-growing-chocolate

Martin, C. (2017, August 31). *Sizing the craft chocolate market*. FCCI. https://www.chocolateinstitute.org/post/sizing-the-craft-chocolate-market

MPIC. (2022a, November 16). *Kementerian Perusahaan Perladangan dan Komoditi.* Academic Press.

MPIC. (2022b, November 18). *Ministry of plantation industries and commodities (MPIC).* Author.

MPIC. (n.d.). https://www.mpic.gov.my/mpi/en/statistic/prestasiperdagangan-main

Nesto, B. (2010). Discovering terroir in the world of chocolate. *Gastronomica, 10*(1), 131–135. doi:10.1525/gfc.2010.10.1.131 PMID:21539057

Nugent, N., & Rhinard, M. (2019). The 'political' roles of the European Commission. *Journal of European Integration*, *41*(2), 203–220. doi:10.1080/07036337.2019.1572135

Perez, M., Lopez-Yerena, A., & Vallverdú-Queralt, A. (2021). *Traceability, authenticity and sustainability of cocoa and chocolate products: a challenge for the chocolate industry. In Critical Reviews in Food Science and Nutrition*. Taylor and Francis Ltd. doi:10.1080/10408398.2020.1819769

Review, H. B. (2022). *HBR Challenges Faced by Cocoa-based Industries*. Academic Press.

Shon, P. d. (2022, June 20). *Bar & Cocoa*. Retrieved from Varieties of Cocoa beans: https://barandcocoa.com/pages/varieties-of-cocoa-beans

Sustainability of Global Cocoa Economy. (2021). doi:10.5772/intechopen.87871

Vivek, V., Bermúdez, S., & Larrea, C. (2019). Global Market Report: Cocoa. *Exchange Organizational Behavior Teaching Journal*, 1–12.

Chapter 19

Study of Regulatory Role and Investors' Protection During the Banking Sector Crisis of 2020 in the Indian Economy: Case of Yes Bank

Partap Singh
Lovely Professional University, India

EXECUTIVE SUMMARY

The case provides an opportunity to evaluate the accuracy of business performance and financial position of Yes Bank, the situation of window dressing in financial statement, and the regulatory role to ensure the investors' protection of Yes Bank, as well as analyzes the role of promoters and different regulators for influencing the retail investors' interest during study period. The major findings of the case indicate that regulators, auditors, independent directors, and rating agencies did not play their effective and active role in preventing unlawful and unethical activities like window dressing regarding business performance and financial position in the financial statements of Yes Bank by promoters and financial manipulators. Retail investors lost their wealth more as compared to other investors. However, RBIs played a critical and remarkable role to avoid complete failure through restructuring of Yes Bank.

INTRODUCTION

Yes Bank is a 7th largest Indian private sector bank which provide the 'Full Service Commercial 'Bank' such as consumer loans, commercial loans MSMEs loans, rural and agri loans. Wealth management, Insurance, technology driven digital offerings, Yes Pay Wallet and various programmes like Yes Premea, Yes First, etc. It has its a wholly owned subsidiary namely Yes Securuties that operates its investment banking, merchant banking andbrokerage businesses. It's headquartered is in Mumbai, and a Representative Office in Abu Dhabi. In present the Bank is making digital investments and maintaining the highest

DOI: 10.4018/978-1-6684-8488-3.ch019

governance and risk management standards. The Bank is also targeting on identifying emerging rural markets to increase value growth and drive profitability and selective opportunities in the infrastructure lending.

Along with his two colleagues Mr Ashok Kapur and Mr Harkirat Singh, Rana Kapoor applied for a license to start YES Bank in India in 2003. The licence was received in 2004 and the initial public offering (IPO) of Yes Bank was bought in June 2005 and the size of the issue was ₹ 315 crore with offer price ₹ 38- ₹45. In 2003, Mr Harkirat Singh quit yes bank due to appointment of Mr Ashok Kapur as non-executive chairman without his consent while Mr Ashok Kapur who held nearly 12 per cent in the bank was killed in 2008 during the 26/11 terror attack. In this way, Mr Rana Kapoor became the lone founder member inescapable at YES Bank since November 2008 and he became aggressive lender and 'lender of the last resort' by offering loans to corporate in their requirements as well as charging and offering higher interest than other banks.

On July 31, 2018, YES Bank share price was at peak with ₹368 due to Mr Rana Kapoor's marketing penetration strategies and market campaign like 'India bole Yes'. But, even than its non-performing asset (NPA) were mounting due to bad loans account like Kingfisher Airlines, Vijay Mallya and Deccan Chronicles. Due to news, 'not letting Rana Kapoor continue in his current post beyond January 31, 2019' there was a decline of 29,92% in the share price of yes bank in a single day while the yes bank's management talking to legal advice on this RBI and Central Government decision. Afterwards, the truth of Yes bank started to come in public domain as bad news.

However, from November 2019, a lot of problems like recession, unemployment, Covid-19 and other economic indicators were reported negatively aggressively and share market was falling continuously and the market price of yes bank share is also falling. There was **a** series of failures of the Non-Banking Financial Companies (NBFCs) namely Dewan Housing Finance Ltd. (DHFL)& IL&FS etc.and the crisis in Indian banks such as PNB bank and PMC Bank during banking sector crisis 2020 was in the news. The case of Yes bank was different than others that involve corporate fraud instead of mismanagement and performance issue, the restructuring of Yes Bank come into force on March 13, 2020 as an effective rescue measure taken by Reserve bank of India (RBI).

First Bad News on Yes Bank and Regulatory Role

The First Negative Report on Yes Bank was published by UBS International financial services in 2015 regarding the asset quality of YES Bank's books. Further it is very interesting that Rana Kapoor quickly filed a complaint against the international firm with the capital market regulator. He tried to manage the bad news by saying that the findings of the USB firm's research are biased and impractical. Due to inefficiency and inactive role of regulatory, he remained successful.

Investors' Protection, Global Research Firm and Regulatory Role

The role of regulatory bodies and global research firm can be judged by the analysis of the impact of bad news:

i. How much is Yes Bank worth? Re 1, say Macquarie,
ii. JP Morgan cuts YES Bank target to Re 1 after stake sale report, March 5, 2020 / 06:47 PM

According to Moneycontrol.com news (2020, March 5, 2020, 06:47 PM) investigated that Yes bank' share rallied 25.79 percent and closed at Rs, 36.84 on account of a Bloomberg report regarding State Bank of India (SBI) to bail out the private lender by forming a consortium of banks and picking up stake 0m March 5,2020. Further, after market close Macquarie and JP Morgan mentioned the news that they have declined its target price on the stock to just Re 1(from earlier Rs.55) due to due to stress book and prospective loss of deposits. As a result of the said news, the market price of shares has declined to Rs.5.65 on March 6, 2020 from Rs. 36.84 as on 5th March, 2020 and closed at Rs. 18.75 on same day while actually SMI has given Rs 10(Rs2 plus Rs 8 premium) per share. And, due to this news, market price of share from Rs. 37.20 as on 5th March, 2020 has sharp declined to Rs.5.65 as on 6th march, 2020.

Reconstruction Scheme 2020 for Yes Bank Ltd and Regulatory Role

On March 6, 2020, the failure of Yes Bank was being accepted by the experts of banking sector and share market, then, Reserve Bank of India gave the assurance to the depositors of the banks that their money will remained safe. Thus, to maintain the stability in Indian banking centre, the restructuring of Yes Bank came into force on March 13, 2020 as an effective rescue measure taken by Reserve bank of India (RBI). Reconstruction Scheme 2020 for YES Bank Ltd is as under:

A. The list of new investors towards investment into YES Bank Limited as per Scheme 2020:
    i. State Bank of India (Rs. 6050 core)
    ii. Housing Development Finance Corporation Limited (Rs. 1000 crore)
    iii. ICICI Bank Limited (Rs. 1000 crore)
    iv. Axis Bank Limited (Rs.600 crore)
    v. Kotak Mahindra Bank Limited (Rs. 500 crore)
    vi. The Federal Bank Ltd. (Rs. 300 crore)
    vii. Bandhan Bank Limited (Rs. 300 crore)
    viii. IDFC First Bank Limited (Rs. 250 crore)
B. Increase in authorized share capital: The authorised share capital of the bank has been increased from the existing Rs. 1100 core to Rs. 6, 200 core. The number of equity shares has been reduced from 450, 00, 00,000 equity shares of Rs. 2 each to 30,00,00,00,000 of 2 each totalling to Rs. 6000 crore and the authorised preference share capital of the bank shall continue to be Rs 200 crore.
C. Issuance and allotment of equity shares: 605 crore equity shares have been issued and allotted to State Bank of India, for an aggregate subscription consideration of Rs. 6050 crore per equity share comprising of Rs.2 face value and Rs.8 (premium).
D. SBI shall not reduce its holding below 26% before completion of 3 years from March 14, 2020.
E. 75% percent of such number of equity shares allotted to each Investor shall be subject to a lock in for a period of 3 years from March 13, 2020 and the remaining 25% percent of the shareholding allotted to each investor shall be freely transferable and shall not be subject to any lock-in.

Indian government has recapitalised PSU banks with Rs 3.5 lakh crore at the cost of taxpayers during previous 8-10 years. Whether it is too high a price for financial failures or not is a billion dollar question in current economic scenario?_

REVIEW OF LITERATURE

Dr Puneet Kumar and Ritee Upadhyay (2021) examined the key reasons of failure of Yes Bank are bad loans, outflow of liquidity, poor corporate governance, and low provisions. He found that he majority of loans were offered forcefully to high pressure organizations in 2008-09 post period and near to bankruptcy namely Anil Ambani Group, DHFL, CG Powers, Café Coffee Day, IL & FS, Radius Developers, Mantri Group Vardaraj Cement, and so forth. These organizations are nearly bankrupt. Uttam Prakesh Agrawal resigned company mentioning poor governance standards and compliance failure at the investor's protection. In interview with Economic Times corporate executive, he discussed his objections on capital raising choices by the management. Further, he disclosed that the bank is surpassing the management.

Moneycontrol (2020) investigated that Yes bank' share rallied 25.77 percent and closed at Rs 36.85 on account of a Bloomberg report. The report was that the government has directed to the State Bank of India (SBI) to bail out the private lender by forming a consortium of banks and picking up stake. He mentioned that JP Morgan on March 5, 2020 lowered the target price on shares of YES Bank to Re 1 (from Rs 55 earlier) assuming that the net worth of the bank may be at near zero value due to stress book and prospective loss of deposits.

Nachiket Kelka (2020) found that Suresh Ganapathy, an analyst at Macquarie Capital Securities has written that the bank's net worth may definitely be zero because of stressed book and suggested that SBI and other PSU banks need to buy the bank at Rs 1. However, there was no there was no confirmation on the reports by SBI. Yes Bank also clarified his unawareness of any such decision. For the moment, Yes Bank shares rallied 26 per cent on March 5, 2020 to close at Rs 36.80 due to the news of Macquarie's expert. On the other hand, he examined that Saurabh Kumar of JP Morgan advised that the rally in the stock of yes bank was unjustified as on March 5, 2020 after close of the market and he further mentioned that JP Morgan has declined its target price on the stock to just Re 1, supposing the new capital to come in at a huge discount to the current share price.

Chief Investment Strategist at Geojit Financial Services (2020) found that the key reason of financial instability in Yes Bank is eternal vigilance. He has studied many serious deficiencies like regulation and supervision, auditing and foreign functioning. Some serious facts like unusually high credit growth of Yes Bank as comparison to the growth of the industry, and the progressively high proportion of fee income, particularly from new corporate borrowers were ignored by the regulatory authority. He mentioned that involvement of promoters and the new type of corporate borrowers are involved in such type corporate failure.

Nayantara Rai (2018) mentioned that RBI has three reasons cited by RBI for sacking Rana Kapoor as CEO - (i) Weak compliance culture in Yes Bank, (ii) Weak Governance In Yes Bank and (iii) Wrong Asset Qualification. According to 121 Articles of Association of Yes Bank, Rana Kapoor cannot be retired from the Board and under Article 110, Rana Kapoor has the right to nominate up to 3 directors to protect his interest. He concluded that the Yes Bank's Articles Of Association were in the favour of Rana Kapoor, which are all subject to RBI approval.

Madan Lal Bhasin (2015) has studied that frauds cases in banks are increasing very speedily by using different innovative methods. He also observed poor employment practices, lack of actual training; work-stress, poor internal control systems, and low compliance levels on the part of bank employees.

Hari Ram A. (2014) studied the detection of fraud and corruption in banking system has become very critical and world-wide phenomenon. He observed that it is very difficult to find these problem in advance as it is done by bank employees of banking& non- banking financial companies, and outsider's customers of banks.

K. C. Chakrabarty (2013) has analysed the impact of frauds and corruption in banking, insurance and non-banking financial institutions and its cost in the form efficient operations in Indian financial sector. The sound banking is the base of economy and sustainability of banking system is a big challenge.

Economics Times (2014) found that Reserve Bank of India has focused on the measures to tackle the problem of window dressing by banks sothat the problem of liquidity pressures in the Indian banking system can be maintained. The window dressing is used to reduce the size of their risk weighted assets to qualify for lower capital requirement and to fulfil others regulatory requirements regarding performance.

Dr. D. V. Ingle (2018) suggested that the bank should focus to match the assets and liabilities on urgent basis and should bring efficiency in liquidity, profitability and risk of the bank. However, he found increasing trend regarding liquidity ratios, profitability ratios and other ratios and recorded the performance satisfactory on the basis of financial ratios.

Yuvaraj Halage (2021) has examined statutory disclosures, principles of governance related to shareholding pattern, board structure, board meetings, risk management practices and auditing to judge the efficiency of the corporate governance practices followed in Yes Bank during a study period. He observed failure to fulfil certain regulatory compliance like the ideal combination of the board should be fifty percent of Non-Executive Directors while this criterion was not fulfilled by Yes Bank. The determined gap criterion was not fulfilled as the maximum gap between any 2 Board Meetings was less than 4 months in case of Yes Bank. However, the annual reports of Yes Bank 2018-19 reveal that Yes Bank has complied fully with all statutory requirements.

Vincent Aebi (2012) studied the risk management related corporate governance mechanisms during financial crisis 2007-08. They had studied the appointment and reporting system of Chief Risk Officer and found that these corporate governance standards are linked to the performance of banks.

Dipika Jain (2019) has studied the comparative performance of bank relating to corporate governance practices regarding Bank of Baroda & Yes Bank. They found that corporate governance practices are sbetter in Bank of Baroda as compared to Yes Bank on the basis of analysis of secondary data like annual reports and bank websites.

Objective of the Book Chapter/Case

- To evaluate accuracy of business performance and financial position of Yes Bank during study period;
- To analyse role of global research firms, investment banks and different regulators for influencing the retail investors' interest;
- To workout the situation of window dressing in financial statement of Yes Bank.
- To study the effective regulatory role of different regulators to ensure the Investors' protection in case of Yes Bank.

RESEARCH METHODOLOGY AND CONCEPTUAL FRAMEWORK

This case is based on secondary data only. The secondary data has been collected from annual reports of Yes Bank for 2010-2020 periods and from NSE websites, and other relevant and reliable site as well as newspapers. The statistical technique Mean and financial ratios like EPS, DPS, ROI, ROE, NIM, Net NPA, Gross NPA, Provision Coverage Ratio and CRAR have been used to analyse the data. The detailed review of literature also helps to get the replies of discussion questions.

Provision Coverage Ratio (PCR): It represents the provision made against bad loans from the profit generated by bank. The given percentage of funds is kept separately by the banks for covering the potential losses due to NPAs. Higher the PCR is good for banks and vice-versa is also true.

Formula:

Provision Coverage ratio= (Equity- net NPA) / (Total assets – intangible assets)

Slippage Ratio: It is the rate at which good loans are rotating to bad loans.

Formula:

Slippage ratio= Fresh accretion of NPAs during the year /Total standard assets at the beginning of the year multiplied by 100

LIMITATION OF STUDY

This study is based on single bank namely Yes Bank. The study can be extended to others private and public sector banks to analyse the stability of Indian banking system and the role of regulatory bodies in Indian banking sector.

RESULTS AND DISCUSSION

Table 1 exhibits that the price of yes bank's share was at Rs 398 on August 18, 2018 at its all life-time high. Afterwards, its stock price decline continuously and it declines to Rs. 36 on March 5, 2020. The next day, its price comes below Rs. 6 and closes to Rs. 18.75. The stock reported 232 percent hike from its bottom on March 6, 2020 while it was down by 84 percent from its previous day closing price. It has taken 18 months to fall from its peak price to its bottom price. During this period, the stock price was at Rs 187 on December, 2018 after fall from its peaks and it increased to Rs 276 on March 2019 and after that it fallen continuously and in the months of March 2020, it was at its bottom after more than 11 months periods.

It has been observed that a lot of good news came and retail investors entered in yes bank. The news about buying of yes bank shares by Rakesh Jhunjhunwala was fake news and a large number of retail investors bought the shares due to the said news and Rakesh Jhunjhunwala also did not object the news. The regulatory body were unable to communicate the fraud in Yes Bank timely to the investors.

The Figure 1 exhibits the volatility and trends in yes bank's shares prices and percentage change in in market price of the share. It shows the greatest volatility in the stock price on March 5 and 6 March, 2020. It was the result of panic created by big global research firm and news agencies.

Table 1. Exhibiting analysis of volatility in market price of Yes Bank stock

Year/Months	Market Price	% Change	Year/Months	Market Price	% Change
Apr-18	319		Apr-19	176	-24.36
May-18	350	9.72	May-19	153	-13.07
Jun-18	335	-4.29	Jun-19	176	15.03
Jul-18	392	17.01	Jul-19	104	-40.91
Aug-18	398	1.53	Aug-19	79	-24.04
Sep-18	343	-13.82	Sep-19	72	-8.86
Oct-18	246	-28.28	Oct-19	70	-2.78
Nov-18	228	-7.32	Nov-19	73	4.29
Dec-18	187	-17.98	Dec-19	64	-12.33
Jan-19	199	6.42	Jan-20	47	-26.56
Feb-19	231	16.08	Feb-20	39	-17.02
Mar-19	276	19.48	March 5,2020	36	-7.69
Apr-20	176	-26.36	06-03-2020	18.75	231.86
				(Rs 5.65)	

Source: Investing.com

Figure 1. Exhibiting analysis of volatility in market price of Yes Bank stock
Source: Table 1 data

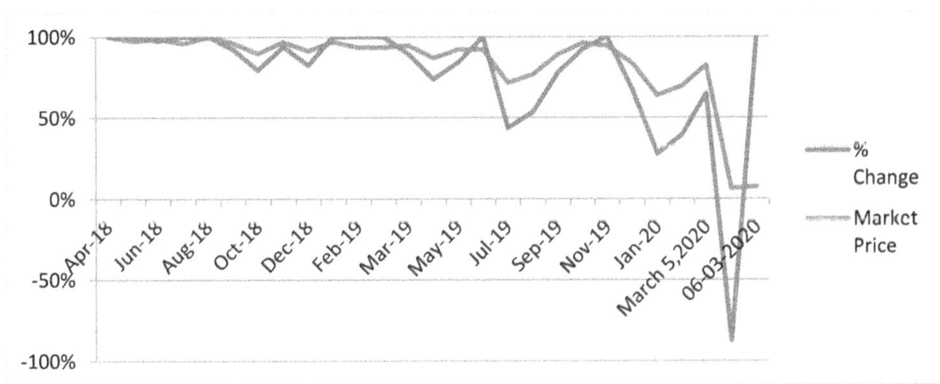

Tables 2 and 3 exhibited that:

- Net Profit after tax of Rs. 4224 crore in March 2018 and other previous years good trend in net profit has converted into net loss of Rs.18560 crore in Q3 FY20 during the corresponding period last year, is a reflection of window dressing in financial statements of Yes Bank. Further, Return on Equity (ROE) is -100.3 percent, return on assets (ROA) is -23.3 percent, and Basic EPS(Rs) is (-72.8) in Q3 FY20 from average ROE of 17.41 percent, average ROA of 16.51 percent and average of Basic EPS(Rs.) of 29.77 percent in10 years study period.

Table 2. Exhibiting financial health of Yes Bank during study period

Financial Ratio	Q3FY20	Mar-19	2018	2017	2016
Basic EPS (Rs.)	-72.8	7.45	18.4	15.8	60.6
Diluted EPS (Rs.)		7.38	18.1	15.4	59.3
Dividend/Share (Rs.)		2	2.7	12	10
Net Profit/Share (Rs.)		7.43	18.3	73	60.4
Net Profit Margin (%)		5.8	20.8	20.3	18.8
Return on Assets (%)	-23.30%	0.45	1.35	1.54	1.53
Return on Equity / Networth (%)	-100.30%	6.39	16.4	15.1	18.4
Net Interest Margin (X)	**1.40%**	2.57	2.47	2.69	2.76
Price To Book Value (X)		2.37	2.73	3.21	2.64
Profit after Tax(Rs. Crore)	-18560	1720	4225	3330	2539
Market Price/share(Rs.)	5.65 (March)	398 (August)	309	303	173

Table 3. Exhibiting financial health of Yes Bank during study period

Financial Ratio	2014	2013	2012	2011	2010	Mean
Basic EPS (Rs.)	44.9	36.5	27.9	21.1	15.65	29.771
Diluted EPS (Rs.)	44.4	35.6	27.1	20.3	14.87	29.026
Dividend/Share (Rs.)	8	6	4	2.5	1.5	5.77
Net Profit/Share (Rs.)	44.9	36.3	27.7	21	14.06	35.094
Net Profit Margin (%)	16.2	15.7	15.5	18	16.77	16.511
Return on Assets (%)	1.48	1.31	1.32	1.23	1.31	1.299
Return on Equity / Networth (%)	22.7	22.4	20.9	19.2	15.46	17.406
Net Interest Margin (X)	2.49	2.23	2.19	2.11	3.47	2.554
Price To Book Value (X)	2.09	2.65	2.77	2.84	2.8	2.702
Profit after Tax(Rs. Crore)	1720	4225	3330	2539	2005	
Market Price/share(Rs.)	79	85	70	62	51	

Source: Annual Report 2010-2020 & Compiled data (including Table 2)

- The market price of shares has declined to Rs.5.65 as on March 6, 2020 from its peak in August 2018 due to its failure of raising funds and negative commentary by many big brokers firm, sale of promoters 'stake and downgrading by Macquarie and JP Morgan due to stress book and prospective loss of deposits. It was a very big loss to retail investors who hold the 48 percent (now just 12 percent) stake in Yes Bank and no regulator authority give the clarification on this news to protect the interest of retail and other investors as the news came on 5th March after stock market close.
- Average Basic EPS and Diluted EPS (Rs.) of Yes bank is Rs. 29.7. Basic EPS is more in the year 2016, 2015, and 2014 and in the year 2013 than average EPS while it is less in the year 2019, 2018, 2017, 2012, 2011 and 2010. But. It is very surprising that It was minus Rs.72.8 in March

2020 which reduced from Rs 49. So, it indicates the situation of window dressing in financial statements.

- Average dividend per share is Rs. 5.77. Dividend per share is more than average dividend per share in the year 2013, 2014, 2015, 2016, and 2017 while it less than average dividend per share in the year 2019, 2018, 2010, 2011, and 2012.
- Average Net Profit per share is 35.09. Net Profit per share is more than average Net Profit per share in the year 2013, 2014, 2015, 2016, and 2017 while it less than average dividend per share in the year 2019, 2018, 2010, 2011, and 2012.
- Average return on assets was observed 1.30 percent. Return on Assets(ROA) is more than average return on assets in the year 2013, 2014, 2015, 2016, and 2017 while it less than average return on assets in the year 2019, 2018, 2010, 2011, and 2012. It is surprising that ROA was -23 percent in Q3 2020.
- Average return on equity or net worth is 17.41 percent. The return on equity or net worth is more than average return on Equity in the year 2011, 2012, 2013, 2014 and 2016 while it less than average return on equity or net worth in the year 2019, 2018, 2017, and 2015. But, ROE was -100 percent in Q3 2020 which reveals some irregularities in the system.
- Average net interest margin has been recorded 2.55 percent. The net interest margin percentage is more than average net interest margin in the year 2011, 2012, 2013, 2014 and 2016 while it less than average net interest margin in the year 2019, 2018, 2017, and 2015.
- Average Price to Book Value has been recorded 2.70. The Price to Book Value is more than average Price to Book Value in the year 2010, 2011, 2012, 2015 and 2018 while it is less than average net profit margin in the year 2013, 2014, 2016, and 2017.

Table 4. Exhibiting shareholding pattern (%) of Yes Bank during study period

Standalone	Dec-19	Sep-19	Aug-19	Jun-19	Average	March-20
Promoters	8.33	13.05	17.97	19.78	14.7825	1.67
Pledged	2.59	35.05	40.78	3.64	20.515	0
Foreign Portfolio Investors(FPIs/ FIIs)	15.17	26.51	31.73	33.69	26.775	1.95
Domestic Institutional Investors(DIIs)	28.53	30.5	27.65	26.07	28.1875	85.05
Financial Institutions	0.42	0.46	0.44	0.32	0.41	67.73
Insurance Companies	8.24	8.98	9.04	10.08	9.085	1.67
Mutual Funds	5.09	9.26	9.29	6.59	7.5575	0.73
Others DIIs	14.78	11.8	8.88	9.08	11.135	14.92
Others(Retail Investors)	47.96	29.94	22.64	20.46	30.25	11.92
Total	99.99	100	99.99	100	99.995	

Source: NSE data and compiled

Table 4 exhibited that:

- From June-2019 to December 2019, the average promoters' shareholding has been recorded 14.78. Out of the promoters' shareholding, 20.52 percent was pledged. Average shareholding of FIIs/FPIs was 26.78 percent while DIIs was 28.19 percent during the same period. The average shareholding of Financial Institutions, Insurance Companies, Mutual Funds, Others Domestic Institutional Investors and others (retail investors) was observed as 0.41 percent, 9.09 percent, 7.56 percent, 11.14 percent, 30.25 percent during study period.
- It has been observed that promoters' shareholding has decreased to 8.33 percent from 14.78 percent. Promoters has pledged share more than average in Sep-19 and Aug-19. Further, pledged shareholding has reduced to 2.59 percent from 20.52 percent.
- Average shareholding of Domestic Institutional Investors (DIIs) has been recorded 28.19 percent. It was increased to 28.53 percent in December 2019 from 26.07 percent in June 2019. Further, It was reduced to 28.53 percent from 30.5 percent in December 2019
- Insurance companies have reduced to 8.24 percent of their shareholding in March 2020 from 10.08 percent in June 2019.
- Mutual Funds have decreased to 5.09 percent of their shareholding in March 2020 from 6.59 percent in June 2019.
- Other DIIs has increased to 14.78 percent of their shareholding in March 2020 from 9.08 percent in June 2019.
- Retail Investors has increased to 47.96 percent of their shareholding in March 2020 from 20.46 percent in June 2019.

Table 5. Showing position of balance sheet as 15/03/2020 (after SBIs partnership) (in INR crore)

	December 31, 2019	September 30, 2019	December 31 2018	Growth % (Y-o-Y)	Growth % (Q-o-Q)
Assets	290985	346576	3,73981	-22	-16
Advances	186099	224505	243885	-24	-17
Investments	61319	67340	83018	-26	-9
Liabilities	290985	346576	373981	-22	-16
Shareholder' Fund	9218	27790	28403	-68	-67
Total Capital Funds	25218	51030	53273	-53	-51
Borrowings	103213	93131	107691	-4	+11
Deposits	165755	209497	222758	-26	-21
CASA	53203	64496	74117	-28	-18

Source: www.nseindia.com

Table 5 exhibited that:

- The growth of CASA, Deposits, Borrowings, Total Capital Funds, and Shareholder' funds, has declined to 18 percent, 21 percent, 11 percent, 51 percent, and 67 percent respectively. On the other hand, the growth of investments and advances has declined to 9 percent and 17 percent.
- It is concluded that there is highly fall in the growth of CASA, Deposits, Borrowings, Total Capital Funds, and Shareholder' fund which shows the negative scenario for investment in banks as well as shows the reason of shareholders wealth minimization. It also indicates the possibility of window dressing in the accounts of bank.

Capital Adequacy in Yes Bank

Table 6. Showing capital adequacy ratio in Yes Bank

	December 31, 2018	September 30, 2019	December 31, 2019
CRAR	17.4%	16.3%	4.1

Source: https://www1.nseindia.com/corporate

Table 6 exhibited that Total Risk Weighted Assets to Total Assets Ratio has decreased to 4.1 percent in December 2019 to 17.4 percent in December 2018. In September 2019, it was 16.3 percent. It is concluded that it was a remarkable fall in the capital adequacy ratio and it shows the inefficiency of banking regulatory bodies that a so big manipulation was made in the books of banks and the wealth of many investors was destroyed. It was more than 75 percent fall that indicates towards manipulation books of accounts in bank.

Assets Quality in Yes Bank

Table 7. Showing assets quality in Yes Bank (in INR crore)

	December 31, 2018	September 30, 2019	December 31, 2019
Gross NPA (%)	2.10	7.39%	18.87%
Net NPA (%)	1.18%	4.35%	5.97%
Provision Coverage Ratio	44.24%	43.05%	72.70%
Slippages Ratio (%)	0.95%	2.58%	11.98%

Source: https://www1.nseindia.com

* Note: After considering capital infusion of ` 10,000 Crores and write down of Basel III compliant AT1 Bonds aggregating to 8,415 Crores

Table 7 exhibited that Gross NPA has increased to 18.87 percent in December 31, 2019 from 2.10 percent in December 31, 2018 while Net NPA has increased to 5.97 percent in December 2019 from 1.18 percent in December 2018. Further, Provision Coverage Ratio (PCR) has increased to 72.70 percent in December 31, 2019 from 44.24 percent in December, 2018. On the other hand slippages ratio has increased to 72.20 percent in December 31, 2019 from 44.24 percent in December 31, 2018. It has been found that the assets quality in yes bank is highly unsatisfactory which indicates failure of regulatory authority.

FINDINGS, SUGGESTIONS, AND RECOMMENDATIONS AND CONCLUSION

Findings

- The key reasons of the failure of Yes Bank were observed like mounting bad loans, outflow of liquidity, poor corporate governance, its failure of raising funds and low provisions, negative commentary by many big brokers firm, sale of promoters 'stake and downgrading by Macquarie and JP Morgan due to stress book and prospective loss of deposits weak compliance culture in Yes Bank and wrong asset qualification. It was found that these bad loans were given to the borrower forcefully by Rana Kapur and his family members. However, Yes Bank stock price reached at its peak due to Rana Kapur's smart marketing strategies; but, the ignorance of granting loan to good account only that was a basic function of management and it became the cause of big NPAs.
- The highest and unexpected volatility was registered in Yes Bank stock price due to much fake news both bad and good by big research firm, news –agencies and websites.
- The situation of window dressing was observed in financial statements of yes bank which was reflected in various financial ratio and parameters like the net profit after tax of Rs. 4224 crore in March 2018 and other previous years good trend in net profit that has converted into net loss of Rs.18560 crore in Q3 FY20 during the corresponding period last year. The market price of shares has declined to Rs.5.65 as on March 6, 2020 from its peak at Rs 398 in August 2018 and basic EPS was minus Rs.72.8 in March 2020 which reduced from Rs 49 in 2018. Further, ROA was -23 percent in Q3 2020 from average return on assets 1.30 percent in 2018, Return on Equity (ROE) was -100.3 percent from average return on equity or net worth 17.41 percent during study period.
- The remarkable decline in promoters' shareholding, fall in FPIs/FIIs' shareholding, unchanged shareholding of DIIs and financial institutions fall in shareholding of mutual funds and insurance companies was recorded while there was remarkable rise(more than double) rise in the shareholding of retail investors. The sale of his shareholdings by Rana Kapoor who is promoter in Yes Bank at goods price is also indicates the failure of different regulators.
- Retail Investors, Domestic Institutional Investors (DIIs), and Other DIIs have increased their shareholding to 47.96 percent, 28.53 percent, and 14.78 percent respectively in December 2019 from 20.46 percent, 26.07 percent, and 9.08 percent respectively in June 2019. On the other hand, Promoters, Insurance Companies, Mutual Funds has decreased their shareholding to 8.33 percent, 8.24 percent, and 5.09 percent respectively in December 2019 from 14.78 percent, 10.08 percent, and 6.59 percent respectively in June 2019.
- Highly fall in the growth of CASA, Deposits, Borrowings, Total Capital Funds, and Shareholder' fund which shows the negative scenario for investment in banks as well as shows the reason of shareholders wealth minimization was observed. It also indicates the possibility of towards window dressing in accounts of bank.

- It has been concluded there was a remarkable fall in the capital adequacy ratio and it shows the inefficiency of banking regulators that a so big manipulation was made in the books of banks and the wealth of many investors was destroyed. It was more than 75 percent fall that indicates towards manipulation books of accounts in bank.
- It has been found that the assets quality in yes bank is highly unsatisfactory which indicates the failure of regulatory authority.

Suggestions and Recommendations

1. On account of increased number of frauds and financial distress in banking and corporate sectors, there is a need of effective and active role of regulatory bodies with transparency to tackle the problems of Indian financial sector. In case of Yes Bank mechanism of regulatory bodies failed to control and monitors the business activities of Yes bank that became cause of yes bank crisis as the first report by USB in 2015 was ignored by the system. If regulatory take the report seriously relating to fraud in yes bank and if timely investigation was started and the reality of the fraud in the bank would come out timely, then the great loss of wealth of shareholders could have been protected.
2. The global and domestic research firm also misinformed and confused the retail investors through various report and news regarding investment by big investors and institutional investors. The SEBI and RBI both remained failed to show the right path to the retail investors by providing accurate and reliable information. Both regulatory bodies should impose restrictions on selling of share- holding by institutional investors in such type typical and special situation for a particular time like in case of ne IPO.
3. The accountability of domestic credit rating agencies like CRISIL, CARE etc, Global Credit rating Agencies, and chief accountants as well as Auditor firm should be fixed sothat they can identify the window dressing in the financial statements so that any company can't cheat to retail investors who buy the shares on the basis of fundamental of company
4. The SEBI should revise the definition of investors' protection relating to corporate governance. Their role should not be like Police that reach at spot after the occurrences of the events. The analysis of shareholding pattern indicates that when big investors were selling by using big research firms' reports in their favour so that they can trap the retail investors by selling their holdings and they were successful in case of Yes Bank due to inactive role of regulatory bodies. The SEBI should actions on all the players like auditors' firm, credit rating agencies who were responsible for window dressing in financial statements.
5. The maximum loan was given to loss making companies which was a doubtful issue, but the regulatory bodies ignored the issue in-spite of involvement of Rana Kapur family at top position of the bank.
6. The mounting NPAs were the key reason of failure of the banks. The basic function of any bank is granting the loan to the right customers; but the loan was given to loss making –businesses that were a matter of effective supervision and monitoring by different regulators. So, reserve bank of India should make the policy for granting the loan for banks and the periodical review of the policy should be made on continuous basis.

7. The RBI should ensure the transparency; accuracy and reliability in financial reporting of the companies and those who believe on fundamental of the company and invest in the company don't have to lose their money.
8. The management of yes bank after rec should focus on retail customer in agriculture sector to give new loan as farmers generally are able to give 5 to 7 times of security of his land' s market value as comparison to the loan amount. It will reduce the possibility of high NPAs in banking sectors as retail take less amount of loan as comparison to big corporate. In present agriculture land and other land in rural area has no issue of marketability and any land can be sold at any time.
9. The yes bank should focus on the effective management of assets and liability. The assets and liability should be matched and bank should increase the deposits and banks.

CONCLUSION

On the basis of the above analysis, it may be concluded that regulators, auditors, independent directors and rating agencies did not play their effective and active role in preventing unlawful& unethical activities like window dressing or manipulation regarding business performance and financial position in the financial statements of Yes Bank by financial manipulators. Items given in financial statements of Yes Bank have been manipulated and this window dressing was unnoticed by different regulators. Yes Bank crisis case indicates a big 'Damage of Wealth of retail investors'. Neither SEBI nor RBI/SBI gaveve their clarification on the negative news given by JP Before the restructuring scheme of RBI, Rana Kapoor sell his shares in profits and after scheme Manju Kapur who is also a key promoter sell his shares when bank was facing crisis and destroying the wealth of investors. There is an urgent need of eternal vigilance for Indian Financial System and different regulators, auditors, independent directors and rating agencies have to be pro-active to pre-empt crisis. The responsibility of promoters should be fixed specially in case of banking as sector as it is a matter of trust in Indian banking system which is the base of Indian Economy. However, Reserve Bank of India has played a critical role for the rescue of bank and to bring soundness in Indian banking sector.

DISCUSSION QUESTIONS

i. Why were borrowers so enthusiastic about Yes Bank? How did Rana Kapoor become the lone founder member at Yes Bank? How do you justify the role of Rana Kapoor in rise and fall of Yes Bank?
ii. What key reasons were responsible in the failure of yes bank? What was the impact of global research firms' news on yes bank's share price?
iii. Why did yes bank's share rise by 25.79 percent and close at Rs 35.84 on March 5, 2020? Further, why did yes bank's share fall to Rs 5.65 as on March 6, 2020 and close at Rs 18.75 on same day?
iv. How did you experience the volatility in the yes bank stock during the crisis?
v. What was the reconstruction scheme 2020 for Yes Bank? Why did SBI bank and other bank's participate in it?
vi. Did you observe the situation of window dressing in yes bank's financial statements? If yes, then what are grounds to prove it?

vii. What was the status of shareholding pattern in yes bank during its crisis in 2020? Are you agreeing that retail investors had lost more than others? How?
viii. Did global research firms and different regulators play their right role in ensuring the investor's' protection in yes bank? If yes, then how would you be agree and if not, then how you would be disagree?

REFERENCES

Bhasin, M. L. (2015). An Empirical Study of Frauds in the Banks. *European Journal of Business and Social Sciences, 4*(7), 1-12.

Chakrabarty, K. C. (2013, July). Fraud in the Banking Sector—Causes, Concerns and Cures. In *National Conference on Financial Fraud organised by ASSOCHAM, New Delhi* (Vol. 26). https://www.bankinfosecurity.com/5-tips-to-reduce-banking-fraud-a-2534

Chief Investment Strategist at Geojit Financial Services. (2020). *Lessons from the Yes Bank saga: Eternal vigilance is the price of financial stability.* https://www.moneycontrol.com/news/business/markets/lessons-from-the-yes-bank-saga-eternal-vigilance-is-the-price-of-financial-stability-5034861.html

Economic Times. (2014). *RBI to propose steps to reduce window dressing by banks.* https://m.economictimes.com/news/economy/policy/rbi-to-propose-steps-to-reduce-window-dressing-by-banks/articleshow/33099560.cms

Jain, D. (2019). Corporate Governance Practices: A Comparative Study of Bank of Baroda & Yes Bank. International Journal of Management. *IT & Engineering*, *9*(6), 237–254.

Kelkar Nachiket. (2020). How much is Yes Bank worth? Re 1, say Macquarie, JP Morgan. *The Week Magazine*. https://www.theweek.in/news/biz-tech/2020/03/05/how-much-is-yes-bank-worth-re-1-say-macquarie-jp-morgan.html

Moneycontrol. (2020). *JP Morgan cuts YES target to Rs 1 after stake sale report.* moneycontrol.com

Nayantara, R. (2018). 3 reasons cited by RBI for sacking Rana Kapoor as CEO and now his board seat in jeopardy. *The Economics Times.* https://economictimes.indiatimes.com/industry/banking/finance/banking/3-reasons-cited-by-rbi-for-sacking-rana-kapoor-as-ceo-and-now-his-board-seat-in-jeopardy/articleshow/65904385.cms

Partap, S. (2017a). Application of financial analysis in evaluation of financial position of IDBI. *Journal for Advance Research in Applied Science*. http://iaetsdjaras.org/VOLUME-4-ISSUE-6-NOVEMBER-2017/ http://iaetsdjaras.org/gallery/41-november-256.pdf

Partap. (2017b). An example of the application of financial ratio analysis: The case of sun pharmaceutical industries limited. *Journal for Advance Research in Applied Science.*

Partap. (2012). An Evaluation of Performance of Indian Banking Sector (With Special Reference to NPAs of Some Indian Public Sector Bankst. *Asia Pacific Journal of Research in Business Management.*

Puneet, K., & Ritee, U. (2021, January). Analytical study of yes bank by considering financial failure: Issues and challenges. *SJBIR Journal*, *10*(1), 54–61.

Shakeb. (2021). YES Bank Fiasco: Arrogance or Negligence. *Emerging Economies Cases Journal*. https://doi.org/ doi:10.1177/25166042211061

Singla & Partap. (2015). An Evaluation of Effectiveness of E-banking in India. *International Journal innovations in Engineering & Technology*, *5*(2), 437-442.

Chapter 20
Disciplined Innovation Conceptual Framework and Adoption Roadmap

Kumar Shalender
Chitkara Business School, Chitkara University, India

Naman Sharma
https://orcid.org/0000-0002-7151-7360
Indian Institute of Foreign Trade, India

EXECUTIVE SUMMARY

The role, importance, and significance of innovation can't be overemphasized in this day and age. While innovators would like to work beyond constraints, the enhanced importance of using resources efficiently is fast fuelling the prospects of disciplined innovation in companies across industries. Studies have shown that the presence of constraints and limits actually spur innovation and can prove instrumental in guiding organisations towards enhanced profitability and greater market share. Using real-world case studies, this research emphasized the importance of disciplined innovation and proposed a framework to integrate this characteristic into the functional procedures and operational mechanisms of the company. The findings of the research suggest that constraining the creativity of innovators within the broader framework of accountability is the optimum approach towards achieving a perfect balance between creativity, innovation, and resource consumption to deliver superior customer experiences.

INTRODUCTION

Creativity and innovation are two important cornerstones behind any successful organisation. Cutting across industries, companies that are creative and innovative are more likely to succeed in attracting prospective customers to their side. The real-world manifestation of creativity is innovation and given its ability to enhance the market share of a company significantly, most organisations across product domains and service categories attach significant emphasis on innovation. There are many approaches

DOI: 10.4018/978-1-6684-8488-3.ch020

that are popular in the corporate world to achieve a desired level of innovation in the organisation. While some are focused on organisational hierarchy in structure, others put emphasis on the training and development of employees to make sure that they create and innovate with the desired rate of success. One of the most commonly used phrases to increase and spur innovation in a company is to think outside the box for bringing new innovations to life. According to this theory of innovation, any kind of constraint that is put on the development and innovation teams can hamper the rate of progress and ultimately decrease the chances of being successful at innovative new things in the organisation (Antioco et al. 2008). This view also subscribes to the axiom that any kind of constraint will ultimately hamper the motivation and inspiration of the development team and will lead to a lower level of innovative capabilities within the organisation. That said, experts across domestic and international businesses have always emphasised the need for having a set of rules and constraints that will help teams to shape their innovations in the context of a particular invention. It is important to consider that without any kind of constraints, it will be difficult for innovators to restrict their thinking on a particular subject and find a coherent way that will lead to successful innovation. In the absence of any clear-cut guidelines and interactive mechanisms with clear boundaries, the entire ecosystem involved in innovative new products and services might struggle to get desired results with proper efficiency and effectiveness. Against this particular backdrop, this research aims to offer guidelines and a conceptual Framework for discipline innovation that will help the top management and innovative teams in a company to guide their innovation efforts in a proper direction that will ultimately make the effort successful and yield desired results for the companies (Micheli et al. 2012). It is absolutely necessary for organisations to stick to a general framework and criteria so that the extensive resources that go into the innovation process will not turn out to be unproductive and futile in the end.

DISCIPLINED INNOVATION: RULES AND REGULATIONS

In stark contrast to the idea of defining the constraints rigidly, this research talks about the simple rules and regulations that can guide innovation towards success in a disciplined and steadfast manner. It is again very important to note that there is no one size fits all approach related to these rules and regulations and depending upon the industry, product category, and service domain a particular organisation is operating will determine the broad framework of the regulations and rules that one has to stick with in order to achieve desired results on the front of innovation (Dalgarno and Lee 2010). However, in order to facilitate the policymakers and teams which are involved with the innovation aspect cutting across the industry we will give a conceptual framework that can be applied across the businesses to facilitate the innovation and help them to stay ahead of the innovation curve. It is a well-accepted fact that in order to innovate organisations have to experiment and in the process of experimentation, it is not uncommon to encounter failures and deficiencies in terms of results achieved by the companies. However, when the innovation is carried out within the broad framework of discipline and rules, the value creation process during the innovation will become more streamlined and seamless. This is particularly beneficial for sustaining the incremental process of innovation rather than getting any kind of breakthrough that has the capability to comprehensively transform the fortune of the company (Sala et al. 2016). Take for instance the example of Maruti Suzuki India Limited. The Japanese car manufacturer is the largest domestic player in the passenger vehicle category and the second-largest exporter of cars from India. It has consistently remained at the forefront of the automobile revolution in the passenger vehicle category and by introducing a string of innovations of incremental nature the company has been successful in dominating the market scenario in the context of India. Taking a close look at the innovation process of Maruti Suzuki, it becomes very much apparent that the company has set the boundaries while devising an operational Framework for creativity and Real-world innovations to help teams maximize their potential while innovating new technology and breakthrough the automobile sector (Shalender and Sharma 2022). The primary idea behind the innovative aspect of Maruti Suzuki is to create value for the customer and this is the most important route each and every organisation need to keep in mind while setting out innovative new product and services for their prospective buyers. Any idea which fails to create value for the customers and rather focuses on the company should be rejected rightly. Not only this will signal of strong message from the top management about the customer orientation philosophy but also give innovating teams the idea that they need to work towards creating a sustainable value proposition for the customers (Eisingerich et al. 2010). Another important learning from the implementing innovation Framework adopted by Maruti Suzuki India Limited is there is an emphasis on a small yet steady stream of innovations rather than disrupting the market with some breakthrough invention. This has helped the organisation to remain committed to the process of innovation for longer periods of time while keeping the inspiration and motivation levels of their innovating teams high all the time. It has also sustained the constant flow of resources money and manpower from the top leadership as shareholders haven't fallen out by the commitment of the top management towards the high level of resources for innovative new tools and technologies. Another example in this regard can be of Lego toymaker which has consistently improved its product innovation by investing in incremental improvisation of the system through disciplined innovation in their functional procedures and operations. The company has always been consistent in terms of putting more effort into disciplined innovation rather than looking for results by applying all its energy and resources to radically different inventions.

DISCIPLINED INNOVATION: ADOPTION FRAMEWORK AND ROADMAP

As mentioned before in the research, the overall Framework for defining disciplined innovation within the constraints of creativity and freedom of expression need to be tailor-made for different companies and different organisations (refer to figure 1). The Framework that you can apply to your organisation needs a slight tweaking and it is only after some kind of alternation you can apply the conceptual Framework developed by the study in your organisation. Having said that the fundamental rules and requirements for sustaining disciplined innovation in a company are the same for all organisations cutting across industries and business disciplines. The first very basic rule of aligning innovation within the broader framework of discipline is to focus on the customers' needs and requirements. In other words, the organization must exhibit the highest levels of customer centricity and whatever functions they perform and whoever performs these functions must have the customer at the epicentre of all their activities (Harmancioglu et al. 2007). This automatically brings into the picture the concept of accountability towards future products that will fit the needs and requirements of the prospective buyers. The second fundamental rule that organisations have to follow is to take care of the expectations that suppliers and partners have from the businesses as the satisfaction of the entire ecosystem will also help companies innovate with the desired level of efficiency and accuracy. In fact, taking a cue from suppliers and partners can significantly enhance the success rate of innovation and make the entire process of innovation more successful than ever before. In fact, it is recommended that organisations must tap into each and every state holder involved in the ecosystem including policymakers, administrators, entrepreneurs, and funding partners to make sure that new products and services under the innovation will align with the overall trends of current and evolving markets (Kelley 2009). This process of taking feedback from each and every stakeholder of the business system evokes confidence among the partners and they will also contribute effectively to make the products and services of the company better in the future.

Figure 1. Disciplined innovation framework
Source: Authors' conceptualization

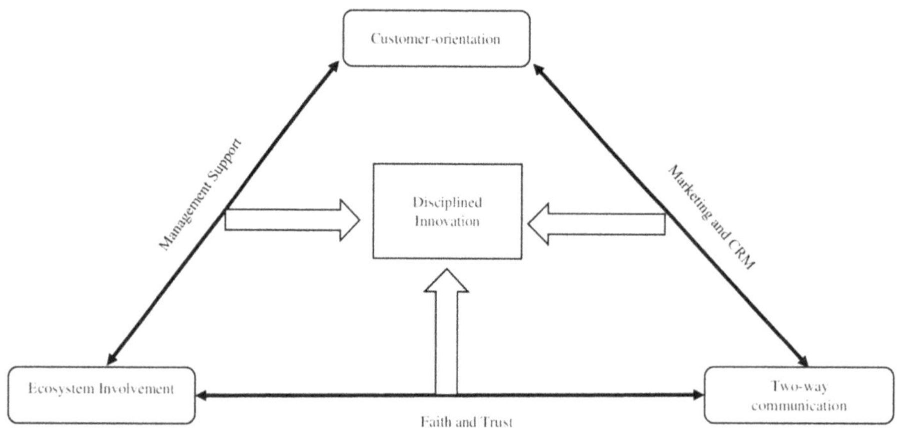

Some of the prominent examples of the company that are using their Holistic network of business partners and suppliers to make innovations in future products include Honda Cars Private Limited and Johnson and Johnson. Both organisations run open innovation programs under which they have created an entire ecosystem for sustainable innovation in their organisations and invite all stakeholders including external collaborators who can come and join the program and contribute in order to make the innovations of the company successful in the long term (Kok and Biemans 2009). These programs are of high value in their own respective industries and now other companies have also started following in their footsteps to enhance the rate of innovation in their own respective categories and domains. The third important variable that should guide disciplined innovation includes the two-way communication between all the participating stakeholders in the business ecosystem. Whether it is communication between top management and the innovative teams, the interaction between collaborators and suppliers or partners, or the exchange of information between policymakers and collaborating teams, this two-way communication will prove instrumental in setting the boundaries and aligning the innovation efforts of the organisation within the frameworks of creativity and innovation. All these three variables have innovation potential for the companies and making some kind of adjustment here and there in this model can allow companies to use this model across businesses operating in different product categories and service domains. Enabling this entire framework of discipline innovation are the three important factors of Management support, faith and trust between the partners, and capabilities of marketing and customer relationship management of the organisation (Kulshrestha et al. 2022). All these three factors will remain instrumental in determining the success rate of innovation in a company and by continually focusing on these three aspects, an organisation can ensure that their innovation will remain in a state of healthy framework and deliver new innovations in the form of products and services that will find favour within the target market.

CONCLUSION AND DISCUSSION

There is no doubt about the transformative potential of innovation to put the organisation on a path of growth and continuous improvement. Innovations are also becoming more and more instrumental in fetching more market share and aligning the long-term goals and objectives of the organisation with the expectation of the shareholders in terms of profits and margins. In such a scenario where the competition is gaining new heights of intensity with each passing day, the relevance and importance of innovation couldn't be overemphasized. That said, it is also very important to understand that innovation is a very costly and resource-intensive process. It requires huge investment and in case innovations don't prove to be as successful as shareholders and companies' top management would have wanted them to then sustaining these processes and procedures is very difficult for the companies. In order to successfully implement the strategy of innovation successfully there is a middle path that has to be taken by the companies in order to remain successful in the path of innovation for a longer time. This middle path is called disciplined innovation where creativity is contained within the product frameworks of constraint and limitations. While the team is innovating according to the changing needs and preferences of customers, they are also required to work within the product framework so that innovation does not go sideways and not lose focus on customer centricity and innovation. In order to apply the framework of discipline innovation, the role and relevance of the top management should be of utmost importance. Once the top management of the organisation is convinced about the prospects of discipline innovation then it will become easy for the entire company to innovate in a manner that is aligned with the long-term strategic objective of the company. The commitment of top management will help with the confidence of the shareholders and this will take away the pressure from innovative teams related to the securing of assets and resources required to innovate in a proper and comprehensive manner. Taking feedback from all participating stakeholders in the business ecosystem will also help the companies to understand the changing reality in a more accurate and precise manner as external communication will help them to show the mirror and break the mould of internal interactions. The Framework given by the study can be used as fundamental criteria for sustaining the process of disciplined innovation the in case of the different companies and industries. That said, the entire scheme of things needs some modification and realignment that can be done quickly without changing the basic and fundamental elements involved in the process of disciplined innovation.

REFERENCES

Antioco, M., Moenaert, R. K., & Lindgreen, A. (2008). Reducing ongoing product design decision-making bias. *Journal of Product Innovation Management*, *25*(6), 528–545. doi:10.1111/j.1540-5885.2008.00320.x

Dalgarno, B., & Lee, M. J. W. (2010). What are the learning affordances of 3-d virtual environments? *British Journal of Educational Technology*, *41*(1), 10–32. doi:10.1111/j.1467-8535.2009.01038.x

Eisingerich, A. B., Bell, S. J., & Tracey, P. (2010). How can clusters sustain performance? The role of network strength, network openness, and environmental uncertainty. *Research Policy*, *39*(2), 239–253. doi:10.1016/j.respol.2009.12.007

Harmancioglu, N., McNally, R. C., Calantone, R. J., & Durmusoglu, S. S. (2007). Your new product development (NPD) is only as good as your process: An exploratory analysis of new NPD process design and implementation. *R & D Management*, *37*(5), 399–424. doi:10.1111/j.1467-9310.2007.00486.x

Kelley, D. (2009). Adaptation and organizational connectedness in corporate radical innovation programs. *Journal of Product Innovation Management*, *26*(5), 487–501. doi:10.1111/j.1540-5885.2009.00676.x

Kok, R. A., & Biemans, W. G. (2009). Creating a market-oriented product innovation process: A contingency approach. *Technovation*, *29*(8), 517–526. doi:10.1016/j.technovation.2008.12.004

Kulshrestha, D., Tiwari, M. K., Shalender, K., & Sharma, S. (2022). Consumer Acatalepsy Towards Buying Behaviour for Need-Based Goods for Sustainability During the COVID-19 Pandemic. *Indian Journal of Marketing*, *52*(10), 50–63. doi:10.17010/ijom/2022/v52/i10/172347

Micheli, P., Jaina, J., Goffin, K., Lemke, F., & Verganti, R. (2012). Perceptions of industrial design: The "means" and the "ends". *Journal of Product Innovation Management*, *29*(5), 687–704. doi:10.1111/j.1540-5885.2012.00937.x

Sala, A., Landoni, P., & Verganti, R. (2016). Small and medium enterprises collaborations with knowledge intensive services: An explorative analysis of the impact of innovation vouchers. *R & D Management*, *46*(S1), 291–302. doi:10.1111/radm.12196

Shalender, K., & Sharma, N. (2022). Integrating strategic flexibility and marketing system to achieve sustainable competitive advantage: Conceptual refinement and framework. *World Review of Entrepreneurship, Management and Sustainable Development*, *18*(1-2), 175–194. doi:10.1504/WREMSD.2022.120794

Compilation of References

9 Rules to Success from India's Richest Man Mukesh Ambani. (2019). www.cnbctv18.com

Abdulsamad, A., Frederick, S., Guinn, A., & Gereffi, G. (2015). Pro-Poor Development and Power Asymmetries in Global Value Chains. *Duke Center on Globalization, Governance & Competitiveness*, (September), 83.

After revenues, Reliance Retail is now biggest in categories too. (2015). www.business-standard.com

Agarwal, S., Alok, S., Ghosh, P., & Gupta, S. (2020). *Fintech and credit scoring for the millennials: evidence using mobile and social footprints.* Manuscript.

Agarwal, S., Basu, D., Ghosh, P., Pareek, B., & Zhang, J. (2018a). *Demonetization and digitization.* Manuscript. doi:10.2139srn.3197990

Aggarwal, A., Chand, P. K., Jhamb, D., & Mittal, A. (2020). Leader–member exchange, work engagement, and psychological withdrawal behavior: The mediating role of psychological empowerment. *Frontiers in Psychology*, *11*, 423. doi:10.3389/fpsyg.2020.00423 PMID:32296361

Aggarwal, A., Jaisinghani, D., & Nobi, K. (2022). Effect of organizational justice and support on organizational commitment and employee turnover intentions: The mediating role of employee engagement. *International Journal of Quality and Service Sciences*, *14*(4), 525–554. doi:10.1108/IJQSS-08-2021-0112

Aggarwal, A., Lim, W. M., Jaisinghani, D., & Nobi, K. (2022). Driving service-oriented organizational citizenship behavior through error management culture. *Service Industries Journal*, 1–40. doi:10.1080/02642069.2022.2147160

Aggarwal, A., Sadhna, P., Gupta, S., Mittal, A., & Rastogi, S. (2022). Gen Z entering the workforce: Restructuring HR policies and practices for fostering the task performance and organizational commitment. *Journal of Public Affairs*, *22*(3), e2535. doi:10.1002/pa.2535

Agus, B. A. P., Mohamad, N. N., & Hussain, N. (2018). Composition of unfermented, unroasted, roasted cocoa beans and cocoa shells from Peninsular Malaysia Chocolate and Cocoa Market Size. In *Cocoa and Chocolate Market* (p. 180). Fortune Business Insight. Retrieved from https://www.fortunebusinessinsights.com/industry-reports/cocoa-and-chocolate-markethttps://www.fortunebusinessinsights.com/industry-reports/cocoa-and-chocolatemarket-100075100075

Ahmad, M., & Shah, S Z A. (2020). Overconfidence heuristic-driven bias in investment decision-making and performance: mediating effects of risk perception and moderating effects of financial literacy. *Journal of Economic and Administrative Sciences.*

Akhtar, S., Alam, M., & Khan, M. M. (2021). YES Bank Fiasco: Arrogance or Negligence. *Emerging Economies Cases Journal*, *3*(2), 95–102. doi:10.1177/25166042211061003

Alexander, S., Becky, Y., & Peter, R. (2023, January 5). Authorities move to seize funds tied to FTX. *WSJ.*

Aljazeera. (2022, December 5). FTX's Bankman-Fried says he will testify before U.S. Congress. *Aljazeera*. https://www.aljazeera.com/economy/2022/12/5/ftxs-bankman-fried-says-he-will-testify-before-us-congress

Alvia, L., & Sulistiawan, S. (2010). The examination of recency and knowledge effect in investment decision making: An experimental study. *Indonesian Journal of Accounting Research, 13*(1), 45–58.

Anand, S. (2014). *RelianceFreshDirect.com to deliver fresh groceries in Mumbai.* economictimes.indiatimes.com

Anthopoulos, L. G. (2015). Understanding the smart city domain: A literature review. *Transforming city governments for successful smart cities*, 9-21.

Antioco, M., Moenaert, R. K., & Lindgreen, A. (2008). Reducing ongoing product design decision-making bias. *Journal of Product Innovation Management, 25*(6), 528–545. doi:10.1111/j.1540-5885.2008.00320.x

Aprayuda R, Misra F, Kartika R. (2021). Does the Order of Information Affect Investors and Investment Decisions? *Experimental Investigation, Journal of Accounting and Investment, 22*(1).

Aston, D. (n.d.). *How The Founder of TaskUs Went From Zero to 1500 Employees in 5 Years.* https://www.incomediary.com/bryce-maddock-interview/

Austin, J., Stevenson, H., & Wei-Skillern, J. (2006). Social and Commercial Entrepreneurship: Same, Different, or Both? *Entrepreneurship Theory and Practice, 30*(1), 1–22. doi:10.1111/j.1540-6520.2006.00107.x

Azizi, M. R., Atlasi, R., Ziapour, A., Abbas, J., & Naemi, R. (2021). Innovative human resource management strategies during the COVID-19 pandemic: A systematic narrative review approach. *Heliyon, 7*(6), e07233. doi:10.1016/j.heliyon.2021.e07233 PMID:34124399

Baack, D. W., Dow, D., Parente, R., & Bacon, D. R. (2015). Confirmation bias in individual-level perceptions of psychic distance: An experimental investigation. *Journal of International Business Studies, 46*(8), 938–959. doi:10.1057/jibs.2015.19

Bailey, R. (2014). *RIL plans to launch Jio with 2,000 Digital Xpress Mini outlets.* economictimes.indiatimes.com

Baker, H. K., & Nofsinger, J. R. (2002). Psychological biases of investors. *Financial Services Review, 11*(2), 97.

Baker, H. K., & Ricciardi, V. (2014). How biases affect investor behavior. *The European Financial Review*, 7–10.

Banker, D. V., & Bhal, K. T. (2018). Understanding compassion from practicing managers' perspective: Vicious and virtuous forces in business organizations. *Global Business Review, 20*(6), 1–17. doi:10.1177/0972150917749279

Bansal, A., Katoch, G., Arora, N., Sharma, A., Bhadula, R. C., & Agarwal, S. (2022, April). Big data analytics in the Indian banking sector: An empirical study. In *2022 2nd International Conference on Advance Computing and Innovative Technologies in Engineering (ICACITE)* (pp. 1624-1627). IEEE.

BansalT. (2020). Behavioral finance and COVID-19: cognitive errors that determine the financial future. SSRN. doi:10.2139/ssrn.3595749

Bashir, T., Mehmood, F., & Khan, A. (2019). *Comforting Investments are Rarely Profitable: Impediments in Investor Decision Making.* Global Social Sciences Review.

Bashir, T., Rasheed, S., Raftar, S., & Fatima, S., & Maqsood, S. (2013). Impact of behavioral biases on investor decision making: Male vs female. *Journal of Business and Management, 10*(3), 60–68.

Bass, B. M. (1985). *Leadership and performance beyond expectations. New York, NY: The Free Press.*

BatesA. N. (2020). Investor Behavior in the Midst of a Global Pandemic. SSRN.

Beg, M. S., Ahmad, S., Jan, K., & Bashir, K. (2017). Status, supply chain and processing of cocoa A review. *Trends in Food Science & Technology*, *66*, 108–116. doi:10.1016/j.tifs.2017.06.007

Ben, C. (2022, December 17). The New CEO of FTX on How to Clean Up a Mess. *WSJ*.

Bennis, W., & Nanus, B. (1985). Leaders: The strategies for taking charge. Harper & Row.

Bhambani, S. (2020). *Challenging corporate policies with people-first practices with Us in India*. TaskUs. https://www.taskus.com/blog/challenging-corporate-policies-with-people-first-practices-with-us-in-india/

Bhasin, M. L. (2015). An Empirical Study of Frauds in the Banks. *European Journal of Business and Social Sciences, 4*(7), 1-12.

Bloomberg. (2022, December 15). FTX downfall: Bahamas challenges the U.S. Case. *Mint*.

Brown, A. L., Bakke, A. J., & Hopfer, H. (2020). Understanding American premium chocolate consumer perception of craft chocolate and desirable product attributes using focus groups and projective mapping. *PLoS ONE, 15*(11). doi:10.1371/journal.pone.0240177

Bruckner, M., LaFleur, M., & Pitterle, I. (2017). Frontier issues: The impact of the technological revolution on labour markets and income distribution. Department of Economic & Social Affairs, UN.

Buller, D. B., & Burgoon, J. K. (1996). Interpersonal deception theory. *Communication Theory*, *6*(3), 203–242. doi:10.1111/j.1468-2885.1996.tb00127.x

Burns, J. M. (1978). *Leadership*. Harper & Row.

Businesswire. (2019). *TaskUs Wins 2019 Best Places to Work For Second Year in a Row*. https://www.businesswire.com/news/home/20191213005067/en/TaskUs-Wins-2019-Best-Places-to-Work-For-Second-Year-in-a-Row

Cacao, B. G. (2021, November 15). *Global Cocoa Market Study*. Retrieved from GAIA CACAO: https://www.gaiacacao.com/

Cadby, J. (2021). Can COVID-19 Melt the Craft Chocolate Industry? *Food Ethics*, *6*(2), 8. doi:10.100741055-021-00087-8 PMID:33937518

Cao, H. H., Han, B., Hirshleifer, S., & Zhang, H. H. (2011). Fear of the unknown: Familiarity and economic decisions. *Review of Finance*, *15*(1), 173–206. doi:10.1093/rof/rfp023

CBI. (2018b). Multisectoral Value Chain Analysis: 'Connecting Central America.' In *Organización de las Naciones Unidas para la Alimentación y la Agricultura*. http://www.oie.sieca.int/documentos/ver/Multisectoral VCA CA – Final report. Pdf

CBI. (2020f, September). *Entering the European market for certified cocoa*. CBI Ministry of Foreign Affairs. https://www. cbi.eu/market-information/cocoa-cocoaproducts/certifiedcocoa/market-entry

CBI. (2021). *The European market potential for semi-finished cocoa products*. CBI Ministry of Foreign Affairs.

Chakrabarty, K. C. (2013, July). Fraud in the Banking Sector—Causes, Concerns and Cures. In *National Conference on Financial Fraud organised by ASSOCHAM, New Delhi* (Vol. 26). https://www.bankinfosecurity.com/5-tips-to-reduce-banking-fraud-a-2534

Chang, C.-H. (2008). The impact of behavioral pitfalls on investors' decisions: The disposition effect in the Taiwanese warrant market. *Social Behavior and Personality*, *36*(5), 617–634. doi:10.2224bp.2008.36.5.617

Chaudhary, A. K. (2013). Impact of behavioral finance in investment decisions and strategies–a fresh approach. *International Journal of Management Research and Business Strategy, 2*(2), 85-92.

Chauhan, C. P. (2016, Sep 29). Premium Motorcycles Gaining in Popularity and Sales. *Business Today.* https://www.businesstoday.in/opinion/perspective/story/premium-motorcycles-gaining-in-popularity-and-sales-144791-2016-09-29

Chen, M., Cheng, H., Du, Y., Xu, M., Jiang, W., & Wang, C. (2021). *Two Wrongs Don't Make a Right: Combating Confirmation Bias in Learning with Label Noise.* Academic Press.

Chen, X., Jiang, K., Zhu, Y., Wang, X., & Yun, T. (2021). Individual tree crown segmentation directly from uav-borne lidar data using the pointnet of deep learning. *Forests, 12*(2), 1–22. doi:10.3390/f12020131

Chief Investment Strategist at Geojit Financial Services. (2020). *Lessons from the Yes Bank saga: Eternal vigilance is the price of financial stability.* https://www.moneycontrol.com/news/business/markets/lessons-from-the-yes-bank-saga-eternal-vigilance-is-the-price-of-financial-stability-5034861.html

Cho, A. H. (2006). Politics, Values and Social Entrepreneurship: A Critical Appraisal. In J. Mair, J. Robinson, & K. Hockerts (Eds.), *Social Entrepreneurship* (pp. 34–56). doi:10.1057/9780230625655_4

Chotalia, P. (2012). Evaluation of financial health of sampled private sector banks with Altman Z-score model. *Circulation in more than 85 countries, 7.*

Claw, J. (2022, June 27). *Malaysia Chocolate & Cacao Culture.* Retrieved from Dame caco: https://damecacao.com/malaysian-chocolate-cacao-culture/

Cocoa and Chocolate Market by Type. (2020, August). Retrieved from https://www.marketsandmarkets.com/Market-Reports/cocoa-chocolate-markethttps://www.marketsandmarkets.com/Market-Reports/cocoa-chocolate-market226179290.html226179290.html

Comparably. (n.d.). *TaskUs Competitors.* https://www.comparably.com/companies/taskus/competitors

Conger, J. A., & Kanungo, R. A. (1987). Towards a behavioral theory of charismatic leadership in organizational settings. *Academy of Management Review, 12*(4), 637–647. doi:10.2307/258069

Consulting, E. (2020). Reseña del Mercado de Cacao Mundial. EUROMONITOR).

Cornelius, C. (2022, December 6). Another year of Crypto Winter likely before turnaround—Anastasios Papakonstantinou. *Kitco.* https://www.kitco.com/news/2022-12-06/Another-year-of-Crypto-Winter-likely-before-turnaround-Anastasios-Papakonstantinou.html?sitetype=fullsite

Corzo, T., Prat, M., & Vaquero, E. (2014). Vaquero E, Behavioral Finance in Joseph de la Vega's Confusion de Confusiones. *Journal of Behavioral Finance, 15*(4), 341–350. doi:10.1080/15427560.2014.968722

Crunchbase. (2022, December 14). FTX Ventures. *Crunchbase.* https://www.crunchbase.com/organization/ftx-ventures

Čuláková, T., Kotrus, P., Uhlírová, A., & Jirásek, M. (2017). *The overconfidence bias and CEO: A literature overview.* Academic Press.

Cummings, A., & Oldham, G. R. (1997). Enhancing creativity: Managing work contexts for the high potential employee. *California Management Review, 40*(1), 22–38. doi:10.2307/41165920

Dalgarno, B., & Lee, M. J. W. (2010). What are the learning affordances of 3-d virtual environments? *British Journal of Educational Technology, 41*(1), 10–32. doi:10.1111/j.1467-8535.2009.01038.x

Dhiresh, & Abhishek, & Sagar. (2022). Analyzing the linkage between GDP, Energy Consumption and Carbon Emission: Evidence from major Economies. *The Indian Economic Journal*, *4*, 67.

Dilla, W., & Steinbart, P. J. (2005). Relative Weighting of Common and Unique Balanced Scorecard Measures by Knowledgeable Decision Makers. *Behavioral Research in Accounting*, *17*(1), 43–53. doi:10.2308/bria.2005.17.1.43

Dubinsky, A. J., Yammarino, F. J., & Jolson, M. A. (1995). An examination of linkages between personal, characteristics and dimension of transformational leadership. *Journal of Business and Psychology*, *9*(3), 315–335. doi:10.1007/BF02230972

Dutta, B. (2022, September 5). *Business standard*. https://www.business-standard.com/article/finance/yes-bank-plans-to-invest-up-to-rs-350-crore-for-20-stake-in-jc-flowers-arc-122071801173_1.html

Economic Times. (2014). *RBI to propose steps to reduce window dressing by banks*. https://m.economictimes.com/news/economy/policy/rbi-to-propose-steps-to-reduce-window-dressing-by-banks/articleshow/33099560.cms

Economic Times. (2022, January 19). *Toyota-Suzuki alliance scales up in India with shared platforms, tech, products*. Retrieved March 3, 2023, from https://economictimes.indiatimes.com/industry/auto/cars-uvs/toyota-suzuki-alliance-scales-up-in-india-with-shared-platforms-tech-products/articleshow/89043745.cms

Economy, F. (2022). *Focus Economy: Over the last month, cocoa prices have decreased, mostly because supply prospects are looking good. May saw a 3.8% decrease in cocoa prices from April, with the average price per metric tonne coming in at USD 2,364. Additionally, compared to the same month*. Author.

Eisingerich, A. B., Bell, S. J., & Tracey, P. (2010). How can clusters sustain performance? The role of network strength, network openness, and environmental uncertainty. *Research Policy*, *39*(2), 239–253. doi:10.1016/j.respol.2009.12.007

Elfaki, I. (2008). *Magic of leadership: How to become effective leader*. Certainty House for Publishing and Distribution.

Elizabeth Holloway, K. A. (2018, May 30). Retrieved from Chocolate Challenges: The Social, Technological, and Environmental Issues Facing the Cocoa Industry. *Red Vere Media*. https://redvervemedia.com/chocolate-challenges-the-social-technological

Elsbach, K. D., & Sutton, R. I. (1992). Acquiring organizational legitimacy through illegitimate actions: A marriage of institutional and impression management theories. *Academy of Management Journal*, *35*(4), 699–738. doi:10.2307/256313

Entrepreneur 360™. (2017). *Entrepreneur India*. https://www.entrepreneur.com/360/2017

Erb, K. P. (2015, August 24). *Debt, Equity and Startup money*. Retrieved 29 May 2023, from Forbes website: https://www.forbes.com/sites/kellyphillipserb/2015/08/24/debt-equity-and-startup-money/

Explainers, F. P. (2022, November 14). Who is Nishad Singh, the Indian-origin techie under scrutiny for crypto exchange FTX's collapse? *First Post*. https://www.firstpost.com/explainers/nishad-singh-indian-origin-engineer-crypto-exchange-ftx-collapse-sam-bankman-fried-11622961.html

Faisal, S., Shurideh, A., Dmour, A. S., & Al-Dmour, R. (2021). *Understanding the Influences of Cognitive Biases on Financial Decision Making During Normal and COVID-19 Pandemic Situation in the United Arab Emirates*. Academic Press.

FE Online. (2020, Oct. 8). *Mukesh Ambani roots for India to become a global leader, says Jio conceived to enable this journey*. Author.

FFC. (2022, January 10). *Federation of Cocoa Commerce*. Retrieved from Agricultural Practices: https://www.cocoafederation.com/education/agricultural-practices#Quality%20control

Fichman, M., & Levinthal, D. A. (1991). Honeymoons and the liability of adolescence: A new perspective on duration dependence in social and organizational relationships. *Academy of Management Review*, *16*(2), 442–468. doi:10.2307/258870

Forbes. (2021). https://www.forbes.com/sites/billconerly/2021/11/13/oil-forecast-2022-and-beyond/?sh=4bc9bf616a67

Fortune. (2022, April 18). Retrieved from Market Research Report: https://www.fortunebusinessinsights.com/industry-reports/cocoa-and-chocolate-

Fund, I. M. (2023, January 6). *International Monetary Fund*. Retrieved from Global price of Cocoa (PCOCOUSDM): https://fred.stlouisfed.org/series/PCOCOUSDM#0

Ganguly. (2019). *Reliance e-commerce venture to be fueled by $1.4 Bn West Bengal investment.* inc42.com

Gansky, L. (2010). *The mesh: Why the future of business is sharing*. Penguin.

Gkritsi, E. (2022, December 6). Goldman Sachs to Spend "Tens of Millions" on Discounted Crypto Investments After FTX Implosion: Report. *Coindesk*. https://www.coindesk.com/business/2022/12/06/goldman-sachs-to-spend-tens-of-millions-on-discounted-crypto-investments-after-ftx-implosion-report/

Gleasure, R. (2015). Resistance to crowdfunding among entrepreneurs: An impression management perspective. *The Journal of Strategic Information Systems*, *24*(4), 219–233.

Global Cocoa and Chocolate Market: Market Segments: By Cocoa Type; By Chocolate Type ; By Application ; By and Region – Analysis of Market Size, Share & Trends for 2014 – 2019 and Forecasts to 2030 . (2022). Academic Press.

Goldstein, M., & Yaffe-Ballany, D. (2023, January 19). FTX assets: Billions in cash and crypto located. *Business Standard*.

Gordon, C. (2019). What is Craft Chocolate? In *Dalloway Chocolate* (pp. 1–6). https://www.dallowaychocolate.com/blogs/news/what-is-craft-chocolate

Grant, A. (2019). A personal perspective on neuro-linguistic programming: Reflecting on the tension between personal experience and evidence-based practice. *International Coaching Psychology Review*, *14*(1), 45–56. doi:10.53841/bpsicpr.2019.14.1.45

Grover, P., Kar, A. K., & Ilavarasan, P. V. (2017). Understanding nature of social media usage by mobile wallets service providers–an exploration through SPIN framework. *Procedia Computer Science*, *122*, 292–299. doi:10.1016/j.procs.2017.11.372

Hall, R. D., & Rowland, C. A. (2016). Leadership development for managers in turbulent times. *Journal of Management Development*, *35*(8), 942–955. doi:10.1108/JMD-09-2015-0121

Haque, A. B., Bhushan, B., & Dhiman, G. (2022). Conceptualizing smart city applications: Requirements, architecture, security issues, and emerging trends. *Expert Systems: International Journal of Knowledge Engineering and Neural Networks*, *39*(5), e12753. doi:10.1111/exsy.12753

Hariyati, W. E. (2022). Farmers' contributions in the establishment of value-added from holistic cocoa processing: A case study in Trenggalek Regency, East Java. *Earth and Environmental Science,* 8.

Harmancioglu, N., McNally, R. C., Calantone, R. J., & Durmusoglu, S. S. (2007). Your new product development (NPD) is only as good as your process: An exploratory analysis of new NPD process design and implementation. *R & D Management*, *37*(5), 399–424. doi:10.1111/j.1467-9310.2007.00486.x

Harte, A. (2020, April 2). 3 HR automation challenges during the Covid-19 pandemic. *FlowForma*. https://www.flowforma.com/blog/3-challenges-faced-by-human-resources-during-the-covid-19-pandemic

Hartono, J. (2004). The recency effect of accounting information. *Gadjah Mada International Journal of Business*, *6*(1), 85–116. doi:10.22146/gamaijb.5536

Henninger, C. E., Alevizou, P. J., & Oates, C. J. (2016). What is sustainable fashion? *Journal of Fashion Marketing and Management*, *20*(4), 400–416.

Henseler, J., Ringle, C. M., & Sarstedt, M. (2015). A new criterion for assessing discriminant validity in variance-based structural equation modeling. *Journal of the Academy of Marketing Science*, *43*(1), 115–135. doi:10.100711747-014-0403-8

High, D. (2020, January 16). *Nestle*. Retrieved from Sustainable Cocoa: https://www.nestle.com/sustainability/sustainable-sourcing/cocoa

Hogarth, R. M., & Einhorn, H. J. (1992). Order effects in belief updating: The belief-adjustment model. *Cognitive Psychology*, *24*(1), 1–55. doi:10.1016/0010-0285(92)90002-J

Hosnan, D. M. (2009, November 13). *Anim Agro Technology*. Retrieved from Cocoa Rehabilitation: http://animhosnan.blogspot.com/search?q=cocoa

Hotten, R. (2015, December 15). *Volkswagen: The scandal explained*. BBC. https://www. bbc.com/news/business-34324772

Hottenrott, H., Rexhäuser, S., & Veugelers, R. (2016). Organizational change and the productivity effects of green technology adoption. *Resource and Energy Economics*, *43*, 172–194.

Hougaard, R., Carter, J., & Hobson, N. (2020). *Compassionate Leadership Is Necessary-but Not Sufficient*. www.hbr.org

House, R. J. (1977). A 1976 theory of charismatic leadership. In J. G. Hunt & L. L. Larson (Eds.), *Leadership: The cutting edge*. Southern Illinois University Press.

Huang, H. H., Hsu, J., & Ku, C.-Y. (2012). Understanding the role of computer-mediated counter-argument in countering confirmation bias. *Decision Support Systems*, *53*(3), 438–447. doi:10.1016/j.dss.2012.03.009

Hütz-Adams, F., Huber, C., Knoke, I., Morazán, D. P., & Mürlebach, M. (2016). Strengthening the competitiveness of cocoa production and improving the income of cocoa producers in West and Central Africa. *Institut Für Ökonomie Und Ökumene*, *49*(0), 156. Retrieved from https://suedwind-institut.de/files/Suedwind/Publikationen/2017/2017-06 strengthening the competitiveness of cocoa production and improving the income of cocoa producers in West and Central Africa.pdf

IANS. (2022, December 12). FTX collapse: U.S. asks listed companies to disclose exposure to beleaguered crypto firms. *Money Life*. https://www.moneylife.in/article/ftx-collapse-us-asks-listed-companies-to-disclose-exposure-to-beleaguered-crypto-firms/69152.html

IBEF. (2022). *Report on IT and BPM*. Retrieved from https://www.ibef.org/industry/indian-it-and-ites-industry-analysis-presentation

ICCO. (2022, October). *Market Report*. https://www.icco.org/wp-content/uploads/ICCOMonthlyCocoa-Market-Report-October-2022.pdf

Ikram, M. (2022). The transition toward green economy: Technological Innovation's role in the fashion industry. *Current Opinion in Green and Sustainable Chemistry*, 100657.

India, S. (2016). *Ministry of Commerce and Industry*. Government of India, Delhi, India https://www. startup India. gov. in/content/sih/en/about_us/about-us. html

IndiaE. https://www.entrepreneur.com/company/taskus

Intelligence, M. (2020). *Chocolate Market (2021-2026) Industry Share, Size, Growth.* Retrieved from https://www.mordorintelli-gence.com/industry-reports/chocolate-market

It is not just about micro-inequities, it is about inclusion: Seema Nair, Reliance Industries Limited. (n.d.). www.peoplematters.in

Jain, D. (2019). Corporate Governance Practices: A Comparative Study of Bank of Baroda & Yes Bank. International Journal of Management. *IT & Engineering*, *9*(6), 237–254.

JainE.JainT. K. (2019). Rainwater Harvesting–The Case Study Related to India's Thar Desert. Available at SSRN 3327743. doi:10.2139/ssrn.3327743

JainT. K. (2019). Concept of Happy City: The Smart Cities of the Future. Available at SSRN 3314531. doi:10.2139/ssrn.3314531

JainT. K. (2019). Smart Cities and Happy Cities in India–A Review Paper. Available at SSRN 3367763. doi:10.2139/ssrn.3367763

Jaiswal, A., & Arun, C. J. (2022). *Working from home during COVID-19 and its impact on Indian employees' stress and creativity.* Asian Business and Management. doi:10.105741291-022-00202-5

Jaiwar, P. (2019). *Mukesh Ambani vs Jeff Bezos vs Jack Ma – The Bulls of Indian e-commerce! Reliance Industries' massive leap of faith.* www.zeebiz.com

Jiménez Tobón, C. S. (2015). Estado legal mundial del cadmio en cacao (Theobroma cacao): fantasía o realidad. *Producción + Limpia, 10*(1), 89–104. doi:10.22507/pml.v10n1a8

Jin, B. E., & Shin, D. C. (2020). Changing the game to compete: Innovations in the fashion retail industry from the disruptive business model. *Business Horizons*, *63*(3), 301–311.

John Makinde, O., Okunade, S., Opoola, E., Sikiru, A. B., O. Ajide, S., & Elaigwu, S. (2019). *Exploration of Cocoa (Theobroma cacao) By-Products as Valuable Potential Resources in Livestock Feeds and Feeding Systems. Theobroma Cacao – Deploying Science for.* Academic Press.

Jonathan, R. (2022, December 15). FTX Executive Warned Funds were Mixed with Alameda's. *Wall Street Journal.*

Joshua, O., & Stefania, P. (2022, December 17). U.S. watchdogs outline sprawling case against Bankman-Fried. *Financial Times Weekend.*

Jun, F., Chunmei, G., & Jun, Z. (2010). *A Study of Oral Communication Re- search Based on Representational Systems.* IEEE. https://ieeexplore.ieee.org/abstract/document/5660840/

Kafayat, A. (2014). Interrelationship of biases: effect investment decisions ultimately. *Theoretical and Applied Economics, Asociatia Generala a Economistilor din Romania-AGER, 6*(595), 85-110.

Kalkreuter, B. (2020). Anyone's Heritage? Indian Fashion Design's Relationships with Craft between Local Guardianship and Valorization of Global Fashion. *Fashion Practice*, *12*(2), 264–287.

Kalm, K., & Norris, D. (2018). Visual recency bias is explained by a mixture model of internal representations. *Journal of Vision (Charlottesville, Va.)*, *18*(7), 1. doi:10.1167/18.7.1 PMID:29971347

Kang, Y., Cai, Z., Tan, C. W., Huang, Q., & Liu, H. (2020). Natural language processing (NLP) in management research: A literature review. *Journal of Management Analytics*, *7*(2), 139–172. doi:10.1080/23270012.2020.1756939

Kapoor, A., Sindwani, R., & Goel, M. (2020). Mobile wallets: Theoretical and empirical analysis. *Global Business Review*. Advance online publication. doi:10.1177/0972150920961254

Kaur, S. (2023). *Simple Kaur.* Chandigarh: Simple Kaur. Retrieved from https://simplekaur.com/Kaur

Kaur, M., Verma, R., & Otoo, F. N. K. (2021). Emotions in leader's crisis communication: Twitter sentiment analysis during COVID-19 outbreak. *Journal of Human Behavior in the Social Environment*, *31*(1-4), 362–372. doi:10.1080/10911359.2020.1829239

Kaur, N., & Parihar, A. (2022). Hybrid Model of Work and Employee Attitudes: Challenges to HR Leadership in the Context of Indian Organizations. *NeuroQuantology : An Interdisciplinary Journal of Neuroscience and Quantum Physics*, *20*(10), 5656–5667. https://doi.org/NQ.2022.20.10.NQ55565

Kelkar Nachiket. (2020). How much is Yes Bank worth? Re 1, say Macquarie, JP Morgan. *The Week Magazine*. https://www.theweek.in/news/biz-tech/2020/03/05/how-much-is-yes-bank-worth-re-1-say-macquarie-jp-morgan.html

Kelley, D. (2009). Adaptation and organizational connectedness in corporate radical innovation programs. *Journal of Product Innovation Management*, *26*(5), 487–501. doi:10.1111/j.1540-5885.2009.00676.x

Kelly, L. (2022). *Overcome Outsourcing Cost Limitations: The Competitive Advantage of Quality Over Price.* https://www.taskus.com/insights/overcome-outsourcing-cost-limitations-the-competitive-advantage-of-quality-over-price/

Kok, R. A., & Biemans, W. G. (2009). Creating a market-oriented product innovation process: A contingency approach. *Technovation*, *29*(8), 517–526. doi:10.1016/j.technovation.2008.12.004

Kotera, Y., & Van Gordon, W. (2019). Japanese managers' experiences of neuro-linguistic programming: A qualitative investigation. *The Journal of Mental Health Training, Education and Practice*, *14*(3), 174–185. doi:10.1108/JMHTEP-06-2018-0033

Kulshrestha, D., Tiwari, M. K., Shalender, K., & Sharma, S. (2022). Consumer Acatalepsy Towards Buying Behaviour for Need-Based Goods for Sustainability During the COVID-19 Pandemic. *Indian Journal of Marketing*, *52*(10), 50–63. doi:10.17010/ijom/2022/v52/i10/172347

Kumar, A. (2013). *Mukesh tops retailer list, too.* www.business-standard.com

Kumar, N. S., Kapoor, S., & Gupta, S.K. (2021). Impact of Covid-19 on the future of HR in India's service sector. *Turkish Journal of Physiotherapy and Rehabilitation, 32*(3), 34941-34949. https://www.researchgate.net/publication/357738038_Impact_of_Covid-19_on_the_future_of_HR_in_India's_service_sector

Kumar, M. (2016). *Reliance Retail shuts 20 stores, to launch Reliance Smart.* FashionUnited.

Kwatra. (2020). Behavioral Finance and Stock Performance: Biases Influencing the Market. *IOSR Journal of Humanities And Social Science, 25*(7), 66-69.

Lathe, A. S., Jain, S., & Anand, S. (2020). An Empirical Examination of the Impact of Locus of Control on Investor Behavioral Biases. *International Journal of Management*, *11*(1), 98–107.

Le Xuan, T. (2019). *Digital marketing strategies of luxury fashion brands in China: The Gucci brand.* Academic Press.

Leong, L. Y., Hew, T. S., Ooi, K. B., & Wei, J. (2020). Predicting mobile wallet resistance: A two-staged structural equation modeling-artificial neural network approach. *International Journal of Information Management*, *51*, 102047. doi:10.1016/j.ijinfomgt.2019.102047

Levy, D. S., Frethey-Bentham, C., & Cheung, W. K. S. (2020). Asymmetric framing effects and market familiarity: Experimental evidence from the real estate market. *Journal of Property Research*, *37*(1), 85–104. doi:10.1080/09599916.2020.1713858

Lim, G. Y. (2019). Barry Callebaut eyes India's fast-growing chocolate industry with new factory. *William Reed*. https://www.foodnavigator- asia.com/Article/2019/08/05/Barry-Callebaut-eyes-India-s-fast-growing-chocolate

Linder-Pelz, S. (2010). *NLP coaching: An evidence-based approach for coaches, leaders and individuals*. Kogan Page Publishers.

Liu, B., Qi, L., & Xu, L. A. (2017). Cross-level impact study of inclusive leadership on employee feedback-seeking behavior. *Journal of Management*, *14*, 677–685. doi:10.3969/j.issn.1672-884x.2017.05.005

Liu, Y., Zhu, W., & Zhao, S. M. (2016). Research on the influence of inclusive leadership on the relationship of the employment relationship and employees' active behavior. *Manag. Rep.*, *10*, 1482–1489.

Loewenstein, Weber, Hsee, &Welch. (2001). *The Role of Emotions in Financial Decision Making*. Academic Press.

Luu, T. B. (2014). Behavior Pattern of Individual Investors in Stock Market. *International Journal of Business and Management*, *9*(1), 1–16.

MacArthur, D. (1944, April 14). Getting facts to the people. *Tuscaloosa (AL) News*. https://www.barrypopik.com/index.php/new_york_city/entry/i_am_a_firm_believer_in_the_people_if_given_the_truth_they_can_meet_any_nat

Mackey, J., McIntosh, S., & Phipps, C. (2020). *Conscious leadership: elevating humanity through business*. Penguin.

Mahony, T. (2007). *Making your words work: Using NLP to improve communication, learning and behaviour*. Crown House Publishing.

Mair, J., & Marti, I. (2006). Social Entrepreneurship Research: A Source of Explanation,BPrediction, and Delight. *Journal of World Business*, *41*(1), 36–44. doi:10.1016/j.jwb.2005.09.002

Malik, A. R., Singh, P., & Chan, C. (2017). High potential programs and employee outcomes: The roles of organizational trust and employee attributions. *Career Development International*, *22*(7), 772–796. doi:10.1108/CDI-06-2017-0095

Manikandan, A. (2020, March 7). *The Economic Times*. https://economictimes.indiatimes.com/industry/banking/finance/banking/digital-payments-hit-cos-tap-alternatives/articleshow/74520306.cms

Martin, C. (2017, August 31). *Sizing the craft chocolate market*. FCCI. https://www.chocolateinstitute.org/post/sizing-the-craft-chocolate-market

Martins, A. T. (2018, February 8). *Advantages/disadvantages of raising fund from angel investors*. Retrieved 29 May 2023, from Profitable Venture website: https://www.profitableventure.com/advantages-raising-fund-angels/

McAndrews. (2017). *How Familiarity Bias May Impact Your Investment Decision-Making*. WrapManager.

Meghmala. (2022, December 12). FTX's Sam Bankman-Fried under Criminal Probe for Market Rig. *Analytics Insight*. https://www.analyticsinsight.net/ftxs-sam-bankman-fried-under-criminal-probe-for-market-rig/

Message from our Chairman and RF Founder-Chairperson to the Reliance Family: WE CARE: Honouring the promise of 'One Reliance Family. (2021, June 3). www.ril.com

Metawa, N., Hassan, M. K., Metawa, S., & Safa, M. F. (2019). Impact of behavioral factors on investors' financial decisions: case of the Egyptian stock market. *International Journal of Islamic and Middle Eastern Finance and Management*.

Michaels, D. (2023, January 20). Crypto lender Nexo settles with SEC. *Wall Street Journal*.

Micheli, P., Jaina, J., Goffin, K., Lemke, F., & Verganti, R. (2012). Perceptions of industrial design: The "means" and the "ends". *Journal of Product Innovation Management, 29*(5), 687–704. doi:10.1111/j.1540-5885.2012.00937.x

Middleton, C. (2011). *Analysis of the Identification and development of High Potential Employees* [Doctoral dissertation]. University of Wisconsin-Stout.

Mile, R. (n.d.). *World's Billionaires' List – The Richest in 2022.* www.forbes.com/billionaires

Milligan, E. (2020 September 15). Uber Tried to Conceal Driver Photo Fraud, London Cabbies Say. *Bloomberg*, https://www.bloombergquint.com/business/uber-tried-to-conceal-driver-photo-fraud-black-cab-drivers-say

Mint. (2021, February 17). *Toyota-Suzuki alliance expands in India with two new models.* Retrieved March 3, 2023, from https://www.livemint.com/companies/news/toyota-suzuki-alliance-expands-in-india-with-two-new-models-11613667886734.html

Mirzaei, S., & Zangiabadi, A. (2021). Studying and Complying Dimensions, Indicators and Variables Related to a Happy City. *International Review for Spatial Planning and Sustainable Development, 9*(2), 94–111. doi:10.14246/irspsda.9.2_94

Mishra, A. K. (2014, Feb 7). Triumph wills sells 1,000 bikes by End of 2014. *Forbes India.* https://www.forbesindia.com/article/auto-expo/triumph-will-sell-1000-bikes-by-end-of- 2014/37117/1

Mitter. (2018). *Mukesh Ambani rides on Jio success to become Asia's richest man, surpasses Alibaba founder Jack Ma.* yourstory.com

Mohanty, D. (2020). Toyota-Suzuki alliance in India: Strategic choices and performance outcomes. *Journal of Business Research, 110*, 297–306. doi:10.1016/j.jbusres.2019.12.044

Moneycontrol. (2020). *JP Morgan cuts YES target to Rs 1 after stake sale report.* moneycontrol.com

MPIC. (2022a, November 16). *Kementerian Perusahaan Perladangan dan Komoditi.* Academic Press.

MPIC. (2022b, November 18). *Ministry of plantation industries and commodities (MPIC).* Author.

MPIC. (n.d.). https://www.mpic.gov.my/mpi/en/statistic/prestasiperdagangan-main

Mukerjee, W. (2019, Jan. 26). *Reliance Retail to open grocery stores in tier III, IV towns.* economictimes.indiatimes.com

Mukherjee, A. (2018). *Amazon's real rival in India isn't Walmart, it's Reliance.* www.livemint.com

Mukherjee, A. (2019). *Jeff Bezos vs Mukesh Ambani is the bout that had to happen.* economictimes.indiatimes.com

Murray, P. (2013). Leading by design: Cultivating self-leadership for sustainability. In Motivating Change: Sustainable Design and Behaviour in the Built Environment (pp. 159-184). Routledge.

Nasution, S. (2017). Effect of Evidence Order, the Cognitive Style and Personality of the Revision Process Confidence. *Accounting National Symposium X.*

Natalie, S. (2022, November 28). Crypto firm BlockFi files for bankruptcy after FTX collapse. *BBC.* https://www.bbc.com/news/business-63786201

Nayantara, R. (2018). 3 reasons cited by RBI for sacking Rana Kapoor as CEO and now his board seat in jeopardy. *The Economics Times.* https://economictimes.indiatimes.com/industry/banking/finance/banking/3-reasons-cited-by-rbi-for-sacking-rana-kapoor-as-ceo-and-now-his-board-seat-in-jeopardy/articleshow/65904385.cms

Nedra, B. A., Sharma, S., & Dakhli, A. (2015). Perception and motivation to purchase organic products in Mediterranean countries: An empirical study in Tunisian context. *Journal of Research in Marketing and Entrepreneurship.*

Nelson, J. A. (2014). The power of stereotyping and confirmation bias to overwhelm accurate assessment: The case of economics, gender, and risk aversion. *Journal of Economic Methodology*, *21*(3), 211–231. doi:10.1080/1350178X.2014.939691

Nesto, B. (2010). Discovering terroir in the world of chocolate. *Gastronomica*, *10*(1), 131–135. doi:10.1525/gfc.2010.10.1.131 PMID:21539057

New York Times. (2022, December 13). Explained: How the collapse of FTX is giving Binance a chance to become the new face of crypto. *First Post*. https://www.firstpost.com/world/explained-how-the-collapse-of-ftx-is-giving-binance-a-chance-to-become-the-new-face-of-crypto-11800601.html

Nickerson, R. S. (1998). Confirmation Bias: A Ubiquitous Phenomenon in Many Guises. *Review of General Psychology*, *2*(2), 175–220. doi:10.1037/1089-2680.2.2.175

Nugent, N., & Rhinard, M. (2019). The 'political' roles of the European Commission. *Journal of European Integration*, *41*(2), 203–220. doi:10.1080/07036337.2019.1572135

Oberholzer, C. (2014). *The role of Neuro Linguistic Programming in improving organisational leadership through intrapersonal communication development* [Doctoral dissertation]. University of Pretoria.

Onsomu, Z. N. (2014). The impact of Behavioral biases on investor decisions in Kenya: Male vs Female. *Impact Journals*, *2*(6), 87–92.

Oruh, E. S., Mordi, C., Dibia, C. H., & Ajonbadi, H. A. (2021). Exploring compassionate managerial leadership style in reducing employee stress level during COVID-19 crisis: The case of Nigeria. *Employee Relations*, *43*(6), 1362–1381. doi:10.1108/ER-06-2020-0302

Our Values & Behaviours. (n.d.). www.ril.com

Overcome, O. C. L. (2017). *The Competitive Advantage of Quality Over Price*. TaskUS. https://www.taskus.com/insights/overcome-outsourcing-cost-limitations-the-competitive-advantage-of-quality-over-price/

Pache, A. C., & Santos, F. (2013). Inside the hybrid organization: Selective coupling as a response to competing institutional logics. *Academy of Management Journal*, *56*(4), 972–1001. doi:10.5465/amj.2011.0405

Panagariya, A. (2022). Digital revolution, financial infrastructure and entrepreneurship: The case of India. *Asia and the Global Economy*, *2*(2), 100027. doi:10.1016/j.aglobe.2022.100027

Parikshit, M., & Oliver, K. (2022, December 12). *U.S. Prosecutors Look to Charge Binance, Executives on Possible Money Laundering Violations: Reuters*. https://www.coindesk.com/business/2022/12/12/us-prosecutors-look-to-charge-binance-and-cz-for-possible-money-laundering-violations-reuters/

Park, J., Konana, P., Gu, B., Kumar, A., & Raghunathan, R. (2010). Confirmation bias, overconfidence, and investment performance: Evidence from stock message boards. *McCombs Research Paper Series, 7*(10).

Partap, S. (2017a). Application of financial analysis in evaluation of financial position of IDBI. *Journal for Advance Research in Applied Science*. http://iaetsdjaras.org/VOLUME-4-ISSUE-6-NOVEMBER-2017/ http://iaetsdjaras.org/gallery/41-november-256.pdf

Partap. (2012). An Evaluation of Performance of Indian Banking Sector (With Special Reference to NPAs of Some Indian Public Sector Bankst. *Asia Pacific Journal of Research in Business Management*.

Partap. (2017b). An example of the application of financial ratio analysis: The case of sun pharmaceutical industries limited. *Journal for Advance Research in Applied Science*.

Patni, I., & Choubey, S. (2019). Behavioral Traits and Investment Decisions: An Empirical Study on Executives of Financial Service Sector. *International Journal of Recent Technology and Engineering, 7.*

Perez, M., Lopez-Yerena, A., & Vallverdú-Queralt, A. (2021). *Traceability, authenticity and sustainability of cocoa and chocolate products: a challenge for the chocolate industry. In Critical Reviews in Food Science and Nutrition.* Taylor and Francis Ltd. doi:10.1080/10408398.2020.1819769

Philip, L. (2015, April 17). Harley Davidson Rolls out Two Years Extended Warranty. *Economic Times.* https://economictimes.indiatimes.com/harley-davidson-india-rolls-out-extended- warranty/articleshow/46837332.cms

Pillai, R., & Paul, B. (2023). Industry 4.0 and the Changing Employment Relations: A Case of the Indian Information Technology Industry. *NHRD Network Journal, 16*(1), 92–110. doi:10.1177/26314541221134849

Pozzo, B. (2020). Fashion between inspiration and appropriation. *Laws, 9*(1), 5.

Pradhan, K., John, P., & Sandhu, N. (2021). AI in healthcare. *Journal of Hospital Management and Health Policy, 5,* 1–10. doi:10.21037/jhmhp-20-126

PTI. (2013, July 24). India to be World's 3rd Largest Automotive Market by 2016. *The Economic Times.* https://economictimes.indiatimes.com/india-to-be-worlds-3rd-largest-automotive- market-by-2016-ihs/articleshow/21306611.cms

Puneet, K., & Ritee, U. (2021, January). Analytical study of yes bank by considering financial failure: Issues and challenges. *SJBIR Journal, 10*(1), 54–61.

Putri, M. D. P. W., Xu, C., & Akwetteh, L. N. (2020). Financial Behavior during COVID-19: Cognitive Errors That Can Define Financial Future. *Open Journal of Social Sciences, 8*(10), 259–269. doi:10.4236/jss.2020.810017

Qadri, S. U., & Shabbir, M. (2004). An empirical study of overconfidence and illusion of control biases Impact on investor's decision making: An evidence from ISE. *European Journal of Business and Management, 6*(14), 38–44.

Qasim, M., Hussain, R., Mehboob, I., & Arsha, M. (2017). Impact of herding behavior and overconfidence bias on investors' decision-making in Pakistan. *Accounting,* 81-90.

Raghavendra Kamath, K. (2013). *Few RIL retail arms still making losses.* www.business-standard.com

Rahayu, M., Rasid, F., & Tannady, H. (2018). Effects of self efficacy, job satisfaction, and work culture toward performance of telemarketing staff in banking sector. *South East Asia J. Contemp. Business. Econ. Law, 16*(5), 47–52.

Ramakrishna, A. (2012). An exploratory analysis of data breaches from 2005-2011: Trends and insights. *Journal of Information Privacy & Security, 8*(2), 33–56. doi:10.1080/15536548.2012.10845654

Rana, N. P., Luthra, S., & Rao, H. R. (2022). Assessing challenges to the mobile wallet usage in India: an interpretive structural modelling approach. *Information Technology & People.* doi:10.1108/ITP-07-2021-0535

Randel, A. E., Galvin, B. M., Shore, L. M., Ehrhart, K. H., Chung, B. G., Dean, M. A. U., & Kedharnath, U. (2018). Inclusive leadership: Realizing positive outcomes through belongingness and being valued for uniqueness. *Human Resource Management Review, 28*(2), 190–203. doi:10.1016/j.hrmr.2017.07.002

Ranganathan, A., & Kuruvilla, S. (2008). *Employee Turnover in the Business Process Outsourcing Industry in India.* https://www.igi-global.com/chapter/management-practices-high-tech-environments/25651

Rangaswamy & Shanka. (2021). The Migh "Tea" Problem of Start-up Expansion. *South Asian Journal of Management, 28*(1), 171-190.

Rangaswamy, U. M. (2021). Chai Thela: The Might "Tea" Problem of Start-up Expansion. *South Asian Journal of Management, 28*(1).

Rangaswamy, U. S. (2021). Chai Thela: The Migh"Tea" problem of start-up expansion. *South Asian Journal of Management, 28*(1), 171–190.

Rangaswamy, U. S. (2021). Chai Thela: The Might "Tea" Problem of Start-up Expansion. *South Asian Journal of Management*, 1.

Rasul & Chakravarty. (2016). *Reliance Industries plan fashion e-commerce site AJIO.com under Jio brand.* economictimes.indiatimes.com

Reese, S. R. (2017). *Leadership Core Values and Beliefs are Keys to Greatness.* Center for Management and Organization Effectiveness. Available at: https://cmoe.com/blog/great-leaders-have-specific-beliefs-and-core-values

Reliance announces e-commerce foray plans; to challenge Amazon, Flipkart. (2019). www.adgully.com

Reliance in process of momentous leadership transition says Mukesh Ambani. (2021). www.indiatoday.in

Reliance Industries adds 2.32 lakh new jobs in FY22, retail business top recruiter. (2022). www.livemint.com

Reliance Industries to raise $ 750 mn overseas. (2015). www.business-standard.com

Reliance Retail leaps to 94th spot on Deloitte's top retailers' list. (2019). www.economictimes. indiatimes.com

Reliance Retail to launch B2B e-marketplace. (2015). www.business-standard.com

Reuters. (2022a, December 9). Insurers shun FTX-linked crypto firms as risk mounts. *Business Line.*

Reuters. (2022b, December 13). Binance under scrutiny by US Justice department, prosecutors split. *Business Today.* https://www.businesstoday.in/crypto/token/story/binance-under-scrutiny-by-us-justice-department-prosecutors-split-356124-2022-12-13

Reuters. (2022c, December 13). Sam Bankman-Fried says lawyers pressured him to name new CEO. *Money Control.* https://www.moneycontrol.com/news/world/sam-bankman-fried-says-lawyers-pressured-him-to-name-new-ceo-9694951.html

Reuters. (2022d, December 22). *Two Bankman-Fried associates plead guilty to fraud.*

Reuters. (2023a, January 5). Bankman-Fried pleads not guilty in FTX fraud case. *Financial Express.*

Reuters. (2023b, January 17). Regulate crypto, Japan tells U.S., E.U. *Business Standard.*

Review, H. B. (2022). *HBR Challenges Faced by Cocoa-based Industries.* Academic Press.

Reviews. (n.d.). https://in.worldorgs.com/catalog/indore/park/taskus-india

Robbie, S. (2017). *Mindful business leadership.* Routledge.

Sabharwal, M. (2014). Is diversity management sufficient? Lead to further performance. *Public Personnel Management, 43*(2), 1–21. doi:10.1177/0091026014522202

Sadi, R., Asl, H. G., Rostami, M. R., Gholipour, A., & Gholipour, F. (2011). Behavioral finance: The explanation of investors' personality and perceptual biases effects on financial decisions. *International Journal of Economics and Finance, 3*(5), 234–241. doi:10.5539/ijef.v3n5p234

Saeedy, A., & Osipovich, A. (2023, January 20). New FTX chief calls reboot of exchange a possibility. *Wall Street Journal.*

Sala, A., Landoni, P., & Verganti, R. (2016). Small and medium enterprises collaborations with knowledge intensive services: An explorative analysis of the impact of innovation vouchers. *R & D Management*, *46*(S1), 291–302. doi:10.1111/radm.12196

Salampasis, D., & Mention, A. L. (2018). FinTech: Harnessing innovation for financial inclusion. In Handbook of Blockchain, Digital Finance, and Inclusion, Volume 2 (pp. 451-461). Academic Press. doi:10.1016/B978-0-12-812282-2.00018-8

Saluja, S. (2022). *Identity theft fraud-major loophole for FinTech industry in India.* doi:10.1108/JFC-08-2022-0211

Saluja, S., Aggarwal, A., & Mittal, A. (2022). Understanding the fraud theories and advancing with integrity model. *Journal of Financial Crime*, *29*(4), 1318–1328. doi:10.1108/JFC-07-2021-0163

Samuel, A. (2023, January 4). FTX failure forces rethink on global sports sponsorship by digital asset groups. *Financial Express.*

Saxena. (2016). Triumph Motorcycles India's Vimal Sumbly says the company has turned down customers wearing slippers. *Economic Times.* https://economictimes.indiatimes.com/magazines/panache/triumph-motorcycles-indias-vimal-sumbly-says-the-companyhas-turned-down-customers-wearing-slippers/articleshow/52613978.cms

Scott, H., & Gulliver, J. (2023, January 19). A Question for Congress: Why Didn't the SEC stop FTX? *Wall Street Journal.*

Shaheen, L., & Ibrahim, M. A. A. (2021). Smart happy city. *WIT Transactions on Ecology and the Environment*, *253*, 527–537.

Shakeb. (2021). YES Bank Fiasco: Arrogance or Negligence. *Emerging Economies Cases Journal.* https://doi.org/doi:10.1177/25166042211061

Shalender, K., & Sharma, N. (2022). Integrating strategic flexibility and marketing system to achieve sustainable competitive advantage: Conceptual refinement and framework. *World Review of Entrepreneurship, Management and Sustainable Development*, *18*(1-2), 175–194. doi:10.1504/WREMSD.2022.120794

Sharma, A. S. (2023). Healthcare IT in India. *Asian Hospital & Healthcare Management.* https://www.asianhhm.com/information-technology/ajaysharma-interview

Sharma. (2018). *Soon Reliance Jio might charge its users for JioTV and JioCinema Applications.* telecomtalk.info

Shaw, B., & Kesharwani, A. (2019). Moderating effect of smartphone addiction on mobile wallet payment adoption. *Journal of Internet Commerce*, *18*(3), 291–309. doi:10.1080/15332861.2019.1620045

Shekhar, S., Manoharan, B., & Rakshit, K. (2020). Going cashless: Change in institutional logic and consumption practices in the face of institutional disruption. *Journal of Business Research*, *114*, 60–79. doi:10.1016/j.jbusres.2020.04.010

Shon, P. d. (2022, June 20). *Bar & Cocoa.* Retrieved from Varieties of Cocoa beans: https://barandcocoa.com/pages/varieties-of-cocoa-beans

Sie, E. (n.d.). *GE Ep 71: How TaskUs CEO Bryce Maddock Went from Living With His Parents to $15M in Revenue.* https://www.levelingup.com/growth-everywhere-interview/bryce-maddock-taskus/

Silzer, R., & Church, A. H. (2010). Identifying and assessing high-potential talent. *Strategy-driven talent management: A leadership imperative, 28*, 213-280.

Simplr. (n.d.). *TaskUs vs Teleperformance? Which is the Better Enterprise Call Center?* https://www.simplr.ai/learn/taskus-vs-teleperformance-which-is-the-better-enterprise-call-center

Singh, S. (2016a). *Reliance Jio 4G: Data plans, prices, how it is different and everything else you need to know.* www. indiatoday.in

Singh, S. (2016b). *Reliance Jio: Free calls forever, Rs 50 for 1GB data, free to try until Dec 2016.* www. indiatoday.in

Singh, S. (2020, September 4). *The Indian Express.* https://indianexpress.com/article/business/banking-and-finance/yes-bank-crisis-rana-kapoor-arrested-bad-loans-6307485/

Singla & Partap. (2015). An Evaluation of Effectiveness of E-banking in India. *International Journal innovations in Engineering & Technology, 5*(2), 437-442.

Speidell, L. S. (2009). Investing in the unknown and the unknowable—Behavioral finance in frontier markets. *Journal of Behavioral Finance, 10*(1), 1–8. doi:10.1080/15427560902719323

Srikant, C. D. (2019). Impression management strategies to gain regulatory approval. *Journal of Business Research, 105*, 136–153. https://doi.org/.jbusres.2019.08.006 doi:10.1016/j

Sulaiman, M. A. B. A., Ahmed, M. N., & Shabbir, M. S. (2020). Covid-19 challenges and human resource management in organized retail operations. *Utopía y Praxis Latinoamericana, 25*(12), 81–92. doi:10.5281/zenodo.4280092

Sull, D., Sull, C., & Bersin, J. (2020). Five ways leaders can support remote work. *MIT Sloan Management Review, 61*(4), 1–10.

Suri, T. (2017). Mobile money. *Annual Review of Economics, 9*(1), 497–520. doi:10.1146/annurev-economics-063016-103638

Sustainability of Global Cocoa Economy. (2021). doi:10.5772/intechopen.87871

TaskUs boosts employee Perks & Benefits amid COVID-19 pandemic. (2020). TaskUs. https://ir.taskus.com/news-releases/news-release-details/taskus-boosts-employee-perks-benefits-amid-covid-19-pandemic

TaskUs Competitors. (n.d.). *Comparably.* https://www.comparably.com/-companies/taskus/competitors

TaskUs Facebook. (n.d.). https://m.facebook.com/TaskUsPH/posts/one-of-our-core-values-is-be-ridiculous-which-is-actually-a-callout-to-all-our-e/1165676483502070/

TaskUs India. (n.d.).. https://in.worldorgs.com/catalog/indore/park/taskus-india

TaskUs vs Teleperformance? Which is the Better Enterprise Call Center? (n.d.). Simplr. https://www.simplr.ai/learn/taskus-vs-teleperformance-which-is-the-better-enterprise-call-center

TaskUs Wins. (2019). Best Places to Work For Second Year in a Row. *Business Wire.* https://www.businesswire.com/news/home/20191213005067/en/TaskUs-Wins-2019-Best-Places-to-Work-For-Second-Year-in-a-Row

TaskUs. (2016). *Facebook official page.* https://m.facebook.com/TaskUsPH/posts/one-of-our-core-values-is-be-ridiculous-which-is-actually-a-callout-to-all-our-e/1165676483502070/

TaskUs. (n.d.a). https://www.taskus.com/

TaskUs. (n.d.b). https://www.taskus.com/locations/india/

TaskUs. (n.d.c). *Entrepreneur India.* https://www.entrepreneur.com/company/taskus

Tepper, B. D., Dimotakis, N., Lambert, L. S., Koopman, J., Matta, F. K., Man Park, H., & Goo, W. (2018). Examining follower responses to transformational leadership from a dynamic, person-environment fit perspective. *Academy of Management Journal, 61*(4), 1343–1368. doi:10.5465/amj.2014.0163

Thacker, H. (2022). *The Definitive CSR Report of Reliance Industries Ltd. The CSR Journal.*

Thakkur, K. (2016). Small Time Buyers Add to Sales of Super Bikes. *Economic Times.* https://economictimes.indiatimes.com/small-town-buyers-add-to-sales-of-super-bikes- like-harley-davidson-ducati-and-others/articleshow/52875844.cms

Tichy, N. M., & Devanna, M. A. (1986). *The transformational leader.* Wiley.

Tirmizi, S. A. (2018). An integrative Framework for responsible Leadership Practice. In *In Enacting values-based change* (pp. 123–136). Palgrave Macmillan. doi:10.1007/978-3-319-69590-7_9

Tosey, P., Mathison, J., Tosey, P., & Mathison, J. (2009). Organisational Applications of NLP. *Neuro-Linguistic Programming: A Critical Appreciation for Managers and Developers*, 25-34.

Trehan, T., & Sinha, A. K. (2021). A study of confirmation bias among online investors in virtual communities. *International Journal of Electronic Finance*, *10*(3), 159–179. doi:10.1504/IJEF.2021.115647

Uber to 'hide' surge pricing notification. (2016, June 24). BBC. https://www.bbc.com/ news/technology-36619414

Vivek, V., Bermúdez, S., & Larrea, C. (2019). Global Market Report: Cocoa. *Exchange Organizational Behavior Teaching Journal*, 1–12.

Von Bergen, C W., & Bressler. (2018). Confirmation bias in entrepreneurship. *Journal of Management Policy and Practice*, *19*(3), 74–84.

Vries, A. D., Erasmus, P. D., & Gerber, C. (2017). The familiar versus the unfamiliar: Familiarity bias amongst individual investors. *Acta Commercii*, *17*(1), 1–10. doi:10.4102/ac.v17i1.366

Vyas, V., Mehta, K., & Sharma, R. (2023). The nexus between toxic-air pollution, health expenditure, and economic growth: An empirical study using ARDL. *International Review of Economics & Finance*, *84*, 154–166.

Wang, T., Wezel, F. C., & Forgues, B. (2016). Protecting market identity: When and how do organizations respond to consumers' devaluations? *Academy of Management Journal*, *59*(1), 135–162. doi:10.5465/amj.2014.0205

Ward, S. (2003, December 13). *The pros and cons of angel investors.* Retrieved 29 May 2023, from The Balance website: https://www.thebalancesmb.com/angel-investor-2947066

Weick, K. E. (1976). Educational Organizations as Loosely Coupled Systems. *Administrative Science Quarterly*, *21*(1), 1. doi:10.2307/2391875

Wong, J. (2017, November 22). Uber Concealed Massive Hack That Exposed Data of 57m Users and Drivers. *The Guardian.* https://www.theguardian.com/technology/2017/ nov/21/uber-data-hack-cyber-attack

Xe: Currency exchange rates and international money transfer. (2019). Retrieved 29 May 2023, from https://www.xe.com/

Yadav, A. (2018, January 30). *Why every Startup should host A crowdfunding campaign.* Retrieved 29 May 2023, from Forbes website: https://www.forbes.com/sites/ajayyadav/2018/01/30/why-every-startup-should-host-a-crowdfunding-campaign/

Zahera, S. A., & Bansal, R. (2018). Do investors exhibit behavioral biases in investment decision making? A systematic review. *Qualitative Research in Financial Markets, 10*(2).

Zaleskiewicz, T., Gasiorowska, A., Stasiuk, K., Maksymiuk, R., & Bar-Tal, Y. (2017). Lay evaluation of financial experts: The action advice effect and confirmation bias. *Frontiers in Psychology*, *7*, 1476. PMID:27729892

About the Contributors

Shefali Saluja is a Ph.D. in Corporate Governance from Chitkara University, Punjab, India in 2021. Post Graduate from Chitkara University, Punjab, India with 10 years of experience in business management education and expertise in finance and ethics. She has 4 years of working experience in Ernst & Young Pvt Ltd prior joining academics. She has published almost 14 research papers/articles in highly indexed Scopus journals in the areas of corporate governance, sustainability, E-learning & other areas. She is a member of several management associations such as Association of Certified Fraud Examiner (CFE) and International Association of academic plus corporate (IAAC) society. She serves as business consultant to several higher education institutions and small enterprises like MSMEs in Cirebon, Indonesia. Dr. Shefali has received Woman Trailblazer Award in 2022 for her work in Community service towards financial inclusion of rural sector in Punjab, India and various appreciation awards from the international universities. She has filed 2 patents and 5 copyrights in diverse areas. Her current job position includes various teaching and administrative related responsibilities in Chitkara university. Dr Shefali was also invited in many teaching opportunities internationally for teaching a module on "Failing corporates" at Emden University, Germany. She was also invited by Telkom University, Indonesia and Providence University Taiwan to deliver sessions on "Fraud Investigation". She has also delivered a module on "Business in Asia" to the students of Mondragon University, Spain. She has successfully presented research papers in national and international conferences. She is also handling Micro finance and Social Activities with United Nations. The activities are also live on YouTube. She has won best paper awards in the field of corporate governance. Her interests include volunteer work/community involvement at social NGOs in India like Khalsa Aid, AIESEC and Sunshine Youth club.

Dhiresh Kulshrestha is Dean of Faculty of Economics, at Chitkara Business School, Chitkara University Punjab. Sir, you have more than 20 + years of teaching and research experience, under your able guidance so far three Doctorates and Five M.Phil Degrees have been awarded. You have so far delivered more than 65 experts talks at various platforms. You are the Executive Committee member of Indian Economic Association from Punjab State, you also hold various members of national bodies such as TIES, MPEA, UPUEA, III and IAA. Prof Dhiresh Kulshrestha has published more than 40 research Publication in various reputed National and International Journals.

Sandhir Sharma is a Ph.D. in strategic Management from Mahatma Gandhi Kashi Vidyapeeth, Varanasi and Post Graduate from Panjab University, Chandigarh with 23 years of experience in business management education and expertise in strategy formulation, sustainability, and leadership. He has 5 years of working experience in telecom industry prior joining academics. He has published 61 research papers/articles in highly indexed Scopus, Web of Sciences and ABDC journals in the areas of strategy, sustainability, Food Science, Energy, Leadership, quality education, Environment, E-learning & other areas. He is a member of several management associations such as AMDISA, AIMS-International, HEF, INFOMS and AACSB. He serves as business consultant to several higher education institutions and small enterprises. Dr. Sharma received Shiksha Bharti Award by Indian Achiever's Forum for his contribution in management education in year 2021, Excellent Researcher Award in 2022 by INSO Awards and Outstanding B-School Director Award by AIMS-International at IIM-Kozhikode in 2020 and 2021. He has filed 23 patents and 11 copyrights in diverse areas. He is visiting faculty to Kedge Business School, France, University of Applied Sciences, Osnabrueck, Germany, Binus University & Telekom University, Indonesia. He is presently serving as Pro Vice Chancellor, Chitkara Business School, Chitkara University, Punjab.

* * *

Muhammad Sallehudin Ali is Faculty of Plantation and Agrotechnology, Universiti Teknologi MARA, Campus Jasin, Melaka. Currently attached to the Department of Plantation Management and Agribusiness. Predominantly focused on agriculture finance, agribusiness management and research methodology.

Abhishek Anand is an M.B.A., M.A., and Ph.D. in Economics. He has 5 years of teaching experience and have more than 12 research papers and 3 chapters in a reputed Journal and books. He is currently working as an Assistant Professor of Economics in Chitkara Business School, Chitkara University, Punjab. He has attended more 10 National and International Seminars.

Neeraj Anand is working as a Professor and Dean at Chitkara Business School, Chitkara University, Punjab since Jan. 2023. His area of specialization is Supply Chain Management, Research Methodology and Operations. Other areas of interest are Entrepreneurship and Project Management. He has 27 year experience in academics and 3 years in industry. He has been instrumental in signing MoU with IATA in Nov. 2022 for Aviation/Hospitality/Business programmes. He has got one patent granted on "Multi-utility Neck Pillow" and another patent filed on "Natural Herbal Powder" with Chitkara Innovation and Incubation Foundation. Organized National Symposium on "Redesigning Supply Chain: Supply Chain: Agile and Sustainable" in April, 2022 supported by WASME and Logistics Insider as the media partner. He has published 15 book chapters in edited books/Springer/IGI Global and 35 research papers in refereed, UGC CARE, Scopus Indexed and ABDC journals. He is a certified Internal Auditor from DNV and has performed the role of Management Representative for ISO 9000 certification for UPES from its inception in 2006 to 2010 and again took over the charge in June 2013. He has successfully faced surveillance audits by DNV. He has been actively involved in Extension/Training and Coordinated an Executive Program for Centre for Aviation Studies for executives of University of Applied Science, Frankfurt a Resource person for "Supply Chain Management" for ISPe and delivered sessions on "Project Management" for engineering graduates of THDC, Tehri (U.K.) in 2011. He has conducted 4 MDPs on and Project Management and SCM. He carried out a research project with UHHDC (Uttrakhand Handloom & Handicraft Development Corporation) and another with a UREDA (Uttaranchal Renewable Energy Development Agency). Conducted ESDP (Entrepreneurship and Skill Development Program) sponsored by Ministry of MSME in partnership with Indian Institute of Entrepreneurship, Guwahati in

2010. Organized ICMI 2013 (International Conference on Management of Infrastructure) in Feb 2013. Convener of the national conference on "Innovation and Entrepreneurship" in 2010. He is a life member of Society of Operations Management and an affiliate Member- Energy Institute, London (U.K). Member – DAAC and BOS (Board of Studies), Chitkara Business School.

Monica Apte is having an experience of 23years in teaching, learning and research. Expertise in Artificial intelligence, machine learning and Deep learning. She is a corporate trainer MCA, MBA, Ph.d and have also worked as an corporate trainer.

Devesh Bathla is a Professor of Business Analytics and Data Science at Chitkara University, Punjab, India. He is an Industry practitioner with vast experience in field of Data Analytics and contributes largely to corporate consulting, besides frequently conducting corporate training modules internationally. He holds a PhD degree in Management, an MBA, and is an Engineering graduate. His areas of expertise are Business Analytics, Marketing Analytics, HealthCare Analytics, Human Resource Analytics, and other Data Science related subjects. He has versatile teaching, corporate training, and industry experience. His academic contributions include fifteen patents and many more in progress, that have already been filed by him and he encourages his mentees to contribute in the domain of invention. Devesh's research publications have been printed by reputable international and national journals. He has also presented research papers in several international and national conferences, and has been presented with Best Paper Award in certain conferences.

Harpreet Bhatia is a Senior HR professional with more than twenty seven years of experience in Human Resources. Extensively worked on building HR strategy in line with business strategy and Building HR Process and policy framework. Has worked in various roles as HR leader, HR Business partner and Head of HR in various manufacturing and services organizations.

Prashant Chauhan is currently associated with Chitkara Business School, Chitkara University Punjab, India as an Assistant Professor of Business Analytics. He has research interest in the domain of Customer Experience Management, Digital marketing and Analytics – How to Develop and Execute the Most Profitable Customer Experience Strategies" and holds visiting professorship at TAPMI School of Business, Manipal University Jaipur. He has been earlier associated with Mittal School of Business, LPU, Punjab, India as an Assistant Professor- MBA Marketing program. Delivered guest session at Jaipuria Intitute of Management, Jaipur, India on "Business research methods and data analytics" for Masters students. He is well versed with research and data analytics tools like, IBM SPSS, AMOS, PLS SEM, R, Python, C, C++, SQL, Tableau and AWS Sage maker. As ingenious researcher, he has presented research papers in national & international conferences, seminars, workshops and faculty development programs at institutions of repute (e.g., MICA Ahmedabad, FMS BHU, IIT- Bombay and TAPMI). He has published research articles and book chapters in ABDC, Scopus and UGC listed journals.

Aarti Dangwal, Ph.D. holder in Management, passionate academician having 10+ years of teaching experience in higher education institutions. She has contributed various research articles in UGC care journals, Scopus indexed and conferences. Currently working as Assistant Professor in Chitkara Business School, Chitkara University, Panjab. Her research areas are Tourism, Marketing, and Business Environment.

Shuchi Dawra is Professor, Chitkara Business School, Chitkara University, Punjab, India. She is a Doctorate in in the domain of human resource management and organizational behaviour from Panjab University, Chandigarh, India. She has varied experience of 16 years in industry and academia with expertise in HRM practices, work-life balance (WLB), TQM, CSR and HR analytics. She is M Com, MBA(HR), UGC(NET); and is HR analytics certified from the IIM, Rohtak. Her area of expertise include Global Practices in HRM, Organizational Behaviour & Research. She has successfully supervised two doctoral research on TQM in Higher Education in Engineering and Work Life Balance; at present she is mentoring 4 Phd Research Scholars(Senior Corporate Executives and academicians) in the Research domains of Self efficacy and Internships, CSR & leadership; and Work life Balance.She has her research publication in reputed international and national journals. She is also a reviewer, and has chaired sessions in the conferences.

Surendar Gade is a Post-Doctoral Fellow in Finance from UGC, New Delhi, currently working as an Assistant Professor of Finance, at the School of Commerce, Narsee Monjee Institute of Management Studies (NMIMS) University, Hyderabad. He has more than 20 years of teaching and research experience. He has published 26 papers in various journals of international and published three books. He also presented 20 papers in various Seminars & Conferences including papers presented in Bangkok, Thailand, and Boston, USA. He is a life member of ICA, IAA, IARDO, TCA, and a Member of AIMA. His research area is Personal and Behavioral Finance and Capital Market developments.

Potnuru Rama Krishna Gupta is working as Assistant Professor at GITAM School of Business, GITAM (Deemed to be University) India. His area of research are Strategic HR, wellbeing, organizational change, and industrial psychology. He has published several research manuscripts in ABDC journals and presented his research in National and International conference. He received Emerald Literati Award 2020 for his paper "Employee engagement for millennials: considering technology as an enabler" published in Development and Learning in Organizations: An International Journal.

Shivani Inder has done Ph.D. in finance. She is a certified Cost and Management Accountant (CMA). She has done M.B.A. (finance) and M.F.C. She is currently working as Associate Professor at Chitkara Business School, Chitkara University, Punjab, India. Her domain areas are corporate finance, accounting and entrepreneurship. She has more than ten years of teaching experience. She is associated with professional bodies and review for reputed journals.

Trilok Kumar Jain is Professor and Dean in International School of Business Management (ISBM) and Director of Ecosystem for Innovation and Entrepreneurship in Suresh Gyan Vihar University Jaipur. He started doctoral research on Social Entrepreneurship in 1994 and since then he has been contributing to the field of social innovation and social entrepreneurship. He is regular contributor to as contributing author. He is also honorary director of Bosch - SGVU Industry Academia Collaboration Centre, which tries to promote Skill Entrepreneurship. He is also Honorary Convener of the Opportunity Lab, which is an attempt to train, mentor and support those who are deprived. He has run many campaigns including "Voters Awareness Campaign in Bikaner", campaign for Heritage Walk, Campaign for reviving Sursagar" etc. He has written biographies on Great (but less known) Personalities. He has written many ebooks, which are available on kdp.amazon.com. He regularly organizes FDPs and Workshops on "Teachers as Transformers". He is on the board of Lokayan, Ajit Foundation for Social Development, Semuno and many impact making institutions / NGOs.He regularly conducts motivation sessions for youth for inspiring them for positivity and creative actions. He conducts career counselling sessions for students. He regularly conducts workshops on Social Entrepreneurship.

Harkiran Kaur is Pro Vice Chancellor Office of Alumni Affairs, Chitkara University. An illustrious alumni of Sainik School Kapurthala. Graduate in Mathematics, English Literature and Psychology. Post Graduate in Management Studies, Post Graduate in Computer Applications and a Diploma Holder in French Language. (Punjabi University, Patiala, India) Certified BEC (Business English Certificate) Trainer by British Council. Certified Trainer by Inlingua School of Languages. An accomplished leader, A dynamic professional with 22 years of ultra-rich experience in Higher Education Management/Consultant. From starting her career as Faculty Communication Skills & French teaching UG & PG Engineering, Pharma, Architecture students, to starting & managing a Business School as Dean, to handling the Office of International affairs as Director, established professional milestones with exceptional performance. She has been with Chitkara since its inception. It is more than 20 years now and has spearheaded all important verticals and contributed with her colossal efforts to the growth of Chitkara as a Brand. Instrumental in establishing collaborations with 150 plus International Partners/ Universities across the World, building trust and association with leading Global Academic schools in span of just 5 years of her stint as Director International Programs. She started and spearheaded the realm of Social Media at Chitkara and was Editor-in-Chief for Chitkara Publication House. Prof. Harkiran Kaur, has been the face of Chitkara University for more than 500 National and International events and brings with her an exemplary wisdom and her stage presence is poise and grace personified. Hosted Nigerian Student Cohorts in Campus for consecutive three years besides heading the vertical of 500 International student mobility from SAARC Countries & students from European Diaspora every Year. Leading Strong and robust Network of 60,000 Alumni spread across six continents. She is a strong woman of substance, precise to core and a perfectionist in her approach. A learned scholar who is widely travelled across the globe. She is the first woman in this region to head an Entourage at Harvard University, The United States of America. Under her dynamic patronage in Bangkok, Chitkara Students defeated 36 countries spanning 5 continents to win the Best Outstanding Paper Award at the Asia-Pacific International Model United Nations, Bangkok. She was invited as Guest of Honour for two consecutive years in Busan, South Korea by IYF World Camp. Honoured by His Holiness Dalai Lama for her exceptional paper written and presented in IIT Roorkee, India on "Buddhism as a Significant means of Global Peace and Harmony". Honoured by H'ble Ex Chief Minister Punjab Captain Amarinder Singh for her "Exemplary Services in field of Education" by Govt. of Punjab, during the 70th Republic Day Celebrations on 26th January, 2019.

Maninder Kaur is a research scholar at Chandigarh University and also an assistant professor at CGC Landran college. She has received her postgraduate degree in finance from LPU and passed the UGC NET exam in management.

Navreet Kaur is an alumna of Panjab University, Chandigarh and a Ph.D. in Motivational Psychology with over 16 years of experience in teaching, both in India and abroad. She was invited as visiting faculty to HEPL University (Belgium), Sup'Biotech (Paris), and DHBW Cooperative State University (Germany) under the Erasmus Exchange Program. As an academic consultant, Dr Navreet has delivered E-learning lectures, conducted workshops and designed course curriculum for pre-PhD Coursework. She has presented research papers at regional, national, and international conferences such as: Conference on

Management and Information Systems (ICMIS-13) at Bangkok; 3rd and 5th International Conference on Managing Human Resources at the Workplace at SDMIMD, Mysore; International Conference on Technology and Business Management (ICTBM-17) supported by AIMS International at Dubai, 3rd International Conference on Facets of Business Excellence - FOBE 2018 at Institute of Management Technology (IMT) Ghaziabad; 3rd International Conference on the Future of ASEAN (ICoFA) 2019 at Perlis (Malaysia). She has also been a session chair in various conferences and is on the reviewer panel of 'Current Psychology' published by Springer. Her current research area is 'digitalization and work behaviour'. Her recent publications are in the Journal of Advanced Research in Dynamical and Control Systems, Webology, Mathematical Statistician and Engineering Applications, Lecture Notes in Networks and Systems and a book chapter in Big Data Analytics for Improved Accuracy, Efficiency, and Decision Making in Digital Marketing. Of late, she has presented a paper on Metaverse at IEEE sponsored conference on Mobile Radio Communications & 5G Networks held at Kurukshetra University. She has also received the Best Researcher Award at IEEE sponsored 2nd International Conference on Recent Trends in Engineering Technology and Management 2022 (ICRETM 2022) at Christ the King Engineering College, Coimbatore held in May, 2022.

Lubza Nihar Khaliq is an Associate Professor at GITAM School of Business, Gandhi Institute of Technology and Management (Deemed to be University), India. Her research areas include Earnings Management, Islamic finance, Corporate Governance, Financial Inclusion, and Mutual Funds. She is a researcher and case writer. She has published in national and international, Scopus and ABDC-ranked scholarly journals, and presented papers at various national, and international conferences. She is on the editorial board of two reputed national academic journals, and regularly reviews research papers of reputed international journals.

Ashish Kumar is a Certified Fintech & Block chain Expert by GBA. International Trade, Forex Management, Portfolio Management, Indian Economy, Indian Banking System, Expertise in Technical Analysis. Heading R& D team in International Institute of Influencers. Revenue model expert for startups Intellectual, self-motivated & self-starter. Strong analytical, problem solving and interpersonal skills.

Ashok Kumar is an Assistant professor in Defence and Strategic Studies at Himachal Pradesh University, Shimla. He is an alumnus of Defence and Strategic Studies, Punjabi University Patiala. He has also qualified UGC NET and JRF. His broader research interests include International Relations, Diplomacy, National Security and Strategic Studies. He has individually authored several research articles in reputed journals, magazines and also edited books. He has recently been awarded Post Doctoral Fellowship by ICSSR, New Delhi.

Sunil Kumar is an Assistant Professor at GITAM School of Business, GITAM (Deemed to be University) Visakhapatnam, Andhra Pradesh, India. He has over 8 years of teaching experience. He earned his Ph.D from Jamia Millia Islamia (A Central University), New Delhi in the area of NGO Management. He has qualified UGC-NET-JRF in Management. His academic qualifications include BA, MBA, DCA and Ph.D. He has published papers in Journals of repute indexed and listed in Scopus, Web of Science, ABDC and UGC care etc. He is a life member of Indian commerce association.

Vijaya Kittu Manda has nearly 12+ years of experience in capital markets, financial planning, and investing. He is an Advocate, a technocrat, an academician, a book writer, and a stock market enthusiast. He has 10 University Postgraduate Degrees, is NISM Certified in multiple subjects and just submitted his Ph.D. thesis on Mutual Funds. Associated with Smart Investment publications for several years, he contributed over 500 articles to the outlet. He is the Chief Editor for a Management Book Series, writers research papers and case studies, and is a speaker for colleges and universities. He conducts Kittu's Wealth Journey Seminars & Webinars in India and abroad on various trading and investing topics.

Sukhjeet Kaur Matharu is an Associate Professor, Prestige Institute of Management and Research, Indore. A Result driven and articulate academician with more than 14 years of academic & research experience in professional institutes. Demonstrated proficiency in writing more than 20 research papers in leading international, national journals and books, including journals listed in ABDC, Scopus, Elsevier and UGC. Reviewer of various reputed journals and has presented research papers in various National and International conferences. Research Supervisor with DAVV, Indore and Pacific University, Rajasthan.

Mankaj Mehta is working as an assistant professor at Chitkara Business School, Chitkara University, Punjab, India. He has done Master of Commerce and Ph.D in finance from Punjabi University, Patiala, Punjab and UGC-NET Qualified. He has more than 7 years of teaching experience. He has 11 research papers in his name. He has attended/participated/organised various national/international conference/seminars/workshops/webinars, etc.

Sushil Nirbhavane has an MBA (Marketing + Retail) from Pune University (PUMBA) and UGC-NET and MH-SET qualified. A Ph.D. Research Scholar at Dr. Vishwanath Karad MIT World Peace University. Over last 12 years, taught various subjects including – Business Communication; Marketing Management; Geopolitics and World Economic System; Distribution & Retail Management; Marketing Research; Consumer & Organizational Buying Behavior, Current Trends in Management; Virtual Marketing; Start-up & New Venture Management; Sales & Distribution Management; Retail Management; Strategic Brand Management; Business-to-Business Marketing; Quality Management System; Marketing Essentials; Professional Communication; Social Media Marketing; Strategic Management; Product & Brand Management; Introduction to International Business; Sales Force and Channel Management, etc.

Ameya Patil is Assistant Professor of Finance and International Business at School of Business, Dr. Vishwanath Karad MIT World Peace University, Pune, India. He has research interest in the areas of Financial Analysis, Behavioural Finance and Banking. His research works have been published in reputed journals and books in these areas.

B. S. Rathore is an instructor of OB & HR with 35 years of experience (20 years of PG teaching and 15 years with the Indian Air Force). He holds a Ph.D. degree from MLSU, Udaipur, as well as an MBA, MPM, and labor law degree from Pune University. He has over 27 research papers and book chapters published in international and national journals. He was an external examiner for the viva-voce of four Ph.D. candidates at prestigious universities like PDPU Gandhi Nagar. He has chaired several sessions of international conferences. Also, the Air Officer Commanding praised him for his role in obtaining the ISO 9002 certificate for the Armed Forces Depot. Three research scholars have been awarded Ph.D. degrees under his guidance, and seven are doing research under him.

Baranidharan S. is specialized in Finance Economics and Econometrics. Having 5 years research experience, 2 years of Industrial experience and 6 years of teaching experience. Published 4 patent, 37 research articles in international and national journal which are indexed in Scopus, WoS, Proquest, ABDC, etc.

Ruhi Sarangal is currently associated with Chitkara Business School, Chitkara University Punjab, India as an Assistant Professor of Business Analytics. She is very Passionate about her interest for Teaching. She has her research interest in the domain of Advertisement and Marketing Including Digital Marketing, Social Media Marketing, Consumer Response Behaviour, Ethics and Privacy issues in Social media marketing. She has been earlier associated with Chandigarh Group of Colleges, Landran, Mohali, India as an Assistant Professor- BBA program. She also has a rich experience of working with Punjabi University (as an Assistant Professor) and Guru Nanak Dev University (as a JRF and SRF). She is well versed with research and data analytics tools like, IBM SPSS, AMOS and SEM. As an ingenious researcher, she has presented research papers in various national & international conferences, seminars and attended workshops at institutions of repute. She has published research articles in various UGC listed journals and also have several book chapters to her account.

Rajeev Sengupta is Associate Professor of Finance at School Business, Dr. Vishwanath Karad MIT World Peace University, Pune, India. His research focuses on the insurance, bancassurance and the technological applications in the area. Prior to joining Academics, he had held leadership roles in various MNC Insurance companies for over two decades.

Kumar Shalender is a Post-Doctoral Fellow of the Global Institute of Flexible Systems Management and a Doctor of Philosophy in Strategic Management. He has more than 14-year experience in the domain of Business Policy, Strategic Management, and Business Model Development and a total of 70 Publications including presentations at international/national conferences and book chapters to his credit. His current research areas include the field of Metaverse, Blockchain Technology, and Sustainable Development with a special focus on sustainable cities and mobility ecosystems in India.

Sandhir Sharma is a Ph.D. in Strategic Management with nearly 22 years of experience in higher education and 5 years in Telecom industry. With more than 43 research papers to his credit published in various journals and conferences at national & international level, Dr. Sharma has developed his core expertise in the area of Strategy formulation.

Tarun Sharma is a PhD (Strategy Management) IIM, Indore, PGDM (Working Exe.) IIM, Raipur, FDP (IIM, Ahmedabad), MBA (Ravi Shankar University), Having 23 years of Industry Experience. Presently working in Dalmia Cement Bharat Ltd. As General manager (Sustainability). Profile handling Risks and ESG function in the group. Research interest: Firm-level resource alignment and competency development.

Partap Singh is committed to teaching and research in Finance and Investment domain since last 16 years+. His qualification is PhD (Commerce), M.Com, MBA. He has rich work experience in the field of Teaching, administration and research as well. He held various responsibilities like Editor, Co-editor, and Editorial Board member, Associate Editor in number of national and international journals. He has regularly been receiving offers for writing books from the top publishing houses of India and received many letters of thanks& compliments for giving valuable suggestions and commendable views concerning improvement of many leading Publications/Books. He has written and published 5 books namely Financial Management, Risk Management, working capital Management, Management Accounting and Analysis of Financial Statements. Further, he has published more than 50 papers and book chapters in good reputed journals and he has also contributed numerous research papers in national and international conferences or seminars. He has good participation in MDPs. FDPs and STCs as well as Life Membership of reputed academic bodies. His future interest area of research is Capital Market, Financial Derivatives, Commodities Market, NBFCs and pharmaceutical Industry.

Sehrish Tariq is a PhD student at the Faculty of Plantation and Agrotechnology, Universiti Teknologi MARA, Malaysia.

Muklesh Kumar Tiwari received PhD in HR in 2019 from MGCGU Chitrakoot (MP). He currently works as Associate Professor at AIT-MBA, Chandigarh University, Chandigarh. He has 16 years of research and academic experience in HR Management.

Shenki Tyagi was bestowed with the Young Influential faculty of the Year award - IISA 2022, bestowed with AND 6th Dr. Sarojini Naidu - The Nightingale of India International Award for working women 2022 in the Category of EDUCATIONIST .She is working an Assistant Prof in ITS Ghaziabad in the domain of Marketing and IIM Certified Digital Marketer. She is a Creative Director at I Transform Magazine by III. A very Dynamic Person who strongly believes in innovative teaching pedagogies while delivering a lecture. She is having rich experience of more than 10 years in Academic and corporate. Her professional and academic areas of Interest Include Digital Marketing, Marketing Management, Sales Management, E-Tailing, Visual Merchandising, Personal Branding, Business Organization, and Business environment. She is also an accomplished researcher with many research papers to her credit, including three case studies and Two Copyright under her name by Govt. of India.

Sunita Verma has been associated with Mody University of Science & Technology since 2006 and currently working as an Associate Professor in the area of OB, HRM and General Management. She has more than 25 publications in her credit. Her papers have been published in ABDC and Scopus listed journals. She has presented more than 20 papers in national and national conferences. She has received the best paper award for the paper titled Factors Influencing Mental Well-Being of Management Students: A Study of Women Exclusive Private Universities of Rajasthan, Two days International Conference on Re-imagineering Business and Management: The Emerging Landscape at ICFAI Business School Jaipur, March 23-24, 2023. One scholar has been awarded Ph.D degree under her guidance and three scholars are working under her guidance.

Index

www.ingramcontent.com/pod-product-compliance
Lightning Source LLC
LaVergne TN
LVHW062142300926
849161LV00010B/2606
* 9 7 8 1 6 6 8 4 8 4 8 8 3 *